Customer Relationship Management

Edited by SCN Education B.V.

HOTT Guide

Edited by SCN Education B.V.
This series of books cover special topics which are useful for a business audience. People who work or intend to work with Internet - at a management, marketing, sales, system integrating, technical or executive level - will benefit from the information provided in the series.

These books impart how new technologies and sales & marketing trends on Internet may be profitable for business. The practical knowhow presented in this series comes from authors (scientists, research firms and industry experts, a.o.) with countless years of experience in the Internet area.

The HOTT Guides will help you to:
▶ Enlarge your knowledge of the (im)possibilities of Internet and keep it up-to-date
▶ Use Internet as an effective Sales & Marketing tool by implementing new technologies as well as future-oriented strategies to improve your business results
▶ Facilitate decision making on a management level
▶ Reduce research costs and training time

These books are practical 'expert-to-manager' guides. Readers will see a quick 'return on investment'.

The Publishing department of SCN Education B.V. was founded in 1998 and has built a solid reputation with the production of the HOTT Guide series. Being part of an international IT-training corporation, the editors have easy access to the latest information on IT-developments and are kept well-informed by their colleagues. In their research

HOTT Guide

activities for the HOTT Guide series they have established a broad network of IT-specialists (leading companies, researchers, etc) who have contributed to these books.

SCN Education B.V., Newtonstraat 37C, 3902 HP Veenendaal, The Netherlands, tel. +31 – 318 – 547000, fax +31 – 318 – 549000, www.scnedu.com, www.hottguide.com.

Books already in print:

Webvertising
Mobile Networking with WAP
ASP – Application Service Providing
Data Warehousing
Electronic Banking

Customer Relationship Management

The Ultimate Guide to the Efficient Use of CRM

Edited by SCN Education B.V.

Die Deutsche Bibliothek - CIP-Cataloguing-in-Publication-Data
A catalogue record for this publication is available from Die Deutsche Bibliothek
(http://www.ddb.de).

658.812 C987

Customer relationship
 management

Trademarks
All products and service marks mentioned herein are trademarks of the respective owners
mentioned in the articles and or on the website. The publishers cannot attest to the
accuracy of the information provided. Use of a term in this book and/or website should
not be regarded as affecting the validity of any trademark or service mark.

1st Edition April 2001

Vieweg is a company in the specialist publishing group BertelsmannSpringer.

Printing and binding: Lengericher Handelsdruckerei, Lengerich
Printed on acid-free paper
Printed in Germany

ISBN 3 - 528 – 05752 – 1

Preface

The rules change when the tools change

Generating traffic to a website and catching the interest of the visitor, in order to make him buy a product or a service, is within everyone's reach today. Intensive research, try-outs and the learning experience of E-Commerce pioneers have helped to uncover the marketing & sales possibilities of the Internet. But now that we have customers visiting our site, how do we keep them coming back? How to get a clear profile of each customer, so we can give him (or her!) the service he's looking for? And offer him other products he could also be interested in?

To achieve this, companies are increasingly turning to Customer Relationship Management: the concentration of sales, marketing and service forces by integrating all dataflows into one data warehouse, thus blending internal processes with technology.

The right way to market, sell and service customers requires a different CRM strategy for every company. Some organizations that reengineered their CRM processes are reporting revenue increases of up to 50%, whereas others have had obtained minimal gains or no improvement at all. The difference between the success or failure of a CRM project lies in the knowledge and ability that an organization brings to its efforts.

This HOTT Guide defines CRM from different points of view: sales, marketing, customer support and technology. By presenting white papers on the technology, business cases, reports sharing the major trends occurring in the CRM marketplace, interviews with experts in the CRM-field, and a special chapter dedicated to the implementation of CRM in callcenters, the reader will have the most complete file on CRM possible at his disposition.

The Editors

Acknowledgements

Many people and professionals have contributed directly or indirectly to this book. To name them all would be practically impossible, as there are many. Nevertheless the editors would like to mention a few of those who have made the production of this book possible.

Executive Editor for SCN Education B.V.: *Robert Pieter Schotema*
Publishing Manager: *drs. Marieke Kok*
Product Manager: *Martijn Robert Broersma*
Editorial Support: *Dennis Gaasbeek*
HOTT Guide Online: *Rob Guijt, Richard van Winssen*
Interior Design: *Paulien van Hemmen, Bach.*

Contents

Contents

Contents

Contents

Chapter 1: Introduction to CRM

Does CRM Really Pay? A General Management Perspective

Title: Does CRM Really Pay? A General Management Perspective.
Author: Simon Caufield, Partner Mitchell Madison Group
Abstract: Customer relationship management (CRM), the most sophisticated of
                  marketing methods, was supposed to transform the way financial institutions
                  generate revenues from customers. And indeed, a few - largely single-
                  product companies and new entrants - have achieved spectacular results. But
                  most have found the development and application of CRM much more
                  difficult than expected. Many have been disappointed and now question its
                  viability. This article explains what's going wrong, describes some successes
                  and distills the key learnings. Its aim is to assist general managers to re-focus
                  their institutions' CRM initiatives to realise their full potential.

What is Customer Relationship Management?

An odd thing about Customer Relationship Management is that it is easier to describe in terms of its objectives than its activities or process. CRM aims to increase the profitability of the customer portfolio. Customer profitability comprises many elements, for example:

▸ Price
▸ Size of balances, assets, premiums
▸ Cross-sales/up-sales
▸ Costs to serve
▸ Number and size of transactions
▸ Expected value of losses
▸ Longevity/attrition

Clearly there are many alternative options for influencing customer profitability. Should you focus on improving the mix by culling unprofitable customers and/or targeting the most attractive ones? Or would there be more to gain from increasing the profitability of current customers? Any of the above factors could be the focus of a separate initiative to increase existing customer profitability. But which would have most impact? Making wise choices from amongst these options is critical.

This description of CRM emphasizes individual initiatives rather than a large-scale, integrated program. So does the term, CRM, have any meaning? Successfully choosing, designing and implementing any of the alternative initiatives in your specific situation require methodologies and capabilities to measure and take advantage of customer behaviour and economics. Implementing CRM is best described in terms of these skills. Their development within your organization will prove the major difference between success and failure.

What's Going Wrong?

In contrast to the focus on capabilities and individual initiatives described above, CRM is often initiated as a holistic program.

Protagonists often justify this approach with sound-bites that are descriptive and directional rather than prescriptive and precise. Without thoughtful adaptation to your specific situation, they are at best irrelevant and at worst misleading.

1. 20% of customers account for up to 120% of profits

Companies such as Direct Line and Capital One, the US credit card issuer, based their initial success on cherry-picking the most profitable customers. But as a large incumbent, it is difficult to avoid both reducing the profitability of current customers and increasing price competition for new customers. Cherry-picking may be hugely successful for new entrants but most incumbents, especially market share leaders, suffer from margin erosion.

Is there one company that, on discovering the Pareto effect, decided to jettison 80% of their customers? In most situations the reality is, of course, that whilst many customers are unprofitable on a fully allocated cost system, the overwhelming majority make a positive contribution.

2. You need to know the individual profitability of your customers

It is valuable to know the factors that drive customer profitability. But individual customer profitability analysis, measured in historic accounting terms, can be a huge wasted effort. It does not address how customers will respond to different marketing mixes. So you risk wasting money on initiatives that add more cost than revenue.

Some retailers use coupons and discounts to persuade customers to trial an item in the hope that they will repeat purchase thereafter. But making such incentives pay-off is based on changing customer behaviour in future not measuring customer profitability in the past.

3. It costs 5 times as much to acquire a new customer as retain an existing one

Of course, customer acquisition can be expensive. But the implication that loyalty programs must be beneficial is simply not true in many situations. For example, a loyalty scheme that gives a 1% discount on gross margins of 20% needs a 5% uplift in sales to make money. Many financial services have neither these margins nor price sensitivities (for existing customers). Loyalty schemes originated in business class air travel and hotels where highly valued rewards can be provided at low marginal cost. But most loyalty schemes achieve no better than break-even.

In many financial services, there are huge differences both in profitability and behaviour between customers. Whilst some are ferociously price sensitive, many are almost completely inert. Universal approaches often lead to cannibalization, i.e. unnecessarily providing incentives or discounts for sales that would have occurred anyway. For example, a universal loyalty program to reduce re-mortgaging by some customers would not be viable due to the cost of providing it to the majority.

4. You need a fully integrated, real-time customer information system

This costs a fortune, takes forever and avoids answering how all the data will actually be utilized by marketing, sales and customer service personnel. In addition, often the most valuable information about customers is, for example, price elasticity, utility for product and service features, propensity to be cross-sold, likely response to various marketing initiatives etc. Whereas many institutions have begun to understand customer economics, very few have collected much data about customer behaviour.

5. You need to organize around customer segments

In consumer businesses, segmentations evolve and change so each time you change your segmentation you would have to rip-up your organization. Unless your organization structure is very flexible and adaptive, this is impracticable. Most retail financial institutions, therefore, should not organize around customer segments. (The alternative approach of cross-functional project teams is discussed in the first example in the following section.)

In short, customer profitability analysis, generic loyalty programs, new systems or re-organization, on their own, will not deliver the results. Indeed, in the face of disappointing results, companies increasingly recognize these arguments and use them to question future investments in CRM.

Despite initial disappointments, to reject CRM now would be a mistake. CRM offers huge potential but requires more a sophisticated approach adapted to specific opportunities and circumstances, as illustrated below.

Successful Examples

The following examples describe different ways that institutions have applied CRM using insight, judgment and precision with great success.

1. New Customer Acquisition

A credit card issuer aiming to improve its mediocre customer acquisition performance put together a cross-functional project team from finance, credit, marketing, and operations together with external support. They believed that the solution lay in aligning product design with customer segments.

- In a month the team had analyzed previous marketing campaigns and developed a new best single product design. It raised customer acquisition productivity by 75%
- In a further month and a half, the team ran and analyzed a marketing test to develop a series of tailored offers that raised customer acquisition productivity by 150%
- After a further 3 months, further tests produced offers tailored and targeted to micro-segments of customers and raised customer acquisition productivity by 800%

The approach required the team to combine analysis, rapid decision making and implementation to get results with extraordinary speed. Their work has been worth £50 million pa to the bottom line. They have learned how a rapid test and learn process and project-based organization can be effective.

2. Differential Pricing

One personal lines insurance company was able to increase profits by 7% of premiums using differential pricing. The company identified customer and product segments with different price sensitivities. Then it optimized prices for each segment separately, raising prices on average by 7% but in a very de-averaged way. The key to successful implementation was enabling customer-facing staff to attribute customers into segments at the point of contact. Despite the price increase, renewal rates improved following implementation.

3. Reducing Customer Attrition

A US mortgage lender was losing customers at a rapid rate due to re-mortgaging. This bank was able to determine, from information collected on the mortgage application form, a measure of re-mortgage risk. To take advantage of the result, it securitised the higher risk loans and sold them off to an unsuspecting secondary market.

One UK retail bank with £3bn of three year fixed rate savings due to mature was worried about possible attrition. Taking advantage of differential price sensitivity and utility for non-price features by customer segment, it developed a range of offers that achieved 95% retention of funds at an average of 25 basis points

lower interest rate than previously thought possible.

4. Risk Assessment and Management

A motor insurer improved its claims ratio by 2-3% by incorporating customer-specific information into its risk assessment and selection procedures. A commercial lines insurer achieved a similar result by investigating how loss adjuster behaviour and incentives contributed to large variations in claims settlements for apparently similar losses.

A credit card issuer with £15 billion in assets was able to save a one-off £40 million plus £80 million annually from collections. It developed advanced scoring models to align and optimize its collection resources and processes for different segments of customers in arrears.

MBNA has long used CRM techniques to target borrowers with lower propensity to default than other credit card issuers. The value of this approach has only become apparent in the last few years as other US issuers' credit losses have increased markedly.

Lessons Learned

Financial institutions seeking to apply CRM must decide how to manage the program and where to focus resources. They should beware. Lack of experience is a handicap and good advice hard to find.

How to Manage CRM

Cross-functional project teams have proven the most successful organization form for CRM. To achieve results rapidly, they seek ways around organizational barriers to implementation. Frequently, they use marketing experiments both to optimize results and develop experience. Often, time-consuming and expensive large-scale solutions are not required to address seemingly insurmountable problems caused by lack of information, inflexible systems, and hierarchical organization structures.

A few financial institutions have achieved one-off successes with cross-functional teams. For them, repeating and sustaining the initial success now requires new approaches to staff career management, performance measurement, and compensation incentives, etc. to reflect a project-based organization. We will have more to say on this topic in a future paper.

Where to Focus the Resources

If institutions would devote a fraction of the resources currently being focused on customer profitability to customer behaviour, they would soon appreciate the vast variations between customer segments. Pretty soon, they would be awash with ideas to exploit these differences through targeting and tailoring.

Empirically, most successful examples seem to be single product applications, rather than cross-selling. There may be two reasons for this. First, our research suggests only 20% of consumers consider one-stop shopping attractive. Second, proprietary customer information, which is CRM's 'raw material', is obtained largely in the context of single product relationships and usually worthless outside that context. For example, most consumers' propensity to re-mortgage is unaffected by their holdings of deposit products with the same institution.

This does not mean that cross-selling cannot be valuable. Identifying those customers with a high propensity to be cross-sold and targeting marketing resources accordingly can pay-off. However, the expectations of many UK institutions may not be fulfilled.

Conclusion

Customized to your specific business and applied with insight, judgment and precision to focused objectives, CRM initiatives pay-off by changing, or taking advantage of, customer behaviour and profitability, and how these differ by segment.

Benefits are sensitive to focus, precision and insight in program design:

- An over-emphasis on customer profitability has left many financial institutions lacking the insights into customer behaviour to design effective initiatives
- There are often huge differences between customers; initiatives aimed at the average fail whilst targeting and tailoring yield substantial gains
- Although cross-selling and loyalty schemes seem to get most attention, experience suggests larger benefits from re-pricing, reducing attrition and new customer acquisition

Chapter 1: Introduction to CRM

It is vital to use cross-functional teams since this is the only way to mobilize the skills and imagination of the entire company. Marketing experiments are also important; not just for optimizing the design of specific programs but also to build capabilities and experience.

Many UK financial institutions need to re-focus their CRM initiatives to avoid disappointment. The prize more than justifies the investment.

We have found CRM results to be sensitive to choice of scope and objectives, detailed design of individual initiatives, and management of the program.

Insight and judgement in choosing scope and objectives are critical because the pay-off from alternative initiatives is situation-specific. In general, cross-selling and loyalty schemes seem the most popular choices, whereas re-pricing, reducing losses and attrition, and customer acquisition often achieve better results.

Program design is important because small changes can yield large impact. Standard approaches may seem attractive but often prove ineffective and expensive. Taking advantage of customer behaviour and/or economics that differ from the average is the source of the largest gains. This requires precise measurement.

Program organization and management are also crucial. It is vital to use cross-functional teams since this is the only way to mobilize the skills and imagination of the entire company. Marketing experiments are also important; not just for optimizing

the design of specific initiatives but also to build capabilities and experience.

Like all strategic initiatives, CRM requires commitment and understanding throughout the company, not just in marketing. Properly conceived and well executed, it offers huge potential. To give up now would be an opportunity lost.

CRM Definitions - Defining customer relationship marketing and management

Title:	*CRM Definitions - Defining customer relationship marketing and management*
Author:	*Professor Robert Shaw, Business Intelligence*
Abstract:	*There is no universally agreed definition of customer relationship management. Find out how leading experts define the term - and what the corporate world makes of the concept.*

Definitions of Customer Relationship Management

The following definitions are suggested by leading authorities in the field of customer strategies and represent different perspectives on the theory and practice of customer relationship management. Until recently, CRM most commonly stood for customer relationship marketing. Currently, it is more likely to be understood as shorthand for customer relationship management. However, there are some important nuances for some authorities, as the following expert definitions suggest. The following selection is not definitive. It does, though, indicate the richness of significance and association that is attached to the concept.

Dr Robert Shaw, Shaw Consulting and author of Measuring and Valuing Customer Relationships.

The following definition of CRM is intended to be both practical, in the sense of being process-based, and actionable, in reflecting what goes on in the real world. It also focuses on the business significance of the activity.

"Customer relationship management is an interactive process for achieving the optimum balance between corporate investments and the satisfaction of customer needs to generate the maximum profit. CRM involves:

▸ measuring both inputs across all functions including marketing, sales and service costs and outputs in terms of customer revenue, profit and value.
▸ acquiring and continuously updating knowledge about customer needs, motivation and behaviour over the lifetime of the relationship.
▸ applying customer knowledge to continuously improve performance through a process of learning from successes and failures.
▸ integrating the activities of marketing, sales and service to achieve a common goal.
▸ the implementation of appropriate systems to support customer knowledge

acquisition, sharing and the measurement of CRM effectiveness.
▸ constantly flexing the balance between marketing, sales and service inputs against changing customer needs to maximize profits."

One of the strengths of this definition is that it should be a provable causal chain: linking inputs to customer motivation to customer behaviour and thence to outputs. Those inputs can be divided into quantity and quality activities. The concentration on emotional aspects of customer relationships has shifted the emphasis onto quality inputs, such as satisfaction. On its own, this may produce higher profits, but it is more likely that both hard and soft aspects need to be addressed. Marketers have tended to concentrate more on quantity issues, such as frequency of TV exposure or volume of direct mail. In isolation, increasing quantity inputs will not create long-term, sustainable increases in profits.

Regis McKenna is founder and chairman of Regis McKenna, advisor to the Stanford Graduate School of Business, Harvard Business School's Science Technology and Public Policy Programs and is an internationally renowned marketing authority.
Regis McKenna has established an international reputation over the past few decades as one of marketing's leading thinkers and advocates. His view is that relationship marketing is the next phase in the evolution of this core corporate activity. He describes it as a fundamental aspect of doing business, something that should pervade the whole business from top to

bottom. What is more, it is not something that can be appropriated by a single function but a practice that should permeate all parts of the organization.

"Marketing is building and sustaining customer and infrastructure relationships. It is the integration of customers into the company's design, development, manufacturing, and sales processes. ... All employees need to be in the business of building customer relationships."
(Source: Relationship Marketing, Regis McKenna, Perseus Books)

Adrian Payne, professor of services and relationship marketing and director of the Centre for Relationship Marketing at Cranfield School of Management.
Payne, one of the leading pioneers of relationship marketing in Europe, has written some of the seminal texts on the subject. He encapsulates his view of relationship marketing as follows:

"Relationship marketing is about maximizing customer value for the firm, by creating, building and lengthening customer relationships with a view to selling more, cross-selling, and keeping customers longer."

He identifies several key characteristics of the relationship marketing approach:

▸ The movement from a transaction-driven to a relationship-driven approach – relationship marketing looks at a continuing series of transactions, rather than an individual transaction.
▸ The movement from a functional to a cross-functional approach – recognizing

that markets other than the customer market need to be addressed.

▸ A holistic customer-centric view, rather than a product-driven view – recognition that customer service, marketing and quality need to be brought together and approached in a coherent way, rather than managed in a disparate way within functional silos.

▸ With the traditional approach, functional objectives are optimized without reference to the needs of the organization as a whole. For example, one department may be striving to conform to a quality specification, but that is not necessarily an optimal objective from the company's viewpoint – or, indeed the customer's.

Martin Christopher, professor of marketing and logistics systems at Cranfield School of Management, and deputy director of the School and chairman of the Centre for Logistics and Transportation.
Christopher sees relationship marketing as a broader view of marketing, one that adds several dimensions to the conventional view. He sees relationship marketing as pan-company – it breaks away from the idea of marketing being the responsibility of the marketing department:

"Probably we should think of it in terms of relationship management as much as relationship marketing – and relationship management necessitates cross-functional, process-based approaches."

At the same time, Christopher and his colleagues have introduced a broader view of the markets themselves – the Six

Markets framework outlined in their book, Relationship Marketing for Competitive Advantage.
The Six Markets are:
▸ internal
▸ referral
▸ influencers
▸ employees
▸ suppliers
▸ customers

This model proposes that to sustain customer value, it is not enough to present a good front to the person to whom you are selling something. The organization has to build relationships with suppliers, individuals within the business, professionals who might recommend your company, and so on.

Christopher says that relationship marketing requires traditional marketers to make changes to the way they work:

"They have to ask what they need to do in order to become a preferred supplier or supplier of choice – to ensure that customers keep coming back, without having to be sold to again every time."

That means marketers have to think about their processes, and about customer value, whereas before they used to emphasize brand value. In the business-to-business arena, consolidation through mergers and acquisitions means that: "…the big guys are getting bigger, and they are seeking to reduce their supplier base – they want to do business with fewer suppliers."

Chapter 1: Introduction to CRM

Chapter 1: Introduction to CRM

How companies see CRM

The amount of coverage being given to the subject of customer relationship marketing and management might be taken to suggest that a stable definition of this activity exists. Yet this is far from being true. In particular, there is a considerable diversity among managers as to the goals and actions that constitute this approach.

A research program was undertaken by Dr Robert Shaw and Business Intelligence in which 131 senior executives in the UK, US and Europe were questioned about a range of key strategic issues, especially those concerning customer management, marketing and measurement. Full results of the survey can be found in the Appendix. As part of the survey, respondents were asked to provide free-form definitions of their understanding of relationship marketing.

A striking feature of this exercise is the sheer diversity of definitions it yielded. Out of the total sample of 131 managers, 53 said they did not know, in itself an indictment of the way this subject has developed without any guiding rigour. Among those who did answer, the most frequently mentioned aspects registered only 11 hits each, revealing that there is far from being a consensus on this subject.

There was also ample evidence both of confusion about the concept of relationship marketing and of hype in the marketplace. A typical answer demonstrating the unrealistic expectations was: "Honouring company commitments to other companies as though they were personal commitments between yourself and other individuals." Similarly, a hype-infected response was: "The non-intrusive capture of customer information leading to the development of compelling service propositions through the revelation of previously unseen demand."

One managing director in the survey provided an answer that accurately sums up the issue of definition: "Term used to described a desired behaviour which usually lacks substance. The sales/marketing teams talk about it, but don't understand it. It is usually indicative of strategies driven by catch phrases." If the genuine benefits of customer relationship management are to be derived, it is critical that board level directors are provided with a coherent, provable set of actions and outcomes.

Definitions of Relationship Marketing

Ranking	Definition	Implications
1=	"Customer needs"	Identifying and meeting customer needs is seen as the primary goal of relationship marketing. Despite this high ranking, customer needs tracking has the lowest level of usage among measurement tools.
1=	"Partnership"	Working in partnership with suppliers and customers is the key focus, both in consumer and business-to-business markets.
3	"Increasing profits"	Maximizing customer retention and value, and so driving up profitability, is the goal. This seems to reflect the popularity of the findings propounded by Frederick Reichheld that increased retention equals substantially increased profits.
4	"Loyalty"	Building loyalty with customers, usually defined as maintaining repeat sales, is the central role of relationship marketing.
5	"Value"	Managing and enhancing the value to both customer and company within the relationship.
6	"Satisfaction"	The focus on satisfaction received a relatively low level of mentions, yet this is the most popular customer measure.

(Source: Measuring and valuing customer relationships, Business Intelligence).

Chapter 1: Introduction to CRM

Customer Relationship Management – An Opportunity For Competitive Advantage?

Title: Customer Relationship Management – An Opportunity For Competitive
            Advantage?
Author: Timothy McMahon
Abstract: There are two fundamental questions you must ask – and successfully answer
            – if you want to develop a customer relationship management strategy, i.e.,
            one that helps you gain new customers, maximize the potential of current
            customers, and protect your most important customers from competitive
            intrusion: What kind of relationship do you want to establish with your
            customer? And What must you do to create and maintain that relationship?

Biography: Timothy McMahon is principal of Timothy McMahon/Worldwide, an international consulting group specializing in
sales and management development, sales process, and sales force automation. He is a leading keynote speaker and the author
of two best-selling books on sales and marketing. He can be reached at (603)424-3387 and by email at
timothymcmahon@usa.net. Web address: http://room.earthlink.net/~labyrinth/

Customer Relationship Management ... it seems there is a new business "buzz word" every year. This year it's "Customer Relationship Management" or "CRM". Not long ago it was Partnering. Added-Value is still around as well. Actually CRM is a pretty good catch phrase simply because there is nothing more important than the relationships we establish and maintain with our customers.

I spoke at a recent sales conference and asked my audience, "How many of you think that customer relationship management is important?". Not surprisingly, every head nodded and every hand went up. Then I asked, "How many of you have a clear strategy in your company for customer relationship management?". Many, but not all, hands again were raised. Finally I asked, "How many of you think that your CRM strategy is being well executed and is making a measurable difference?" Now only a few hands could be seen, half-raised, among the crowd.

There's the problem. We all embrace CRM as a good idea but when it comes to developing a customer relationship strategy and then executing it ... well, we're a bit less confident. We shouldn't feel that way about something as critical to the success of our businesses as CRM.

What kind of relationship do you want to establish with your customer?

When we think about relationships, many of us – and most salespeople – think of the personal one-on-one relationships we establish with key customer personnel. Without question, personal relationships are important. The axiom "People buy from people they like" is still true. The problem is that people come and go in the business world, both in the customer's company and in our own. So, as useful as personal relationships may be, they're dangerous to depend on for long term success.

The real question is:
*What kind of relationship do you want
your Company to establish with your
customers?*

▸ Your customers will directly or indirectly
interact with many different people in
your company across the enterprise, not
just your sales representatives. How do
you want your customer to feel about
his or her overall interaction with your
company? What do you want your
customer's to value about you as a
result?
▸ What are the Key Values you bring your
customers; that is, what are the reasons
your customers should only want to buy
from you? Your key value(s) should form
the basis of the customer relationship
you want to create. Can you clearly and
succinctly define and communicate your
key values?
▸ Are your Key Values unique and
important enough to your customers
that if they fully understood and
appreciated them they would clearly
prefer you over your competitors? Take
a few moments before you answer this
question and take a hard look.
Remember that you simply cannot build
a powerful business relationship if you
can't offer something the customer
needs and values better than your
competition. You may need to rethink
your key values.
▸ Does the customer's every interaction
with your entire company support, sell,
and enhance this key value message?
Does each interaction enhance and build
the relationship?

Let's look at the mythical ABC Company.
ABC believes its key values are the quality
of its products and the responsiveness of
its people. ABC must first ask itself if its
customers feel these key values are
important – important enough to establish
an exclusive business relationship with
ABC. ABC must then ask itself if its quality
and responsiveness are unique enough to
base its customer relationships upon. If the
answer to both questions is "Yes", they
must then ask whether every customer
interaction – with sales, service, billing,
delivery, etc. – actively supports the
messages of quality and responsiveness.
Finally, does the customer consistently feel
that their relationship with the company as
a whole is so strong that it can easily
survive any change in ABC's personnel?

What must we do to create and maintain that relationship

Step 1: Definition & Action Plans

Creating and managing the customer
relationship is clearly an enterprise-wide
task. The company as a whole must define
– and clearly communicate to every
employee -- what it wants to be the basis
of the customer relationship (key values).
Each function of the company must clearly
define:

1) how it contributes and impacts
(positively or negatively) the customer
relationship,
2) develop a specific action plan of what it
can do to provide a greater contribution,
and

3) how it depends upon and needs to interact better with other functions.

Step 2: Customer Communication & Internal Change

If there is a "single point of failure" in CRM, this is it! Too many companies do a good job of defining why customers should buy from them (other than just product or price) but seem to forget to tell the customer! In other words, we create a potentially powerful message that could help build stronger customer relationships but fail to clearly establish it in the mind of the customer. So in the final analysis it's still business as usual.

It is an important consideration that unless your company's customer relationships are already exactly as you want them, you will have to do something different than you are today. Different results are the result of different actions. This means that everyone in your company – and especially the sales force – will have to do some things differently than in the past. As the prime point of customer contact – and as the people who set the direction of the customer relationship -- this directly impacts your sales organization.

Look again at ABC Company. They did a fine job defining their key values upon which to base the customer relationship. They determined what each job function and each employee needed to do and they communicated it well to their organization. New marketing and advertising focused on the unique value ABC offered. Unfortunately nothing really changed – sales and win/loss ratios stayed the same and the company won and lost the same number of new and old customers as the year before. Clearly customer relationships were not strengthened or enhanced. What went wrong?

The problem was ABC's salesforce. It wasn't that they weren't good salespeople. The problem is they were excellent salespeople! In fact, they were so good that they were not about to change what had worked for them in the past. Their "sales pitch" stayed the same and they continued "building" the customer relationship one-on-one, not "company-to-company". To a lesser degree the same was true with employees in other job functions; they continued to do their jobs they way they always had with lip service to the company's CRM initiatives.

Step 3: Managing the Initiatives as a New Product

So in the end it's all about execution. Companies successful in Customer Relationship Management have learned that results happen when employees actively embrace new initiatives (much like they would an exciting new product) and carry out the prescribed action plan (to sell it).

In other words, try viewing and positioning your Customer Relationship Management initiative as a true product, the cost to the customer of which is embedded in the price of the "standard" products you sell. After all, your CRM program is designed to first benefit your customer and through them your company. It is the responsibility of every employee to both "sell" and "deliver" the CRM product successfully to the customer.

Package your CRM program as you would a product, supported with marketing collateral, support, and a strong selling strategy. Put the same effort and enthusiasm into teaching your salesforce your CRM product and how to sell it as you do teaching them to sell any new product.

Make sure that managers in all functions clearly understand the initiatives and action plans and how each employee is expected to perform. Assure that each manager understands that it is his or her responsibility to manage their business as expected.

Finally create a series of metrics or measurements of how you will measure the success of CRM – and tie an element of employee compensation (sales, managers, and others) to achieving those metrics. Aggressively track and measure.

Customer Relationship Management – it's a good phrase and a good idea. While simple in concept, however, developing a CRM program is a complex initiative which will require enterprise-wide input, communications, and commitment ... if it is to become your company's most powerful tool for increased sales, customer loyalty, and competitive advantage.

Build relationships with customers that competitors find difficult to break

Title: Build relationships with customers that competitors find hard to break
Author: Bryan Black, Chief Executive of Recognition Systems
Abstract: This article entails an opinion by Bryan Black, Chief Executive, Recognition
                       Systems, that talks about the possibilities a CRM project can give a company
                       and the issues that need to be considered before installing a CRM project.

Biography: Bryan Black, Chief Executive, joined Recognition Systems from Oracle Corporation UK where he was the Business
Alliances Manager for Applications. Prior to joining Oracle, Black was Managing Director of decision support software company,
Pilot Software. Before this he spent 10 years with business applications software company, McCormack & Dodge, where he
became Regional Vice President, Americas, responsible for all operations in Canada and South America.

Protagona, the flagship CRM product of Recognition Systems, delivers unique customer experiences consistently across all channels, including the Web, call centres, direct sales, and traditional direct marketing communications. The product delivers a true bricks and clicks solution by providing both functional and multi-channel integration. With its ability to support high volume, complex marketing campaigns, Protagona is turning customer and prospect transactions into profitable customer relationships for global 500 organisations worldwide. These organisations represent a cross-section of industry including financial services, insurance, retail, utility and non-profit.

Traveling on the train I couldn't help but overhear a conversation two friends were having about coincidences. During their idle chat one mentioned he'd recently surfed the Web viewing holiday information about Hawaii and the USA, only to have a travel brochure come through his door a few days later and give further details about such journeys.

That was good timing, his friend said, then gave a similar account of an experience he'd had. After buying a £5 and £7 bottle of wine from an off-license the previous weekend a pamphlet from the same shop had come through his door the following week. It had outlined special offers on wines priced between £5 and £10. While the man said he was not a great wine drinker he decided to try some of the offers because he'd liked the bottles he'd bought before.

So were these two happenings coincidence? Probably not. These two men will most likely find such occurrences will become a regular event in their lives as the years go by. Letters from their insurance companies will ask if they'd like family insurance on their cars at about the time one of their children has a 17th birthday and their banks may begin to deliver loan offers shortly after they get a job promotion or pay increase. In general, the direct mail they receive through their doors will become more and more relevant to their needs.

This is because advancements in CRM technology allow companies to establish systems that will help them build strong individual customer relationships - no matter how large their client base. CRM makes it possible for all organisations to instantly respond to individual customer needs and will soon no longer be a niche practice.

Information systems can capture customer communication whether through e-mail, direct mail, call centres, point of sale or Web site analysis. Customer confidence can then be built by tracking changes in each consumers life circumstances such as marriage, divorce, children, the purchase of a new house, job change or retirement. All these factors affect a persons needs and their ability to pay. Having such information allows companies to better target customers at the right time according to their individual needs.

Collecting data of this type on individual customers is not new. Today, almost every organisation does it but they usually segregate the different data into separate departments within the company. CRM groups the customer details into one source and enables quick access to all the information held on individual clients or potential consumers. Companies are then able to compute the value of each customer and know what they buy, how much is made from their purchases and what it costs to acquire them.

Firms using CRM can also focus on the best and most intelligent way to deal with their customer databases. For example, if someone rang a company twice in two

days they would not want to give, or be given, the same information on each occasion. With CRM the information exchanged during previous conversations would be recorded and easily accessed by any staff member a customer speaks to. This ensures each transaction is up-to-date, unique and a continued evolvement on the previous contact.

CRM will also add operational customer workflow by ensuring certain steps are taken to better the chance of a customer making a purchase. For instance, if a potential consumer responds to an advertisement by faxing or emailing a request, the next step might be to send a product kit out to them. Workflow-enabled CRM will automatically send reminders to staff to ensure this happens and then again to ensure follow-up calls are made and personalised by the data held on each individual.

So what does adopting a CRM project entail?

In the first instance companies will have to hire a professional project manager or have in-house staff with the necessary skills to handle large system projects. A viable alternative would be to employ a consultative group with specific expertise in data warehousing or CRM. A general IT consultant shouldn't be hired as IT requires a very different area of expertise from that needed to implement a successful CRM system.

Once the proper expertise has been acquired, data from every department within the organisation will have to be integrated so every employee can access it instantaneously. Pulling data from legacy systems is the most complex part of establishing a CRM programme. It involves connecting documentation stored in different forms on incompatible systems or in separate political territories. An ETL (Extract, Transform and Load) program has to be written to move data from one or more source systems to a single receiving system and the whole process is usually the biggest budget item when installing a CRM program.

Sometimes company politics also have to be overcome when establishing a CRM service. For instance, one department may decide it doesn't want to share its records with other employees. This maybe because it believes extra work may result or its role within a company may be lessened should its sole control of the information it has collected be lost. Company directors need to explain to department heads that a CRM programme will bring all sectors into a team with a cohesive focus. The result will be increased synergy with business, technical and marketing users making joint decisions.

Other considerations that need to be taken into account include various departments having different file calendars or one group finishing its month on the 25th, and another on the 31st. There may also be problems with territories and codes. But only when all company data is brought together will instant access to all information be possible. Otherwise a company will effectively have only a database marketing system with batch programs.

When considering the cost of ownership of a CRM service I'd advise companies to talk to external organisations or expert consultants as there is no set formulae for pricing an implementation. The expense is often higher than companies expect when they initially start to investigate but if a company has to merge several systems total project costs will be somewhere in the lower range of six figures. A large organisation may have to pay several millions of pounds but the payback from the most CRM projects will be achieved very quickly and certainly between one and two years.

Plenty of time must also be allowed to install a CRM programme. In fact, the best advice anybody can give is to allow enough time. Many companies expect to have a CRM campaign running in weeks, but, depending on complexity, it can take between four and six months to become fully operational. A CRM system needs to be built to evolve easily and with changes in mind. It cant just be formed for the present and it will take a lot of time to find the expertise and people who can merge documented data successfully and maintain quality assurance.

Once in place, a company should have a CRM system with administration standards, back-up, security, database training and user administration all rolled into the one package, and if a business rule or a data code is changed all staff should be notified automatically.

Then the company will be able to begin to understand the life stage each customer is at. It will be able to personalise the

information it sends to individual
customers and prospective consumers and
ensure its direct mail and marketing
promotions are relevant to or alerts them
to their needs. The organisation will also
realise which are its most valuable clients
and be able to plan, schedule and control
pre and post sale activities in a targeted
fashion.

In all, it adds to a sense of expectation and
loyalty being instilled within the consumer
and the development of a relationship
between company and customer that
competitors find hard to break.

Chapter 1: Introduction to CRM

Implementing the Customer Relationship Management Foundation – Analytical CRM

Title: Implementing the Customer Relationship Management Foundation –
                 Analytical CRM
Author: SAS Institute
Abstract: In today's highly competitive business environment, companies must
                 continuously learn from interactions with customers and respond to the
                 knowledge gained from those interactions. A shift from product-driven
                 business strategies to customer-driven business strategies has become
                 essential. This white paper discusses the technological and business issues
                 involved in implementing progressive techniques in managing customer
                 relationships. It details the practice of using advanced data management and
                 analysis techniques to transform a large amount of carefully chosen customer
                 data into reliable information to support strategic and tactical business decisions.

A Changing World

The business world is changing. Widespread deregulation, diversification, and globalization have stimulated a dramatic rise in competition between companies. And customers themselves are changing—natural customer loyalty is a thing of the past. The more consumers understand the marketplace, the more they want to be recognized and understood as individuals, and they will give their business to the companies that do the best job of understanding and responding to their needs.

In response to these changes, competitive companies are abandoning ineffective business philosophies of the past and adopting new and innovative ways to maintain customer loyalty and profitability. Rather than focus on internal considerations like reducing costs and streamlining operational systems, companies are seeking to maximize profitability by focusing on the many facets of the customer relationship. Guided by the concept of customer profitability, an economic view of customers that measures how profitable a customer is to a company rather than measuring the profitability of product lines, companies are adopting a customer-centric strategy, stressing the importance of optimizing the value of each customer relationship. In this significant shift from product-driven strategies to customer-driven strategies, customer retention is becoming more and more important, in some cases eclipsing customer acquisition as the primary focus. Reacting to increasing acquisition costs and acknowledging the value of analyzing customer profitability, many enlightened companies have realized that the key to success is this: know everything you can about the customer.

The goal is to define the profitability of customers based on customer lifetime value (LTV)—a measurement based on the fact that the past value of a customer, though useful information, does not itself determine future profitability. It is what that customer is going to do and spend in

Chapter 1: Introduction to CRM

the future that will contribute to the bottom line for the next year and beyond. This enables companies to not only manage profitable customers in a way that optimizes the customers' LTV, but also manage non-profitable customers. A notion of future or lifetime value is essential when prioritizing and focusing resources to ensure they are directed where they will benefit most.

One key approach in transitioning to a customer-centric strategy is to gather enough information to group customers into categories and tailor your interaction to each group. Segmentation is an important starting point for understanding individual customers. Through analytical segmentation techniques, customer information such as demographic data and lifestyle information can be combined with historical customer information to help identify differences in behavior among various groups, or segments, of customers. For key segments, these can continually be filtered and differentiated to become segments of one, with the goal of creating unique, individual customer profiles.

So why do many companies settle for a fuzzy definition of who their customers are, when a detailed profile of individual customers allows for vastly improved opportunities to meet the customers' needs? The answer for some is an unwillingness to tackle what may appear to be an incredibly complex data management and analysis task. After all, if you gather 100 pieces of information about each of 1000 customers, you then have to store, manage, retrieve, and analyze 100,000 pieces of data in real-

world, operational scenarios. Even in a small-scale example like that, the numbers can be a little daunting. This is where data warehousing technology comes into play—it's the foundation on which successful CRM strategies are built.

What is Customer Relationship Management?

Customer Relationship Management (CRM) is a process by which a company maximizes customer information in an effort to increase loyalty and retain customers' business over their lifetimes. The primary goals of CRM are to

▸ build long term and profitable relationships with chosen customers
▸ get closer to those customers at every point of contact
▸ maximize your company's share of the customer's wallet.

CRM combines a progressive approach to gathering customer data with advanced database and decision support technologies that help transform that data into business knowledge. By maximizing the use of customer information, companies can better monitor and understand customer behavior. In response to newly gained customer intelligence, companies retool their front- and back-office systems to ensure that they are providing what the customer really desires. CRM calls for increasing customer share—that is, retaining customers and selling them an expanded set of products that has been tailored to their wants. This requires amassing data from every customer

Figure 1: CRM Overview

integrated customer view can feed a wide variety of data analysis processes, from call behavior analysis and needs analysis to segmentation and campaign analysis.

In addition to the application of state-of-the-art data management and analysis techniques, CRM implementation often involves a significant change in a company's business strategy—changes that require not only retooling back-office processes, but in many cases, reorganization of the business functions closer to the customer. Operational processes designed to support a product-driven strategy become ineffective when the company's marketing focus shifts to a customer-centric strategy. Companies must adjust those processes to allow all information coming from customer contact points and other customer related information to be consolidated and analyzed. Then, newly acquired customer intelligence is translated into real-world changes in how the company manages customer relationships. From implementing Web-based solutions for communicating with customers to initiating automated campaign management strategies, effective and flexible front-office processes are vital in any CRM implementation, serving as both the initial conduit for customer data,

contact point, analyzing that data to find ways to better serve customers, and then effecting changes based on the new business knowledge.

Effective CRM depends on data—data about who customers are, their preferences, their behavior, their status with the company (both past and current), their purchase history, and their classification, based on demographic and psychographic information. Much of the data-intensive work involved in CRM initiatives begins with back-office processes. A repository of customer data must be created within a single, customer-centric data warehouse. Then, this

Chapter 1: Introduction to CRM

and then, after the data is analyzed, affecting changes based on the resulting customer intelligence.

As we explore the central concept of CRM—the notion that customer information fuels analytical processes that in turn yield business knowledge used to improve company processes—a clear division begins to emerge between the primary elements of a CRM initiative. Two halves of CRM, one focusing on operational initiatives and the other focusing on analytical initiatives, can be further defined as follows:

▸ Operational CRM, which, building on the notion that customer management plays an important role in a company's success, calls for the automation of horizontally integrated business processes involving customer contact points via multiple, interconnected delivery channels and integration between front- and back-office operations.

▸ Analytical CRM, which involves the implementation of the advanced data management and analysis tools that make progressive customer relationship management possible. This is the analysis of data created by Operational CRM for the purpose of business performance management.

As this paper focuses primarily on Analytical CRM, let's take a closer look at the advanced analytical technologies that contribute to an effective CRM initiative.

The Technologies behind Analytical CRM

The technologies most commonly involved in the analytical portion of a CRM initiative are

▸ data warehousing
▸ data mining
▸ online analytical processing (OLAP)
▸ advanced decision support and reporting tools.

Before we examine each of these technologies, let's first examine the general flow of data and information in a CRM initiative to get a feeling for where each technology comes into play. Initially, operational data (records of business transactions that have occurred between the company and the customer) is gathered from customer contact points. This operational data, along with legacy customer data and market data from external sources, is compiled into a data warehouse. At this point, OLAP tools and data mining techniques are used to extract relevant patterns or trends in the data. Finally, utilizing sophisticated reporting tools such as Web-enabled dynamic reporting systems and executive information systems, the business knowledge gleaned from this process is used to improve operational effectiveness at customer contact points, and the knowledge is also deployed to back-office business activities for use in tactical decision making.

Data Warehousing

A data warehouse is an implementation of an informational database used to store shareable data that originates in an operational database-of-record and in external market data sources. It is typically a subject database that allows users to tap into a company's vast store of operational data to track and respond to business trends and facilitate forecasting and planning efforts.

Typically, before a data warehouse can be created, a data cleansing phase must occur. Data cleansing is the process of manipulating the data extracted from operational systems to make it usable by the data warehouse. When loading data from existing operational systems, it is likely that few if any of the operational systems will contain data in a format that is compatible with the data model developed for the warehouse. For example, a product number may be stored as a numeric field in one system, while a second system appends an alphabetic suffix to the number for reporting purposes. Data cleansing is an extremely important part of creating the integrated customer view, often exposing unexpected inconsistencies in operation data from disparate sources.

It is during the creation of the data warehouse that an IT department adds metadata, or data about the data. Metadata includes descriptions of what kind of information is stored where, how it is encoded, how it is related to other information, where it comes from, and how it is related to your business. The disparity in content and format of the data, coupled with the sheer volume of information, requires the creation of metadata that will tell users and analysts important details about the source, format, and purpose of the data.

Figure 2: A Closed-Loop CRM Architecture

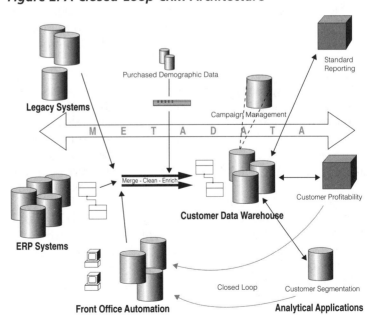

Chapter 1: Introduction to CRM

For business users, metadata is essential to the management, organization, and exploitation of the data that feeds a CRM initiative. It is very helpful for business users to be able to see, for instance, how the profit variable was calculated, or that perhaps sales territories were divided differently prior to a certain date, or even just when the data was last updated. This type of metadata, such as documented business rules, helps extend the value of your repository of customer information. Given the complexity of the relationship between operational systems and decision support systems, metadata should document all data elements from data source to data exploitation as completely as possible.

SAS software is widely recognized as the de facto standard data warehousing technology, highlighted by its ability to capture and integrate data from a large number of sources and its support for a broad range of hardware platforms and operating systems. SAS software allows you to access, manage, and organize all relevant customer data from operational systems, legacy systems, value-added data providers, and market research sources— both internal and external.

Data Mining and OLAP

Data mining involves specialized software tools that allow users to sift through large amounts of data to uncover data content relationships and build models to predict customer behavior. For many years, statisticians have manually "mined" databases looking for statistically

significant patterns. Now, data mining uses well-established statistical and machine learning techniques to build models that predict customer behavior. Predictive modeling can segment and profile customers, and this information can be integrated into the data warehouse and with other marketing oriented operational applications. SAS Institute's data mining offerings, including the recently released Enterprise Miner™ software, are acknowledged market-leading technologies that enable analysts to model virtually any customer activity and find patterns relevant to current business problems. This technology enables you to define a set of comprehensive and consistent customer profiles to better understand customer needs, behavior, and profitability and construct predictive models of customer behavior to fuel target marketing and campaign management activities.

OLAP (Online Analytical Processing), also known as multi-dimensional data analysis, offers advanced capabilities in querying and analyzing the information in a data warehouse. In some CRM initiatives, OLAP plays a major role in the secondary analysis that takes place after initial customer segmentation has occurred. For example, in CRM-based campaign management systems, OLAP is an excellent tool for analyzing the success or failure of the promotional campaigns. A pioneer in OLAP technology, SAS Institute offers the SAS/MDDB™ server, a powerful tool that allows analysts to work with multidimensional views of the data and surface information that will aid in decision support processes.

Decision Support and Reporting Tools

Web-enabled reporting tools and executive information systems are used to deploy the business information that has been discovered. This enhanced customer knowledge is distributed to executive decision-makers as well as to the operational customer contact points. Applications equipped with some of the same sophisticated modeling routines developed in the data mining phase are applied to individual contacts in real time. In some companies, the World Wide Web and Internet/intranet technology are critical components in managing customer relationships. They not only use Web technology to share business knowledge from the CRM process, giving every employee a better understanding of customers at every point of contact, but also to collect additional information about customers and prospects, thus fueling further CRM activities. You can create advanced information delivery systems like Web-enabled OLAP, query, and reporting tools using SAS/IntrNet™ software. Additionally, SAS/EIS® software viewers and our Web-based data warehouse exploitation tool called MetaSpace Explorer™ software are also powerful reporting tools that help put fresh, valuable business intelligence into the hands of those who need it.

Summary

As corporate competition continues to increase due to external market factors and a market-savvy customer-base, companies must discard their business philosophies of the past and adopt new and innovative ways to maintain customer loyalty and profitability. Building loyalty among customers involves understanding the various ways that they are different and using that knowledge to tailor appropriate behaviors towards those customers. Companies must adopt a customer-centric strategy that stresses the concept that success over time comes from customer loyalty—that long-term profitability lies in fostering unique lifetime relationships with small numbers of carefully chosen customers. Companies must continuously learn from interactions with each individual customer and be prepared to dynamically respond to information and knowledge gained from those interactions. What makes this possible is CRM, a method of processing a large amount of carefully chosen customer data in order to obtain reliable information to support strategic and tactical business decisions. Utilizing advanced data warehousing, data mining, OLAP, and decision support technologies, companies can create an integrated customer view and extract relevant patterns or trends in the data. Business decisions based on complete and reliable information about your customers are very difficult for your competitors to replicate and represent a key and sustainable competitive advantage.

SAS Institute offers the only software and services solution that spans the entire decision support process for managing customer relationships. SAS software is recognized as the de facto standard data warehousing technology, providing the capability to capture and integrate data from a large number of sources on a broad range of hardware platforms and operating systems. Our data mining offerings are acknowledged market-leading technologies that enable analysts to model virtually any customer activity and find patterns relevant to current business problems. As a pioneer in OLAP technology, SAS Institute offers powerful tools that allows analysts to work with multidimensional views of the data and surface information that will aid in decision support processes. And finally, SAS software enables you to create advanced information delivery systems like Web-enabled OLAP, query, and reporting tools so you can deploy the valuable business intelligence reaped from your CRM implementation into the hands of those who need it.

e-Everything: Technology-Enabled Customer Relationship Management

Title:	*e-Everything Technology-Enabled Customer Relationship Management*
Author:	*Web Associates*
Abstract:	*Customer Relationship Management can be widely defined as company activities related to developing and retaining customers through increased satisfaction and loyalty. In this white paper Web Associates refers to online CRM activities—all customer-facing processes integrated via the Internet—as e-CRM: Electronic Customer Relationship Management.*

Biography: Web Associates, Inc. is an Internet technology integration team specializing in implementing the e-CRM services outlined in this document. Web Associates has provided systems specifications development, production, and other services for Hewlett-Packard, Lucent Technologies, DHL, Sybase, Apple Computer, and other top companies.

"Dynamic trade will push the traditional model of customer relationship management (CRM) beyond its limits. Companies need a new approach—eRelationship Management—to leverage the Web's unique strengths for capturing and publishing a single view of customers."

--Forrester Research

"Outsourcing mission-critical e-Customer Relationship Management lets experts design and maintain online systems while the company focuses on its core business."

--Dave Swan, CEO, Web Associates

Going "e" with Customer Relationship Management

CRM's traditional focus is on managing and increasing the value of business-to-customer relationships. But while CRM practices help to acquire and retain customers, historically CRM activities have increased rather than reduced operations costs. Managing customer relationships is expensive and cumbersome, especially where cross-divisional communications are required to link customer needs to fulfillment channels.

Web-based CRM uses the Internet to integrate and simplify customer-related business processes, drastically reducing costs of customer-facing operations while achieving CRM's primary goal: to enhance the customer experience.

A Single View for Customers

A complete, integrated e-CRM system is characterized by faster, automated services available online or on the desktop 24 hours a day. Typically the greatest challenge a global company faces in accomplishing this level of service is providing a seamless experience between different departments and business units; therefore, a focus of e-CRM is integrating front- and back-office activities and cross-divisional functions.

Chapter 1: Introduction to CRM

Table 1: Cross-Divisional eCRM Functions

PROCESS	FRONT OFFICE	BACK-OFFICE
Sales	Customer-directed E-commerce Dynamic, interactive catalog integration	→ Sales Force Automation → Product database
Marketing	One-one relationship Proactive notification	→ Data mining & analysis → Lead generation/routing
Service & Support	Customer self-service	→ Communications channel/ call center management
Product Development	Direct customer feedback	→ Product knowledge base integration
Distribution & Supply Chain	Direct information transaction	→ Integrated management systems

As Web use becomes a way of life for more and more people, online customers' demands are increasing and their tolerance for internal communications deficiencies is decreasing. Customers want instant gratification, and if they can't get it from your company they will go elsewhere. In fact, defecting to a competitor is easier than ever, and researching options is a breeze, even for an inexperienced Internet user.

More than ever before, it is imperative that a company's various divisions share a single view of the customer, and project a single view of the company back to the customer. e-CRM systems, then, need to be designed fundamentally from a customer's perspective, and with a holistic approach to integrating lead generation, lead conversion and customer fulfillment processes.

Increasing ROI

The more complex a company's CRM needs are, the more difficult and expensive it is to implement e-CRM systems. However, once deployed, e-services are as easy to deliver to low-dollar customers as high-dollar ones, and the more customers served by automated customer services and transactions, the less costly per customer the system becomes.

Figure 1: eCRM as a Continuous Sales Cycle

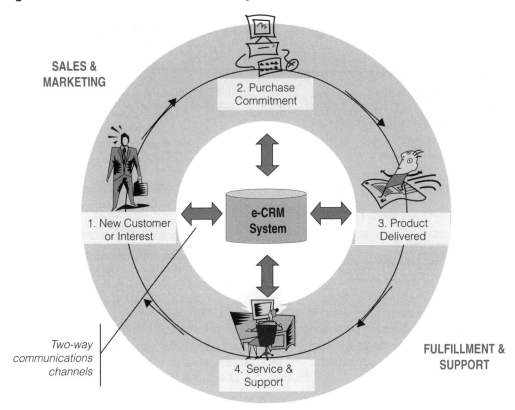

Success Criteria

The primary goal of e-CRM is met when e-services and transactions are more convenient and less expensive for customers. This in turn facilitates the company's fundamental goals: increasing revenues and reducing costs. Specific e-CRM initiative goals, then, can be viewed in the same terms:

Improved Customer Satisfaction
1. E-services are always available, accommodating any schedule
2. Services take less time to render, adding to customers' convenience
3. Orders can usually be processed and delivered more quickly
4. Online self-service is immediate, private, relevant, and easy to access (customers don't always have to go to the Internet to get help; e-CRM services can be integrated directly to users' desktops as well)

5. Customer feedback to the company is immediate, and customers are gratified by knowing they can easily communicate their needs
6. Automated software delivery eliminates users' having to monitor and update software applications
7. Shopping and purchasing is easier and more time effective than ever
8. Electronic services are generally free or cost less for the consumer

Reduced Operating Costs
1. Electronic automation results in companies' being able to render 24-hour services without incurring 24-hour operating costs
2. Use of more efficient data transfer technologies results in less expensive, more efficient communications
3. Automated sales systems result in lower cost-per-transaction for purchases
4. Shared knowledge bases result in greater accuracy and simplified processes in multidivisional collaboration
5. Easy viewing of customer behavior results in better business intelligence and better business decisions
6. Global data delivery systems result in drastic reductions in software packaging and distribution costs

Increased Revenue
1. Better customer satisfaction results in better customer retention
2. Online commerce transactions often enable broader market reach
3. Online services drive demand-generation mechanisms (e.g., the need to update software or upgrade software)
4. Dynamic metrics analysis tools provide real-time effectiveness reports for faster

market response
5. The Web creates new sources of per-service and per-transaction revenues for many companies
6. Enhanced services can drive new sales; improved customer and business relationship management enhances value of deliverables

Services-On-Demand

As the global base of regular Internet users continues to increase, so do online consumer expectations; better and faster services on a wider scale is part of every e-Business survival strategy. From new product information to service manuals, if it's not on the Web your staff will hear about it. But information services offered in an e-CRM environment are about more than posting static Web pages regularly; users need information to be easy to access, easy to browse and search through, and completely up-to-date.

State-of-the-art electronic relationship management solutions include a growing variety of services that are increasingly industry-focused. Users want and have come to expect specific services on demand, requiring that information availability and transfer is a reflex, not a process.

Online Information Services
Online information systems provided for users can include a variety of features, including automatically published content, user groups and bulletin boards, catalogs, event notifications, and other database-driven content. Information can also be

delivered directly to users' PC screens or right to their printers. Online publishing can be also automated with content responsibilities distributed among departments or regions.

Simplified Searching
Smart search capabilities in an e-CRM environment can help customers to solve problems or find products more easily. Key word searching is a standard, but natural language search engines are also available, and many users find it easier to type in a sentence or phrase that narrows the search criteria and often requires less technical knowledge about the subject. Multi-variable searching and step-by-step product fitting are ideal for online sales, particularly when numerous product options are available or custom quotations are required.

Customer-Directed Online Transactions
Commerce transactions on the Internet are now a standard expectation for customers, and less costly sales can be facilitated through efficiencies created by electronic technology. Well-planned and well-managed e-CRM systems can also provide new sales opportunities through a better understanding of customer behavior and more interactive involvement.

Online Technical Support
Technical support processes can be far more effective when users are provided with in-context Help information that empowers them to solve their own problems. Support technologies can include methods for self- and auto-diagnoses, automatic software updating, and direct interaction through connected devices. Ideally, a customer support Web site is easily available from the main company Web site via an obvious link or a customer support log-in.

Desktop Integration: Closer e-CRM
Providing a desktop icon for users can solve a number of problems associated with online support; desktop applications as the entrance to the customer service "corridor" offer immediate product and support information, and can connect with Web-based e-CRM systems when updates or transactions are required. This can in turn speed customer service issues, create sales opportunities and offer a closer level of support; with an integrated desktop application, the company has the ability to communicate directly with users through their desktops instead of just through email.

Information and Software Updates
Customers also expect to be able to download current software from your Web site, but customers approving automatic updates can receive software updates during idle connected time.

Information can be added to users' desktop applications without user's instigating an update, and software can be updated transparently, depending on permission levels (which should be set by the users).

Call Center Integration
Web sites and desktop applications should connect with the call center, even if the connection must be loose in the initial phases of e-CRM deployment. Ideally an e-CRM system should begin with a common

Chapter 1: Introduction to CRM

knowledge base and data structure, but if that's impractical for the first phase, call center integration can be as general as including links from within the e-CRM application.

e-Feedback Channels

Feedback directly from customers combined with pure metrics analysis delivers the business intelligence needed to continually improve online CRM services. Constant end-user feedback is part of an integrated e-CRM system, and immediate user feedback in e-CRM can do a lot more than make improvements; it can help detect costly mistakes early and provide insight into fixing problems.

Feedback collection and management following system deployment can be accomplished through a variety of types of field surveys such as Web site feedback forms, desktop message inquiries, and YES/NO questions following transactions and support activities. Large quantities of user feedback can be managed by administrative interfaces allowing managers to search for specific types of feedback over particular periods and view reports of users' responses.

Intelligent Commerce

Electronic commerce is a closely integrated part of e-CRM. Understanding customer behavior and anticipating needs through online activities tracking provides the ability to offer users the right kind of sales information at the right time.

Whether from a new or an existing customer entering the system from the Web site, their desktop, CD or other commerce portal, all transactions in an integrated e-CRM environment share a common knowledge base driving a network application. A single product and customer database can be used for all sales channels, and distributed retail outlets and field sales operations can share the same system simply by being connected.

Personalization

The ability to customize network-based software and make it dynamic creates new opportunities to improve customer relationship management. Applications can "know" users' needs, creating a shorter path for sales and support activities. Customer interface aspects that can be personalized include:

1. The name or alias the customer uses; a personalized e-CRM system can recognize users and call them by name
2. The content available; content can be customized according to products the user has or as specified by the customer, so customers have the same apparent channel for support for any and all products they purchase
3. The look-and-feel and branding; many Web-based electronic service and commerce applications create different interfaces for different targeted demographic groups, providing the same features and using the same network server application
4. The level of interaction; e-CRM systems should allow users to decide when and how and when they receive and respond to sales information

Depending on the permissions allowed by the end user, a desktop extension of an e-CRM system can also provide additional intelligence about user preferences and activities.

Demand Generation

Part of the need for close collaboration across company functions is the inherent connection between sales and post-sales support. Technology-enabled customer service and support creates sales opportunities in the process of solving users' problems or returning information. A user trying to find a particular solution, for example, may be more inclined to purchase immediately if the solution offered in context meets the immediate needs of the customer and can be purchased (and often delivered) on the spot.

An Online CRM Specification

The goals of e-CRM are not difficult to understand, nor are e-Business endeavors generally hard to cost-justify. Still, realizing a complete and fully-integrated e-CRM solution is a huge challenge, and the specification is the starting point—the blueprint for success of any system.

Knowing your customer is critical to an e-CRM system's success. Prior to developing a specification, companies implementing e-CRM should organize current customer data to completely understand the uniqueness of their segment's customers and their specific needs. Features defined in your specification will be in direct response to those defined needs.

Metrics showing costs of current customer sales, service and support channels will provide a referent for setting specific revenue and cost-saving objectives, including lead referrals, delivery costs, and costs per transaction for sales and support activities.

Specification Considerations

Developing an effective e-CRM specification requires experience in network-based systems implementation, interface design, information architecture, and e-CRM applications. For a typical large company, generating a specification internally simply takes too long.

Still, in-house management and company-wide participation are required. Companies expecting to succeed with their e-CRM solutions need commitment from each department to develop a complete specification for e-CRM to move forward effectively. Piece-by-piece approaches are ultimately costly if individual systems don't fit compatibly into the whole.

Pressure from Sales & Marketing and Customer Service to deliver solutions quickly leads most implementers to a phased approach to e-CRM systems deployment. However, this can only work if all systems are designed within the same specified platform and data structure, and all use the same knowledge base.

Questions to Ask

QUESTION 1: WHAT WILL OUR e-CRM SYSTEM DO?
A preliminary specification should be discussed at the executive management level, determining the fundamental system goals and priorities, beginning with the basic question, How will this system serve our unique customers?

From the answers, a long list of specific functionality can be developed and a specific set of features defined. The resulting feature set is the preliminary specification that describes the scope of the e-CRM objectives, the starting point for a more complete specification development.

Once basic functional goals are determined, each department involved should be identified and a resource designated to represent that department or business unit's needs during the specification development process.

QUESTION 2: WHAT DO WE KNOW ALREADY?
The next question to address is what parameters can be automatically assigned. One general assumption that most e-CRM developers would begin with is that the e-CRM system be network-based and accessible from the Web. Other constraints may be product-specific or customer-directed, or based on demographics, budget and other strategic considerations.

QUESTION 3: WHAT WILL IT LOOK LIKE?
Based on the intent and the constraints identified in the first two questions, a system and information architecture can be specified and the user interface defined. It is critical at this point to know exactly what the system does and what information transactions need to occur to facilitate that functionality; mock-up interfaces provide clarity and detail for technical teams to completely understand system functions and data tables before they make implementation decisions.

QUESTION 4: HOW DO WE BUILD IT?
Finally, specific technology solutions can be proposed. Vendors who have performed online customer service implementation should be able to offer a specific solution for the specification defined. A practical approach divides the final specification into two parts: What we can do now and What has to wait. Some aspects of an e-CRM solution can take months to develop, and in order to stay competitive, businesses have to provide online services as quickly as possible. Taking one step at a time allows them to begin executing their e-CRM Plan immediately, then add services as they are ready to integrate into the same system.

All e-CRM systems have to consider the three basic e-Business solution elements: software applications, network servers, and implementation and support expertise.

e-CRM Software
Integrating software applications is a basic requirement of technology-enabled customer relationship management. Ideally, a comprehensive, integrated software application would be better than a hodgepodge of unrelated applications,

optimizing the functionality-versus-cost trade-off.

Forrester Research reports that veteran client/server CRM software programs will not suffice as a core e-CRM system engine because they are not Web-based and tend to manage customer records and workflow rather than managing relationships. Still, applications like SAP and Siebel lead in preference among IT managers surveyed by Forrester.

But Internet channel managers are inclined toward Web-based software such as BroadVision and SilkNet, which offer a whole new class of applications that attempt to build a real-time understanding of customers in a wider context.

In either case, integration of multiple applications is required. Customized Web applications for customer and partner interaction can be effectively built and integrated within the same, compatible environment using the same intranet- or extranet-based knowledge base as the internal client/server architecture. These customer-facing applications supplement internal client/server applications to serve specific e-CRM-related functions such as banner ad tracking, feedback management, or other transactions.

Existing databases can be converted to provide the basis of the new, extranet-based Web system.

Application Servers and Network
The backbone of a Web-based e-CRM application infrastructure will be the network itself. Network and server operations should be specified last to accommodate the needs of the software, database applications and content delivery requirements specified. The primary issues involved in server and network decisions are

1. Performance, especially where global content distribution and processor-intensive operations are a consideration.
2. Security, including firewall protection and intranet versus extranet considerations.
3. Reliability, especially minimized down time and removal of all single points of failure through redundant equipment and backup power
4. Backups, including a rotation strategy for backing up all databases, content and logs

Implementation Expertise
Depending on the extent of the e-CRM task, and disregarding specific industry expertise, at least four separate skill sets apply to a successful e-CRM deployment team:

1. Business development and project management
2. Content organization, management and publishing
3. Internet-based systems architecture and development
4. Interface design and cross-platform, multi-device implementation

Implementation plans should include an online system for file sharing and collaboration, as well as reviewing specifications, designs and other documentation.

Chapter 1: Introduction to CRM

Finalizing a Specification

Most companies turn to outside sources for implementing e-Business and e-CRM because of the wide range of skill sets required and the learning curve involved if an in-house team is assembled (often, consultants are brought in to develop a specification as well).

The caution here is that outside consultants are often predisposed to a particular solution or part of a company providing implementation services. A specification should focus on specific, high-value functionality rather than particular products or methods.

Properly defined specifications should be integrated into Requests for Proposals and sent to multiple vendors, creating more options for achieving the company's specified objectives before making a final commitment.

A final specification should describe the system well enough for a vendor to provide a complete proposal for the e-CRM solution described. In table 2 are final checkpoints that e-Business or e-CRM specifications should address in order to receive a predictable solution in a realistic time frame.

Companies specializing in online Customer Relationship Management should be able to demonstrate strong experience producing Web-based applications and have an implementation plan that addresses each of your requirements and specified features.

Table 2

e-CRM Specification		Vendor Proposal
1. Functionality requirements	➡	1. Implementation
2. Desired time frame	➡	2. Schedule with milestones
3. Content structure	➡	3. Electronic publishing plan
4. Content sources	➡	4. Communications strategy
5. Design requirements	➡	5. Design production plan
6. End-user requirements	➡	6. Application server & network
7. Compliance standards	➡	7. Adherence plan
8. Testing requirements	➡	8. Testing strategy
9. Q/A & approval needs	➡	9. Deployment plan
10. Security standards	➡	10. Security plan
11. Metrics requirements	➡	11. Reports definitions
12. Budgetary constraints	➡	12. Implementation cost
13. Maintenance role	➡	13. Maintenance costs
14. Evaluation criteria	➡	14. Customer service plan
15. Future requirements	➡	15. Vendor market focus

Measuring Results

Positive results of a successful e-CRM implementation will be tangible, and reflected in metrics reports. Metrics analysis tools are available from a variety of vendors, but most e-CRM applications and solution providers will include or specify a reporting solution.

Ultimately an e-CRM system's impact can be quantified in terms of 1) value as customer service system (by measuring cost per user and customer satisfaction levels) and 2) revenue growth. Evaluating costs per user, per lead and per transaction is relatively straightforward and calculable through client/server metrics reports.

Gauging customer satisfaction with an e-CRM system can be accomplished through field surveys that prompt users for feedback (electronically) provide insight into the effectiveness of specific customer sales and support objectives.

Application-based field surveys are contained in the e-CRM application interface, typically accessible from the customer's desktop. A feedback form is easily accessible and available at all times.

Push- and pull-based systems provide questions dynamically to the user through an active Internet connection and implementation of a direct-to-user update technology such as BackWeb.

User responses can then be used to gauge the overall user experience, determine the effectiveness of the application and its services, and assist in product research and development. Most importantly, every single transaction in a true CRM environment, whether a sales- or a support-related transaction, is an opportunity to build loyalty and profit.

The Importance of Marketing Data Intelligence in Delivering Successful CRM

Title:	The Importance of Marketing Data Intelligence in Delivering Successful CRM
Author:	Emma Chablo, Marketing Director, smartFOCUS Limited
Abstract:	The purpose of this white paper is to discuss the issues and opportunities surrounding the value of Marketing Data Intelligence. It reviews how Marketing Data Intelligence delivers marketers with the levels of access and knowledge of the customers required to drive successful Customer Relationship Management strategies that widen, lengthen and deepen the customer relationship.

Widening, lengthening and deepening the customer relationship:

Widen
- Acquire new customers
- Identify new segments
- Identify under served segments

Lengthen
- Develop longer term relationships
- Reduce churn and attrition
- Increase perceived and purchased product value

Deepen
- Cross and up sell
- Enhance the propensity to buy
- Sell more profitably

This paper covers the role of Marketing Data Intelligence in delivering effective CRM.

The whole area of Customer Relationship Management and the need to widen, lengthen, deepen customer relationships is much discussed at this time. There are a huge number of articles discussing the systems and processes to deliver quality CRM, however very few address the first step, intimately knowing who your customers are and the factors influencing their behaviour.

The essence of CRM is to move organisations from a product centric to customer centric philosophy to gain control over these influencing factors based around three key drivers, market, technology and economic. In addition, the widely accepted principle that it costs between five and ten times more to recruit a new customer than to retain a current customer brings the CRM philosophy to life. In a highly competitive global environment holding on to good customers is key to continuing business success, the economic opportunity of maximising the customer and new and emerging technology solutions all conspire to drive the CRM marketplace.

Figures in a recent KPMG report found that 70% of leading UK companies admitted

Chapter 1: Introduction to CRM

that it was either not easy or impossible to find out who their customers are and what products they buy.

In a recent Business Intelligence (1999) survey 70% of leading UK companies stated that customer retention is a significant issue. In the same report 90% of companies believed that CRM was of strategic importance to their organisation today but that there were many obstacles to the successful implementation of CRM.

Barriers identified included:
▸ operational barriers
▸ poor marketing practises
▸ inadequate, un-integrated information systems
▸ the ability to access and understand customer needs
▸ the possession of sufficient information on customers
▸ effective segmentation of customers
▸ lack of marketing tools to manage the customer relationship including loyalty schemes

However, the research indicated that the overriding barrier effecting good marketing practise with regard to successful CRM was the need for access to real customer knowledge.

Definition of CRM

A myriad of CRM definitions are being espoused however, our belief is that the following best sums up the essence of CRM:

"A comprehensive approach which provides seamless integration of every area of business that touches the customer – namely, marketing, sales, customer service and field support – through the integration of people, process and technology, taking advantage of the revolutionary impact of the internet."

Ovum, leading technology analysis use the following:

"CRM is a concept, or management discipline concerned with how organisations can increase retention of their most profitable customers, simultaneously reduce costs and increase value of interactions, thereby maximising profits."

For the purposes of this report either definition is valid, both definitions are driven by sophisticated marketing data intelligence.

Definition of Marketing Data Intelligence

Marketing Data Intelligence is the key to successful delivery of any CRM marketing decision support activity. Marketing Data Intelligence delivers access to real customer knowledge. It is the point at which all companies should start when defining the corporate CRM strategy.

Marketing Data Intelligence is defined as:

"Combining data driven marketing and technology to increase the knowledge and understanding of customers, product and

*transactional data to improve strategic
decision making and tactical marketing
activity, delivering the CRM challenge."*

Customer Data Transformation
The extraction and transformation of raw
data from a wide source of internal and
external databases, marts or warehouses,
pooling the total data value and
information into a place where it can be
accessed and explored.

Customer Knowledge Discovery
Providing marketers with the tools and
processes to discover the true value of
data, converting information into usable
customer knowledge deployed to enhance
marketing decision making and customer
relationship management initiatives.
Closing the feed back loop with results
from marketing and customer relationship
management activities and strategies
continues the process of learning and
knowledge acquisition enhancing the ongoing value of marketing data intelligence
and its role in delivering successful CRM.

The final part of marketing data
intelligence is measuring the results of
campaigns driven by marketing data
intelligence. It is critical to measure
performance and feed results back into the
feedback loop delivering greater
intelligence in the future.

Customer Relationship Management Drivers

This section covers the main factors driving
the demand for CRM including market
drivers, technical drivers and economic
drivers.

Market Drivers
The single clear driver for CRM is
increasing competition. Markets are
becoming saturated and communication
channels delivering marketing messages
are saturated. Because of this customers
are demanding to have a different
relationship with suppliers than the
traditional sales model.

Market research suggests that customers
want to develop a closer relationship with
suppliers and are happy to pay a premium
to do so for as long as they feel they are
getting superior value/service. However it is
also true that customers want to have
different types of relationships with
suppliers depending on what they are
buying and at what point they are at in the
customer life cycle. Add to this the fact
that access to information of all kinds is
getting easier through technologies like the
internet means that the customer can
easily discover the range of options
available and the prices they are available
at. The whole traditional marketing model
where product is centre stage clearly does
not address this change.

Marketing gurus such as Peppers & Rogers
have for several years been proposing that
the theories of mass marketing and mass
media will disintegrate making way for a
one to one relationship driven relationship.

The key enabler to this change in the same way that the industrial revolution led to mass marketing in the first place is the availability of technology to deliver one to one relationships.

Modern database technologies putting the information into the hands of the people who can use it best enables the delivery of customer centric relationships. This is delivered through knowledge of which the customers are, what they buy, when they buy and even predictions based on historical behaviour and socio/psycho/geodemographic data of future behaviour. These technologies lead to new marketing techniques that put the control back into the hands of the consumer to choose.

Successful companies in the future will use customer information intelligently to build relationships with their customers on the level that the customer wants and will work towards developing a long-term relationship through retaining customers by delivering delighted customers.

Now more than ever, the ability to understand and manage a close relationship with the customer is central to delivering these business goals. It is the ultimate challenge for marketing in any business. A challenge that can not be ignored in fact, one in which businesses must excel.

It is essential to widen the customer base through acquiring new customers, identifying and targeting new segments, finding new or under served markets.

Lengthening the customer base is important in developing the life cycle value of the customer, maintained through a longer term relationship, increasing the perceived value of products, identifying and introducing new products whilst reducing churn and customer attrition. The depth of relationship with the customer must increase identifying different customer and product profitability, understanding the cross selling and up selling opportunities, the propensity of different customer segments to purchase and increase sales.

Knowing what data is available

Data warehousing has been promoted as the key to getting all organisational data together under one roof and making it accessible to the people who need it. In many cases this is true although the time it takes to achieve this panacea can be a great deal longer than initial expectations. Even where the data warehouse is up and running, accessing and analysing the data is not as easy, fast or as accessible as it should or could be. Having the information easily available to marketing can make the difference between a successful campaign and a failure. Potentially huge amounts of data is available, but unless this data is available in a useful format, is available in a timely fashion (not weeks later) and enables the train of thought analysis that marketers rely on, your data is of no value at all.

Analysing your data

Having the right marketing information available to do full customer analysis is key to better understanding of customers and potential customers. Being able to use that information to make decisions has influence on marketing campaigns and inevitably marketing spend. To achieve profitable campaigns the marketing department needs to ensure that customers receive the information that they want in a timely fashion and target the right people with new information.

Enhancing your data

If the picture of your customers is incomplete you can enhance the data with externally available information. For example geodemographic, lifestyle and psychographic data can help in developing the full image. All this information can be pulled together to a single source and over time a historical perspective can be developed.

Predicting the future

The use of data modelling & mining techniques can take customer information one step further, the future behaviour of your customers can be predicted by analysing their historical behaviour. Predicting which customers are most likely to buy your products or customers who are most likely to move to a competitor enables you to campaign these people more effectively, growing the customer base or reducing attrition rates.

Technology Drivers

Dr Wolfgang Martin, Senior Research Analyst, Meta Group states that the successful businesses of the future have changed the rules by introducing mass customised interaction with their customer base. CRM is defined as business systems for acquiring and retaining customers. According to the Meta Group, analytical

CRM is about knowing your customers and being able to measure your CRM business performance. Analytical CRM provides the value-added knowledge. In Marketing Data Intelligence terms analytical CRM maps to the customer knowledge discovery and customer data intelligence stages. The goal is to deliver integrated operational and analytical CRM solutions, in Marketing Data Intelligence terms Customer Data Transformation acts as the closed loop processing link to operational systems.

The Aberdeen Group takes a different view of the CRM technology space and defines it at a much more technological level. The diagram below shows the CRM Application Spectrum.

Marketing Automation consists of:

Lead Management

▸ Acquisition of prospects from sources
▸ Web sites, trade shows, print/telemarketing campaigns
▸ Management of leads
▸ Passing leads to Sales Force Automation or call centre automatically
▸ Monitoring and controlling success/failure of lease
▸ Correlation of success/failure back to campaign or source of lead

Campaign Management

▸ Plan, manage and monitor the campaign project
▸ Monitoring the success or failure of leads generated through the campaign (end to end timescales of campaigns can be reduced)

Chapter 1: Introduction to CRM

Chapter 1: Introduction to CRM

Marketing Effectiveness System
▸ Electronic repository of company, product, collateral information
▸ Designed for access by both internal (sales) and external (partner or customer) constituencies
▸ Uses web technology to push (distribute automatically) or pull (deliver upon request) information

Commerce Centre
▸ Internet based successor to the call centre
▸ Provides a customer point of contact for customer enquiries, support, purchases
▸ A superset of both e-commerce and call centre

Data Mining and Decision Support
▸ Evolution of CRM & Data Mart based systems – real time marketing data analysis surrounded by campaign management
▸ Enable the search of internal and external data
▸ Internal data from ERP, SFA and legacy systems
▸ External data from third party lists
▸ Applied to
▸ Identify potential customers from databases
▸ Tailor highly targeted campaigns to prospects

Management of Distributor and Channel Promotion
▸ Keep the channel partners informed, enthused and fed
▸ Integrated and automated marketing effectiveness and lead distribution

Marketing Data Intelligence falls within the Marketing Automation spectrum of the Aberdeen model. Lead management falls into the feedback loop delivered from Customer data intelligence activities. All other areas within the Aberdeen model fall into the customer knowledge discovery sector of MDI excepting marketing effectiveness that falls into the customer data transformation area.

Economic Drivers

Customer Loyalty
Studies show that maintaining loyalty can increase customer profitability between 25% and 85%. Knowing who customers are and what they're buying is one step towards ensuring their loyalty without necessarily increasing costs. Using customer knowledge to make marketing decisions ensures that better decisions are made. Mass unfocused marketing is a thing of the past, marketing spend needs to show a higher return on investment, something that can be best achieved through longer term relationships.

It is the marketing department who is responsible for developing and maintaining the long-term relationships with customers. Marketing manages the day to day communication with them and it is marketing that the organisation will turn to for the delivery of a "one to one" customer relationship.

Customer Retention
It is proved that it is between five and ten times more cost effective to retain customers than to attract new customers. The cost of losing profitable customers to

the competition is very high and it is unlikely that once lost the customer will return.

Customer Life Time Value

Extending the life time value of customers is also key, knowing who your customers are and what they buy enables analysis and modelling to identify what other products those customers may buy. The key is to identify those customers who match the profile and then to predict response to cross and up selling opportunities.

Customer Case Studies

The following case studies highlight areas where smartFOCUS customers are already using Marketing Data Intelligence to drive elements of CRM campaigns.

The Financial Services case study particularly shows how Royal & SunAlliance use MDI to identify and segment customers by profitability and how this information is used to feed their campaigns.

The FMCG case study shows how MDI is used within a very difficult marketing environment to target specifically the market segment with loyalty offers.

The Telecomms case study shows how getting knowledge from customer data has driven business and marketing decisions effecting the whole customer strategy including channel strategy.

These companies and over 200 others are using smartFOCUS Marketing Data

Intelligence to improve customer data transformation, customer knowledge and finally customer data intelligence.

Financial Services
Royal & SunAlliance Corporate Partnership Division delivering better customer service

Royal & SunAlliance is a leading global force in insurance and financial services with over £9.2bn in revenues of which 59% is generated in the UK. Offering a strong service and tailor made product portfolio, Royal & SunAlliance have built a secure and highly respected business based on professionalism, teamwork and customer focus. Royal & SunAlliance concentrate on three main areas of business, life insurance, asset management and personal insurance lines including motor, home and health.

The corporate goal is to become a dominant global force in insurance and financial services in the years to come by being responsive to customer needs whether it's an individual, small business or multinational. Within Royal & SunAlliance the Personal Financial Services Division is divided into four main divisions of which Corporate Partnership Division is accountable of more than one third of the total personal financial business in the UK.

Corporate Partnership Division is the area of Royal & Sun Alliance responsible for providing "own brand" insurance services through a diverse range of businesses including banks, building societies, retailers, credit card companies and motor organisations. They have a large product portfolio which includes Household insurance both buildings and contents, Motor insurance, Travel, Extended Warranty, Creditor Insurance and Domestic Mortgage Indemnity. All of which can be tailored to specific requirements and sold through the corporate partners as branded products, providing a large and varied distribution channel for Royal & SunAlliance products and an extensive customer base to service.

Back in 1996 Corporate Partnership Division identified the need for a customer database capability. CPD saw that providing database marketing services to their partners and delivering them with customer analysis information for marketing campaigns and to improve customer relationships would be beneficial.

The business problem required CPD to overlay different data-sets, sourced from various Royal & SunAlliance systems (both operational and marketing intelligence), data from those partners wishing to engage in collaborative analysis plus enhanced data from external sources (ACORN & MOSAIC). A data mart strategy was identified to provide the solution because it offered the flexibility needed and could be provided on a PC platform.

An initial demonstration of the Viper portfolio from smartFOCUS showed that it met the challenge, this was followed by a one-week evaluation of the software. Objectives were set to load and build a CPD database, to undertake limited analysis and gain further experience on the products usability. The next stage involved the Viper portfolio being benchmarked against another product. The tests included a database, meta data and query build,

measured by the speed of operation, ease of use and accuracy of results. Viper emerged the faster and easier to use of the two products and benefited from a familiar look and feel through the Windows interface. Following this successful evaluation, Royal & Sun Alliance purchased the Viper portfolio including Viper, Asp, Sidewinder and Viper Viewer plus all supporting training and implementation services.

Customer Relationship Marketing with the Viper Portfolio

RS&A CPD uses Viper today because of its ability to perform one way analysis to help identify those variables that appear significant when explaining particular customer behaviour. Analysis is typically focused on the individual customer but may be segmented by product (e.g. household insurance) or by client (e.g. Banking Partner).

Viper is used to undertake portfolio analysis by customer profitability. For example within one client portfolio, the definition of a value score for each customer led to customers being sorted into ten bands. From this CPD have established that the top 10% of customers for this client are worth 38% of the total value and that the bottom 10% group made up minus 28% of total value. This example shows the importance of segmenting and targeting for customer relationship campaigns. This information is then provided to the call centres that handle the direct relationships with the customers and use it to determine customer strategy on a case by case basis.

Conclusions

The key strengths of the Viper portfolio identified by Royal & SunAlliance have been speed of implementation and the ability to deliver usable results quickly. In addition to products Royal & SunAlliance have benefited from the support services that smartFOCUS deliver around the product including implementation consultancy and Marketing Information Analysis and Discovery services providing data analysis and modelling skills.

Sidewinder provides RSA with excellent CHAID modelling capability whilst Viper provides the exploratory train of thought analysis. The Viper products are used alongside other modelling tools such as SAS which is needed for linear modelling and working closely with the Actuaries on pricing models using the customer value scores.

" *the use of smartFOCUS Viper portfolio has made a significant contribution to bettering our understanding of our customers. We are now in an excellent position to identify profitable customer segments in order to better target our conversion and retention activities and thereby increasing overall customer value.* "

Vince Mason, Customer Database Marketing Manager, Royal & SunAlliance, Corporate Partnership Division

FMCG

Leading FMCG Company Improving Marketing Segmentation & Campaign Planning through Viper

A leading UK FMCG company working in a restricted marketing environment has seen significant benefits to its direct marketing initiatives from using the Viper products within their marketing department and agencies. As an early adopter of Viper technology this company has benefited from improved targeting of campaigns, resulting in lower campaign costs and higher campaign redemption rates.

The household name brands manufactured by this company are sold through all major high street FMCG retailers, newsagents and supermarkets.

The past five-ten years have seen the company shift from a very strong above-the-line advertising strategy, to a much more mixed strategy incorporating direct marketing and sales promotion as well as the traditional advertising and sponsorship activities.

The Marketing Database Project

The company established a consumer database in 1991. With no access to transaction information the database was built from promotional responses and questionnaire information. The database primarily is used for direct mail and consumer research activities and now holds details on several million individuals.

In the summer of 1996 the company commenced a marketing database improvement project. The existing mainframe system was held by a third party bureau and managed via a direct marketing agency, a set-up that had become inappropriate for the company's direct marketing plans and activities. In addition the existing database solution was expensive and cumbersome to manage.

A dedicated database marketing professional was employed to manage this project and then manage the resulting solution.

A requirement specification for a new database marketing system was published in September 1996. Key objectives were the provision of a faster system with better access for the whole marketing team and at a lower cost to manage and maintain. This brief was sent to a broad range of database bureau including several major players as well as smaller operators and the companies in-house IS resource. After a detailed evaluation process the chosen solution involved an outsourced database plus Viper tools for analysis. This offered the most effective achievement of the speed, access and cost objectives.

The initial Viper implementation included two copies of Viper and four copies of Adder. Since then a further 12 Adders and one copy of Sidewinder have been installed. The marketing database now has over 25m records covering over 7m customers. Customer information is relatively sparse, consisting largely of brand preferences plus consumption and purchasing behaviour, with limited demographic and lifestyle information.

Considerable liaison between smartFOCUS and the database bureau ensured an effective implementation. A large PC database server provides the platform for the Viper marketing analysis database with fortnightly refreshes independently undertaken by the bureau and sent via DAT tape.

The users were trained by smartFOCUS over three training courses and now a number of people within the FMCG Company and their various direct marketing agencies regularly use Viper to plan & initiate direct mail campaigns. One of the main ongoing challenges is to increase the frequency of use of the products to reinforce the skills learnt and extend the usefulness of the database.

Marketing Analysis
The Viper products are now used regularly for campaign planning, to define direct mail campaign volumes and to analyse the campaign response rates. Pre-campaign analysis in Viper/Adder results in a mailing list definition being provided to the database bureau for production.

Campaign responses typically are loaded back to the database within six-eight weeks of mailing and then automatically will be incorporated within the next Viper refresh. Once the campaign has been completed, various response analyses are undertaken to determine the profile of the responders. This post campaign analysis allows the next campaign to be more tightly defined.

More effective targeting and analysis have led to significant improvements in direct marketing activity. Response rates have improved from reduced mailing volumes. Improved segmentation and customer understanding has enabled more effective mailings to be created.

Future Plans

As previously mentioned the marketing activities of this Viper user are being increasingly regulated. Focus is moving to promotion to the distribution channels or trade rather than the consumer. A database of over 200,000 retail and distribution establishments has been established to support the direct salesforce and trade marketing initiatives. The use of Viper to access and examine this database is being considered to better understand the profiles of retail outlets and assist in growing sales through campaigns focused on these channels.

"The company's Database Marketing Manager states that "using Viper has enabled us to enhance our marketing strategy under difficult trading and marketing conditions. We have really improved our ability to target our customers and have seen genuine improvements in campaign performance. Our next challenge is to grow our understanding of the trade channels and Viper could be a key part this."

Telecomms

Marketing Data Intelligence Drives Martin Dawes Business Information

Martin Dawes is the UK's largest Independent Mobile Service Provider. Established as a result of the OFTEL decision to implement a layer of competition between the end service provider in mobile telephony and the end-user, Martin Dawes' role in the early days of mobile telephony was to manage the customer relationship. Martin Dawes Telecommunications was established in 1987 and now has over 1 million customers. The law changed a few years later, at the time the Orange and Mercury licences were allocated and since that time the leading service providers have followed a policy of buying out the Independent Service Providers to gain access to the end user bases. In February 1999, BT Cellnet purchased Martin Dawes Telecommunications.

In early 1997 the customer base was growing enormously but the management information system developed for connecting new customers and billing did not provide the information necessary to drive marketing. Martin Dawes recruited a Database Marketing Manager whose first challenge was to understand better the fast growing customer base. The information available from the corporate information system was not sufficient to allow large scale analysis to take place, it was also difficult to obtain information due to a high reliance on the IT Department whose main responsibilities lay elsewhere.

The Marketing Database

The database marketing strategy was defined by working alongside an independent consultant and smartFOCUS were approached to assist in delivering the marketing database analysis tools to provide the required customer information to drive business and marketing decisions. Before Viper could be implemented however the marketing database needed to be built and cleansed. This stage is now completed and over 1.6m records including all subscribers, connects and disconnects from the start of the Martin Dawes business are now stored in the marketing database. A monthly extract is provided from the marketing database for loading into Viper for the analysis to be done.

Marketing Analysis

The main analysis to date has been to identify trends in customer loyalty and trends in churn. For example Martin Dawes run a Diamond Club scheme for high value service users. The Viper analysis showed that the average churn was a great deal lower for Diamond Club members than those people who exhibited the same high usage levels but were not members. Further analysis was undertaken to find out why Diamond Club members had a lower churn rate. The results indicated a mixture of elements, including the fact that members of the Diamond Club priority service were handled by a specific team allocated to Diamond Members (Group dynamics), the psychology of being in a club and the recognition of value. The results of the analysis proved the value of the Diamond Club outweighed the costs of running it and enabled the level of spend by each member to be calculated and measured.

Other analysis undertaken regularly using Viper concentrates on connections and disconnections over a six month period by channel. Martin Dawes uses a number of channels to sell its services to market including the Carphone Warehouse, Dial a Phone, Amway, Telesales, Direct Sales and retailers. Recent analysis has shown that some channels have a much higher churn and further research indicated that some channels were actively churning customers at the end of one year fixed contracts in order to get re-sign revenues. This valuables information enables Martin Dawes to make business decisions on channel strategy and on product offers to ensure that churn rates are kept low.

Viper has also been responsible for identifying a data entry error that led to approximately 500 customers not receiving bills for up to three or four years. The cost of this error has been calculated at approximately £120k per annum and would have gone unnoticed if Viper had not been used.

Finally, Viper is also used to drive telemarketing campaigns by identifying simple customer segments. For example Viper was used to identify all customers who were signed to old tariffs (these have a high propensity to churn). These customers once identified were targeted with an upgrade campaign, the result being a very high conversion rate.

The customer understanding that Martin Dawes now has is driving key business decisions. All the results from Viper analysis are sent to the Chairman and Managing Director as part of their business information. The credit reference group within Martin Dawes also uses Viper to analyse the trends in credit reference rejection. In addition the Finance department will use Viper in the near future. Further developments will include analysis at call record level of up to 30 million call records per month, the plan being to analyse two to three months at a time.

Viper within Martin Dawes has already proved its worth by giving information to the people who need it in a very digestible format. By identifying trends in the data Martin Dawes has been able to ring fence their most valuable customers.

Paul McQuaid, Database Marketing Manager, Martin Dawes: "Viper has provided Martin Dawes with an excellent view of our customer information enabling us to make business decisions that have made a real difference. We have already recouped the cost of our investment and are growing our use and the value of Viper all the time. Viper will be used increasingly to manage our customer relationships to ensure minimal churn and maximum customer value."

Further growth in the use of the Viper portfolio is anticipated in the future, not every product has yet been analysed against every customer. More questions arise as more analysis is done and there is always a need to delve deeper. The team has now grown to four people all using Viper products on an almost daily basis.

Following earlier successes, new partner databases are being built in order to exploit the skills and techniques over as broad a customer base as possible.

Surviving the future

The future success of businesses will be greatly influenced by the ability to harness and use customer data and the knowledge they derive effectively. Delivering successful Customer Relationship Management will depend on the intimate customer knowledge marketing data intelligence delivers the marketers.

It is marketing that lead the way in delivering this. The winners and losers will be determined by the investments made in marketing and marketing driven technology and marketing's ability to deliver clearly targeted activity focused on managing the relationship through whatever channel the customer chooses and whatever relationship the customer wants.

Deploying software tools that unlock the invaluable knowledge trapped in potentially huge amounts of data is the key. These tools must deliver data that can be easily manipulated, analysed and modelled, easily implemented and used by the people who can deliver the most value from understanding it, marketing.

smartFOCUS experience in deploying marketing data intelligence through PC based database analysis and modelling software tools is dramatically improving the customer relationships of over 200 organisations in the UK, including Royal & SunAlliance, Dun & Bradstreet, Royal Mail, Lloyds TSB, Comet, Proctor and Gamble and Microsoft. smartFOCUS provide software solutions & supporting professional services designed by marketers for marketing people that put them in control of the customer relationship and in control of future business success.

Making every customer relationship count. Exploring the business drivers and technology enablers of customer relationship management

Title: Making every customer relationship count. Exploring the business drivers and technology enablers of customer relationship management

Author: Bill Schmarzo, IBM NUMA-Q

Abstract: Competition in all industries, as well as increasing customer sophistication, is forcing organizations to rethink how they do business. Products are no longer the key differentiator — competitive advantage comes from utilizing all knowledge within the organization to treat customers as individuals and maximize their lifetime value. As organizations shift their business models, success is based on the ability to identify, acquire, retain, and grow the most profitable customers. Until now, information technology has not enabled this process. Most systems have reflected a product and functional focus, and customer data has resided on multiple systems with no ability to link together. A fresh approach is required, one that utilizes a completely integrated and flexible information architecture to support a customer-centric business strategy.

Chapter 1: Introduction to CRM

"Historically, the hotel business has been very focused on product and the physical package of the hotel. Today there's a far greater focus on customer relationship management: getting to know the customer, serving the customer individually and personally. From an information systems side, this means we have to store and manage information about the customer. We have to make information accessible to the organization; some on a real-time basis and some on a less real-time basis for marketing purposes. It is changing our focus significantly, moving us into information warehouse management and making that information available very, very quickly."

—Scott Heintzeman
Vice President of Knowledge
TechnologyCarlson Hospitality Worldwide

"In a retail business we focus on product and understanding the product demands for customers. But the view of how you market, how you sell, is very customer-focused. And the combination of that product/customer mix is always part of the retail solution. As that evolves —once you have a strong product base and control, which is the infancy of retail —you focus more and more to refine your customer aspects. And that's a phase we're moving strongly into."

—Tammy Lowe
Director of Product Distribution Systems
Hollywood Entertainment

Introduction

In today's increasingly competitive business environment, sophisticated customers aren't just making their buying decisions on the basis of product comparisons. They're making those decisions on the basis of the relationships that they have with their suppliers.

Sophisticated businesses, in turn, are using advanced information technology solutions to analyze the status of their sales and profits, to learn more than ever about their customers, and then to put that knowledge to work. Armed with a strategy for Customer Relationship Management (CRM), these businesses are winning new customers, delivering highly targeted solutions to existing customers, and building the type of customer loyalty that will increase sales and profitability for years to come.

Although many companies recognize the value of CRM, not all of them are adept at it. Customers want recognition, value, quality and respect for their patronage. They don't always get it. Banks issue ATM cards that know your name — but not which language you prefer to speak. Technology companies make you punch in your customer ID number when you call for customer support —and then have the support engineer request the same information when you finally get him or her on the line. Phone companies are offering an increasing array of services to give customers more convenience —but still require them to call during business hours, when most people are busy working at their own jobs, to order those new services.

CRM recognizes that not all of a business's customers are of equal value —and that it is essential to pay the most attention to the most valuable customers. For example, a leading U.S. airline estimates that six percent of its customers represent 24 percent of all miles flown and 37 percent of all revenue. Given that industry's high fixed costs, these customers probably represent half or more of the airline's profits. Other companies and industries have similar statistics. A major retailer, for

example, estimates that five percent of its customers represent 75 percent of its revenue.

But CRM also applies to the rest of a company's customers — to the majority who now comprise a minor share of a company's sales and profits. That's because this majority on the periphery represents a company's future income stream. CRM helps to identify ways to bring these occasional customers into the tier of more valued and more-profitable customers. It also helps to identify those who do not fit the profile of present or potential profitable customers, enabling businesses to essentially "fire" them as customers.

A historical perspective

CRM represents the culmination of a long-term, evolutionary shift in the traditional thinking of business. Until the past few decades, the business of the global economy was, essentially, manufacturing. That focus on goods rather than services led to a product-focused, mass-market marketing strategy in which businesses tried to sell the same product to as many people as possible. The result: a high cost of acquiring new customers, and a low cost for customers switching to other brands. When all the value is in the product —rather than in the relationship with the vendor — there's little reason for customer loyalty if a better price or new feature pops up somewhere else.

To counter the negative aspects of this situation and to increase customer loyalty, companies are moving toward a more customer-centric perspective. Recognizing that their most profitable or potentially profitable customers are among their existing customers, companies are trying to learn to sell multiple products to those same customers. The result: lower cost of acquisition and some increase in the customer switching cost. But even the best customers in this model can still be lured away by new products or promotions elsewhere.

The challenge for all companies that sell products or services—and that means all companies—is to take this customer-focused approach to the next step: a long-term, relationship-centric perspective. Instead of adding some relationship value to a product-based customer interaction, companies need to focus first on the customer, and on adding maximum value to the customer's relationship to the company. Selling multiple products to the same customer, generally through campaigns or promotions, gives way to developing an understanding over time of who each customer is and what he wants, and then using that knowledge to sell better service to him. This is the basis for a learning relationship, in which the accumulated knowledge about a customer's activities and preferences enables the company to engage in a more intimate, value-added relationship.

The result will be fully interactive, one-on-one tailored approaches in which each customer's needs govern how and when and to what extent he interacts with the company. Some companies are getting very close to this model, such as retailer Nordstrom, known for the pro-active, highly personalized service that its sales staff provides to turn customers into loyal family members.

Figure 1: Relationship-centric focus

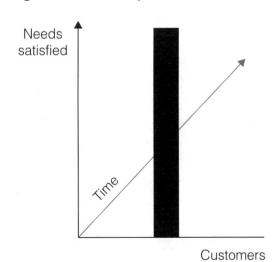

Goal: Sell complementary products to same customer

Near-zero cost of acquisition
Increased customer switching costs
"Experiience" is based on the relationship
Value to the customer defined by the company

Result: One-to-one marketing approach

Other companies don't quite have it right yet, like the consumer electronics company whose sales clerks put customers through a detailed marketing questionnaire in order to buy low-cost, commodity items such as batteries. Not all customer interactions need to be personalized or relationship-based. Which makes it crucial for businesses to identify when and where to apply personalized, relationship-based marketing.

Researchers Don Peppers and Martha Rogers have provided a marketing model that helps to identify what marketing approaches are best for a given industry, and which industries can best benefit from CRM, or what the researchers call "One-to-One" marketing.

The horizontal axis measures the diversity of customers' needs; as one moves farther to the right, the graph conveys that customers have an increasingly diverse set of needs. For example, a gas station — where people are relatively limited in their choice of products (a few grades of gasoline, motor oil, etc.) — has low diversity and falls toward the left end of the axis. A bookstore — where consumers can buy any of thousands of titles in scores or hundreds of categories — has high diversity and falls on the right end of the axis.

The vertical axis measures the differentiation in "customer valuations." Businesses in which a small concentration of customers provides high profits have a highly differentiated customer valuation; the airlines are an example.

Businesses where customers contribute relatively equally to profits — again, such as the gas station — have low or uniform customer valuation. The more a business can implement targeted interactions with its valued customers, the higher it falls on this axis.

According to Peppers and Rogers, businesses with relatively undiversified customer needs and relatively uniform customer valuations —e.g., the gas station —will do best with mass marketing techniques. Those with diversified customer needs but uniform valuations —

Figure 2: Right marketing strategy for the industry

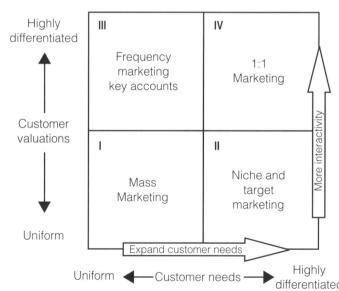

such as a bookstore —can benefit from target marketing. A package goods company selling to retailers will benefit from a key accounts marketing approach. And a pharmacy or computer systems company with diversified customer needs and highly valued customers will benefit from one-to-one marketing or CRM.

Since CRM reduces costs, and increases customer loyalty and profitability, it would be a shame to think that many industries can't take advantage of it based on where they are on this chart. Happily, they can. Companies can move along the horizontal axis by expanding their customers' addressable need sets. But it is also possible for a company to affect its position on the vertical axis. This is done by increasing the level of interactivity that the company has with its customers, in order

to distinguish the value derived from that customer. For example, gas stations can add a convenience store, ATM machine and other services —from dry cleaner to key duplication —to address a wider range of their customers' needs.

For example, Mobil Corp. is using electronic smart cards to identify customers and their purchases, in order to facilitate target marketing or CRM, as appropriate. Telephone calling cards, superstore "membership" cards, and bonus-buy cards from the corner bakery or bookstore are additional ways that businesses attempt to build loyalty and gain more information about their customers. But gaining more information isn't enough. Companies also have to be able to analyze and act on this information in a timely way to influence customer purchases and relationships.

Figure 3: Driving customer relationships

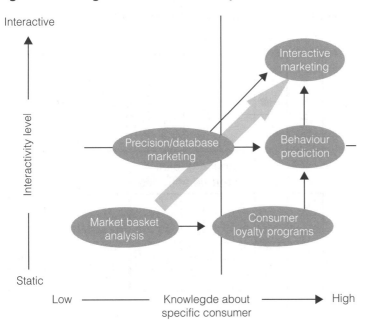

The business drivers of CRM

Companies are spending $3.5 billion per year on relationship marketing, according to the Gartner Group. They're doing so because CRM is delivering quantifiable business benefits. Value-chain analysis helps to show why.

For most companies that sell products, the value chain includes processes and activities that are capital intensive, but don't add value from a customer perspective (e.g., inventory, distribution centers). Forward-thinking companies are increasing their profits by reducing their investment in these capital intensive, non-value added links of the chain, and redirecting those investments into activities that do have value to the customer. Companies as diverse as Dell Computer, Amazon.com and Cisco all exemplify this trend. For example, both Dell and Amazon.com have vastly reduced their inventories, an aspect of the value chain that provides no obvious value to the customer. Dell has reduced its inventory to 7 days from the industry average of more than 80; Amazon.com has decreased its inventory to 17 days versus the industry average of 176. With the money they're not spending on inventory, these companies are investing in innovative service and

support activities —through new channels such as the Web—that build customer loyalty and company profits.

A variety of factors are driving businesses to adopt CRM and realize its benefits. For example, the Web puts tremendous product and supplier information into the hands of consumers and corporate buyers. A range of reporting and analysis services —from Consumer Reports to million-dollar consultants —do the same. Customers have more information than ever before on which to base their purchase and relationship decisions, which makes those customers more sophisticated.

Customers also have more access and interaction points with their suppliers. In addition to getting more information from the companies with which they do business, customers today have more ways

Figure 4: CRM value chain ramifications

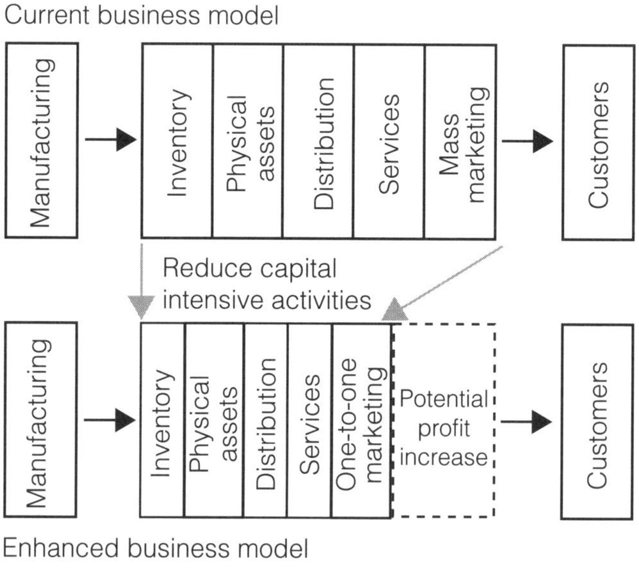

Current business model

Enhanced business model

to interact with those companies — including phone, fax, email, Web, mail, on-site and more. That's encouraging businesses to customize and maximize their use of each of these venues and to build profitable relation-ships with customers who prefer to use these new channels of interaction.

As a result, business processes themselves are changing. And boards of directors, recognizing all of these changes, are mandating companies to respond in order to establish, or maintain, a competitive advantage.

The customer management cycle

Businesses have a range of compelling reasons to adopt CRM. Once it has made the decision to adopt CRM, a company needs to integrate this approach into all of its customer-related processes, so making these processes a pervasive part of operations. That requires marrying or aligning business drivers with the company's technology base. The company that does so will be able to incorporate CRM into three key steps or stages:

▸ Assessment starts the process. The company uses the unprecedented amount of data it has about its customers to identify churn and retention rates, to segment customers according to sales and profitability, and otherwise gain understanding of customer behavior.

▸ Planning continues the process, with the company devising a marketing plan, or customer treatment plan and related media plan to target customers with a specific value proposition that will build loyalty and customer value.

▸ Execution is the culmination of the process. A broad range of techniques and technologies come into play here, including inbound customer service, outbound telemarketing, sales force automation, point-of-purchase terminals, sales kiosks and more. Regardless of the specific technique used, the company ensures that every execution of customer interaction is customized and targeted based on the customer information gained during the assessment and planning phases.

The IT legacy problem

Most companies adopting CRM face a huge IT challenge. Their systems were designed for product-related processes, not customer-related ones. Their customer data is scattered across a range of stove-piped product systems with no ability to link that data together.

It's seldom practical to scrap an entire, existing information infrastructure and adopt a completely new one. So, businesses must find ways to adapt their current infrastructures and integrate new, customer-related system components. To fulfill the vision of an agile enterprise, and to make this transition from product-to customer-centric systems, businesses need to consider the following key requirements:

▸ Focus on the needs of the customer. The infrastructure must provide a single

Figure 5: Example of product-related systems

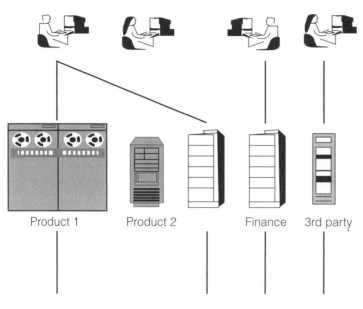

Product 1   Product 2   Finance   3rd party

▸ Increase the organization's knowledge of the customer. Every customer interaction must be remembered. More than that, the infrastructure should facilitate dialogue so that the organization is able to build a wealth of valuable information about the customer.

▸ Exploit knowledge. The organization's knowledge of the customer must be used intelligently at every interaction. Every contact should be seen as a possible sales opportunity, not as a random event, offering the most appropriate product at the most appropriate price. Knowledge should also be used to enable every function within the organization —for example, to allow sales to have an understanding of any outstanding customer care issues before engaging with a customer.

▸ Efficiency. In today's highly competitive world, cost is always a major driver. As a result, this new customer-centric infrastructure needs to be highly efficient. It should maximize the use of new technology and isolate the customer from the inadequacies of the existing systems.

point of contact for the customer for all products and services, whether for customer service or sales. The infrastructure must help enforce business processes so any issue can be dealt with correctly the first time. It must use all the data that is known about the customer so that the customer does not have to continually provide the same information. Most importantly, it should be the customer who decides how to interact with the organization and who chooses both the time of day and the mechanism for that interaction. Lastly, those crucial, highly valued customers must be treated with the special degree of service they deserve.

▸ Flexibility. Moving forward, the infrastructure's flexibility is going to be key. The infrastructure should support the rapid introduction of new product systems to reduce the time to market and to allow the organization to exploit new channels, such as the Internet.

This approach has some positive, practical implications for CRM. For example, take an insurance company that offers home, life, health and auto coverage. It will have many telephone-based customer service or call center representatives that deal with separate systems for each major product line. When they're on the phone with a customer, the agents must spend time

toggling back and forth among the screens for each system. They don't have real-time access to all relevant company information about the customer, may not be able to manage the system even with expensive training, and will likely rotate out of their jobs within 18 months, boosting training costs and reducing efficiency even further.

This detracts from the time they could otherwise spend obtaining insightful customer information. Moreover, the agents could be selling complementary products that boost customer loyalty by increasing the cost of customer switching, and building positive customer relationships. And that diverts from the

Figure 6: NUMA-Q's integrated and customer-centric architecture

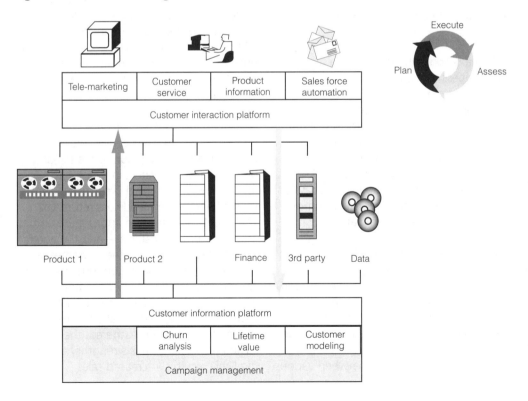

increased revenue, increased loyalty and increased profitability that are the three key benefits of CRM.

With a relationship-centric approach, a customer service representative —who doesn't have to toggle among screens when adding a new driver to an automobile policy —can ask some useful questions and collect important customer data. The new driver is a female —did the customer get married recently and, if so, has the couple considered adding life insurance, or does the new wife have adequate health and disability coverage? If the driver is a daughter, has the customer considered a new insurance product that will help pay college tuition costs? Does the customer have other lifestyle changes that might be reflected in new insurance needs?

Adding a second driver can mean adding new business in many ways —but too often, the customer service representative is too busy with his software to ask the probing questions that lead to this better understanding of the customer and his needs. With more effective systems, the service representative can make the link between better service and increased sales. This link represents a major execution of the CRM-based marketing plan.

Of course, the customer service representative isn't deciding on the spot what customer information is relevant and which complementary products might be offered. The company establishes the specific nature of the service-marketing link through the use of data analysis tools that show the exact correlation between various demographics and sales. For example, these tools can establish the probability that a customer with two drivers (or two cars) on his policy will also be open to a homeowner's policy. This in turn can lead the company to set-up call center scripts to take advantage of the link—and to obtain even more information about the customer as part of the company's efforts to continually expand the customer relationship.

For example, if the call center agent determines that the second driver is a new spouse, that can lead to questions about the customer's need for homeowner's or renter's insurance. Because the customer already has several policies with the company, the agent can offer a "valued customer discount"—adding to the customer's perceived value in the relationship—and calculate the discounted price on the spot. He can also be asked about key possessions, children, and other factors that can lead to additional sales.

Does the customer want to buy the added policies? No? If the call center agent doesn't make the sale during the initial call, his script and software can prompt him to ask the customer if he'd like a quote sent via mail and when he'd like a return call. The agent can make the appropriate entries in the customer database —and the agent is prompted to call back the customer at the prearranged time to continue the conversation. The customer has been wowed—and wooed—by highly effective customer service, additional customer information has been gathered, the customer relationship is strengthened, and the likely result is in-creased sales.

Chapter 1: Introduction to CRM

NUMA-Q's technology foundation for CRM

NUMA-Q ® 's CRM solution combines industry-leading software and a range of services with IBM's highly scalable, fully integrated NUMACenter™ environment, which provides the foundation for this customer-centric solution.

A NUMA-Q customer-focused data warehouse solution consolidates data from multiple systems into a single, customer-centric data store, where it is accessed and analyzed by sophisticated tools to provide insight into customer behavior. The CRM solution then enables a company to utilize this knowledge in all customer interactions. It provides a platform for the latest generation of customer interaction applications, enabling these applications to access customer data to support customer-specific treatment, and seamlessly integrates the applications in real time with underlying product and functional systems, overcoming any limitations in the underlying systems.

In addition, NUMA-Q's CRM solution enables organizations to capture customer data at every interaction, enhancing the quality of customer data throughout the business. When used in conjunction with a customer-focused data warehouse, the knowledge gained from the data warehouse can be exploited in every future customer interaction to enable, for example, highly targeted cross-selling after a customer care call or Internet request.

Smart CRM Solutions: The Key to Competing in the Net Economy

Title: Smart CRM Solutions: The Key to Competing in the Net Economy
Author: SUN Microsystems
Abstract: This paper describes some of the issues associated with maintaining personal
                  interactions with customers in the age of electronic commerce, and explores
                  how corporations can begin to integrate more smart information
                  technologies to solve the traditional business challenge of acquiring and
                  retaining loyal customers while increasing business profits. Integrating Smart
                  Customer Relationship Management (CRM) solutions into the overall
                  enterprise information architecture enables companies to more effectively
                  target, interact with, sell to, and retain loyal customers. As a leading provider
                  of solutions for the Network Economy, Sun Microsystems delivers both the
                  technologies and the expertise to help companies build profitable CRM solutions.

The Economics of Customer Retention

Retaining a strong customer base has always been a vital component of running a successful business. Industry experts agree that it costs far more -- possibly ten times as much -- to acquire a new customer as it does to retain an existing one. According to one major investment banking firm, "U.S. organizations lose one-half of their customers every five years, and a five percent incremental improvement in the customer retention rate could have the effect of doubling profits."

The increasingly competitive economic climate dictates that companies take a close look at the effectiveness of each marketing dollar. In addition, companies must look beyond the initial sale and implement cohesive programs for generating repeat business through improved levels of post-sale customer service and communication. That is, rather than continuing to flood prospective customers with expensive mass-marketing campaigns, companies may do better to invest in technologies that enable them to increase the level of one-to-one customer contact, even across the highly-impersonal medium of the Internet.

Unfortunately, most organizations are paralyzed in their ability to effectively use information technologies to identify, attract, and retain profitable customers. Although companies have multiple points of contact ("touch points") with each customer, the information gleaned from each contact is rarely incorporated into a single data system that merges historical data with intelligent analytical models. As a result, companies cannot easily pinpoint which customers are profitable and which are not, which are likely to default on a loan, or which are likely to respond to particular products or promotional offers. More importantly, few companies can identify those customers or prospects that have the greatest potential to become profitable customers over time.

The Role of CRM Solutions in the Enterprise

With the increasing popularity of the Internet and Web-based commerce, the challenge of retaining customers is greater than ever. Customers can compare alternative products and services with a mouse click, making it difficult for companies to "close the sale" through traditional selling techniques. In the new Net Economy, successful companies will understand how to harness the power of advanced information technologies to "personalize" every electronic interaction with a customer.

Integrated into core enterprise information systems, Customer Relationship Management (CRM) solutions can help companies increase customer loyalty and retention rates by enhancing customer service before, during, and after the initial sale. For example, CRM solutions can be designed to look at a customer's long-term value to the company, analyze customer consumption patterns, and track areas of customer complaints. Among other questions, companies using effective CRM strategies are better equipped to answer such vital business questions as:

- Who are the low-risk, high-profit customers?
- Which products produce most profits?
- What is the lifetime value of a particular customer to the company?
- Who are our most loyal customers?
- How effective are our marketing programs for capturing qualified sales leads?

- How quickly do we respond to customers via electronic media such as the Web and e-mail?
- What types of post-sale services are most likely to increase repeat business?

CRM encompasses more than just the technology required to automate business functions such as sales, marketing, and customer service. To be used as an effective competitive strategy, CRM solutions must be integrated throughout enterprise information systems and business processes. Identifying target customers requires leveraging the customer information hidden in traditional operational systems such as customer order entry systems, enterprise resource planning (ERP) systems, and transaction processing systems. The foundation for this is a robust data warehouse environment that can gather, store, and cross-reference the enormous amounts of customer data generated through each touch point.

Other components of a successful CRM solution include:

- Business intelligence systems (BI) to collect, transform, analyze, and distribute data for better decision-making, and personalized customer interaction
- Analytical engines for understanding customer's preferences and buying patterns
- Campaign management for reaching customers with personalized marketing promotions
- Multi-channel communication (Web, fax, e-mail, voice, etc.) enabling the customer to respond in the most convenient and appropriate form

Smart CRM Solutions: The Key to Competing in the Net Economy

- Two-way asynchronous and real-time communication with the customer leveraging Web and personalized e-mail communications
- Processes and systems for integrating customer information from sales, marketing, services and ERP systems into a historical and cross-functional data warehouse
- Workflow management tools to automate marketing, sales and customer service business processes

Real-time, secure and reliable customer interaction requires integration of CRM solutions with operational and analytical systems. By integrating CRM with core enterprise information systems, corporations can personal every customer interaction, resulting in more opportunity for sale and improved customer retention.

A complete CRM solution would consist of a customer knowledge base of both structured data (such as sales data) and unstructured customer information such as e-mails and contracts. An estimated 85 percent of business information is unstructured. This information is spread around the organization in e-mails and documents locked in personal computers, not generally available to the enterprise. Any viable CRM solution should enable capture and re-use of unstructured information. A number of companies are offering technologies for capture, reuse of unstructured information, usable by anyone in the enterprise with a Web browser. Typically, these products are referred as Knowledge Management applications, or Enterprise Information Portals.

All the components of a CRM solution must work together in a cohesive architecture that supports the business's plans for both immediate success and sustainable, long-term growth. Broad and ubiquitous user accessibility, scalability, flexibility, investment protection, and interoperability with other business systems are critical. In the ideal world, companies will build CRM solutions into the core enterprise information system architecture; however, the reality is that most companies will need to find ways to modify and extend legacy operational database systems to support new CRM solutions. In either case, working with a trusted team of experienced network business leaders can make it easier to plan, develop, and deploy powerful CRM solutions in the shortest possible timeframe.

Building a Successful CRM Solution

With innovations such as Java™ technology for ubiquitous customer communication from anywhere, reliable and scalable servers for real-time personalized customer interactions via the Web and e-mail, and world-renowned expertise in assembling teams of industry experts and mix of technologies, Sun Microsystems has taken a leadership role in driving the Net Economy. In addition to offering the products and services required for net-based business strategies, Sun also works closely with leading suppliers of complementary CRM, database, and business intelligence technologies to help companies build successful CRM solutions.

Sun's professional consultants and world-class service partners offer technical assistance and Best Practice models based on their proven experience in building effective CRM, BI, and e-commerce solutions for forward-thinking global corporations. Here are just a few tips Sun offers for companies in the initial stages of defining a CRM strategy:

Best Practices for CRM Solution Implementation

▸ Start small and plan for expansion and ensure scalability: Implement CRM technology in phases to allow users ample time for training and becoming familiar with new processes and tools.
▸ Perform cost justi_cation and ROI analysis. Select the initial projects based on availability of customer and product information and the anticipated ROI resulting from the CRM solution.
▸ Focus on the business, not the technology. De_ne your company's customer relationship management goals. Articulate how information will be used to support marketing, sales, and customer service goals.
▸ Find the right business sponsor. Get senior management on board and out front to endorse the technology-enabled CRM strategy and ensure its adoption throughout the organization.
▸ Put end-users on the implementation team. This assures development of CRM solutions with cross-department functionality and practical usability.
▸ Form a cross-functional committee involving representatives from every department who will use or manage the CRM systems.
▸ Align information technology strategies with marketing, sales, and service strategies to support the company's customer development and management objectives.
▸ Develop a CRM solution with multiple communication channels customized for based on customer preferences.
▸ Integrate marketing communications contacts for both direct and indirect communications channels to synergize programs, maximize customer interaction, and improve marketing ROI.
▸ Consolidate essential customer, sales force, and sales channel information in a central data warehouse to support both customer interaction operations (sales, call centers, campaign management) and business intelligence operations (query and reporting, customer segmentation, predictive modeling).
▸ Make it easy for customers to provide the information you need to serve them through multiple interactive communication channels.

Working with system integration partners and third-party solutions providers, Sun is able to develop complete CRM solutions. In addition to delivering reliable, high performance servers, storage systems, and network technologies, Sun's staff of professional service enterprise consultants offers expertise in the areas of project management, needs analysis, data modeling, enterprise information systems architecture design, and infrastructure design and management.

Smart CRM Solutions: The Key to Competing in the Net Economy

With the invention of Java technology and successful implementation of many reliable and scalable enterprise ERP and BI solutions for world-class companies, Sun has the proven expertise and credibility to help you build CRM solutions with predictable schedule and functionality and therefore minimize risk for real-time and reliable customer interaction via the Web and traditional communication channels.

For More Information

To learn more about Sun's vision, technologies, and best practices for implementing advanced customer relationship management and business intelligence solutions, contact a local Sun Microsystems sales office, or direct your Web browser to www.sun.com.

Chapter 2: How to Integrate CRM in Your Business

The CRM Lifecycle. Without CRM Analytics, your customers won't even know you're there.

Title: *The CRM Lifecycle. Without CRM Analytics, your customers won't even know you're there.*

Author: *Hyperion*

Abstract: *In this paper Hyperion applies the CRM lifecycle to three common business problems: customer profiling, call center improvement and e-business effectiveness. In each scenario the three stages of the CRM lifecycle will be applied to the business problem and the solutions will demonstrate how essential CRM analytics are to customer success.*

Customer relationship management (CRM) is one of the fastest growing business technology initiatives since the web. Each year companies pour millions of dollars into CRM application suites and front office automation systems. CRM vendors such as Siebel, Vantive, Onyx and Clarify are growing at rates of 30-70% annually on the corporate dollars flowing into CRM projects. That growth rate will only climb higher as businesses increasingly recognize that in order to achieve sustainable competitive advantage, they must first understand and then delight their customers.

Yet despite widespread recognition of the need, the willingness to fund a solution and the urgency driving CRM projects at a relentless pace, businesses are finding themselves short. At the end of the process and several million dollars later, companies are no more customer facing then when they started. And in this winner-take-all playing field, the ultimate winners are not standing still.

The problem doesn't lie with the imperative -understanding your customers and strengthening your relationships with them is essential in today's demand driven economy. Your customers aren't just buying your products; they're buying their relationship with you. Nor does the fault lie with the front office automation suites. Integrated sales force automation, contact management, marketing automation and call center integration provide unprecedented productivity and shared communications to front office departments. These applications are enabling one shared, consistent view of front office activities and customer data, much as ERP systems have integrated back office activities and centralized HR, manufacturing and financial data.

The failure of CRM initiatives to even affect, let alone manage a business's relationships with its customers, is a problem of incompleteness. Integrating sales, marketing and customer service activities is the first stage in the CRM lifecycle. It is necessary, but not sufficient.

Without CRM analytics and the strategic process refinement that they drive, a company can certainly enjoy a higher level of integration and productivity, but their customers will still be out in the cold - strangers to them.

The CRM Lifecycle

The CRM lifecycle begins with the integration of front office systems and the centralization of customer-related data. This is the Integration phase (figure 1) and its benefits include improved front office efficiency and productivity. The output from this phase is a centralized source of all relevant customer data. Reporting is typically summary level only, showing what activities have occurred, but failing to explain their causes or impact. This is, unfortunately, as far as most CRM initiatives get. This phase certainly provides business value, but alone it doesn't improve your understanding of your customers, nor strengthen your relationships with them.

The second phase, Analysis is the most critical to CRM success. CRM analytics enable the effective management of customer relationships. It's only through analysis of the customer data that you can begin to understand behaviors, identify buying patterns and trends and discover causal relationships. Together these help more accurately model and predict future customer satisfaction and behavior and lay a quantified foundation for strategic decision making.

The final phase, Action, is where the strategic decisions are carried out. Business processes and organizational structures are refined based on the improved customer understanding gained through analysis. Business and financial planning is revised and integrated across all customer facing activities, including sales, marketing and customer service. This final phase closes the CRM loop and allows organizations to cash in on the valuable insights gained through analysis.

Without CRM analytics your customers remain a mystery and you might as well read tea leaves to try figure out how to please them. Conversely, the well considered analysis of customer behavior and causal influences can take the guesswork out of business strategy. Your understanding of your customers will no longer be based on thin anecdotal evidence. Rather, solid quantifiable conclusions will guide the business process refinements that will delight your customers and improve the lifetime value of your relationship with them.

"META Group believes that a CRM initiative lacking the analytical component will fail to provide a panoramic customer view long-term."

"In 100%of the CRM projects we've seen that lack CRM analysis, there was a total and complete inability to effect change in the customer relationship and improve the return on the customer relationship."

-Elizabeth Shahnam, Senior Program Director, Application Delivery Strategies, META Group

The CRM Lifecycle. Without CRM Analytics, your customers won't even know you're there.

Figure 1: The CRM Lifecycle

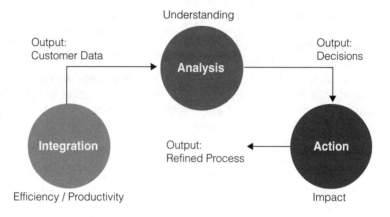

Lifecycle: Phase I - Integration provides efficiency and productivity and outputs centralized customer data. Phase II - Analysis provides a deeper understanding of customer behaviour and needs and outputs strategic business decisions. Phase III - Action provides positive impact and strengthening of customer relationships and outputs a refined business process.

CRM Success: Customer Profiling

The Business Problem

A major cellular phone company is ready to market test a new service offering that will integrate voice and e-mail on cellular phones. The company is excited, not only because this service will differentiate them from their competition, but also because it will enable e-mail for individuals that don't already own computers or lack Internet access.

The company is particularly interested in how this campaign effects customer profitability and retention within the test population. They specifically want to know if the new service results in more airtime, the sale of additional services and if it decreases the current rate of customer churn.

For the results of this market test to be meaningful, the test population will need to be chosen carefully. The first question that must be answered is, who's likely to

use this service? It would be a waste to test the new service on a group with little or no interest in e-mail. Second, test customers should be selected based on profitability and retention scores. It would be more meaningful to measure the response of more profitable customers, rather than less. Similarly, it wouldn't be worth testing customers with such a low retention score they were expected to defect regardless.

Finally, the company hopes to use the results of this market test to fine tune their pricing strategy for this service. The ultimate price structure and bundling options will be based on the responses of different population segments to different offer treatments, the product profitability of each offer treatment, its impact on customer profitability and retention, and customer demand. Integrated analysis ensures that the impact of these pricing adjustments on sales forecasts and margins can be accurately predicted. By correctly balancing each of these components, the company can best lower marketing program costs, increase profitability, and increase customer loyalty and satisfaction.

The Solution: Required Integration

▸ Profitability analysis requires customer transaction detail, both current and historical, integrated with product detail and financial records. Customer records across multiple business divisions need to be linked to show an aggregate customer profitability score. By deriving and assigning direct and indirect costs to customers, a customer P&L can be calculated. When modeled forward in time, it's possible to calculate a total lifetime P&L for each customer. This derived profitability data typically does not exist in financial systems at the customer level. It is an extremely valuable and distinguishing benefit of CRM analytics.

▸ Customer profiling requires as broad a range of data as possible for each customer. Sales force records including customer profiles and contact management detail need to be integrated with each customer's transaction history. External demographic and psychographic data may also be required. In addition, external data on customer web, ISP and e-mail use is necessary to identify customers that currently use e-mail.

▸ Integrated sales and marketing automation systems accessing customer data help target customers that are more likely to respond to particular campaigns. By targeting the test campaign to promising segments, and

measuring the specific responses of customers within those segments, the company can fine tune their sales and marketing strategies before the new service is formally launched.

The Solution: Required Analysis

The solution of this business problem requires a number of different types of analysis, including customer profitability, retention, segmentation and customer clustering, promotional and pricing analysis. Each of these is not separate and distinct, but rather offers a different perspective of the customer and their value to the business. When viewed together, the aggregated results provide a whole picture of the customer.

Customer profitability usually begins with a ranking of customers relative to their percent contribution to total revenue. By analyzing profitability across a number of business dimensions (typically including products, time, geography, demographics and channel) the organization can uncover the factors that most influence profitability.

Segmentation defines how the test population is broken down for more targeted marketing and product offerings. Finer segmentation allows more personalized marketing. Multidimensional analysis is an extremely effective segmentation technique, since each grouping of dimensional values essentially represents a unique segment (for instance, households in a particular region with income >$100,000, two or more children and two cars).

In addition, statistical regression analysis and data mining clustering algorithms help predict how particular segments may respond to the promotion, based on past promotional behavior. This is known as promotional analysis, and is an effective method of fine tuning campaign strategy.

Retention analysis is particularly important to companies in the Telco industry, as customer churn is very high and customer acquisition programs are considerably more expensive per customer, then retention programs.

The Solution: Required Business Actions

The initial segmentation of customers based on their profitability and predicted loyalty scores provides a good ruler with which to measure the results of this test market campaign.

The company is looking closely for customer segments that are promoted upward, either for profitability or loyalty, in response to this campaign. Conversely, they want to identify any segments that result in worse than average profitability and loyalty scores. Once these segments are identified, statistical regression analysis and data mining clustering algorithms should be applied. These help the company identify any common customer characteristics within each population that are believed to impact the profitability and loyalty scores.

The segments with the greatest positive response to the campaign represent those customer groups who best respond to the new product. By identifying common characteristics, similar customers from the much larger population of total customers can be identified. Customized marketing and advertising can then be tailored to these various customer groups when the service is finally offered.

Pricing and bundling options can also be balanced for these targeted customer groups to make the offering more attractive without undercutting profitability.

What is Customer Profiling?

Sales and marketing analysis involves many techniques that analyze different aspects of customer populations.

No single technique gives a composite view of the customer, their behavior and their descriptive characteristics. Customer profiling is this collective set of analysis that best describe our customers. It includes:

Segmentation -The subdivision of customer populations into finer groups. These groups are then targeted with specific marketing and advertising, based on their characteristics.

Customer Profitability -The measurement and ranking of customers based on their profitability -typically measured by accumulating customer revenue and assigning direct product costs, indirect customer acquisition costs and operational costs.

Customer Retention -The measurement of how likely a customer is to remain loyal to your company. Customer churn is the lack of retention.

Customer Clustering -The identification of common characteristics within a customer segment that are associated with a measured behavior.

Response Analysis -The measurement of a marketing campaign's effectiveness within a specific customer segment.

"CRM analysis isn't about making companies more productive, although that's often a side benefit ..."

"...Its real value is as a key enabler for broad strategy change."

-Michael Emerson, VP Marketing Recognition Systems

"Complex customer analysis is essential to understanding the effects of all the various attributes that can contribute to customer behavior."

-Dan Lackner, Chief Operating Officer Paragren Technologies

CRM Success: e-Business Effectiveness

The Business Problem
A leading department store chain has recently introduced an on-line shopping mall that allows customers to purchase the same products via their web site that are available in their stores. This e-commerce site has enjoyed early success, and during its first six months of operation has contributed 7% to total revenues.

Corporate headquarters is ecstatic, and is hoping e-business revenues will grow to reach 20% of total revenue within the first two years. Unfortunately, however, management doesn't really understand who's visiting their web site, and what's motivating visitor behavior enough to feel confident in their revenue growth predictions.

The company would like to better understand the composition and behavior of their web customers. Are the web purchases being made by existing store customers who prefer the web as a shopping venue? This would shift revenue from one channel to another, without increasing overall revenue. If that's the case, then under what conditions, or for what products, do these customers purchase over the web versus in a store?

Do some existing customers browse on the web and subsequently purchase at stores within several days of their web site visit? This may indicate that these customers prefer on-line product selection, but still choose to purchase in person.

What web-based advertising is most effective for what product purchases among existing store customers and for new web customers? Are there certain products that new web-only customers tend to purchase? Is it possible to identify new web site visitors who are likely to purchase, based on their click stream behavior, and what advertising would be most effective for them?

The Solution: Required Integration

▶ When available, web site cookie data and customer data should be integrated to identify web site visitors by name.

▶ By integrating web transaction records with store transaction records, web site customers who are also store customers can be identified.

▶ The web-based shopping behavior of existing store customers (using click stream data) can be compared with shopping behavior through non-web channels. Response rates to banner ads can also be compared with response rates to non-web advertising.

▶ Web-based market basket analysis software (shopping cart analysis) can be applied to click stream data to help identify what products tend to sell together and what products may be left in a visitor's shopping cart if a visit is abandoned before purchase.

The Solution: Required Analysis

The first question to answer, and perhaps the most important, is whether the web-based revenue is, in fact, new revenue or simply shifted from the stores channel to the web channel. To answer this, web customer data must be broken down by existing customers vs. new customers (through any channel).Certainly all the new customers represent revenue growth. But even existing customers can contribute to revenue growth if their total purchases through all channels increase over a period of time.

Total purchases of existing customers now buying online, need to be analyzed by sales channel. This is a straightforward dimensional analysis (with customer class, channel, time and products as the basic dimensions)that helps identify the preferred purchase venue of existing customers.

Store purchases of existing customers who have visited the web site, but not purchased via the web, also need to be analyzed. Here additional dimensions would include click stream detail associated with specific product information on the web site. If there's a correlation between the referenced web site product information and subsequent store purchases, it may indicate that the web site can contribute to revenue growth in other channels.

Dimensional analysis can provide insight into the effectiveness of e-marketing campaigns such as banner ads, direct e-mail campaigns, affiliate networks and search engines, and their correlation with specific product purchases among different classes of customers. In addition, this analysis can benefit from the application of statistical regression analysis and data mining techniques.

Predictive models can help identify web site visitors who are most likely to purchase certain products based on their click stream behavior. This can be used to drive the specific content of e-marketing programs that are most likely to lead to purchases.

The Solution: Required Business Actions

Click stream data becomes exponentially more useful when the web visitor can be identified by name. This enables the integration of click stream data and customer data, providing a much fuller view of customer behavior and preferences. The company needs to develop a mechanism to capture web visitor names, and other descriptive data, together with an incentive for web visitors to provide that information.

If analysis indicates that multi-channel customers follow predictable browsing, selection and purchase patterns, then the company can alter their marketing strategies to appropriately incent these customers. For example if certain customers prefer to browse on-line, but actually go to the store to purchase products, customers might be able to request via the web site that a particular item be held at a given store location. This would ensure the item's availability when the customer goes to the store.

Advertising, incentives and product placement can be personalized and delivered through each customer's channel preference. This degree of personalization makes the shopping experience more intimate and more convenient for customers. The strengthened customer relationships, in turn, result in greater customer loyalty, lower customer acquisition costs and greater sustainable profits for the company.

e-Business Terminology

Click Stream -The series of sequential web page selections (usually via a mouse click) that a web visitor makes before they arrive at a particular page or purchase a particular product.

Click streams are extremely valuable and unique to the web. Through no other channel can you see the exact sequence of events and choices that led a customer to a product.

Click Stream Data -The collected data is very granular and can include the number of hits on a server and the sequence of links or areas on a web page selected by the visitor.

The raw data is practically meaningless, and only reveals valuable information when analyzed in sequence at a summary level.

Cookies -Small text files stored on a web visitor's PC that contain any personal information they've entered into web forms. This information can be retrieved upon subsequent visits and used to personalize their visit to that site. It's also extremely valuable in identifying who a visitor is.

Content Personalization -The dynamic creation of banner ads and other web content around the web visitor's identified preferences.

"CRM analytics effectively get the customer into the board room ..."

"...Rather than driving business strategy based on thin anecdotal evidence (i.e., this

customer said this or that), strategy can now be based on quantifiable measures of customer behaviors and needs..."

-Larry Goldman, Director, Braun Consulting.

What Does A Balanced CRM Solution Require?

In each of the three business problems presented, the problem could not be solved without the quantified understanding of customer needs and behaviors provided by CRM analytics. This understanding then drove the business actions that closed the loop, strengthening both customer relationships and each business's bottom line. How can an organization ensure that it has a balanced CRM solution that will provide the customer insight necessary for survival? A short checklist identifies the key components required in a well balanced CRM solution:

1. Integration
Customer data from all sources must be accessible and integrated across all channels and departments within the enterprise. Integrated reports show summary level customer activity but don't offer any explanation for cause or impact. Front office automation suites can provide effective integration, data access and reporting for many business activities and can be particularly effective in providing this integration. However, they are rarely sufficient and are usually only one of several integration mechanisms.

2. Analysis
Analysis provides the critical customer insight that results in the positive benefits promised by CRM. This analysis is usually dimensional in nature. This makes OLAP products particularly well suited for a CRM analytics platform. Furthermore, they can be complemented with statistical and data mining tools that provide predictive modeling and forecasting.

3. Action
A CRM solution is only effective if the valuable lessons learned through CRM analytics are turned back onto the business process through action. Business process refinement and business planning revision close the CRM loop. Customer relationships can only be strengthened by using what's been learned about customer preferences and behaviors to improve the customer's experiences with and perceptions of your business.

Conclusion

The key to sustainable competitive advantage in today's business markets is the customer. Companies must know who their customers are, which customer populations most directly drive their profits, and what will keep these customers loyal and happy over time. Customers drive business success and the winners on this playing field will be those organizations who most effectively and positively manage their relationships with their customers.

Chapter 2: How to Integrate CRM in your Business

Despite the millions of dollars invested to date in CRM systems, many companies are failing to impact their relationships with their customers at all. These businesses can see their customer's activity, but they don't understand what's driving it nor how to appropriately respond to it. Their CRM initiatives are incomplete, and hence, ineffective.

CRM analytics move an organization beyond the obvious. They provide the understanding of customer behavior, interests and value, and enable the business process refinement and business planning revision that closes the loop and touches the customer. CRM analytics enable the effective management of customer relationships. With a balanced CRM solution, well grounded on quantifiable analysis, not only will your customers know you're there, but they'll value their relationship with you and make a point to bring their business to you, again and again.

"...Analysis of your customers will drive corporate change from the inside out at the grass roots level..."

"...Learning who your customers are and what they want will disrupt your business process ..."

"...But the disruption and the change will be fact-based. Your business can then lign itself around what the customer wants."

-Dan Graham, Solutions Business Executive, IBM Global Business Intelligence Solutions

Closing the Loop to Optimize Customer Relationships

Title: Closing the Loop to Optimize Customer Relationships
Author: Henry Morris, Research Vice President, Data Warehousing and Information
                Access at IDC

Abstract: What are the requirements for a solution that optimizes customer
                relationships? A customer relationship management (CRM) system should
                combine transaction processing with the analysis of customer interactions,
                leading to the optimization of each future interaction via integrated customer
                touchpoints. Sequent has packaged software, hardware and services to
                deliver one of the most impressive closed loop systems available on the
                marketplace.

Customer Relationship Optimization: Linking Information to Actions

Companies are turning to data warehousing and powerful analytical tools in order to maximize business opportunity. Through the use of techniques that lead to more personalized customer relationships, companies can more readily retain and grow business with existing customers, as well as attract new customers.

The marketplace is beginning to understand that optimizing customer relationships requires the strategic use of customer information in every customer interaction via multiple customer-facing channels. But data pertaining to a company's relationship with its customers is typically scattered, maintained by separate applications written to support each major type of customer interaction. Hence, a requirement for optimizing customer relationships is to bring this information together into a data warehouse for analysis, and then to strategically use the results of the analysis during the next interaction.

Data warehousing is a process that integrates data from multiple sources organized for decision support. IDC forecasts that the data warehousing software market will surpass $12B by 2002, a compound annual growth rate of 24.3 percent. (See "Data Warehousing: Worldwide Overall Market, 1997-2002," IDC #17797). Customer relationship management will be the leading subject area for data warehousing as businesses seek to gain better intelligence on their customers as a source of competitive advantage.

But integrating data in a data warehouse and analyzing patterns in customer data are not sufficient for optimizing customer relationships. These activities are only useful if the results of the analysis can be linked directly to actions that affect the quality of a business's relationship with a customer. For maximum impact, the results of the analysis should be made usable right at the time of each customer interaction, through whichever channel the customer uses to touch the organization. IDC projects that the market for packaged applications that manage customer interactions—sales, marketing and customer support—will grow to nearly $8B by 2002, a compound growth rate of 43.9 percent.

Closing the Loop: The Business Improvement Cycle

Figure 1 shows the link between transaction processing (i.e. operational) and analytic systems as a cycle that IDC calls the business improvement cycle. Within a particular process or family of processes (such as customer relationship

management or procurement), operational applications cover the adjust/act and track phases, while analytic applications cover the analyze and model phases. Analytic applications are supported by a data warehouse which integrates internal and external information relevant to the business problem.

The business improvement cycle for a process that impacts business performance covers the following tasks:

▸ **Adjust/Act:**
Adjustments are made to business rules (such as changing pricing or compensation) in order to achieve specific objectives. These are then put into action governing the transaction of business.

Figure 1: Closed Loop Systems: Business Improvement Cycle

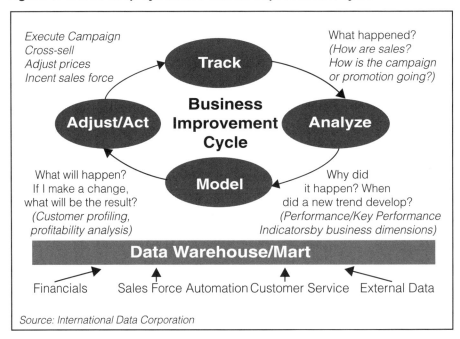

Source: International Data Corporation

> **Track:**
> Transactions are applied to the operational database, and production reports reflect the events that have occurred. Business programs such as marketing or sales campaigns are monitored regularly.

> **Analyze:**
> Business trends are probed by analyzing recent data in order to understand why events have happened. This need is met by providing a view that shows key performance indicators (such as profit or return on equity) by business dimensions (such as organizational or product hierarchies).

> **Model:**
> Predictive models are built to help understand what will happen. A manager explores alternative scenarios (such as new policies on customer service) before putting the changes into effect. This completes one iteration of the cycle.

When the constituent tasks of a business process are being performed, this cycle is traversed in a clockwise direction. However, it makes sense in a customer-oriented environment to design the process (and its supporting data flows) in a reverse direction. That is:

> - Identify the opportunities for action (Adjust/Act).
> - Calibrate the analysis and modeling to yield results that are actionable (Model and Analyze).
> - Design the data flows to the data warehouse (from Track to Analyze) to ensure that the data necessary for the analysis is present.

The rate at which a business is able to move through these phases improves the velocity of information. A business will seek to traverse the cycle as rapidly as possible for processes that have a significant impact on overall performance and where trends can shift unexpectedly. Customer-centric pro-cesses fit this description. First, they are key determinants of business performance. Second, the data that records the behavior of customers is notoriously volatile.

This volatility requires that a business be able to respond as quickly as possible to the latest customer information. The velocity of information can be increased by automating the links that pass data between each phase of the cycle and by increasing the level of performance and availability for each link. The need for speed and the impact on business performance makes closed loop customer relationship management a business-critical system.

System Implementation Requirements

A business-critical system such as closed loop customer relationship management has demanding implementation requirements:

> **Scalability with Performance:**
> A customer interaction system, such as a call center application, requires the processing of a high volume of transactions with good response time. Meeting these response time requirements for a complete business transaction can require the coordination

of database read and update operations for multiple systems in parallel, rather than having each execute separately. The related customer information system requires the movement and transformation of large data sets to a data warehouse for analysis of customer behavior patterns.

Yet the need for scalability will only increase as customer-facing channels merge into an integrated contact center and as we move into the e-commerce era. For example, beyond data on what was ordered, on-line retailers can analyze data on which catalog pages were touched by a Web shopper and which ads were displayed to that shopper. All of this is potentially relevant for predicting future customer behavior and tailoring treatment strategies within a current customer interaction, as well as for the next interaction with those target customers.

▸ **Availability:**
Real-time customer interaction systems (such as call centers or contact centers) require near 7x24 availability. In general, businesses will find that with the introduction of e-commerce interaction solutions, availability requirements will be much higher than the availability of underlying operational systems. The supporting infrastructure for off-line analysis (populating and managing the data warehouse) is linked to this real-

Figure 2: Sequent CRM Architecture: Closed Loop Customer Relationship Management

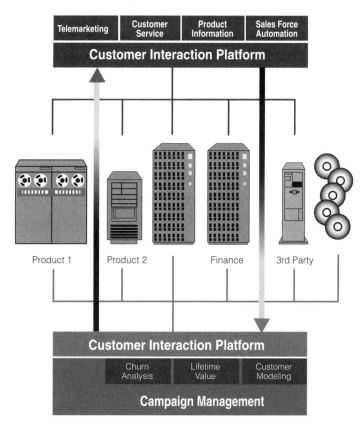

Source: Sequent Computer Systems, Inc. 1999

time system.

The demand for up-to-date, actionable information based on customer analysis drives higher levels of availability for the data warehouse and related analytic processes. IDC surveys have shown that availability is frequently cited as an implementation challenge for data warehousing.

▸ **Integration:**
A closed loop is an extended business process supported by a complex information system. The overall system has many independent elements that must be brought together to solve a business problem. Domain knowledge and implementation expertise are needed to design and build the information flows at every step. A robust architecture is needed to ensure the smooth flow of information across the steps within a closed loop system.

Sequent's CRM Solution: A Closed Loop Implementation

Sequent's customer relationship management solution is a packaging of systems, software and services to facilitate the implementation of a closed loop system for customer relationship management. It was developed with these requirements in mind. Figure 2 provides a high-level view of the relationship between the customer interaction and customer information parts of the total system. The architecture enables a closed loop because data flows from the point of on-line customer interaction to the analytic systems and then back to the on-line system to direct future interactions.

The goal of the system design is to bring to bear the results of the analysis of customer behavior directly to those who interact with customers in a real-time environment. These could be the call center agents and sales representatives who need information that is directly related to their activities at precisely the time they must act.

This solution encompasses two related systems:

▸ **A customer interaction platform** supporting sales, marketing and customer service applications. These transaction processing applications manage real-time interaction with customers. Sequent calls this solution Contact Advantage.

▸ **A customer information platform** supporting customer-centric and analytic applications, such as lifetime value, campaign management, customer modeling and segmentation and churn/retention analysis. These analytic applications analyze the data trail of customer interactions, developing actionable information to optimize customer relationships. This is Sequent's Decision Advantage solution.

Chapter 2: How to Integrate CRM in your Business

Contact Advantage: The Customer Interaction Platform

Figure 3 shows the customer interaction platform in more detail.

The customer interaction platform needs to support multiple applications and channels, including new Web-based points of contact, that record the events that directly touch a customer. These are heavy-duty, transaction processing systems that need to handle a large volume of work. To ensure customer satisfaction, good response time is required so as not to keep a customer waiting while data records are being accessed and updated.

A key element of the system is message-based middleware (the "message broker" in Figure 3) that manages queues which ensure the delivery of information between the customer interaction application, the customer interaction platform and core business applications such as inventory management and procurement.

The "message broker" also ensures the delivery of the customer scores (based on predictive modeling of data warehouse

Figure 3: Contact Advantage: The Customer Interaction Platform

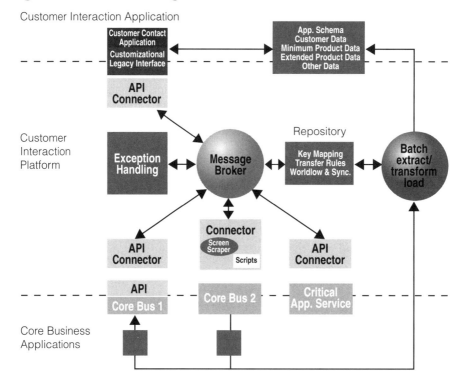

Source: Sequent Computer Systems, Inc. 1999

information) to the customer interaction platform where they are saved in customer data records. Applications such as customer service can then reference these scores in directing the way the current customer is to be served. For example, branching in call center scripts or personalization of Web pages must be made dependent on the customer's potential to churn or lifetime expected value. In this manner, the course of each new interaction is adjusted in real-time with reference to the collective intelligence owned by the business on that customer's expected behavior.

Decision Advantage: The Customer Information Platform

Figure 4 shows the customer information platform in more detail.

Data flows from the customer interaction platform and its transaction-oriented databases (along with data from financial and product-centric applications, and external sources) to a data warehouse that forms the foundation of the customer information system.

Figure 3: Contact Advantage: The Customer Interaction Platform

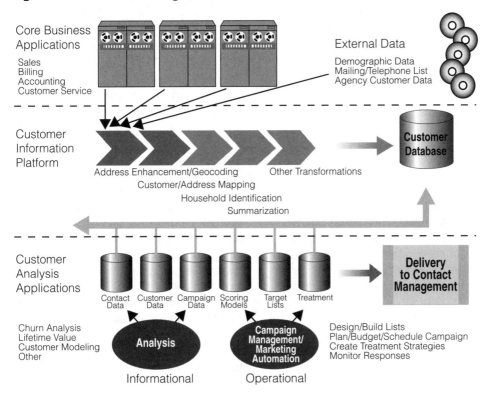

Source: Sequent Computer Systems, Inc. 1999

The data warehouse supports the development of analytical models, yielding results such as customer segmentation, assessment of lifetime value and propensity to churn for individual customers. Scores are then assigned by applying each of the models to each customer and later are transferred to the customer interaction platform.

New data is collected based on the latest interactions and the cycle continues.

Meeting System Implementation Requirements

With the delivery of Contact Advantage and Decision Advantage, Sequent brings together many separate system components in a manner that supports the demanding requirements of closed loop system implementation:

▸ *Scalability with Performance:*
Sequent's NUMACenter provides a scalable Intel-based processor architecture. A mixed mode design is possible that employs a highly scalable UNIX data server with Windows NT application servers. This design utilizes the operating environment best suited for its function within the system. Based on the Intel Architecture, it also enables easier migration from UNIX to Windows NT at the data server level as a future deployment option.

In addition to system scalability and per-formance, the Contact Advantage framework contributes additional performance benefits. The architecture

supports the pre-fetching and caching of customer and product data records likely to be needed in support of transactions to multiple opera-tional systems.

▸ *Availability:*
The system architecture supports high availability at the software, processor and storage levels. For example, from a software perspective, middleware ensures the reliable delivery of data between the customer interaction platform and operational systems, as well as the customer information platform. Records of the most recent customer interactions can be queued (if the operational systems are not available) and then delivered to the operational system when it is running. In addition, storing the results of analysis in an operational data store eliminates the need to directly access the data warehouse during a customer interaction. This design ensures both greater overall availability and higher performance.

▸ *Integration:*
The integrated architecture provides a single view of the customer, bringing the information together from multiple sources. From a systems integration perspective, Sequent acts as the prime contractor. This is a highly complex system from a software perspective alone, ranging from the call center application and its database, to the data movement programs and associated message-oriented middleware, to the data warehouse software and analytical tools, to the operational data store. And this doesn't include servers and storage properly tuned to meet system

requirements. Sequent takes
responsibility for testing and certifying
the interoperability of the many
elements of the solution.

Unified Customer Interaction

Title: Unified Customer Interaction
Author: Easyphone Portugal
Abstract: *We can classify the way we interact with our customers as either assisted or self-care. IVR (Interactive Voice Response) technology and mostly the spectacular growth of the Internet as a communication medium have been dramatically increasing the volume of self-care interaction, mainly at the cost of assisted and face-to-face contact. Sophisticated and cost-effective as it can be however, there comes a time when self-care interaction is not enough and human assistance is necessary to satisfy a request, answer a query or close a sale. Unified Customer Interaction then becomes a major business differentiation, allowing the right blend of human assistance and self-care interaction.*

THE CONVENTIONAL BUSINESS MODEL

We are all more aware than ever how important it is to establish a relationship with every single customer. Companies have long realised that it is approximately seven times more difficult to win a new customer than it is to do business with an existing one. This reality has been impacting the business world for the past decade and has forced companies to invest more heavily in building long term relationships with their customers.

The Customer Relationship Management (CRM) concept has been invaluable in setting up a framework that helps companies building their front-ends around a relationship concept. Three major functional silos are considered within this framework: Service, Sales and Marketing. These functional silos usually emerge as departments.

Each one of them today has mature supporting technologies: Knowledge management software for service, sales force automation for sales and data warehouse and data mining for marketing.

Figure 1

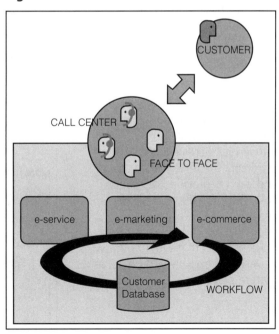

The silos rely on a common customer database, so that a unique and consistent view of the customer is developed and may be leveraged. A workflow engine must also be in place, enabling processes and work items to flow within and between silos.

Supporting CRM solutions have been deployed with the assumption that company representatives would be the only users. This was in line with another assumption that all customer interactions were to be performed by a customer representative, or to put it another way, in assisted mode.

We call this approach, the conventional business model. Within this model, all customer interactions are assisted interactions. The supporting software solutions are inward applications as they are designed for use with a company representative as intermediary.

E-BUSINESS

The advent of the Internet has brought an immense opportunity for companies willing to invest in self-service. Self-service can be incredibly convenient to customers and yet it is provided at reduced cost. Also, the Internet allows companies to escalate geographically and exposes them to huge markets that would otherwise be reserved exclusively to large and mature players.

The emerging e-business model has introduced an abrupt paradigm shift in the way customers access organisations, since all interactions are now performed in self-care mode. Within this model, the customer himself accesses the Company's front-end application, now in the form of a Web site.

A new framework has been emerging to support this model, eCRM, where interactions are conducted electronically and without assistance. The corresponding functional silos still exist, but now they don't necessarily map into departments. Their philosophy dramatically changes also: The marketing silo, for example, assumes a much more online characteristic: it allows the projection of a customised company image on the Web site, which depends on

Figure 2

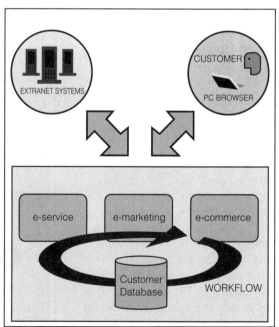

the accessing customer. It is this one to one marketing that allows mass-customised messages and even products. We can call these e-business applications outward applications, since they are designed for use by people outside the organisation.

CONVERGENCE

Most people enjoy shopping in supermarkets because of the self-service model. We all appreciate to freely handle and compare products, as well as to check product prices against one another. That experience is much enhanced by the fact that we are tempted into impulse buying by original new products that supermarket

managers judiciously display along the aisles.

But regardless of how well designed and informative the supermarket is, we frequently encounter situations where we want to be assisted by a supermarket employee. And we have all felt exasperated while looking around for someone to help us find a product or understand the difference between two apparently similar products.

The same principles apply on the Internet within e-commerce sites. The significant difference is that it is much easier to walk way if we can't find assistance: we are always only a couple of mouse-clicks away from a competitor that might provide a more helpful and convenient service.

Figure 3

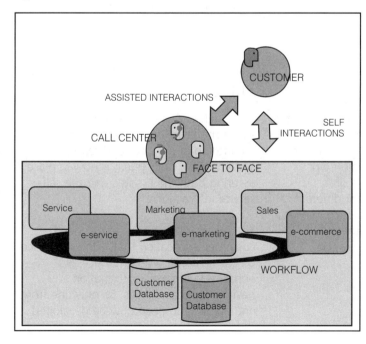

As more and more companies became aware of these phenomena, a convergence process began: conventional businesses started offering self-care options, while e-business sites started offering assisted help. The urgency to move was such that usually the solution implied a duplication of systems, processes and, worst of all, data. As a response to the urge to converge, companies started integrating monolithic systems that had seldom been designed with that objective in mind. Several problems usually arise from this approach:

1. There is no support for transferring the interaction from self-care into assisted mode. The context is lost in the process and so the customer has once again to identify himself, validate his access and set the whole context of the interaction. This can be rather disturbing and time-consuming for the customer, depending on the richness of the interaction context.

2. The tracking of all customer interactions is spread across different systems. The call centre representative is therefore unaware of previous interactions through the web site. Once again this can be frustrating for the customer who has to update the representative on previous interactions.

3. E-mail, web collaboration interactions and phone calls are routed to representatives by different routing engines. No discipline or minimum service levels can be set and the result is that e-mails may end up never being answered because they have a lower priority than other interaction types. Alternatively, different sets of representatives are used for different interaction type. This approach implies a low utilisation of costly human resources, with negative financial impact.

4. Two different applications are now in place: one to be used internally by the representative and another, the web site, to be used by the customer. Coherence is hard to achieve, with different answers being provided to the customer, depending on the media he selects to access the company. Time to market suffers, as two applications have now to be upgraded when the company launches new products. Also, whenever the customer asks for help while surfing the Web, it provides hurdles for the representative who is accustomed to a different application. So in order for the representative to be familiar with the Web site, extra training is required. Finally, the IT department now has two different systems to maintain instead of one.

All these problems can be somewhat overcome with the help of costly professional services.

UNIFIED CUSTOMER INTERACTION AND U-BUSINESS

The Unified Customer Interaction model solves the problems presented by the integration of assisted- and self-service systems. Only one system is now in place, assuring both the assisted and the self-service interactions.

The representative uses an extended customer application that, although based on the customer Web interface, is enhanced with extra information and navigational capabilities. So only one front-end application need now be developed

Figure 4

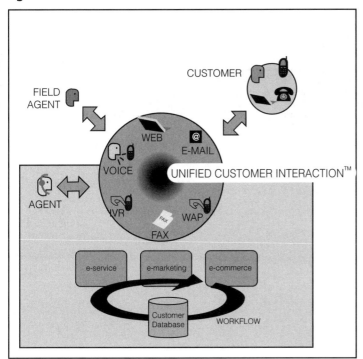

an interaction session so the customer never has to repeat himself while he moves from self-service to a human representative or when the representative changes. Finally, since only one customer database exists, there is only one log of interactions, which the representatives access while contacting customers, providing a complete picture of the customer history.

With Unified Customer Interaction, the customer experiences a consistent and current image of the company that is absolutely fundamental for relationship building. Unified Customer Interaction sets up the basis for u-business (unified business) which is destined to become the prevalent business model of the future.

and maintained. Besides experiencing the same interface as the customer, the representative also has the ability to impersonate a customer, in order to experience exactly the same interface behaviour as the customer. This goes a long way in helping the representative to assist the customer.

A common routing engine exists, assuring the blending of calls, e-mails and co-operative web sessions. Routing disciplines can be defined that ensure optimal resource usage while pre-defined minimum service levels are met.

The binding between the interaction and respective data is maintained throughout

Biography: Easyphone who will enter the next millennium as Altitude Software is the market leader in complete software solutions for unified customer interaction. It is a complete solution in the sense that it provides full blown CTI; a management information system; script screen pops; synchronised voice and data transfer; wrap-up control; Interactive Voice Response; digital recording; predictive dialling; reactive and Internet blending; skills-based routing; Internet security and content management; e-commerce and electronic billing. Easyphone is also completely software-based and open, so will always be complementary to other applications and hardware already in place. It interfaces with a wide range of external PBX platforms from major vendors such as Lucent, Nortel, Alcatel, Ericsson, Siemens, Philips and Panasonic. The solution is based on a tiered architecture where the presentation applications run on Windows workstations or Windows terminals, the CTI and transactional server runs on Windows NT, Solaris and AIX and the relational database relies on a DBMS such as Oracle, Informix, SQL Server, Sybase or DB/2.

Implementing a CRM-based Campaign Management Strategy

Title: *Implementing a CRM-based Campaign Management Strategy*

Author: *SAS Institute Inc.*

Abstract: *A shift from product-driven marketing to customer-driven marketing has become essential in today 's highly competitive business environment. Companies must continuously learn from interactions with customers and respond to the knowledge gained from those interactions. This white paper discusses the technological and business issues involved in implementing a marketing campaign management initiative based on progressive techniques in managing customer relationships. It details the practice of using advanced data management and analysis techniques to transform a large amount of carefully chosen customer data into reliable information to support strategic and tactical marketing decisions. This paper illustrates one instance of integrating analytical CRM with operational CRM for competitive advantage.*

CRM and Campaign Management

Widespread changes in the business landscape and a change in the way customers view the marketplace have caused companies to shift their attention away from internal considerations like reducing costs and streamlining operational systems, and instead to focus on the concept of customer profitability. By taking an economic view of customers that measures how profitable a customer is to the company rather than measuring the profitability of product lines, companies are adopting a customer-centric strategy, stressing the importance of optimizing the value of each customer relationship. The technology-driven process that makes this possible is called Customer Relationship Management (CRM).

CRM is a process by which a company maximizes customer information in an effort to increase loyalty and retain customers ' business over their lifetimes. It combines a progressive approach to gathering customer data with advanced database and decision support technologies that help transform that data into business knowledge. By maximizing the use of customer information, companies can better monitor and understand customer behavior.

Note: For a more detailed discussion of CRM and the data warehousing, data mining, online analytical processing (OLAP), and advanced decision support technologies it involves, refer to the SAS Institute white paper Implementing the Customer Relationship Management Foundation — Analytical CRM.

CRM initiatives can be applied in a wide range of business functions, one of which is marketing campaign management. The CRM process, coupled with the advanced campaign analysis tools that are available, can help companies execute marketing campaigns that are more tightly focused and automated, directing costly marketing efforts toward only those customers who will maintain or increase their value to the company.

Chapter 2: How to Integrate CRM in your Business

Figure 1: Campaign Management Data Flow

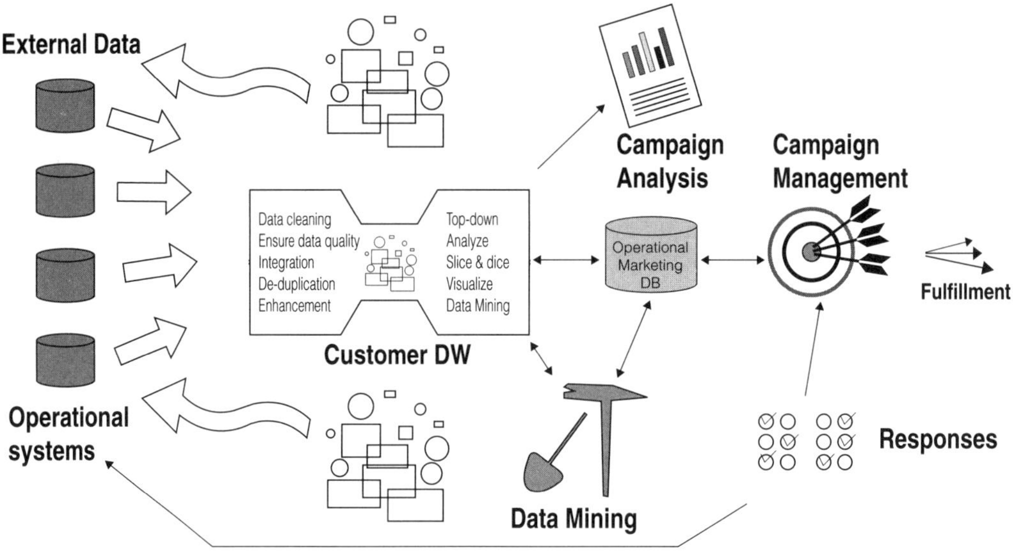

Sharing one of the basic tenets of CRM, that it is at least as profitable to focus on customer retention as new customer acquisition, modern marketing campaign management is an ideal application of the CRM process. With the power of a CRM-based campaign management solution, we can extend that basic tenet one step further: marketing efforts can be directed not toward all existing customers but toward only those customers who, if retained, are likely to maintain or increase their value to the company.

To be successful, database marketers must, first, identify market segments containing customers or prospects with high profit potential and, second, build and execute campaigns that favorably impact the behavior of the individuals in these segments. Segmentation is the key starting point in understanding individual

customers. Through analytical segmentation techniques, customer information such as demographic data and lifestyle information can be combined with historical customer information to help identify differences in behavior among various groups, or segments, of customers.

Because segmentation involves analyzing huge amounts of customer data, data mining is a key component of campaign management. But before we discuss the importance of data mining in detail, let 's step back and take a look at the entire CRM-based campaign management process.

In a CRM-based campaign management initiative, operational data is combined with legacy data and market data from external sources, plus, because of campaign management 's focus on predicting reactions to an upcoming campaign, information about the customer 's history of responses to campaigns is added as well. Data from each of these sources is cleansed and compiled into a customer information warehouse.

Utilizing the customer information warehouse, target groups are selected for promotional campaigns. This is accomplished through OLAP analysis. The multidimensional views that OLAP technology affords make it easier to identify customer segments with regard to their historical response to campaigns.

Marketers could stop there and simply market to the customers who historically respond. But there 's a better way. Through advanced data mining techniques, you can create complex models that segment customers into groups with predictable buying or consumption behaviors. You can take into account a much more accurate view of whether a given customer is likely to respond to the campaign. Marketers using data mining tools can find new ways to categorize customers and more efficiently identify those customers most likely to respond in any number of ways, whether it be to buy more products, buy different products, or even discontinue as a customer.

After mining the data, marketers must feed the resulting models into campaign management software that manages a marketing campaign directed at the defined customer segments. Then, once a precisely targeted campaign has been defined, campaign management software can help ensure that the details of the campaign are communicated to each customer contact point involved and coordinate ongoing management of the campaign until its completion. Finally, campaign management software and OLAP tools are both used to facilitate the back-office processes of communicating, analyzing, and managing data about the campaign results.

Data Mining: The Key to Successful Campaign Management

In order to function as a customer information warehouse, a CRM data warehouse must contain massive amounts of disparate customer data. When viewed though conventional techniques, the value of some of the data may not be apparent. Only when it is analyzed using data mining techniques does the data yield hidden information about your customers and their buying behaviors. It is these discoveries that will enable you to exploit marketing opportunities that your competitors are missing. When you use data mining technology to automate the process of searching through large amounts of data, you can find patterns that predict customer behaviors more efficiently.

Data mining creates models by using information from the customer information warehouse to predict customer behavior. The prediction is usually called a score. A score is assigned to each customer and indicates the probability that the customer will exhibit a particular behavior. Scoring is a method that direct marketers use to determine which individuals or households are most likely to respond to a particular offer. Scores can be based on a large number of variables, all of which are stored in the customer information warehouse. After scoring a set of customers, the scores are used to select the most appropriate prospects for a targeted marketing campaign.

Tight Integration between Data Mining and Campaign Management Software

Campaign management software uses the scores generated by the data mining model to zero in on a particular segment of customers, the goal being to improve campaign effectiveness. But the campaign management software can be even more useful if it can work with customer models directly instead of with the scores the models generate. Integration between the two processes can help solve logistical problems associated with running a large number of frequently changing campaigns, as well as enabling dynamic scoring, which improves scoring efficiency by ensuring only target segments are scored. Dynamic scoring not only saves time but also ensures that the scores are completely up-to-date.

Some of the benefits of integration between data mining processes and campaign management software are as follows:

- Enables dynamic scoring
  - Eliminates need to score entire database
  - Improves efficiency and simplifies refinement of campaigns
- Enables the execution of many multi-event campaigns

- Accelerates the campaign cycle
- Improves targeting
  - Improves response rates
  - Builds relationships
  - Reduces costs
- Provides campaign analysis and feedback
- Reduces manual intervention
- Introduces a process to maintain and develop models by linking the two applications

Integrating data mining and campaign management can accelerate marketing cycle times, reducing costs and increasing the likelihood of reaching customers and prospects before competitors. Scoring takes place only for records defined by the customer segment, eliminating the need to score an entire database. This is important to keep pace with continuously running marketing campaigns with tight cycle times. Plus, new campaign results can be immediately factored into ongoing campaign management activity. Fresh data enables marketers to refine scoring information within defined market segments and improve ongoing campaign results. The end of each campaign cycle presents another chance to assess results and improve future campaigns.

Partners in Campaign Management

To build a complete campaign management process that takes advantage of the latest technology, it makes sense to examine the individual components of the process and obtain the right solution for each. When looking at analytical CRM — the data warehouse, data mining, OLAP, and decision support components —the optimal choice is software and services from SAS Institute. As a recognized leader in each of these areas, SAS Institute can provide you with world-class solutions to address a wide range of business requirements.

In an effort to provide a total solution to customer interested in campaign management, SAS Institute is currently collaborating with some of the industry 's leading producers of campaign management software to seamlessly integrate SAS analytical software with campaign management software. When implemented as part of a closed-loop cooperative effort with the SAS CRM solution, campaign management software will be able to access the customer information warehouse; automate the planning, design, execution, and scheduling of multiphase marketing campaigns; profile customers; create target segments; develop sophisticated, targeted campaigns; measure and test new strategies; and track the complete history of each customer communication.

Integrating SAS Institute 's analytical data warehousing technology, model-development architecture, and pre-and post-campaign analysis engine with powerful campaign management tools effectively automates the process of evaluating and managing campaigns and making them better focused. The result is a more intelligent basis for campaign management that can shorten the cycle time for both campaigns and for analytics.

A Study in Success: One Company's Campaign Management Initiative

The telecommunications industry is one of many that has had to react to changes affecting its markets. The changing business landscape has stimulated a dramatic rise in competitiveness, and many telecommunications companies have experienced a loss of market share as a result. One of the nation 's largest telecommunications companies, with more than 20 million customers, is no exception. When their research showed that they were selling to only a third of the customers in their market, the company reacted in a way that many forward-thinking competitive companies are reacting: taking steps to maximize customer profitability by optimizing the return on marketing investment in acquisitions and retention. They adopted a CRM-based campaign management strategy. In 1998,the company developed an enterprise marketing plan that laid the foundation for what is now a highly successful system for managing customer relationships. The system optimizes the profitability of customer relationships via continuous one-to-one customer management processes that maximize retention and cross-selling rates. And the key component of their initiative was the marketing automation solution provided by SAS Institute. By utilizing models generated from Enterprise Miner™ software as input to Exchange Application 's ValEX campaign-management software, the company 's system became one of the first complete, fully automated, CRM-based campaign management initiatives.

The marketing automation solution from SAS Institute, which integrates sophisticated predictive modeling and campaign management software, provided a dynamic, customer value scoring capability. When presented with a complete picture of the customer by continually gathering data from all customer contact points, the company was better able to understand and predict customer behavior, needs, and profitability and then feed this knowledge back to customer contact points. Instead of high-volume untargeted mailings, this forward-thinking telecommunications company now delivers many more small, highly targeted, customized mailings through marketing automation.

Summary

In a world where corporate competition continues to increase due to external market factors and a market-savvy customer base, companies must discard their business philosophies of the past and adopt innovative ways to maintain customer loyalty and profitability. Companies must adopt a customer-centric strategy that stresses the concept that success over time comes from customer loyalty—that long-term profitability lies in fostering unique lifetime relationships with small numbers of carefully chosen customers. Companies must continuously learn from interactions with each individual customer and be prepared to dynamically respond to information and knowledge gained from those interactions. What makes this possible is CRM, a method of processing a large amount of carefully chosen customer data in order to obtain reliable information to support strategic and tactical business decisions.

Campaign management is one operational application of CRM that improves a company 's ability to evaluate its customers' needs and respond with marketing programs that foster prolonged customer loyalty. A successful CRM-based campaign management initiative allows companies to identify market segments containing customers or prospects with high profit potential and create marketing campaigns that favorably impact the behavior of these individuals.

By utilizing advanced data management and analysis techniques coupled with powerful campaign management software, companies can create a true one-to-one marketing environment that targets customers based on an optimal balance of needs and customer economics. This requires working with extremely large volumes of disparate customer data, but the analysis capabilities of today 's data mining and OLAP software make the required customer segmentation and modeling possible.

SAS Institute offers the only software and services solution that spans the entire decision support process for managing customer relationships. Companies can collect data at all customer contact points and turn that data into knowledge for understanding and anticipating customer behavior, meeting customer needs, building more profitable customer relationships, and gaining a holistic view of a customer 's lifetime value through all

Chapter 2: How to Integrate CRM in your Business

possible interactions with the company. While SAS technology provides the key ingredients for successful CRM, we recognize the need to deliver a solution that incorporates decision support, operational feedback systems, system implementation services, and business process expertise. That 's why we are partnering with companies producing campaign management software to provide the most complete solution. These partnerships will make an integrated CRM-based campaign management solution much easier for our customers to implement, speeding their return on their marketing investment and resulting in increased customer loyalty.

Modeling customer relationships - A flexible, integrated architecture enables customer-centric marketing

Title: *Modeling customer relationships - A flexible, integrated architecture enables customer-centric marketing.*

Author: *David Puckey, IBM NUMA-Q*

Abstract: *This white paper draws upon the lessons learned by IBM NUMA-Q ® in implementing large-scale technology platforms to support customer relationship management (CRM) strategies within major organizations worldwide. Interested readers are likely to be concerned with how they might model customer relationships in a way which will support the transition from present product-focused views of marketing intelligence to more useful (and profitable) customer-focused views. This paper provides the data architect or modeler with a generic template for modeling customer data. This paper also highlights commonly faced problems that occur when modeling customer data.*

1.0 Introduction

The strategic importance of managing customer relation-ships both drives and is driven by technology. In particular, this applies to data and the increasingly sophisticated and useful ways in which data is used to model relationships and to drive contact strategies. At the core of any technology enabler for CRM is the customer database. The customer database represents the data hub that integrates the various statistical modeling, campaign management, contact history and response tracking components of the marketing campaign lifecycle. This is true whether the database is used for the execution of marketing strategies (e.g., generates mailing lists), or whether it exists purely as an analysis engine that passes contact strategies and information to a separate customer interaction platform for execution (e.g., customer call centers).

The technology layer and its integration with emerging business processes is therefore key to the successful implementation of a data-driven Customer Relationship Management strategy. This paper describes, in a generic way, an approach that IBM NUMA-Q has successfully used to ensure that the core data structures in the CRM technology layer support the integration of the various components of the marketing process and reduce the time required to design and execute a campaign. This approach enables the creation of a complete model of customer relationships over time.

2.0 The evolution of the customer database

Current approaches to the design of the customer database fall broadly into two camps. The first —the flat earth view of the world —hails from the glory days of target marketing in the late 1980s. This approach, which is popular with list providers and bureau operations, utilizes the concept of the customer file or list. Such a list tends to offer a current snapshot of the customer or prospect base

Figure 1: Customer databases evolve with integration of technology and business processes (Source: Raab and Associates)

Evolution of customer database

	Campaign management	Customer relationship management
• contact horizon	• one-shot	• sequence
• output	• offer	• information
• systems	• mail/phone	• touchpoint
• execution	• manual	• scheduled
• departments	• marketing	• front-office
• data types	• purchases	• contacts
• update interval	• monthly	• daily
• reaction time	• billing cycle	• transaction
• goal	• reduce waste	• add revenue

and is often the product of much tortuous cleansing, de-duplication and point-in-time segmentation. This approach makes it difficult to analyze the ups-and-downs of an organization's relationship with a customer over time due to its current snapshot view of the customer and prospect base. Further, it typically lacks the transaction-level detail and promotional history needed to model customer behavior.

The second approach has evolved from the data warehousing movement and IBM NUMA-Q's experience in helping hundreds of organizations design and implement data warehouses (see Figure 1). NUMA-Q has developed a mature methodology for delivering rapid business benefit by integrating sophisticated analytical tools with subject-oriented and time-consistent central databases. Such systems typically concentrate on the delivery of business intelligence and are generally not designed to plug directly into an organization's day-to-day operations. However, the modeling techniques employed by NUMA-Q for the delivery of successful data warehousing projects represent a radical shift in emphasis from both flat earth views of data and the microscopic views of data used in Online Transaction Processing (OLTP) Systems. NUMA-Q's dimensional view of data provides the optimum combination of analysis of facts over time and high system performance when dealing with large data volumes.

IBM's approach to successfully delivering large-scale technology platforms to support CRM strategies uses the best attributes from both of the previous approaches. This

Chapter 2: How to Integrate CRM in your Business

approach incorporates the maximum degree of analytical flexibility for the marketer and marketing analyst with the efficient scoring, segmentation and extraction of data to execute marketing campaigns or contact strategies. It also places the customer or prospect at the center of the model and seeks to model all facets of a relationship with that customer over the known lifetime of the relationship. NUMA-Q's approach to the design of customer databases is not list based and is not designed to simply support ad-hoc, point-in-time marketing solutions. Rather, the objective is to give the marketer true insight into the variability of his relationship with a customer or customer segment over time and to deliver seamless integration with the widest possible choice of campaign management and statistical modeling tools available.

▸ All relevant facets of the relationship over time
▸ Integration of external prospect lists
▸ Integration of external data classifications
▸ Integration of external data enrichment
▸ Ability to directly score the database and segment the database many times
▸ Ability to evaluate different campaigns and treatment strategies over time and across millions of transactions and customers
▸ Campaign management, prioritization, etc.
▸ Ability to predict future customer behavior based on past behavior

It is not possible to achieve all of the above features using either a flat file approach or a standard data warehousing approach alone.

3.0 Elements of a customer relationship management database

There are a number of required features of a CRM database that the architect must integrate in order to support the marketing lifecycle (see Figure 2). These are (in no particular order):

▸ Customer or prospect focus

Figure 2: Typical facets of a customer relationship that need to be tracked over time

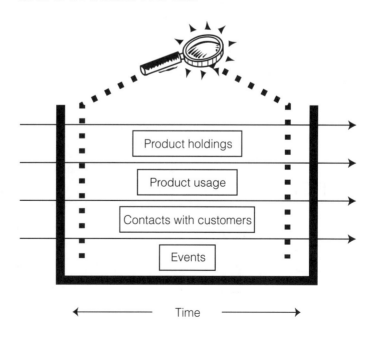

Product holdings

Product usage

Contacts with customers

Events

◄——— Time ———►

4.0 Taking a lifetime view of the customer

In order to fully realize a CRM strategy, the marketer must have information that enables him to take a lifetime view of the relationship. A relationship is most usefully defined as the starting point at which the organization has an initial interaction with a prospect. This relationship then needs to be tracked as the prospect is encouraged to climb the loyalty ladder from prospect to customer and eventually to highly valued customer. The marketer needs to see and understand past events, contacts and purchase information in order to assess the current and future profitability of the relationship. The commonly used marketing analysis of recency, frequency and monetary value of transactions indicates some of the facets of the relationship that should be tracked.

In IBM NUMA-Q's experience of facilitating client work-shops to establish the business requirements for a CRM solution, four relationship facets appear common to most organizations (see Figure 3). These facets are:

Product Holding–What products has a customer purchased and what products do they currently hold?

Figure 3: Customer focus is key. Each facet of a relationship may be treated as an island of analysis, linked centrally to the customer

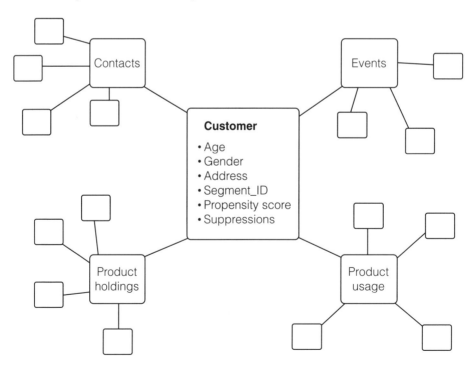

Contacts

Events

Customer
- Age
- Gender
- Address
- Segment_ID
- Propensity score
- Suppressions

Product holdings

Product usage

Product Usage–How has the customer used that product? For example, can an increase in credit card usage be attributed to some prior interaction with the customer or some promotional activity?

Contacts–What has the organization's interaction with the customer been over time and what were the outcomes?

Events–What other events have occurred, either within the life of the customer (e.g., marriage) or externally to the relationship (e.g., competitor activity)?

Each of these facets may be treated by the modeler as an island of analysis linked centrally to an individual customer at a given point in time. For example, the marketer may take a point-in-time view of the relationship, a view over time or make prescient predictions for the future. Information about these four facets of a customer relationship enable the marketer to answer questions such as: How many customers have bought product X? How many customers display a repeatable purchasing pattern? How often have I contacted this customer and when? Who are my most profitable customers? What events or contacts occurred prior to customer defection?

The approach taken by NUMA-Q to support this kind of questioning is to place a customer table at the center of the model and to surround it with satellite dimensional schema (star schema) representing each facet of the relationship to be modeled. Modeling the facets of the relationship dimensionally allows who,

what, when, where style analysis. For example: Which segment bought which products and what contacts preceded which purchase? Where do the contacts live, and how do they like to be addressed?

The customer-centric nature of the model also lends itself well to the prudent de-normalization of often-used facts, such as disposable income estimates, onto the customer table and helps facilitate the efficient extraction of contact lists and integration with statistical modeling tools, such as SAS or Unica. The customer-centric model also supports very well the iterative nature of the marketer's questioning, such as: How many customers hold product Y? Which of those customers are profitable? Which of those customers did I contact last week and which of them complained about the contact? It is also possible to assess what behavioral changes are exhibited as a result of identifiable interactions with the customer. Once the marketer has exhausted his questioning, which helps refine the contact list names, addresses and salutations may be simply extracted from the customer table using the relevant keys. Current suppression indicators and propensity scores may also be stored against the central customer record, allowing the possible automation of standard hygiene filtering.

Chapter 2: How to Integrate CRM in your Business

5.0 The customer-centric model at an insurance company

To see how this model might work, take the example of an insurance business (see Figure 4). The firm's relationship with Mr. Jones begins when he makes an initial inquiry about health insurance via the organization's call center. This initial inquiry is the result of a press advertising campaign that reached Mr. Jones; this fact is recorded.

In response to his interest in the company's health insurance offering, the insurance business sends Mr. Jones an information pack. This step is also captured and recorded in the database. At this point, Mr. Jones does not have a product holding, but his name and address and contact records exist within the database.

Mr. Jones does not respond to the receipt of the information pack, and after three months the marketer plans a campaign targeted at Mr. Jones and all the other Mr. Joneses who have interacted with the organization but not purchased any products in the last three months.

In this case, a query can be run against the database asking, Who has contacted us in the last three months with a contact type of inquiry? This query will generate a list of keys into the customer or prospect table, which, without further refinement, could be used to generate a contact list. However, it is more likely that the marketer's questioning will continue further —How many of these customers or prospects were sent an information pack? The result set from this query will be matched against the result set from the last query to further refine the list of keys. This process may be further refined by asking, How many people in this list do not have a

Figure 4: Example—The customer-centric model at an Insurance company

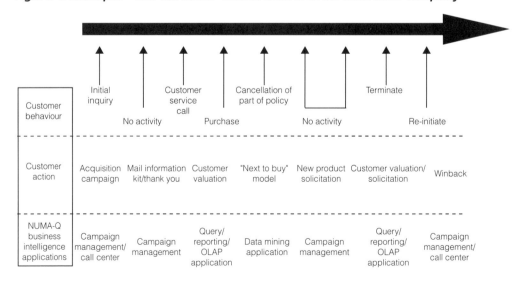

product holding? Once the marketer has completed his refinement of the list, it is a simple, and highly performant, exercise to take the resulting list of keys and extract the name, address, salutation data, etc. from the central customer or prospect table and perform further filtering based on suppressions on the customer table or assigning customers to campaign cells for different treatments based on segmentation keys on the customer record. Once the contact list is finalized, the customer keys are used to populate the contact table and to record the fact of the outbound contact. By storing all of this data in a centralized Relational Database Management System (RDBMS), it is a relatively simple matter to make this data available to sophisticated campaign management tools and statistical modeling tools. These tools interface easily with an open RDBMS, such as Oracle, and almost without exception, such tools feature native connectivity options.

Those readers familiar with the processing dynamics of most RDBMS will immediately spot a major dependency of this model — the various software components deployed to support the marketing lifecycle must allow the generation of interim result sets. This is absolutely crucial in order to support the marketer's analytical processes as he constantly shrinks and expands potential target lists, possibly to generate the required list size to match a budget allocation. Already, a number of tools vendors are acutely in-tune with the mindset and thought processes of the modern marketer.

6.0 Integrated infrastructure supports

In the past, database marketing solutions often focused on individual user communities participating in the overall marketing process. While this focus has managed to hit the sweet spots of these often isolated communities (e.g., marketing analysis or campaign management) and to temporarily satisfy parochial needs, it has left a troublesome legacy for the integrator of the technology layer who seeks to accelerate the marketing cycle, empower the marketer and reduce the marketing department's dependency on highly skilled and expensive (and often obstructive) database experts. Such function-focused solutions have ensured that the walls that block the implementation of a virtuous circle of continuous improvement in the marketing process remain solid. The proliferation of file formats, APIs and unnecessary processing layers needed to integrate these elements have delivered a full employment charter for those who wrangle with the complexity of the technology layer at the expense of marketing responsiveness and creativity.

NUMA-Q's solution to such technical anarchy is to focus firmly on a technological infrastructure that supports and integrates the overall marketing process, and underpins the progressive development of a relationship management strategy (see Figure 5). The use of a centralized relational database and open systems to manage customer data, contact history and relationship history

Chapter 2: How to Integrate CRM in your Business

Figure 5: Example—The customer-centric model at an Insurance company

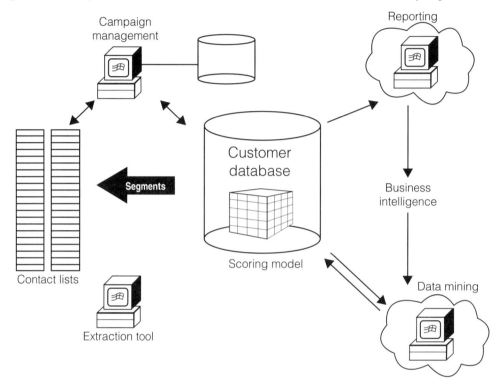

allows the easy integration, at the data level, of the various technologies deployed at different stages in the marketing process. Analysts' models may be stored alongside the actual data, and scoring and segmentation keys can be made directly available to campaign management and campaign scheduling software. The automation of routine communications is simplified and database triggers can be utilized to make marketing more event driven.

7.0 Typical data modeling challenges

This section details some of the data modeling challenges, which, in IBM NUMA-Q's experience, are common across a number of industries and organizations.

Householding
The grouping of individuals by household or relationship patterns is often a difficult process in product-focused legacy systems. These systems often have great difficulty in even identifying the individual responsible for purchasing a given product. The benefits of groupings for the relationship marketer are many:

- Avoidance of unnecessary duplicate contacts per household
- Understanding loyalty patterns among relationship groups
- Identification of cross-sell and up-sell opportunities (e.g., family policies, etc.)
- Identification of significant life events (coming of age, birth, marriage, etc.)
- Analysis of geodemographic data by household

Multiple households can be problematic for both the marketer and the system designer. Individual customers may have multiple addresses, each of which is related to the customer via the product holding. For example, Mr. Jones has a main residence in the city and a weekend retreat by the coast. Mr. Jones has a household insurance policy for each address. An insurance marketer may wish to sell Mr. Jones a life insurance policy. However, for the modeler, a household is just a simple grouping of individuals. Specific business questions must be answered in order to track the household movements of individuals. The difficulty is in the actual identification of a household—particularly in high-density urban residential areas or areas with a highly transient population.

There are several approaches to handling customer householding, de-duping and geocoding challenges.

These include:
- Service Bureau operations
- Integrating specialized software tools to perform this function on a regular basis (this also requires process integration for proper and effective handling)

A number of marketing data processing bureau services perform household identification, based on, for example, electoral register information, etc. However, such matching is never 100 percent accurate.

Products held by groups of people
Certain types of products, for example joint bank accounts, introduce a many-to-many relationship between product holdings and persons. This fact, if modeled literally, can cause performance problems in the database and confuse campaign management and extraction tools seeking to identify a single prospect. This is particularly true in cases where organizations are transitioning to a customer-focused marketing strategy yet still require the ability to market in the interim period based on product holding attributes. This situation is common in large businesses that cannot possibly switch from a product to a customer focus overnight. The only answer to this problem is a business one. Identifying a primary marketing contact for a product holding can simplify the problem in some cases.

Person matching
Another key challenge for the designer of a CRM database is the identification of individuals. Often, seemingly multiple individuals on the database are in fact the same person, albeit at a different point-in-time, or with a different product holding, or at a different address. Organizations with multiple operational systems serving multiple customer touch points often find that the non-uniformity of input validation across these systems leads to situations where Mr. John Jones, Mr. J. Jones and Mr.

J. B. Jones at the same address could perhaps be one, two or three actual people. This problem is further exacerbated when external prospect lists are brought into the database. Once again, the modeler can incorporate a simple grouping of people within the database design but the problem is identifying the actual grouping. In some cases, IBM NUMA-Q has allowed a "degree of confidence" value to be assigned to the grouping record to provide the marketer with a coefficient that validates assumptions. The business rules for deriving this coefficient clearly evolve over time, and can result in the creation of specific profiling questions targeted to specific customers during interactions.

As with householding, some marketing data providers can perform unique person identification based on postal lists, real estate listings, electoral rolls, and other data. This identification activity can be cumbersome as it involves exporting and re-importing data periodically. If the grouping of seemingly multiple individuals into one is handled as a grouping table, the impact on, for example, referential integrity within the database can be minimized. However, this kind of group can also make the model more complex — with a possible impact on performance.

Unfortunately, there are no magic cures for the problem of person matching, and the database modeler should be wary of the purveyors of such cures.

Classing and banding

A number of marketing database designs use fields such as "date of birth" or "age" on the customer record. Though there is a clear use for such fields, marketers rarely wish to contact people who are, for example, 51 or 23 years of age. Usually, the marketer wants to target people aged between 25 and 35 or those who are past retirement age. Such targeting calls for some sort of banding of customers to reduce wasted processing and simplify the process for the marketer.

Age is not the only candidate attribute for banding. The modeler should seek to understand other candidates and include these in the model.

Regularly used measures

Initially, and over time, the modeler of the customer database should seek to identify those frequently asked marketing questions, such as: Who earns more than $20,000? Who has made more than four insurance claims in the last period, etc.? It makes little sense to have multiple marketing campaign designers all scanning the product usage table over and over again. This can be avoided by denormalizing regularly used measures directly onto the customer or prospect record.

Suppressions

Most organizations are able to identify a number of standard reasons for suppressing marketing communications. Suppressions can range from blanket "do not communicate at all" indicators to "do not market a specific product" to this individual. These suppressions should be held directly on the customer or prospect record to enable swift and easy filtering of targets.

and cost reengineering the organization's marketing databases —sometimes comprising many terabytes of data.

8.0 Summary

While both flat file and standard data warehousing approaches to the customer database will allow analysis of customers and the selection of target lists, neither approach will, on its own, support the management of customer relationships over time. Likewise, neither will integrate all components of the marketing process in the most efficient way.

The template presented in this paper may form the basis of the data architect or analyst's initial attempts to define data structures, which will support both of the above objectives. This template reflects the work IBM NUMA-Q has done with a number of major organizations to support their database marketing activities and to drive the strategic implementation of Customer Relationship Management at both the business and the systems levels.

CRM requires a fresh approach to systems design, along with the flexibility to accommodate unexpected change. Many piecemeal or point solutions in the market fail to take an integrated view of the entire marketing lifecycle and focus only on data structures to support their own specific components of that lifecycle. As CRM matures as an operational reality, it is imperative that organizations have an integrated view of business processes and data. Failure to take an integrated view of requirements will lead to significant effort

Customer Relationship Management: Choosing the appropriate strategy and Data Warehousing technology to win and retain customers

Title: Customer Relationship Management: Choosing the appropriate strategy and
                    Data Warehousing technology to win and retain customers
Author: Professor Adrian Payne of Cranfield University for Oracle

Abstract: This White Paper sets out to offer practical guidance by suggesting that
                    companies approach CRM in two stages:
                    - determine the business's CRM strategy and
                    - select and combine the appropriate technology options

1. EXECUTIVE SUMMARY

"Customer relationship management" (CRM) is increasingly viewed as a major element of corporate strategy. This is due partly to new opportunities presented by information technology. In particular, IT - in the form of customer databases, data warehouses and secure Internet technology now enables companies to target chosen market segments or micro-segments more precisely.

The Internet, in particular, can be seen as a technology that is both a threat and an opportunity. By removing barriers to entry it is turning some markets on their heads. For any organisation, operating in this new environment, it is imperative that they retain their hard fought for customer base, while also exploiting the new emerging market opportunities. CRM is therefore becoming increasingly important as the Internet begins to make an impact.

Despite the Internet becoming a household word, its use as an effective channel to market is still relatively low. According to the Bathwick Group's research published in 'the Countdown to a Connected World', while 54.2% of the organisations surveyed provided passive information to customers, only 20.8% are executing any type of business transaction with them. However, as successful examples of using the Internet more proactively, like Dell Computer and Amazon.com begin to pervade business folklore, we should expect this number to rise dramatically.

Another explanation for the popularity of CRM relates to the limitations of traditional marketing: this activity has typically been the sole preserve of the marketing function, which has focused on "marketing mix" elements such as product, price, promotion and place. These activities have been largely directed at winning new customers rather than retaining or maximising existing ones.

Many companies have now recognised that long-term relationships with customers are one of the most important assets of the whole organisation. Put another way, improved customer retention and an ability to grow the customer's value - some call it "customer ownership" - is the key to competitive advantage and profitability.

The problem is that there is still a great deal of confusion about what CRM (also referred to as relationship marketing, or customer management) is. To some it means direct mail or a loyalty card scheme, to others a help desk or a call centre. Others see it as a relational database for key account management. As a result, many organisations are adopting CRM on a fragmented basis. To make matters worse, only a few businesses have a clear idea about how IT is best exploited to implement CRM, or how to do so in the most cost-effective way.

This White Paper sets out to offer practical guidance by suggesting that companies approach CRM in two stages:

Determine the business's CRM strategy
Depending on the core business and a number of related strategic issues, each organisation needs to consider precisely which CRM strategy is appropriate now and in the future. We have identified four broad strategic options facing organisations - product-based selling, customer-based marketing, managed service and support, and 'individualised relationship marketing', or what Peppers & Rogers have term '1 to 1 Marketing'. The latter is the most sophisticated - it requires collection and analysis of extensive information about customers, and also the ability and desire to give customers individualised service. Various migration

paths are possible over time from one option to another.

Select and combine the appropriate technology options
Once the appropriate CRM strategy, for now and the future, is decided the business needs to select the technology that will enable it to implement the chosen strategy. We describe four key information technology elements - databases, data marts, the 'enterprise data warehouse' and 'integrated CRM solutions'. The last option, which is the most complex, (but of course delivers the most value), will typically involve the integration of several customer-facing operational systems, such as Call Centres and electronic commerce applications with an enterprise-wide data warehouse.

Finally, we offer some suggestions regarding implementation.

2. DETERMINING A CRM STRATEGY

With much current attention being directed at CRM, some managers are advocating the quick introduction of a particular technology solution. However, organisations' experiences with IT are mixed. Some are hostages to out-of-date legacy systems, and others have inherited a culture where IT is inappropriately viewed as an ever-escalating cost rather than as a source of competitive advantage. The result is either inappropriate investment in new technology which may fail to break free of the legacy "chains" or a focus on the technology challenge alone, rather than the underlying business issues. In turn, organisations may adopt one particular technology too rapidly; focus insufficiently on building customer relationships; or resist using new technologies for improved CRM. Rather than focus immediately on technology, managers should determine the role of CRM within the overall business strategy. They should start by clearly defining core business and what they would like it to be in the future. This will involve the review of a number of specific business issues - (see box below).

The role of CRM - specific business issues to consider

Your Company and your Industry
What is your strategic intent? What are your organisation's resources and competences?
What is the current state and possible future changes in your industry structure?
Where does your company fit within that structure?
Are there new strategic alliances that may disrupt the market?

Competitive Position
What is the nature of your competitors? How do they compete?
How will new competitors evolve in the future?
Are there new entrants on the horizon that are not hindered by the same legacy architecture?

Channel to Market
What is the current and future role of different distribution channels?
What opportunities exist for disintermediation?
What opportunities exist for new forms of electronic distribution and delivery?
How are your products/services purchased? How important are they to your customers?
Who constitutes the decision-making unit?

Your Customers
Who are your existing and potential customers? What are the major segments?
What are the opportunities for micro segmentation, one-to-one marketing and mass customisation?
What kinds of relationship do you have or want to have with your customers?
Do you feed customer communication back into the business so we can relate to customers on a one-to-one basis?
What is the appropriate information technology platform to serve present and future customer and corporate needs?

A review of these issues, which may vary from industry to industry, will have implications for a business's present and future CRM strategy. In particular the organisation needs to determine the amount of customer information it requires, as well as how closely it should interact with its customer base both now and in the future.

The CRM Strategy Matrix shown in Figure 1 illustrates this process well. The vertical axis of the matrix shows completeness of customer information, a combination of (a) how much information is held about customers, and (b) how sophisticated is the analysis of that information. The horizontal axis shows the degree of customer individualisation - the extent to which the organisation uses whatever information it has on customers to give them individual or customised service.

The CRM Strategy Matrix shows four broad strategic positions which may be appropriate for a particular organisation depending on the business issues outlined above and its specific characteristics. A shift from the lower left to upper right position reflects a movement away from a transactional approach (a very unsophisticated form of CRM) to individualised relationship marketing (a much more sophisticated form of CRM). Many would argue that there is a strategic advantage in being the first to reach this individualised (or one-to-one) position within a given industry as competitors will have to offer significant inducements to get customers to switch .

The question remains when and how fast the trend will gather pace. The rate at which companies mature to this position of course varies from industry to industry: supermarkets and telecommunication suppliers are obviously fairly advanced. However, it is likely to be some time before

Figure 1: The CRM Strategy Matrix

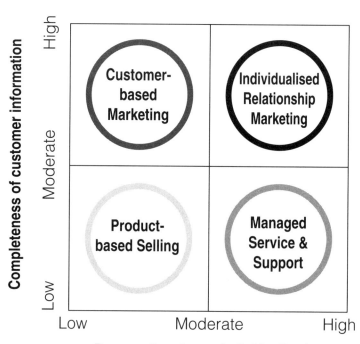

Completeness of customer information (vertical axis: Low, Moderate, High)

- Customer-based Marketing
- Individualised Relationship Marketing
- Product-based Selling
- Managed Service & Support

Degree of customer individualisation (horizontal axis: Low, Moderate, High)

we see a used car dealer develop a loyalty card programme! The most advanced Internet booksellers and electrical component distributors are examples of where top right-hand corner positions have been achieved. Each business will need to consider where it is now and where it must migrate to in the future.

These four positions on the CRM strategy matrix are now outlined in more detail.

2.1. Product-based Selling
At the bottom left-hand position of the CRM Strategy Matrix is 'product-based selling'. Here the organisation has information about transactions and wishes to do simple analysis of variables such as product sales over time, channel productivity, etc. The organisation will have basic information such as a customer mailing list (often many), but there is probably little or no detailed information on individual customers behaviour.

With product-based selling, the emphasis is on product and channels, not on the customer. It is highly unlikely that any segmentation undertaken would be based on the customer except in single product organisations or those with a very simple set of related products. The level of sophistication in terms of CRM is fairly low. Nevertheless this approach may represent a perfectly appropriate strategy for some organisations.

2.2. Managed Service and Support
On the bottom right-hand corner of the CRM strategy matrix is 'managed service and support'. In practice, most companies tend to move from product-based selling to managed service and support as their

first extension into CRM by setting up a call centre or help desk. Here the business is seeking both to identify which specific customers it wishes to retain and to place greater emphasis on its most important customers.

Essentially this approach is about applying customer service to selling. The business is seeking to build improved relationships with customers through enhanced levels of service and support. This form of CRM does not need comprehensive information on customers, but the communication is person to person, or individualised.

An example is banks, who know quite a lot about their customers, but do not make this information available to their sales force to enable them to change pricing to take account of their customers' risk profile, or to make marketing decisions based on customers' expected lifetime value.

Investment in these systems can be high and whilst the productivity gains can be significant, many organisations fail to fully analyse the customer information they collect. The result is that organisations fail to take advantage of the more strategic opportunities that this information can reveal.

2.3. Customer-based Marketing
In the top left-hand corner of the matrix is 'customer-based marketing'. Organisations undertaking customer-based marketing shift their emphasis from individual product sales to a focus on the customer. Here the organisation seeks to develop a more detailed understanding of its customers by

Chapter 2: How to Integrate CRM in your Business

undertaking a range of analyses including:
▸ Customer profitability
▸ Competitor responses
▸ Loyalty and churn management
▸ Credit scoring
▸ Customer loyalty
▸ Fraud detection and management
▸ Risk management
▸ Delinquency detection.

Not all of these analyses will be relevant for every company. Their relevance will depend on the industry sector, the company's position in the market and other factors.

A move from product management to customer management, will allow an organisation to:

▸ make different offers to different customers - the essence of CRM.
▸ monitor the organisation's progress towards this goal
▸ identify individual cross selling and up-selling opportunities to maximise customer profitability

Whilst customer-based marketing is a more advanced form of CRM, those businesses that adopt this approach will not be offering the highly individualised customer service and support found on the right-hand side of the CRM strategy matrix.

2.4. Individualised Relationship Marketing
In the top right-hand corner of the CRM Strategy matrix is 'individualised relationship marketing', or what Peppers & Rogers have termed '1 to 1 Marketing'. This usually requires both sophisticated data platforms and sophisticated

applications running on them. Such applications include:

▸ Advanced one-to-one marketing (both business-to-business and business-to-consumer), like Amazon.com and Dell Computer's web site.
▸ Advanced computer telephony integration (CTI) which enables the business to use the computer interactively during telephone contact with a customer creating individualised service to the customer

In particular, this strategic position is relevant for organisations that are seeking to adopt a wide range of channel options. These may include direct selling, selling through indirect channels, such as distributors or brokers, and sales over the Internet using electronic commerce. This latter channel option represents considerable opportunities for building one-to-one marketing systems, which can learn from electronic interactions with customers and which develop a differentiated service for every individual customer that comes onto the system. At the most advanced level of individualised relationship marketing, the business is able to respond instantaneously to customer enquiries. And, as the communication or transaction with the customer takes place, information feeds back into the operational systems. The whole process becomes a dynamic form of CRM rather than a static one.

Organisations adopting the individualised relationship marketing approach to CRM will be able to offer a complete, individualised and customised service. This could be via telephone, mail, face-to-face, or it may take the form of electronic commerce via the Internet, where customers can use a web browser to make enquiries or purchases.

An illustration of a company adopting this approach is RS Components (see box below).

This form of CRM does not have to be personalised, (i.e. have direct person-to-person contact with the customer) but it must be individualised. For CRM to be individualised, the business needs to develop IT systems that "know" the customer and then extend that knowledge throughout the enterprise. If the business develops a 'corporate memory' of the customers it is dealing with, whenever they contact it (and whomever they contact) they will feel that the business knows all about them. The relationship is then continually strengthened through on-going

---

RS components - towards individualised relationship marketing

RS Components, an international distribution company is an example of an organisation that has shifted its focus to individualised relationship marketing. Its electrical component catalogue weighed 4 kilos, was nearly 8 inches thick and contained over 100,000 products. Upgraded quarterly and despatched to over 150,000 account customers, the cost of the printed catalogue was a good reason to embrace first a CD ROM version and then an Internet site.

With a direct presence in 13 countries, the company's ability to find and service customers was constrained economically by the costs associated with catalogue-based business. Today, the Internet gives it global reach, with close to zero engagement costs.

A key differentiator for the Internet site is the customer personalisation, which is driven by profile questions such as job type, industry type and product interests. On entering the site, each customer has his or her own dynamically generated welcome page showing tailored editorial, advertising and new product alerts relevant to that particular customer.

The Internet site has been designed to provide individualised relationship marketing, including direct customer access to 10,000 documents in the RS technical data library. With its customer service, personalised operation, downloadable technical information and tools for navigation (to make finding the required products easier), there is clearly an improved value proposition for customers.

RS confirms that the site is meeting and exceeding its sales expectations.

interactions. In addition, customers are likely to build an emotional bond with the organisation that has invested time in the relationship, and they may be unwilling to invest that time again with competitors.

2.5. Migration Paths for CRM

Using the CRM Strategy Matrix you can position your own organisation. Many will not be where they want to be and will want to shift towards more sophisticated forms of CRM as their markets become more competitive. Only a few, such as the most developed Internet booksellers, are already adopting advanced forms of individualised relationship marketing.

So what are the options for migrating? Organisations starting with product-based selling should initially be concerned with integrating their key existing customer-facing activities. They need to look forward in time to see what business benefits would be realisable through a more advanced form of CRM. A range of possible transitions is shown in Figure 2. The choice of migration paths from product-based selling will depend heavily upon the specific business issues outlined

earlier. Two paths are common. In some cases the transition will emphasise building increased customer intimacy through elements such as call centres and computer telephony integration (Path 1). In other cases, it will involve developing greater database completeness and exploiting clearly targeted but relatively simple marketing approaches (Path 2). This latter path focuses on improving the quality, management and utilisation of data.

Despite this, as yet very few organisations have begun to shift towards one-to-one marketing. There are two reasons why some organisations might not want, or might not be able, to do so:

Figure 2: Transition Paths for CRM

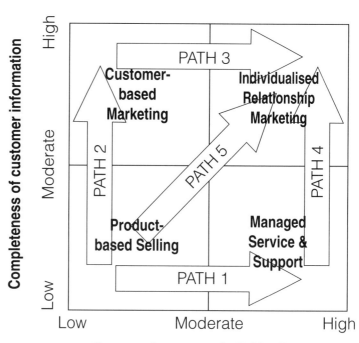

1. Some lack the necessary direct interaction with customers: for example, a manufacturer who sells through wholesalers and/or retailers, or through a dealer network may not have direct contact with its final customers.

2. Others are not culturally ready: even if they had comprehensive information about customers, they wouldn't make real use of it. This may be because they are more focused on selling an existing product than understanding customers needs; or because they are organised around individual product lines with little sharing of information between product managers.

Those organisations wishing to adopt one-to-one marketing applications may do so by migrating from customer-based marketing - Path 3, or from managed service and support - Path 4. (RS components is a case of the latter transition).

A few organisations may undertake a more radical transformation directly from transaction-based selling to individualised relationship marketing - Path 5. This radical shift will be easier for a start-up or smaller company without existing investment in legacy systems, or an organisation that has strong leadership and is willing to undertake heavy investment to make a range of different and new initiatives work together concurrently.

Whichever path taken, the organisation must choose technology solutions that enable it to grow from one position on the CRM matrix to another without undue difficulty.

3. SELECTING AND COMBINING TECHNOLOGY OPTIONS FOR CRM

Having determined the appropriate migration path for the organisation on the CRM Strategy Matrix, managers can now consider the relevant IT solution. There are four broad technology options for facilitating the adoption of a CRM approach. These include: a tactical database with decision support systems; sales and marketing data marts; an enterprise data warehouse; and integrated CRM solutions (incorporating both data warehousing and electronic commerce technology). These options, which progressively extend the range of CRM applications available, are outlined in Figure 3.

It is not necessary to choose one of these four technology options to the exclusion of others. On the contrary, most organisations will need to blend these solutions creatively as they adopt more sophisticated forms of CRM, moving from product-based selling to individualised relationship marketing on the CRM strategy matrix.

We now describe how these technology options can be used to assist in CRM. As we discuss these options we will refer back to the strategic positions on the CRM Strategy Matrix.

3.1. Tactical Databases and Decision Support Systems

Most organisations at some time or another, will have developed a tactical sales & marketing database to support specific needs like mailing list management. These

Figure 3: Technology Levels for CRM

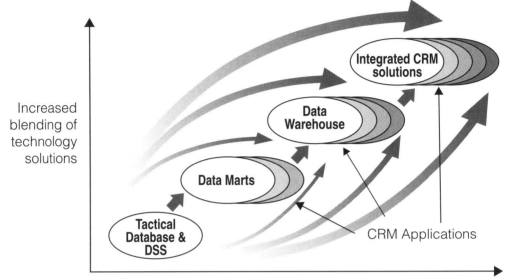

databases are typically built to meet short-term needs and are often built, owned and managed by the marketing department. The database and software technology used is often held on a personal computer (PC). Most organisations also carry out analysis of product sales and other transactional data directly upon the operational systems. The structure of such systems is shown in Figure 4.

Advantages

These systems can be quick to establish and require very little investment in terms of IT. However, even at this level, more in-depth analysis can provide significant benefits, such as better targeting of direct marketing activity or a better understanding of market buying behaviour.

The use of modern query and reporting tools or more advanced analysis tools (referred to in the IT industry as On-Line Analytical Processing (OLAP) or Data Mining tools) can help to identify new sales and marketing opportunities. These modern end-user tools provide multi-dimensional views of the data which better reflect the business and provide advanced user interfaces that allow the users to directly interact with the data.

These analysis tools are important elements of any technology solution used by a marketing organisation for CRM purposes, because they will help it to unearth the 'nuggets of gold' in the data, and help analyse customers either as individuals, or in product-based segments.

Figure 4: Tactical Database and Decision Support System

Operational systems

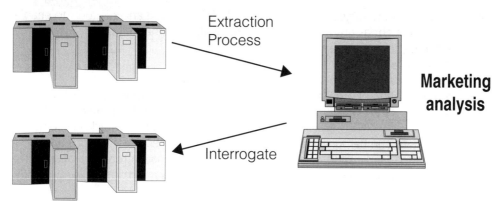

Disadvantages

1. However, using such simple systems will severely limit the sophistication of the sales and marketing strategies that an organisation can deploy. Tactical marketing databases inevitably require extensive manual work to load and maintain. This diverts resources away from the key role of analysis and often makes the extension of the system prohibitive..

2. Using query and analysis tools directly on existing operational systems also limits the scope of analysis, i.e. it is impossible to link data which is kept on different operational systems. While significant query and analysis activity can adversely affect the performance of the operational system themselves and therefore may not prove to be popular with the IT department maintaining them.

3.2. Sales and Marketing Data Marts

It is the ability of computers to act as an enormous memory and capture all the information on a customer that has been the driving force behind the adoption of CRM IT applications. This ability, coupled with the rapidly decreasing cost but increasing power of computers, that has lowered the entry point for many organisations and has made the applications affordable.

Moving from 'product-based selling' to 'customer-based marketing' requires a more advanced CRM system. Users need more complex analysis power and the business needs a much more structured approach to the collection, sorting and storage of data regarding the customer. This typically involves building what is termed a 'data warehouse'. This is a separate database from the operational systems and it is built solely to 'warehouse' all the data that needs to be collected in order to support a CRM system. The simplest form of data warehousing is called a 'data mart'.

A data mart is a 'single subject' data warehouse, i.e. it is not as grand in scope as its big brother - the enterprise data warehouse, which is built for the entire organisation (discussed in the next section). A simple representation of a data mart is shown in Figure 5.

Data Mart solutions can be purchased as part of a 'packaged' application or as an integrated suite of software products

which allow the extraction of data from operational systems. The sorting, organising and design of that data is done in a form which is optimised for analysis of data. The data mart package may also include query and analysis tools to enable the analysis of that data.

Advantages

Data marts are proving popular for organisations with departments (or lines of business) that want to quicklyrespond to a new market or business opportunity. Other organisations may introduce a data mart to get a pilot system up and running quickly

Figure 5: Data marts

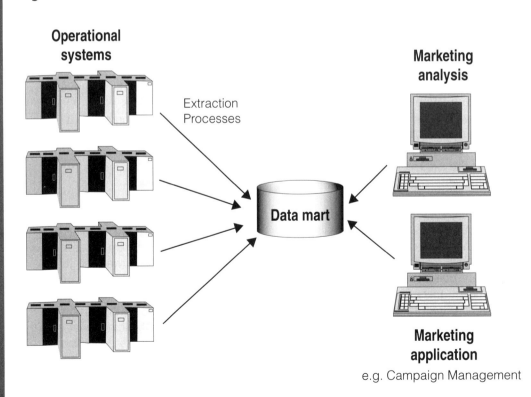

Operational systems

Extraction Processes

Data mart

Marketing analysis

Marketing application

e.g. Campaign Management

and achieve easily identifiable paybacks. However, there are several considerations which need to be taken into account when installing data marts.

Disadvantages

1. Organisations must be careful that multiple, unconnected data marts do not spring up in many areas of the company making a 'single customer view' across multiple systems difficult to achieve.

2. In order to achieve a customer-centric view across the entire organisation, multiple subject data must be held (i.e. financial and transactional data on the customer). This implies that an enterprise data warehouse will ultimately need to be constructed that brings all relative customer information into one consistent store.

3. Most data warehouse solutions start as data marts forming part of a pilot scheme, with the aim of achieving an initial win within the organisation. However, it is important that, although on the surface they are a data mart, they should from the start be architected as a data warehouse.

4. Any analysis is only as good as the quality and breadth of data that is available. If only product sales and financial data are available then this may be useful for recognising the best customers and their profitability, but it does not help the company build up a consolidated 'single view of the customer' so every department in the business sees the "same picture".

3.3. Enterprise Data Warehouse

As business shifts from product-based selling to more developed forms of customer-based marketing or managed service and support, there is a requirement for more data and greater integration of data, both from the front office (call centres, customer-facing applications) and the back office (general ledger, human resources, operations). As the volume of data expands and the complexity increases, this may result in many databases and data marts. Therefore, it is much more logical and beneficial to have one repository for data, i.e. an enterprise data warehouse as shown in Figure 6.

Once the enterprise data warehouse is loaded with 'cleansed' data, it represents the 'single version of the truth' for the whole organisation. The appropriate query and analysis tools and data mining software can then be applied to better understand customer behaviour, and the organisation can plan more advanced CRM strategies.

Data Warehouses can often evolve into a multi-tier structure where parts of the organisation take information from the main data warehouse into their own departmental systems. These may include tactical databases or dependent data marts (i.e. data marts - dependent on the central version of the data warehouse).

In fact, Data Warehouses in reality rarely look as straightforward as in the diagrams. Acquisitive or multi-business organisations will often have several data warehouse initiatives at the same time. It is often not possible to incorporate them into a single

Chapter 2: How to Integrate CRM in your Business

Chapter 2: How to Integrate CRM in your Business

Figure 6: Enterprise Data Warehouse

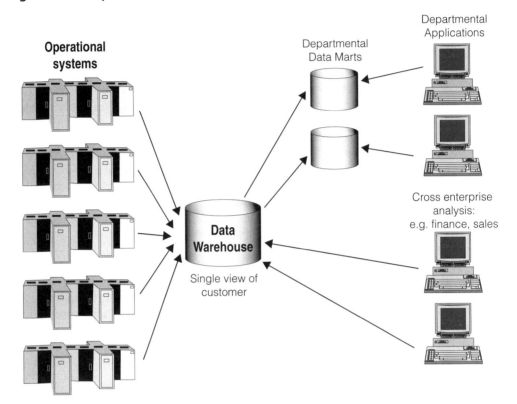

'warehouse', hence the organisations adopt what is called a 'federated' warehouse approach. However, the key is that from a user's point of view it appears as one logical system.

And, as the data warehouse evolves and the organisation gets better at capturing information on all interactions with the customer, so the CRM strategies that can be employed get more sophisticated.

Advantages
The key advantage of the enterprise data warehouse approach is the fact that an

organisation can refer to one 'single version of the truth' which can then feed numerous data marts with consistent data.

Disadvantages
Enterprise data warehouses are large and complex IT systems that require significant investment.   The business however, cannot wait for the data warehouse to be implemented, it needs to make decisions today.

The key to success will be the ability for organisations to 'Think Big but start small'. The organisation needs to have a vision of what it wishes to achieve and what will be required in the future. However, this vision must be broken down into achievable steps. Each step must deliver practical returns on the investment, giving clear 'Wins' to the organisation, while moving closer to the long-term aspiration. This approach avoids the pitfalls of implementing numerous unconnected data marts, that prevent an organisation taking a single view of the business and which can result in significant integration costs, while also avoiding the pitfalls of the 'Big Bang' approach, that often flounders because it is impossible to define all that is needed today and involves significant initial investment

3.4. Integrated CRM Solutions

The Internet, can potentially connect any individual to any other individual or organisation around the globe. The attraction of using this as a customer relationship management tool is apparent. However, electronic commerce web sites are at widely differing levels of sophistication, some of them are relatively simple, but some of them, such as Amazon.com, are relatively sophisticated. The most advanced use their web site to regularly collect information from the customer and provide highly individualised service back to the customer. This advanced technology-enabled approach to CRM has created greatly increased opportunities to interact with large numbers of customers on a one-to-one basis.

However, in order to use the Internet effectively for sophisticated CRM applications the organisation must have

integrated its e-commerce systems with a customer-orientated data warehouse which is able to push and pull customer intelligence from the Internet.

Figure 7 shows an outline of the final stage of CRM systems development - an integrated CRM solution.

To implement such a solution, the organisation may not need to add further data marts or data warehousing technology. In fact, .the business may have all the data and sophisticated architecture that is needed, but it has to deal with it in a more intelligent way.

The enterprise data warehouse is the backbone to this approach. It serves both as a capture device and as the memory for the system, enabling the customer to be given a totally individualised and co-ordinated service across all CRM interfaces. To achieve total integration means linking this tightly into both the front and back office applications. Complete systems that provide this high-level of integration are beginning to appear. They provide organisations with the potential for a quick implementation path for the adoption of CRM and significantly reduce the potential development risks.

Advantages

An integrated CRM solution will enable an organisation to move to the top right-hand corner of the CRM Strategy matrix i.e. 'individualised relationship marketing', or what Peppers & Rogers have termed '1 to 1 Marketing'. A range of sophisticated CRM strategies can be adopted, which are appropriate for the organisation without

Figure 7: Integrated CRM solutions

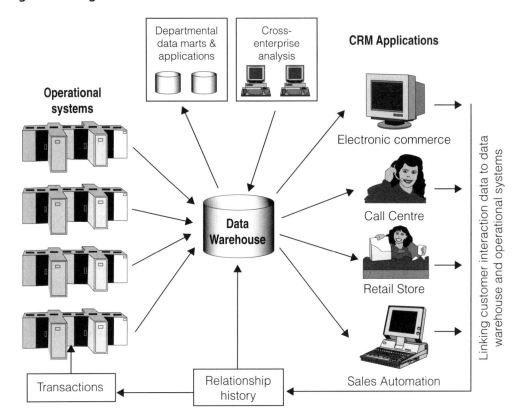

being handicapped by IT. The business opportunities are enormous for those who can get to this position first.

Disadvantages
Like the enterprise data warehouses, integrated CRM systems are complex and require significant investment in both the warehouse and operational systems.. Organisations need to reduce the risk and cost of these systems by buying packages where available and working with established and proven technology suppliers.

Examples of organisations that have adopted such electronic commerce mainstream solutions include:
▸ British Airways' airline ticket purchase
▸ Virgin's Internet travel service
▸ Waterstones - the UK book seller
▸ Amazon.com - the US book seller
▸ CD Now - Internet sales of CDs
▸ E*trade - electronic share brokerage
▸ RS Components - the electrical components supplier described earlier.

In choosing technology solutions, 'scalability' and 'flexibility' should be an important consideration. The business needs to create a flexible technology architecture suitable for both present and future needs. In doing so, it needs to take account of the building blocks in place at present as well as requirements which may exist in two years time. Managers may not yet know what will be needed and perhaps the technology does not exist at present., however It is necessary to create an architecture which will be responsive to the increasingly sophisticated requirements of CRM in the future.

4. CONCLUSIONS AND IMPLEMENTATION ISSUES

In summary, companies that wish to use the new technology to enable them to increase their customer retention and thus profitability should approach Customer Relationship Management in two stages:

▸ First, determine the precise CRM strategy appropriate to their particular business and competitive position.

▸ Then select and combine the technological options needed to implement the chosen strategy.

To achieve implementation of CRM three key issues should be considered:

▸ Plan the evolution of the solutions. In order to succeed an organisation will need an appropriate strategic vision for the future (to enable them to make a wise choice-of-technology solutions) and they must use appropriate analytical techniques to exploit the data. As

organisations increase their sophistication they will need to integrate these technologies creatively. "Planned evolution" is a good way of summarising the approach to building the technology backbone to support the CRM strategy that has been mapped out for the business.

▸ Utilise a pre-built industry model or Packaged Application. Adoption of a data warehouse requires a well-planned project. If available, a pre-built industry data model will have already defined the data required and the structure of the data warehouse. It will also save considerable time and money, as many of the requirements will be common to all companies within an industry sector. Integration between data warehouse and the front-office and back-office systems will be key to enabling the more advanced CRM strategies. Packaged application suites can provide this and also reduce implementation time and risk. Where available these should be considered as a first option.

▸ Select appropriate vendors. In selecting vendors or partners to help the business design and build the appropriate IT architecture, it is clearly important to consider technological capability and price, but it also pays to take into account whether the vendor has a sufficiently strong and stable position in the market. A recent article in the McKinsey Quarterly quoted an example of one company which was developing a data warehouse and which had rejected a market-leading vendor in favour of one whose product was marginally faster. Unfortunately, within three years the latter vendor had fallen behind its more prominent competitors and its system had proven unreliable and costly to maintain. The company was then faced with high costs in moving to another supplier.

In the new millennium, Customer Relationship Management will have advanced considerably and we will have reached much more sophisticated levels of one-to-one marketing. There is now a great opportunity for organisations to develop a clear advantage by being amongst the first to improve their 'customer ownership' through an integrated set of activities which addresses all the key strategic elements of CRM.

High-Availability Networks Enable Business-to-Consumer E-Business

Title: *High-Availability Networks Enable Business-to-Consumer E-Business*
Author: *3COM Corporation*

Abstract: *CRM programs involve three basic business processes: marketing automation, sales force automation, and customer service. This paper describes the business benefits and challenges of CRM initiatives. It then describes these three functional areas in some detail. It concludes with a discussion of network infrastructure implications of each of these areas and how a secure, scalable, high-performance network infrastructure can facilitate a successful CRM implementation.*

The Changing Marketing Landscape

Historically, marketing efforts could be content to focus on product awareness and product identification. Programs that simply "freshened" product awareness in a given market segment and initiated a flow of new customers, even if transitory, were considered successful. Now, channels are often effectively saturated with awareness messages, and marketing programs must focus on value-oriented differentiation to be successful. Increasingly, businesses are seeking to leverage relationship themes to achieve this value-oriented differentiation. Businesses are reaching out to say more than "we are here"; they are saying "we are here for you, and here's how we deliver value over time."

Specifically, businesses have become increasingly aware of the problems with customer churn, whereby marketing efforts are failing to improve customer loyalty, even though they may be attracting new customers. Businesses have learned the hard way that it is more efficient to retain customers than to merely attract new customers. Furthermore, loyalty is desired primarily in a specific category of the client base. Studies show another manifestation of the old "80/20 rule": most organizations find that roughly 20 percent of their client base generates 80 percent of the profits. Customers with whom the business has constructively established a relationship--the customers who bring their business back, time and again, and/or meet other criteria--are the most profitable. It is now critical that businesses identify the salient characteristics of this group, retain these highly desirable customers, and find ways to increase the size of this category.

The idea behind customer relationship management is to have a single, enterprise view of the customer for the purpose of cultivating these high-quality relationships that lead to improved loyalty and profits. This means being able to identify all the products, services, and intermediary relationships that customers have with the organization, as well as knowing all the interactions that have taken place between

Chapter 2: How to Integrate CRM in your Business

the customer and the company since the start of the relationship. It means being able to maintain "consistency of experience" for the customer through all forms of interaction (such as inquiry, order, delivery, and service). The distinguishing feature of modern CRM is the emphasis on an enterprise view of the customer, not simply a departmental view.

Business Benefits of CRM

In addition to the cultivation of loyal customers who exhibit the profitability profile businesses seek, CRM brings other benefits to the enterprise. An improved and detailed understanding of customers, their needs and expectations, and how the company interacts with them is emerging as a critical success factor of both supply chain management (SCM) and electronic commerce (e-commerce). For example, a successful CRM initiative will provide a better ability to model and classify various customer market segments, leading to improved business-to-consumer (B2C) e-commerce performance. Alternatively, real-time order processing, whether to meet periodic or aperiodic customer needs, will require integration with SCM systems.

Other benefits of CRM initiatives include improved ability to:

▸ Adapt to the effects of globalization and deregulation
▸ Position offerings that hold up to increased customer scrutiny (for example, Web-enabled comparative analysis and research)
▸ Control costs associated with customer acquisition and retention
▸ Sustain competitive differentiation

Business Challenges of CRM

Although CRM initiatives enjoy high return on investment (ROI) compared with other IT initiatives such as SCM or enterprise resource planning (ERP), there is also a high purported "failure" rate (55 to 75 percent). This failure rate applies specifically to the sales force automation (SFA) dimension of CRM; call center, marketing automation, and data warehousing application projects typically fare better. In such cases, the failure rate is often due to a failure to account for cultural issues associated with the sales organization. Poor executive sponsorship is another significant contributor.

CRM projects are more than just SFA projects; they are truly cross-functional, cross-departmental initiatives, requiring meaningful collaboration at the executive level. Some advocate that a distinct COO/CFO-level position should exist specifically to address CRM functions and processes. Careful planning and executive direction can help identify and manage the key cultural concerns for the organization.

Technical complexity is also a challenging area. CRM initiatives currently require a degree of best-of-breed integration to meet functional objectives. Some organizations are not positioned to tackle such integration efforts, either because of a lack of capability in the application infrastructure, or simply because of an inability to leverage a form of component-engineering discipline.

CRM initiatives can encounter significant challenges in a number of key areas:

▸ **End user-driven methodology.**
IT departments may lack either the knowledge base or the political clout to influence corporate decision making. Product selection may be driven entirely by end-user considerations, neglecting critical integration considerations like architectural adaptability.

▸ **Lack of appropriate executive sponsorship.**
Unlike other initiatives (such as back-office ERP), COOs/CFOs are rarely involved in CRM mandates, primarily because the business performance metrics associated with CRM are often not quantified in the corporate balance sheet. CRM projects are more likely to be driven by a functional head such as the vice president/director of sales or marketing, and consequently rarely produce the desired result: an enterprise view of customers.

▸ **Lack of cultural preparation.**
Investing in CRM technology without a customer-oriented cultural mindset, inherited hierarchically throughout the enterprise from the CEO, will typically fail to yield an acceptable ROI.

▸ **Inappropriate application design approach.**
Designing CRM applications to model a single functional view rather than an enterprise customer view will often result in failure. A component-based methodology should be used--one that models customer interactions from the customer's perspective to facilitate an adaptive application architecture.

▸ **Over-automation.**
Making functionality the primary design driver leads to over-automated business functions. This is particularly problematic in sales, because the sales process benefits more from unobtrusive, minimalist automation; and in call centers, where turnover is high and skill-level maintenance difficult due to minimal staff investment. CRM systems are best served by incremental function implementation.

▸ **Poor accounting for extensibility.**
The range of constituents and functions required calls for extensible application architectures. IT departments should examine component models and other flexible technologies (such as XML and Java) to maximize long-term successes.

▸ **Poor support for mobile synchronization.**
For field sales and field service applications, mobile synchronization is a critical architectural requirement. Support must include mobile CRM requirements involving electronic software distribution, data base schema changes, publish-and-subscribe services, incremental error recovery, and team-level security/authorization.

▸ **Lack of appropriate network infrastructure.**
The network infrastructure must be capable of providing total network availability to support the enterprise CRM application. Whatever is needed--a strong remote access system for mobile sales personnel, a robust LAN/WAN for CRM package users, or a voice-capable network for customer service representatives--no CRM endeavor can succeed without a robust, high-performance network solution already in place. Inadequate infrastructure is a leading cause of failure for CRM implementations.

Chapter 2: How to Integrate CRM in your Business

Businesses cannot afford to fail when implementing CRM. Delaying the initiative until the window of opportunity is lost or implementing a system that does not meet the organization's objectives or is not accepted by users can be disastrous for the entire enterprise. Many businesses are looking for vendors that can help them meet these challenges and ensure that a successful CRM initiative is delivered in a timely manner.

CRM Business Processes

There are three primary CRM business processes:

▸ Marketing automation (MA)
▸ Sales force automation (SFA)
▸ Customer service

These processes are operational in nature, and play a critical role in businesses. They are described in the following sections.

Marketing Automation
Traditional data base marketing has been static; it often takes months to tabulate the results of a campaign, and other key opportunities are often missed in the interim. The new class of campaign management software is built on the premise of multiple overlapping campaigns, with the ability to react to customer activity or inactivity, triggering responses to smaller prospect groups.

Modern MA is based on the premise that, in addition to all phases of campaign management, many core marketing functions (for example, customer scoring,

trade show management) can be improved through increased automation. MA encompasses lead management, campaign execution, and marketing collateral management. Campaign planning functions--critical functions, demographic analysis, variable segmentation, and predictive behavior--are primarily analytical in nature.

Enterprises must be able to coordinate marketing communications across channels such as sales force, telesales, telemarketing, direct mail, fax, e-mail, and Web; and prevent campaign overlaps or conflicts within channels. Additionally, conflicts across products and lines of business (LOBs) (for example, a customer simultaneously receives offers for discounted long-distance service and a cellular package) must be identified early and prevented. MA systems communicate directly with the customer through direct mailings or telemarketing and learn directly from the customer through point-of-sale data and surveys.

MA systems must ensure a smooth handoff of generated leads and relevant supporting collateral (such as marketing encyclopedias and call scripts) to a variety of sales channels. In return, sales must return a history of the prospect/customer interactions so that campaigns can be evaluated and improved. With established customers, MA systems should be tightly integrated in both a sales and service context to:

▸ Manage cross-sell and up-sell opportunities.
▸ Personalize customer and prospect

interactions (1:1 target marketing).

▸ In a business-to-business (B2B) context, ensure that hierarchies within and relationships among LOBs are known.

▸ In a B2C context, ensure that householding issues are understood, as well as discover possible relationships between B2C and B2B (such as a B2C customer who is the spouse of a valuable B2B client).

Overall, MA can be divided into three areas:

▸ High-end campaign management
▸ Web-driven campaign execution
▸ Marketing-oriented analysis

High-end campaign management is primarily focused on companies involved in B2C marketing (such as financial services and telecommunications); its focus has typically been to assist campaign planning, management, and tracking (but not execution). B2C companies have a prospect base that can easily number in the tens of millions, with resulting data bases exceeding one terabyte. The scale of these databases and the required infrastructure has not escaped the attention of hardware vendors such as Digital/Compaq, IBM, NCR, and Sequent, which have built "cradle-to-grave" enterprise MA (EMA) offerings to serve the B2C market. High-end campaign management consequently requires adopters to have already implemented a corporate hub-and-spoke data warehouse architecture and to have a mature infrastructure for managing large data warehouses.

Web-driven campaign execution focuses mostly on the B2B market (smaller volumes, all targets having readily available e-mail addresses) and use the Internet as a major campaign execution vehicle, in addition to direct mail, fax, and telephone. Campaign execution can include mass e-mailings (with embedded URLs) that enable the prospect to gather more information, Web site hits that become events in a continuous series of campaign steps, and personalization of Web pages for certain target audiences.

Marketing-oriented analysis focuses on measuring all major aspects of sales and marketing (such as customer profitability and customer churn) and relating it to customer activity data and ERP data.

Sales Force Automation

SFA is the fastest-growing CRM segment, with critical functions including lead/account management, contact management, quote management, marketing encyclopedia, forecasting, win/loss analysis, and sales administration. The sales function has proven to be the most difficult process to automate, not only because of its dynamism (changing sales models, geographies, product configurations, etc.), but also because of its culture. Sales departments typically operate with a degree of autonomy and are often resistant to externally mandated change. There are four components of the sales process that organizations must analyze and re-engineer as part of every SFA initiative:

> Lead generation and tracking
> Order management
> Order fulfillment
> Integration of marketing and customer service functions

The complexity and distinctiveness of SFA is such that it often requires an entirely separate (and sizeable) endeavor from CRM. 3Com has explored SFA in greater detail in a separate white paper, "Sales Force Automation," available at www.3com.com/technology/tech_net /white_papers/500690.html.

Customer Service

Customer service focuses primarily on post-sales activities, though some presales information functions are also present. Post-sales activities occur primarily in office-oriented call centers, but field-oriented activities are also part of the picture. Product support is typically the most significant function. It is usually delivered from large offices where customer service representatives providing support to customers require operational integration with field service personnel (who must share/ replicate customer interaction data and dispatch availability) and the sales force. The integration of these groups with the operational organization as a whole and the unification of customer interaction data is what distinguishes this area in modern CRM.

CRM Application Landscape

There is a relatively rich assortment of vendor offerings on the market for each of the three business process areas discussed above. For example, in addition to full-blown SFA product packages, simpler contact management software is available for a less-demanding customer segment (fewer than 300 users and 50,000 contact records, uncomplicated sales cycle, etc). Products in each of these areas will continue to develop individually, and vendors will increasingly offer capabilities that cross category boundaries.

The product architectures vary for each application category. MA systems, for example, are typically analytical in nature, requiring integration with the enterprise data warehouse architecture and decision-support tools. Data warehouse/mart characteristics prevail and the MA system exhibits two-tier or N-tier architecture characteristics, but is often restricted to a single corporate campus serving a small user population. Sales systems exhibit an online transaction processing (OLTP) transactional profile and large user population. Sales systems also tend to exhibit N-tier characteristics, since they serve more decentralized user populations and have stronger synchronization/ replication requirements.

Finally, customer service systems reflect typical call center environments that are largely restricted to a single corporate/regional campus with a medium-sized user population. Transactional requirements are mixed because query support is needed to augment understanding of the client's history, but OLTP characteristics are seen in the way customer information is gathered.

Overall, there is a strong enterprise application integration (EAI) theme that applies throughout these application categories for CRM. The complete CRM view requires integration of marketing automation, sales tracking, customer service, ERP, SCM, and other systems. There are no complete CRM application packages on the market, and adopters must address an application integration scenario of some form. Table 1 lists sample vendors with their general areas of focus.

Network Infrastructure to Support CRM

In the face of these business and application challenges, one point emerges clearly: the network must become a utility. The concept of value over time, which is inherent in CRM, implies creating excellent and constantly improving customer service. To support this goal, the network

infrastructure must be constantly available, flexible, and secure.

The nature of the business will largely dictate how CRM business processes are implemented and how applications are used to enable them. For example, CRM for one business may be more effectively enabled by the utilization of a custom marketing data warehouse and for another by utilization of a call center equipped with a CRM package, telephony, and e-mail. This section examines the network implications of CRM in terms of the business challenges and application categories previously discussed rather than the business processes they support.

Network Infrastructure to Support CRM Business Challenges

The challenges previously outlined fall into one of two basic categories: technical challenges and cultural issues. Network technology, in conjunction with application solutions, can be used to overcome both these common hurdles.

Table 1: Sample CRM Application Vendors by Area of Focus

Application Area	Sample Vendors
Customer support	Aurum, Clarify, Onyx, Pivotal, Siebel, Vantive, IBM/Corepoint, Chordiant, IMA, Pegasystems, Silknet
Marketing automation	Annuncio, Epiphany, Exchange Applications, MarketFirst, Paragren, Prime Response, Rubric, Broadbase, RightPoint (formerly DataMind), Quadstone, Sagent, SAS
Sales force automation	Siebel, Vantive, Clarify, Baan/Orum, PeopleSoft, Saratoga, Pivotal, Onyx, Borealis, Firstwave, MEI, Proscape, SalesLogix

Technical Difficulties.

As the applications that support CRM grow in capabilities and complexity, the network infrastructure must be continuously tuned to deliver total availability. One of the most common concerns regarding the design and implementation of a new or expanded network infrastructure is inappropriate technology application. How does an organization avoid overbuilding the network while maintaining high availability and meeting target service levels? Will the cost of network maintenance negate the cost savings from the enterprise CRM application? How can a business provide a clear transition path to accommodate future technologies and application requirements?

One way to avoid overbuilding the infrastructure is by using scalable network products that are designed and configured to deliver the highest levels of both device and environment-wide availability. These systems should also provide a modular approach to networking, allowing the organization to choose those technologies that are right for today's application-support requirements.

The 3Com CoreBuilder® family of network switches is flexible and highly reliable, and their chassis design allows cost-effective additions to the network infrastructure when the need arises. For smaller branch offices or mobile user support, 3Com offers a wide array of cost-effective branch office routers, WAN access products, and security software.

By applying this 3Com technology, companies can benefit from the powerful Transcend® network management software suite. Transcend applications ease the operations burden and help network managers maintain availability and meet target service levels. Further, Transcend applications can help organizations plan (and justify) their next network upgrade. Where should IT dollars be spent? Which parts of the infrastructure would benefit most from additional capabilities? Transcend applications can help answer these questions by providing insight into the traffic patterns of business-critical applications. By providing an in-depth understanding of the network environment, 3Com helps companies save time and money in their CRM implementations.

3Com solutions also have a positive influence on operations and support costs. In the face of an ever-moving sales force and the heavy infrastructure demands of a customer service call center, network maintenance becomes a major concern. 3Com has a proven track record of making complex tasks simple. 3Com CoreBuilder switches, PathBuilder™ WAN access products, DynamicAccess® technology-- enabled network interface cards (NICs) and OfficeConnect® product lines all provide simple configuration options. Standard RMON-1 and RMON-2 support in these devices enables network monitoring and troubleshooting from a single console. Software upgrades and device reconfiguration can be performed remotely, reducing the need for costly site visits.

When customer needs change, business software must adapt to the new environment. The network must therefore be able to support, or adapt to support, new application demands. Features such as Class of Service (CoS) support, priority queuing, virtual private networks (VPNs), security options, and traffic shaping increase the flexibility, adaptability, and overall availability of the network.

Sponsorship, Acceptance, and Other Cultural Issues.

Implementing a system that users won't use can be disastrous. Before they will commit critical sponsorship for the CRM initiative, decision-making executives must be clearly shown the benefits of the CRM application and the supporting network infrastructure investment. Although some factors may be difficult to quantify, a flexible, forward-thinking solution that includes network infrastructure as well as application migration can help gain sponsorship for the entire CRM initiative.

If the network cannot forward traffic with the proper prioritization and speed, call center employees will notice the slow response. This can lead to frustration with a system they perceive to be failing them in this fast-paced environment. Providing these applications with a fast, fault tolerant, properly managed network infrastructure will increase productivity and acceptance of the CRM application.

3Com addresses these needs by offering robust Class of Service prioritization and redundancy features in their enterprise routing and switching equipment. This backbone technology gives administrators speed and control to maintain a smooth flow of vital traffic. Through LAN telephony integration using the 3Com® NBX® 100

Communications System, organizations can eliminate costly parallel communications infrastructures and realize greater value from current and new network investments.

Mobile and remote users need reliable access to centralized resources without being inconvenienced by network problems or cumbersome access procedures. By applying an end-to-end security technology, a mobile sales force can use and benefit from the CRM application data. One powerful way to satisfy this requirements is with 3Com DynamicAccess NIC technology supporting IPSec and encryption. This end-to-end security allows confidential communications without extra passwords, login screens, or other labor-intensive processes.

Network Implications of Marketing Automation

Marketing automation applications usually exhibit data warehouse/mart and two-tier or N-tier architecture characteristics. Whether the application is intended to provide high-end campaign management, Web-driven campaign execution, or marketing-oriented analysis, the core is typically a data warehouse aggregating customer information. As with most data warehouses, the interaction between client and server or server and server tends to be highly transactional and restricted to a single campus.

This type of reactive communication requires a highly reliable and flexible infrastructure. The 3Com CoreBuilder 9000 enterprise switch provides the ability to prioritize and monitor the multitude of

Chapter 2: How to Integrate CRM in your Business

traffic types in this environment. As the traffic types and patterns evolve, Transcend software lets the network manager modify prioritization instructions to all 3Com core devices and monitor the effects of the change.

The modular design of the CoreBuilder 9000 switch makes it highly scalable as the network grows. Layer 3 switching (high-speed routing) modules can forward and groom traffic as fast as the Gigabit Ethernet or ATM backbone can carry it. As more intelligence is required, more Layer 3 modules can be added.

In addition to abundant bandwidth and flexibility, a redundant, intelligent Gigabit Ethernet or ATM core enables a reliable network backbone. Super-fast, intelligent switches connected via multiple, aggregated high-speed Gigabit Ethernet or ATM links eliminate bottlenecks and provide redundancy in case of link or device failure.

Server network performance benefits from load balancing and Resilient Server Link (RSL) technology in 3Com NICs. Traffic to and from the servers can be evenly distributed across all NICs (forming a large aggregate "pipe"), and redundant NICs also ensure that a single NIC or link failure does not disconnect a critical resource in this highly transactional environment. Further performance, scalability, and efficiency optimization can be achieved through the use of storage area networking (SAN) technologies (for example, Fibre Channel) for the transport between the data warehouse systems and their primary storage.

High-end campaign management and Web-driven campaign execution applications require that the customer data warehouse integrate with other systems such as Web and e-mail servers. The high-speed, intelligent switched network should be used between the data warehouse and these systems, as well as "within" these systems to ensure timely delivery of information to customers. As with any Internet-related effort, security is critical.

3Com firewall technology augments existing security capabilities and even provides for packet-by-packet examination of incoming traffic. High-speed VPN termination devices like the PathBuilder family of WAN access switches allow companies to collaborate with business partners or clients over the Internet using secure, IPSec-standard encryption and authentication. These 3Com solutions will help companies build a secure "demilitarized zone" (DMZ) through which future Web-driven marketing campaigns can be launched and monitored.

Network Implications of Sales Force Automation

SFA applications come in a wide variety of shapes and sizes, from simple, file-based contact management to N-tier quote management or sales forecasting packages. On the corporate network, they behave much like other file-based and N-tier applications and can be accommodated in a similar way--for example, via robust, efficient WAN/LAN connections. However, they can greatly impact infrastructure developers and network planners because of the mobile and distributed nature of the user constituency they support.

High-Availability Networks Enable Business-to-Consumer E-Business

Sales groups are increasingly decentralized, with small office/home office (SOHO) and mobile arrangements becoming more popular. At the same time, these groups are also experiencing increasing pressure to be tightly connected. In response, SFA applications are being designed to incorporate synchronization, replication, messaging, and/or Internet technologies. Companies will need to provide their sales force with access to these applications, whether through a 3Com Palm Computing® handheld organizer with a wireless Internet connection, through remote access to the corporate network via dial-up or VPN connections; or through a high-speed Internet connection using 56K analog, ISDN, xDSL, or cable modem technology.

The cultural aspects of SFA are extremely important. These SOHO and mobile users are often extraordinarily busy people who must function in rapidly changing environments. They cannot afford to be burdened by network complications when they attempt to use new applications or access resources on centralized servers. At the same time, mobile and remote access to business-critical applications can pose a significant security risk that must be managed carefully by the organization.

3Com innovation provides an elegant solution for these SFA issues. From robust firewall protection to full routing support to multiple WAN access options, 3Com OfficeConnect products enable small or home offices to connect securely and cost effectively. The remote-management capabilities of the OfficeConnect routers and firewalls help ensure network availability while lowering the cost of operations and support. Also, corporate policies can be downloaded and enforced through the Transcend suite of network management software.

At the corporate DMZ, the 3Com Total Control® multiservice access platform and PathBuilder WAN access switches will accept, authenticate, decrypt, and authorize these incoming communications from the mobile workforce. This central and powerful DMZ, provided by 3Com innovation, addresses the need to monitor and track activity on your network. As application and client needs change, so will the network traffic load and patterns. By maintaining historical data, Transcend network management applications can provide compelling business case support for augmenting network capabilities to meet changing requirements.

Network Implications of Customer Service
Because of the many different ways that customer service is delivered, there is no single network infrastructure that is best suited to support it. The advent of customer interaction centers that utilize more than just a single application highlights the need for cross-application integration and the associated network infrastructure. Although call center technologies have been used for a while, only recently has there been a push to integrate these technologies with other CRM components such as electronic mail, the Web, and CRM packages.

The convergence of voice and data on corporate networks will open up a new set of CRM possibilities such as live electronic customer chat and whiteboarding, Web-enabled call center agents, Web-based automation and knowledge engines, and cross-platform quality monitoring customer interaction recording systems. And each of these options has network infrastructure implications. Infrastructure developers and network planners can facilitate this integration by ensuring that the network provides solid performance, reliability, and manageability, as well as features such as Class of Service and telephony capabilities that will be required for these new applications.

3Com is dedicated to providing voice-over-packet technology options and subsequent network transport capabilities. By using an intelligent, CoS-capable network infrastructure, network personnel can channel the converged traffic across a common set of network resources. LAN telephony technology can be applied to this backbone via the 3Com NBX 100 communications system (Figure 1), an integrated, Ethernet-based product that supports advanced features like computer telephony integration (CTI) and call detail recording. Such a system can not only support the emerging call-center applications, but also ease the maintenance burden of supporting multiple, disparate networks.

Customer Interaction Center

A customer interaction center (CIC) is a critical component of operational CRM, whether implemented for sales, marketing, or customer service functions. The CIC accommodates multiple channels for customer interaction and critical functions, including customer service/support, field service dispatch, quality management, intelligent routing, case-based reasoning, and knowledge repositories. Critical technology integration includes computer telephony integration, automated call dispatch, and integrated voice response. Many CRM application technology solutions use mobility as the critical design point, but with customer service/support, high-volume processing capability is the critical component. The CIC is the key to consolidating customer interaction and developing a unified, enterprise view of the customer.

Figure 1: The 3Com NBX 100 Communications System Supports LAN Telephony

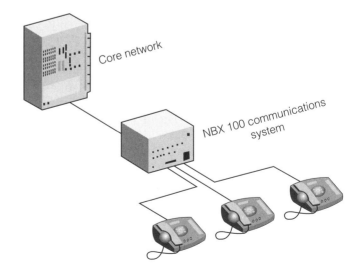

Core network

NBX 100 communications system

Conclusion

Customer relationship management enables improved business performance at all stages of the customer relationship. As the Web-based marketing campaign reaches out to the potential client base, some individuals want more information. Marketing automation applications not only track this interest, but can manage overlapping campaigns and trigger responses to groups of interest. The underlying network infrastructure permits various policies to be enforced, supplying appropriate bandwidth and priority where needed.

As the sales force is dispatched to follow up on the interested parties, it is able to securely upload client information. With this SFA toolset, they can also get up-to-the-minute information regarding product availability, order processing delays, and discount strategies. After the calls, the sales team can download any proposals, refreshed client information, and customer orders. The back-end databases can be updated to reflect changing customer needs and preferences. Everything from what was ordered to how it was paid for, as well as contact information and service agreements purchased, can be compiled into a unique client profile. The underlying network enables secure remote communications and protects the enterprise from viruses, illegal activity, and data interception.

Customer needs change and grow as their own business needs change. The established client profile enables post-sales support staff to provide customized service for every customer who calls. The call-tracking application can be linked to these profile databases to keep customer records as fresh as possible. The network provides reliable and highly available service for these application requirements. Computer telephony integration can further integrate the call center with the data infrastructure.

Although the CRM environment is challenged to implement, manage, and upgrade, the business benefits are clear. Network and application suites must complement each other in every area of this environment. 3Com provides robust, high-availability network infrastructure solutions to facilitate successful CRM initiatives in businesses of all kinds.

Chapter 2: How to Integrate CRM in your Business

Acronyms and Abbreviations

ATM: Asynchronous Transfer Mode
B2B: business-to-business
B2C: business-to-consumer
CIC: customer interaction center
CoS: Class of Service
CRM: customer relationship management
CTI: computer telephony integration
DMZ: demilitarized zone
EAI: enterprise application integration
EMA: enterprise marketing automation
ERP: enterprise resource planning
IPSec: Internet Protocol Security
ISDN: Integrated Services Digital Network
IT: information technology
LOB: line of business
MA: marketing automation
NIC: network interface card
OLTP: online transaction processing
RMON: Remote Monitoring
ROI: return on investment
RSL: Resilient Server Link
SAN: storage area network
SCM: supply chain management
SFA: sales force automation
SOHO: small office/home office
URL: Uniform Resource Locator
VPN: virtual private network
xDSL: Digital Subscriber Line
XML: Extensible Markup Language

Extended Enterprise Applications. Spotlight Report

Title: Extended Enterprise Applications. Spotlight Report
Author: Cherry Tree & Co
Abstract: This report will define the concept of the extended enterprise and explain its
              relevance to IT services firms. Cherry Tree will then highlight two of the
              hottest segments in the extended enterprise space — Customer Relationship
              Management and Supply Chain Management — to demonstrate how the
              functionality of corporate IT systems is being extended beyond the
              "enterprise." Cherry Tree will then review how Enterprise Application
              Integration tools are being utilized in extended enterprise environments to
              enable the connectivity of multiple applications both within and between
              businesses.

This Spotlight Report is Cherry Tree & Co.'s first quarterly research report for 2000 and our first in-depth examination of the "Extended Enterprise." This Spotlight Report is part of a regular series of research reports that are prepared and published by Cherry Tree & Co. Please see our web site at www.cherrytreeco.com for additional research published in 1999 regarding Application Service Providers (ASPs), Professional Consulting, Project-Based Service Providers, and IT Staff Augmentation.

We have broadened our coverage for this report to include emerging segments of the extended enterprise software and software integration industries that are creating opportunities for IT services firms. We strongly believe that as new, web-enabled technologies arise to connect traditional enterprise software packages with sup-pliers, distributors, and customers, a new and more complex set of skills will be demanded of IT services firms to facilitate this evolution

Relevance for Privately Held Firms

Although we will review the evolution of the underlying technology, the main thrust of this report will center on the enormous opportunities that have been created for External Service Providers (ESPs) by the increased demand for extended enterprise applications. We believe that with proper planning and execution, privately held IT services companies can be well-positioned to take advantage of this new wave of opportunity. Consistent with our previous research, we will conclude this report with potential strategies that private IT services firms can use to exploit these new opportunities. Included in this section will be strategic business development considerations including:

▸ Partnership opportunities with CRM, SCM, and EAI software vendors;
▸ How to leverage vertical industry expertise;
▸ How to leverage an existing ERP implementation practice; and
▸ Utilizing EAI expertise to open other web application development opportunities

Chapter 2: How to Integrate CRM in your Business

Table 1: IT Services Composite Stock Price Index

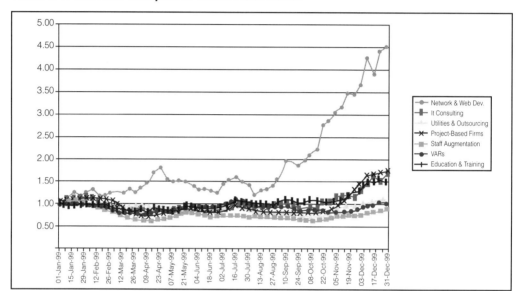

Stock Market Performance

As a component of our quarterly research, Cherry Tree & Co. provides a brief review of the previous twelve months' market performance for all the different IT Services sectors that we follow.
(A listing of the Cherry Tree & Co. IT Services Universe and Sector Definitions are provided in the appendices to this report).

The Network & Web Development companies have been separated from the other Project-Based companies to illustrate Wall Street's ongoing enthusiasm for "all things Internet" as these firms continue to trade at multiples far in excess of their IT Services counterparts. The rest of the IT Services sector has staged a comeback in the last several months, which we fully expect to continue into the foreseeable future. While the Web Development firms

continue to dominate the stock market, the IT Consulting companies, Project-Based Service Providers, and Education & Training firms have also performed particularly well.

The Extended Enterprise

Before we jump into our analysis we should first define what we mean by an "extended enterprise." An extended enterprise is a business whose information systems operate within a distributed application architecture. This architecture is arguably the most critical component of the new e-business environment. IDC projections indicate that business-to-business e-commerce revenue is expected to increase from $80 billion in 1999 to over $1 trillion in 2003. Given this explosive growth potential, Cherry Tree &

Co. believes that the market for the extended enterprise applications that enable this e-business environment will expand dramatically.

At the core of the extended enterprise sits the core ERP backbone or other core accounting, manufacturing, and HR applications. These applications reside within the enterprise and can be described as being primarily inward facing applications that track the internal flow of information. An enterprise starts to become "extended" when its information systems face outward by enabling connectivity with customers, suppliers, and distributors. Examples of extended enterprise applications include Customer Relationship Management (CRM) and Supply Chain Management (SCM) software that will be described in detail below. A company completes its evolution and becomes a truly extended enterprise when this connectivity with its business partners

becomes fully integrated into its ERP backbone. Notably, this final step in the evolution is the missing link for most companies since this integration task has been very elusive even for the most highly respected systems integrators.

As we have illustrated in Figure 1, traditional ERP packages are now being viewed not as a comprehensive solution but as the backbone to which customer- and supplier-facing applications may be linked as a means of extending the functionality of enterprise software. Once accomplished, the complete connectivity between the sales and supply chain arms of the business will manifest itself in a fully-integrated "Value Chain" - indicative of the value that each component of the business adds during the delivery of products and services to the client. While the traditional large ERP software providers recognize this trend and are rushing to add this capability to their product offerings, a

Figure 1: *"The Extended Enterprise"*

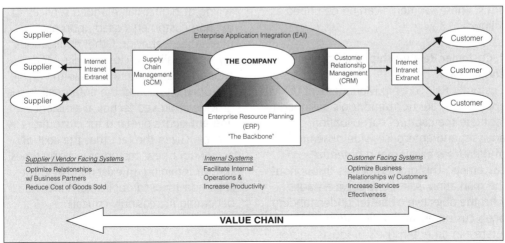

Source: Cherry Tree & Co. Research

Chapter 2: How to Integrate CRM in your Business

new group of packaged software providers have emerged as early leaders in these segments.

Extended Enterprise Applications Overview

Extended Enterprise Applications and Tools: Three "Hot Zones"

We are well aware of the fact that the extended enterprise software market encompasses a number of categories of applications designed to connect with and extend an enterprise's ERP backbone. To restrict our discussion of this market to only three segments may appear to be something of an oversimplification. Nonetheless, we have chosen to confine our focus to two high-growth, high-profile areas — Customer Relationship Management and Supply Chain Management — and one emerging area — Enterprise Application Integration — as it is our belief that these three segments are highly relevant to the owners of IT services firms. These segments can be described as follows:

1. Customer Relationship Management
Overview
Customer Relationship Management (CRM) applications are front-end tools designed to facilitate the capture, consolidation, analysis, and enterprise-wide dissemination of data from existing and potential customers. This process occurs throughout the marketing, sales, and service stages, with the objective of better understanding one's customers and anticipating their interest in an enterprise's products and/or

services. A CRM software deployment has two primary goals:

1. Enable the company to more effectively identify, contact, and acquire new customers. Certain CRM applications automate the process of generating customer and market profiles, tracking marketing campaigns across a variety of media, and managing the quote/proposal process through negotiation to close. By accelerating and refining the process by which prospective clients are identified, these applications allow companies to focus limited marketing resources on the most promising target markets and thus maximize top-line growth.

2. Leverage existing customer relationships. The two primary means of accomplishing this task are identifying cross-selling opportunities and increasing retention through improved post-sale service. By tracking and analyzing sales patterns, CRM applications are able to generate suggestions for the cross-selling of higher value-added services to existing customers based upon past purchasing behavior. Other applications document all post-close service- and support-related interactions with customers, enabling the enterprise to provide improved technical assistance and anticipate demand for customer service. Given the fact that the cost of acquiring a new customer is many times that of retaining an existing one, these retention-focused applications are becoming increasingly critical.

To accomplish these objectives, a fully integrated CRM system obtains data from any number of customer touchpoints (e.g. phone contact with a salesperson, interaction with the enterprise's Web site, responses to mail or e-mail marketing materials, etc.) and consolidates the information into a central data reservoir. Once collected, stored, and organized, this information can be analyzed and accessed in a number of ways by various users within the enterprise — as shown in Figure 2.

The central value proposition of a comprehensive CRM system is the ability to seamlessly integrate customer information from across the enterprise into a user-friendly, real-time format, and transform the entire enterprise into a single integrated sales net-work. This model requires sufficient cohesion such that at

every instance of contact with a customer or prospect, enterprise personnel have access to a comprehensive overview of the marketing/sales/service relationship. Such an overview would include but would not be limited to the customer/prospect's initial contact with the enterprise, their current status within the sales cycle, account status, post-sale interactions with customer service and support personnel, and suggestions for additional sales opportunities based upon previous purchases and inquiries.

Segmenting the CRM Landscape
Cherry Tree & Co. has identified three major segments within the broader CRM market: Marketing Automation, Sales Force Automation, and Customer Service & Support. Although several major vendors in the CRM space attempt to offer comprehensive customer relationship software suites (e.g. Siebel and Vantive), most major players tend to specialize in one of these sub-sectors (a detailed segmentation of CRM vendors may be found in Appendix 3).

▸ *Marketing Automation* applications optimize an enterprise's marketing process, with the objective of allocating resources to target markets with the highest potential value. These applications, which evolved from earlier data mining and database marketing systems, assist in the planning and execution of marketing campaigns by

Figure 2: CRM Process Diagram

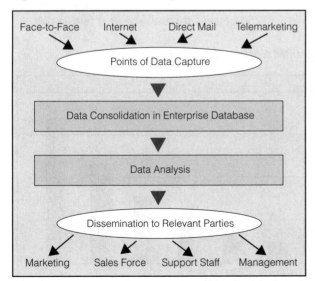

Source: Cherry Tree & Co. Research

managing customer and market profiles, identifying target markets with high revenue and profitability potential, generating leads, selecting appropriate contact media (i.e. mail, phone, print ads) and tracking initial customer contact efforts across these channels.

▸ *Sales Force Automation* software manages and optimizes an enterprise's sales cycle, increasing its productivity by accelerating the contracting process and improving revenue velocity.
These applications manage and track the presentation and negotiation process, generate product/service proposals and preliminary quotes, and create final sales packages based on auto-mated price and product configuration. They also link the enterprise's sales force (field and internal) with the corporate office and enterprise database, and facilitate improved communications between the sales force and management.

▸ *Customer Service & Support* applications developed apart from other CRM packages as automated help desk and call center systems but are in the midst of a convergence with other customer-centric software

packages. These systems were originally custom-designed to reduce headcount in an enterprise's customer service/ technical support department by automating such functions as order tracking and account status checks. Today these applications offer advanced customer service centers integrated with other front-office applications and are capable of receiving and tracking customer requests and feedback from a variety of communication channels. The primary objective of these capabilities is to document all post-close interactions with the enterprise's client base in order to maximize customer satisfaction and retention while minimizing customer service staff.

CRM Software Market Forecast
As shown in Figure 3, the CRM packaged software market is expected to continue expanding dramatically. The US market alone is expected to grow at a compounded annual growth rate of nearly 50 percent through the next five years,

Figure 3: US CRM Software Market Forecast

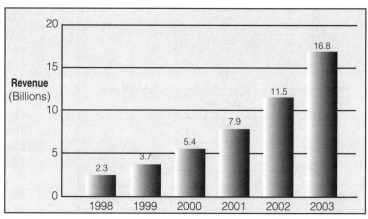

Source: AMR Research

from $2.3 billion in 1998 to almost $17 billion by 2003.

Implications for External Service Providers

The exploding demand for web-enabled CRM applications is creating a myriad of opportunities for services companies to add value. Quite simply, demand for CRM-related services far out-strips available talent, and in-house IT departments are generally incapable of providing the intellectual capital needed to implement such complex applications. This disparity between corporate needs and available resources will continue to drive tremendous demand for CRM-oriented implementation and integration services.

As shown in Figure 4, CRM-related services represent a growing opportunity. Gartner Group estimates that through 2004, 80 percent of enterprise-level CRM initiatives will be outsourced to External Service Providers, and IDC forecasts that the global CRM services market (including consulting, systems integration, out-sourcing, and training) will reach nearly $90 billion by 2003.

The high-end of the CRM services market is currently dominated by the usual systems integration giants — Andersen Consulting, Deloitte & Touche, Pricewaterhouse-Coopers, and the like. However, Cherry Tree & Co. is of the opinion that more agile, focused firms have the opportunity to compete effectively with the generalists to be the service providers of choice by taking advantage of several trends detailed below.

Enterprises Face a Complex CRM Environment.
Given the extreme complexity behind the development and implementation of CRM applications, it will be difficult for any single software vendor to offer a comprehensive solution that provides complete functionality across all segments of the customer relationship spectrum. There are simply too many variables to take into account across industries, business processes, and functional requirements for any one vendor to emerge with the definitive CRM package.
While certain firms that are more conservative in their adoption of new technologies may be content with the basic functionality

Chapter 2: How to Integrate CRM in your Business

Figure 4: CRM Services Forecast

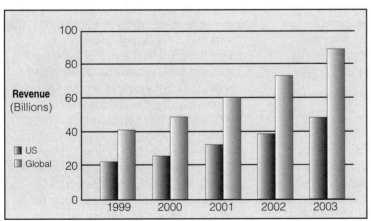

Source: IDC and Cherry Tree & Co. Research

provided by generic application suites, we believe many enterprises will turn to "best-of-breed" applications from specialized vendors. Gartner Group research confirms this trend and indicates that over the next four to five years, a variety of factors, including industry-specific requirements, business process and functionality requirements, and various financial and cultural influences will drive procurement of multiple CRM components from different vendors.

Seamlessly linking all of these components is an extremely complicated process that will drive demand for customized integration work performed by services providers with demonstrated domain expertise in CRM applications. A small- to mid-size firm with a solid track record of providing specialized CRM services in accordance with deep functionality requirements will often present a much more compelling value proposition to a prospective client than a larger systems integration generalist. While it is probably unrealistic to expect private ESPs to win Fortune 500 engagements over the largest consultancies on a regular basis, the opportunity exists for these firms to establish a defensible niche with mid-market companies and begin to make inroads towards the larger corporate clients.

There is a Growing Need for Vertical Market Expertise.
The complexity of the technological environment created by the use of best-of-breed solutions as discussed above will be compounded by an enterprise's need for industry-specific expertise. As the CRM

software market develops and matures, vendors will be forced by widely varying user requirements across industries to offer applications tailored to specific vertical markets. It is highly unlikely, for example, that a discount retailer could effectively use the same Sales Force Automation application as a high-end financial services firm tracking investment, credit, and insurance information; the relevant customer data points and purchase behavior patterns are simply too divergent for any one application to track and analyze.

As CRM software vendors tailor their products to meet industry-specific requirements, this trend will fuel demand for ESPs to develop similarly tailored service offerings. Competitive differentiation through vertical focus has always been a sound strategy for firms seeking to add value, and it becomes even more compelling given the significant customer relationship challenges we see in certain markets.

Demand for CRM applications is especially pronounced in those industries that have undergone major shifts in their competitive environment, as deregulation, consolidation, and the rise of Internet commerce have dramatically intensified competition. For example, in the financial services industry, the elimination of regulatory barriers between commercial banking, insurance, and securities, along with increasing industry consolidation and the rise of new sales and delivery channels (e.g. online banking and stock trading), has significantly intensified competition for customers among full-service financial institutions. The rise of the comprehensive "financial supermarket" has created a need for these firms to transition from a product-centered business model to a customer-centric, integrated financial services delivery system facilitated by CRM technology.

For private IT services firms, the development of core competencies based on these and other vertical markets should prove to be an effective means by which to add value and create competitive advantage through strategic differentiation.

2. Supply Chain Management
Overview
Supply Chain Management (SCM) packages are back-end applications designed to link suppliers, manufacturers, distributors, and resellers in a cohesive production and distribution network and thus allow an enterprise to track and streamline the flow of materials and data through the process of manufacturing and distribution to customers. SCM applications represent a significant evolution from previous enterprise planning systems, such as MRP, in terms of their ability to integrate an enterprise's business partners into the production process. By enabling greater data sharing between these supply chain partners, SCM applications improve production efficiency and flexibility. The three primary goals of an SCM system are:
1. Decrease inventory costs by matching production to demand. SCM forecasting applications utilize extremely complex planning algorithms to predict demand based upon information stored in the company database. These applications also incorporate any changes in supply

chain data into the forecast much faster than previous modes of calculation, allowing companies to more accurately predict demand patterns and schedule production accordingly.

2. Reduce overall production costs by streamlining the flow of goods through the production process and by improving information flow between an enterprise, its suppliers, and its distributors. Logistics-oriented systems such as transportation management, warehouse management, and factory scheduling applications all contribute to reduced production costs. By ensuring real-time connectivity between the various parties in a supply chain, these applications decrease idle time, reduce the need to store inventory, and prevent bottlenecks in the production process.

3. Improve customer satisfaction by offering increased speed and adaptability. SCM applications allow enterprises to reduce lead times, increase quality, and offer greater customization, enhancing the customer relationship and improving retention.

The SCM process begins with forecasting and data mining applications analyzing information consolidated in the enterprise's database. Planning algorithms are used to generate a demand forecast upon which to base subsequent procurement orders and production schedules. Figure 5 illustrates this process.

Supply Chain Management represents the convergence of all facets of the manufacturing and sales process:

Figure 5: Simplified Supply Chain

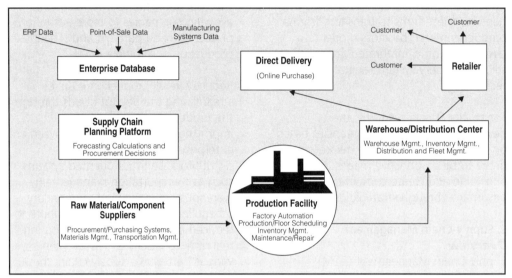

Source: Cherry Tree & Co. Research

anticipated demand, production and storage capacity, capital resources, time constraints, and profitability objectives. The value proposition of a SCM application is the capacity to integrate suppliers, manufacturers, and distributors into a dynamic Internet-, intranet-, or extranet-enabled system that takes all of these factors into account.

Through the increased collaboration between supply chain partners permitted by such a system, an enterprise in effect extends its operational boundaries. Suppliers are better able to anticipate the enterprise's need for materials, the enterprise is better able to schedule production processes and manage inventory levels, transportation companies are better able to coordinate material delivery and product distribution, and customers are better able to place and track orders.

Segmenting the SCM Landscape

We have segmented the Supply Chain Management market into two sectors: Supply Chain Planning (SCP) and Supply Chain Execution (SCE). Although SCM market leader i2 Technologies is expanding beyond its core SCP business into SCE and even some customer-facing offerings, most SCM firms have remained specialists in one sector or the other (a full segmentation of SCM vendors may be found in Appendix 3).

▸ *Supply Chain Planning* applications are tools used to access and analyze information stored in the company database in order to forecast product demand and plan manufacturing accordingly. Sophisticated computing platforms run data through extremely complex planning algorithms and optimization routines in a comparatively

Chapter 2: How to Integrate CRM in your Business

short time frame to produce anticipated demand figures and corresponding procurement and scheduling requirements, the calculation of which used to take days. These systems may be applied to both operational decisions (such as shop-floor scheduling) and long-term strategies (such as factory construction and quarterly forecasting).

▸ *Supply Chain Execution* applications use the information generated by SCP tools to guide the physical production, storage, and movement of raw materials, assembly components, and completed products. These applications are able to interface with SCP and order management systems to determine production capacity, including cost or time constraints, and calculate a production plan which satisfies all requirements and can adapt quickly to any change in variables.

Both Supply Chain Planning and Supply Chain Execution applications can be further segmented along functional lines. While the scope of this report does not permit an in-depth exploration of these subdivisions,

Figure 6 illustrates the major points of functionality involved.

SCM Software Market Forecast
As is the case in the CRM market, demand for Supply Chain Management applications is expected to continue its rapid growth. The US market is expected to expand at a compound annual growth rate of almost 50 percent and reach an estimated total value in excess of $18 billion by 2003.

Implications for External Services Providers
The market for supply chain solutions, much like the CRM market, is a case of too much demand chasing too little talent. In addition to the enormous challenges associated with integrating web-based back-end applications with legacy mainframe and client/server systems, SCM adopters face the daunting task of linking their systems with those of their supply chain partners. Internal IT divisions rarely have either the staff or the technical knowledge to deal with this level of complexity. Figure 8 illustrates the exploding demand for SCM services provided by ESPs.

Chapter 2: How to Integrate CRM in your Business

Figure 6: Supply Chain Functionality by Segment

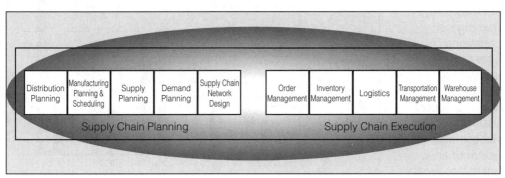

Source: Cherry Tree & Co. Research

Figure 7: US SCM Software Market Forecast

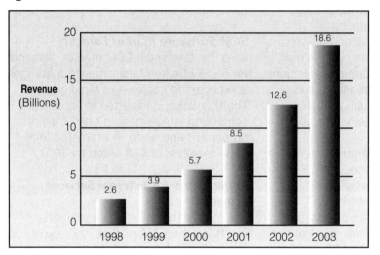

Source: AMR Research and Cherry Tree & Co. Research

ERP applications and other internal systems is only the first step in a painstaking and complex process. The bulk of the implementation work occurs beyond the boundaries of the enterprise and involves the integration of the SCM application with the systems of an enterprise's supply chain partners: raw materials and component suppliers, distributors, and shippers. Full integration involves linking incompatible and heretofore non-communicative software, hardware, and infrastructure systems. This connectivity increases collaboration in the

As is the case in the CRM market, Cherry Tree & Co. believes that private ESPs are well-positioned to compete for supply chain engagements, particularly in the middle market. Several factors are creating dramatic opportunities for services firms that are willing and able to develop significant SCM competencies.

Enterprises Face a Challenge in Integrating IT Systems with Supply Chain Partners. Linking a Supply Chain Management system to an enterprise's legacy

Figure 8: SCM Services Forecast

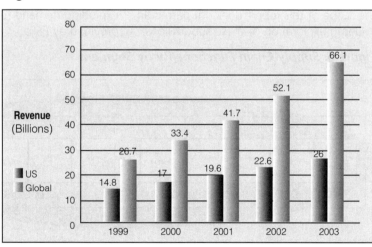

Source: IDC and Cherry Tree & Co. Research

forecasting, purchasing, production, and inventory management processes, and in synchronizing delivery and distribution schedules.

The difficulties associated with this task can be exacerbated depending on the financial condition, level of technical sophistication, and overall mindset of the supply chain partner. Partners constrained by financial, technological and cultural considerations can complicate integration immensely. Increasingly, SCM adopters will require the services of specialized integration partners who have the technical knowledge and experience to effectively surmount these and other obstacles.

Reconciling the Disparity Between Customer Functionality Demands and Vendor Offerings.
As adoption of SCM systems accelerates, customers are increasingly demanding both Supply Chain Planning and Supply Chain Execution functionality in their back-end systems. These demands have led to a disconnect between the solutions desired by the marketplace and the solutions that vendors are actually capable of providing; although certain SCP vendors are beginning to branch into SCE applications, the supply chain market is far from fielding a unified SCM suite encompassing both planning and execution.

In addition, there is a lack of complete functionality even within the SCE segment, as the major vendors have yet to offer a fully functional execution suite spanning inventory, warehouse, and transportation management. In order to bridge the gap between functionality desired and

functionality available, enterprises often purchase from multiple supply chain software vendors, which requires work performed by ESPs to ensure compatibility and full integration. With the introduction of the first comprehensive SCM suite several years out, we expect demand for integration services to remain strong for the near- to medium-term.

Vertical Market Expertise and Familiarity with Business Processes are Increasingly Critical.
The supply chain functionality required by a given enterprise varies widely across vertical markets. Discrete manufacturing demands different production optimization techniques than process manufacturing, and inventories of consumer goods cannot be managed in the same manner as inventories of industrial components. As the SCM market matures, it will mirror the CRM market in that applications will become increasingly specialized along vertical industry lines, fueling demand for vertically focused service providers.

Since SCM solutions have implications for both cost-containment and revenue enhancement, demand is strongest in those industries in which increasing competition has resulted in a need to enhance growth and margins through improved inventory and production methods. As an example, the wholesale/retail distribution sector, which has been comparatively slow in implementing supply chain solutions, is being forced to transition to a more agile production model as Internet vendors with fully integrated supply chains chip away at traditional retailers' top- and bottom-line

Chapter 2: How to Integrate CRM in your Business

growth. As a result, distributors will increasingly require SCM implementation to improve logistics, enhance supply chain collaboration, and thus bolster their margins and regain market share.

Cherry Tree & Co. believes that a growing number of SCM-related consulting and integration engagements will be awarded based on vertical market experience and that private services firms that move quickly to establish themselves within a set of vertical markets will have a distinct advantage over their competitors.

3. Enterprise Application Integration
Overview
Despite the value that extended enterprise applications such as CRM and SCM bring to the table, their full potential can never be realized without the technological "glue" that integrates them into the core of the enterprise. Most legacy or client/server-based enterprise applications, whether packaged or customized, were not designed to inter-operate with external applications or browser-based, end-user clients.

Consider that the vast majority of web applications augment rather than replace existing transaction management systems. This integration challenge often results in disconnected applications throughout an enterprise that are referred to in a number of different ways including "stovepipes," "islands of automation," and "vertical application silos." These islands of automation, in their native state, are oblivious to what exists outside of their domain. In order to solve this problem, a diverse set of tools and technologies have

evolved out of the general category of middle-ware that are loosely grouped together under the rubric of Enterprise Application Integration — or EAI.

Differentiating EAI from Traditional Middleware Solutions
It is critical to understand that EAI and traditional middleware solutions are not one in the same. Whereas traditional middle-ware facilitates the integration of individual applications and discrete transactions between them, EAI enables an enterprise to manage relationships among multiple applications and the surrounding network of transactions that constitute a business process. To better illustrate the difference between EAI and integration utilizing traditional middleware it is helpful to think through a couple of different integration examples. In Figure 9, we have selected a CRM / Sales Force Automation example to highlight the two different types of integration challenges that can arise during the utilization of the same web-based application.

Although our example is a bit of an oversimplification, the central point made in Figure 9 is that different integration challenges arise depending on how the sales force automation application is utilized. In Scenario #1, the sales person uses his/her browser to check the status of a customer order. This end-user request drives a tightly integrated front-to-back office communication that can be thought of as a discrete task. The computer processing required to answer this question can be thought of as an extended transaction. This type of "straight-through" processing between two programs requires

Figure 9: Sales Force Automation Integration Challenges

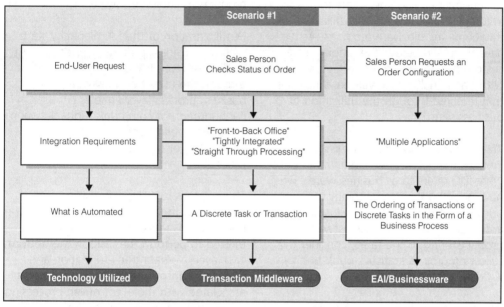

Source: Cherry Tree & Co. Research

the use of traditional middleware products. The advent of the Internet as a platform does not eliminate this type of integration challenge — in fact, it increases the volume of end-user requests that drive the need for this type of integration. While this type of integration is absolutely crucial for the utilization of Web-based applications, this type of integration is not EAI. Although we are not including this type of integration within our definition of EAI, we do not want the reader to lose sight of the fact that there is also a tremendous demand for consultants who can effectuate tightly-coupled / point-to-point integration between front-end Web-based applications and back-end legacy systems.

In Scenario #2, the salesperson requests that an order be configured for a customer.

Order configuration, once broken down into all of its component parts, can be thought of as 5 or 10 or 20 different discrete transactions that, when grouped together, constitute a business process. Depending on the situation, the processing of all of the different discrete tasks that constitute a business process - such as order configuration - will require communication between several applications. A new brand of middleware, often referred to as businessware, has recently been introduced that enables business process automation by integrating numerous applications. *It is essential to keep in mind that it is the chaining together of discrete transactions, in the form of a business process, from one application to the next that constitutes EAI.*

Chapter 2: How to Integrate CRM in your Business

Before we move forward, we do not intend to suggest that it is impossible to accomplish EAI through the utilization of traditional middle-ware products. As we have discussed below, the amount of custom coding required to effectuate EAI with traditional middleware far surpasses that required through the utilization of businessware.

The Introduction of Businessware

Perhaps the hottest new area within EAI is what IDC refers to as businessware - we have adopted their terminology for purposes of this analysis. To illustrate the anticipated value that businessware products bring to the table, consider the following growth statistics published by IDC (see figure 10).

Although favorable growth has been projected for several of the middleware product segments, we cannot give each of these equal time within the framework of this report. Instead, we will focus primarily on businessware as we believe it will become the most integral component of the new EAI paradigm. In essence, EAI can be thought of as a hierarchy of functionality that is predominantly controlled by the new businessware products as shown in Figure 11.

Our illustration of the EAI hierarchy starts with the business process layer on top. At its highest level, EAI is being facilitated through the use of businessware. The business process layer enables configuration of communications between disparate applications in a manner that automates, or replicates, a business process.

The business rules layer is also controlled by many of the businessware products. The rules layer dictates the rules that are utilized to perform the tasks in the bottom two layers — data trans-formation and message transportation. The rules layer is associated with the event driven processing component of businessware that we will describe more fully below.

Figure 10: Middleware & Businessware Growth Projections

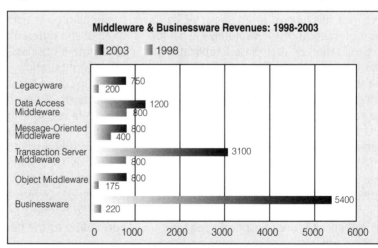

Middleware & Businessware Revenues: 1998-2003

■ 2003   ▌ 1998

	2003	1998
Legacyware	750	200
Data Access Middleware	1200	800
Message-Oriented Middleware	800	400
Transaction Server Middleware	3100	800
Object Middleware	800	175
Businessware	5400	220

Source: IDC

Figure 11: EAI Hierarchy

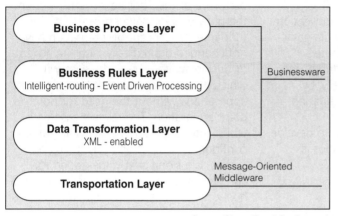

Source: Cherry Tree & Co. Research

1. Application integration within an independent system infrastructure;
2. Event driven processing; and
3. Business process automation.

1. Application Integration Within Independent System Infrastructure
As mentioned above, the integration challenge centers on uniting the many different "islands of automation" that exist within an enterprise. Businessware vendors have taken the position that the only real solution to this problem is to facilitate integration without introducing conditions that lead to new islands of automation — which is often the case when individual Application Program Interfaces (API's) are authored for point-to-point integration of two programs.

The data transformation layer interprets and transforms the large number of different types of data into a usable format that can be communicated between applications. When XML is mentioned in the context of EAI, it is typically in reference to this process. Most businessware and traditional middleware products are now embedding XML functionality into their product offerings. Finally, the transportation layer, consisting primarily of message-oriented middleware, handles routing of messages and guarantees delivery of messages between applications. Within our EAI hierarchy, the transportation layer is the only layer that arguably falls outside of the domain of businessware and into the realm of message-oriented-middleware.

The dramatic growth projected for businessware is predicated on the fact that these products offer three unique value propositions that can be summed up as follows:

In this vein, businessware contemplates an independent system infrastructure designed specifically for the integration task. By "unbundling" or "decoupling" the integration task a new "thin" computing layer is created. In the context of an Internet-enabled "n-tier" architecture, an enterprise's distributed application architecture can be illustrated as in figure 12.

In this vision of a distributed application architecture, the role of application integration receives its own tier or layer of computing power. This has several advantages, not the least of which is the realization of integration without interfering with the stovepipe application's ability to operate unchanged in its native environment. In addition, separate processing power can be directed at the integration tier as needed. Finally, by centralizing the application integration infrastructure in a generalized businessware solution, the cost to develop and maintain integration scenarios is greatly reduced.

2. Event Driven Processing
In the vocabulary of businessware, a "business event" is a piece of information generated by an application (such as an order entry by a customer) that must be shared with other applications (such as a requisition system with a supplier). Middleware has facilitated the transportation of this information on a point-to-point basis for a long time with the assistance of considerable custom coding. Today, businessware allows business analysts, not custom developers, to configure applications so that the "business events," once published into the separate integration infrastructure, become available to all of the other applications

within the enterprise that have a need to be aware of the "business event" — hence the phrase event driven processing. The fundamental concept of integration has not changed dramatically with the advent of businessware — only the ease with which it can be executed between multiple applications without the need for point-to-point integration. The relative ease with which inter-application processing can be configured, without an army of custom coders, is a significant value-added for companies seeking connectivity between a host of web-applications and core systems.

3. Business Process Automation
Businessware automates business processes by again taking advantage of the separate tier of computing for the integration infrastructure. Simply put, rather than having business processes hard coded into applications, the business processes are configured by business analysts into the businessware itself. In other words, the business process, like the integration itself, is "decoupled" from the native application. The advantage to this approach is that new processes can be configured into the integration infrastructure on the fly

Figure 12: Distributed Application Architecture

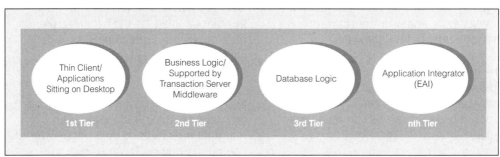

| 1st Tier | 2nd Tier | 3rd Tier | nth Tier |
| Thin Client/ Applications Sitting on Desktop | Business Logic/ Supported by Transaction Server Middleware | Database Logic | Application Integrator (EAI) |

Source: Cherry Tree & Co. Research

without having to re-code any of the distributed applications.

Other Integration Products
Although we don't have space within the framework of this report to fully describe all of the different tools that could possibly be pulled into an integration project, we want to reiterate the fact that there will continue to be tremendous demand for integration of web-based applications without the use of businessware products. As depicted in Figure 9, different uses of applications present different integration challenges — many of which cannot be solved with businessware. Businessware should not be thought of as the "silver bullet" that solves any and all integration problems.

Many other tools besides businessware will continue to be very useful in different integration scenarios. For example, we should mention the importance of application servers, transaction servers, XML, and other message brokering technologies. Without getting tangled in too much technical detail, application and transaction server vendors, such as BEA Systems and SilverStream Software, support the middle tier of the distributed application architecture where the business logic resides and therefore are an essential component of most Internet centered integration solutions.

Also, XML is making headlines as the glue that facilitates the data formatting and conversion necessary to connect Web-pages to world class databases. We believe that XML will likely become part of the answer within the data transformation

layer of most integration solutions — both within the context of EAI and traditional point-to-point integration. Finally, despite the advent of business-ware, there will undoubtedly be situations where point-to-point integration using traditional message-oriented middleware is the preferred approach. This brand of integration, although not as flexible as that accomplished with businessware, may be favored in certain situations where tighter integration is important.

Implications for External Service Providers
At first glance, it appears that the advent of EAI represents a threat to ESPs and to the traditional revenue streams associated with systems integration work. If EAI in fact delivers on its promise to greatly simplify the integration of multiple enterprise applications, systems integrators may experience a decrease in demand for custom coding that has heretofore accompanied point-to-point systems integration assignments.

Despite this potential threat, we believe that in the end there will be two very substantial integration opportunities for IT services firms:

1) EAI — the chaining together of discrete transactions, in the form of a business process, from one application to the next; and
2) Tightly-coupled integration of web-based applications to back office systems utilizing more traditional middleware products and methodologies.

Chapter 2: How to Integrate CRM in your Business

Our conversations with the pure-play Web Development companies lead us to believe that there is a severe shortage of firms that truly have the ability to deliver on both types of integration.

We should also note that there is considerable upside for the utilization of businessware tools by IT services firms. Although new businessware tools lend themselves to more rapid deployment than was previously possible, the task of selecting the appropriate EAI tools and then configuring business processes within the integration infrastructure is still beyond the abilities of the vast majority of internal IT departments. Indeed, Cherry Tree & Co. is of the opinion that the ultimate result of EAI will be increased demand for integration-related services, for the reasons outlined below:

▸ By demonstrating how the new EAI technologies make it possible to truly leverage all of the applications within a distributed application architecture, ESPs with command of EAI technologies will be better able to sell their clients on new extended enterprise initiatives. As businessware allows services firms to better demonstrate ROI associated with new web-application initiatives, these services firms will enhance their credibility and their foot-print within a given market.

▸ Developing EAI-related competencies represents a means by which services firms will be able to differentiate themselves from their competitors. Businessware will provide agile, first-to-market ESPs with a competitive

advantage as an emerging core practice area upon which to build vertical and/or domain expertise in integrating best-of-breed extended enterprise applications. Integrators who can leverage business process expertise and embed that expertise within standard methodologies surrounding the use of the new businessware products will gain a tremendous competitive advantage as vertical industry expertise becomes an increasingly important point of differentiation.

▸ Given that client companies demand differing degrees of intra- and inter-enterprise integration, businessware enables ESPs to tailor their offerings to the level required by a given customer. This ability represents a significant enhancement to an ESP's value proposition and provides them with the opportunity to establish leadership in different integration scenarios. For example, e-commerce integration involves establishing connectivity between an enterprise's front-end, web-based sales engine and its back-office systems. Integration work is primarily intra-enterprise and does not involve linking with external suppliers or distributors. In contrast, inter-enterprise integration is externally-focused and requires that an enterprise's systems be connected with those of its business partners. The central point is that different integration challenges require different EAI tools and different levels of business process expertise. The complexity of these integration tasks, even without the custom coding, will require IT consultant involvement.

▸ Finally, integration projects that fall outside of the scope of the EAI contemplated by businessware will continue to be extremely important. Very few companies have truly mastered the art of effectuating tightly coupled communication between web-based applications and legacy transaction systems. Integrators who have strong skills in this area will continue to be highly valued in the marketplace.

We believe that as standardized integration technologies, such as businessware, mature and proliferate, systems integrators focusing on enterprise application integration will evolve from custom-coders to application component assemblers and configuration experts. IT services firms will likely remain at the hub of the process, but the business analyst with business process knowledge will ultimately supplant the expert custom-coder as an IT service company's most valued asset in EAI projects.

At the same time, we believe that demand for point-to-point integration will remain strong despite the advent of businessware. The custom-coders will remain as valued contributors on point-to-point integration assignments. Standardized middleware products will continue to evolve to simplify these integration tasks as well, but the complexity of selecting and utilizing the correct middleware tools will bolster the value of those companies that have mastered this complex practice.

Significant News & Events

A review of the past four quarters' news and events for software and services firms within the extended enterprise application market reveals that the pace of partnering and merger and acquisition activity is accelerating. Newcomers to this market are attempting to acquire or develop new customer- and supplier-centric competencies, while companies with an established presence are leveraging and refining existing skill sets. Appendix 4 contains a comprehensive listing of major transactions announced during this period; this section will highlight several major trends that are most relevant to owners of private services firms.

Major ERP Vendor Migration to the Extended Enterprise Space

Faced with a slowdown in demand for full-scale enterprise systems as a result of the Year 2000 lockdown and a maturing Fortune 1000 market, the major ERP vendors are attempting to stimulate sales by developing competencies in extended enterprise applications through acquisitions, strategic partnerships, and in-house development. Oracle and J.D. Edwards have been the most aggressive vendors in this regard, adding capabilities in both SCM and CRM over the past several quarters. Focusing on customer management, Oracle has launched a front-office suite offering functionality in all three CRM segments as well as integration with the company's ERP applications. The company has also launched a Supply Chain Planning application targeted at the manufacturing industry, and has entered into partnerships with EAI vendors TSI and TIBCO.

J.D. Edwards has focused on adding supply chain capabilities to its ERP suite, agreeing to acquire major SCP vendor Numetrix for $80 million and entering into a partnership with IBM and SynQuest to develop supply chain solutions for the industrial manufacturing industry.

SAP has moved into the extended enterprise application space, partnering with supply chain software vendor Aspect Development and launching a web-based sales configuration engine. SAP also acquired a 9.7 percent stake in Catalyst International and announced that the two companies have entered into a strategic alliance to develop Supply Chain Execution solutions for mySAP.com.

PeopleSoft has also begun to move aggressively in recent quarters, agreeing to acquire CRM vendor Vantive for $433 million (2.4 times trailing revenues) and partnering with Supply Chain Execution vendors Optum and McHugh.

Software Vendor Merger & Acquisition and Partnering Activity
As companies have accelerated efforts to introduce new product and service offerings into the enterprise application space, the majority have selected acquisition or partnering strategies rather than internal development as the preferred means of obtaining the necessary intellectual capital and technological infrastructure. One of the major trends that has emerged has been major EAI software vendors partnering with other market leaders or acquiring smaller software vendors to extend their footprint in this market. EAI vendor New Era of Networks

(NEON) has been at the forefront of this trend, acquiring five integration software vendors and entering into an alliance with BEA Systems, a provider of integration and networking software. SilverStream Software announced that it will acquire two private firms, GemLogic and ObjectEra. GemLogic's primary product offering is an XML-based integration suite, while ObjectEra is a provider of distributed computing solutions using Java-based object request broker technology.

SCM and CRM vendors have also been active in expanding their product offerings via acquisitions and strategic alliances. i2 Technologies announced a partnership with SCE vendor Aspect Development and acquired CRM vendor SMART Technologies. SalesLogix acquired marketing automation software vendor Enact, while Clarify acquired Newtonian Software, an interactive selling and sales configuration software firm.

Demand for vertical industry expertise has been a key driver of acquisition activity among software vendors. Demonstrating this trend, two of the enterprise software firms acquired by NEON, VIE Systems and SLI International, had vertically-focused business models — VIE specializes in the transportation, financial services, and retail industries, while SLI focuses on retail, manufacturing, and consumer goods. In addition, TSI Software International, an EAI vendor, announced its acquisition of Braid Group Ltd., a UK-based provider of EAI software to banking and securities firms.

IT Services Merger & Acquisition Activity

Another major trend visible in this sector is the acquisition of small, niche service providers by larger ESPs as a means of migrating into the extended enterprise market. CIBER recently announced its acquisition of Waterstone Consulting, a Chicago-based management consulting firm with strong competencies in SCM and CRM solutions. The transaction was valued at $31 million, 2.1 times Waterstone's revenues of $15 million. Metamor Worldwide acquired PrimeSource Technologies, $10 million services firm specializing in ERP and SCM implementation, and Interliant acquired Sales Technology, a CRM and groupware implementation firm, to augment its CRM practice.

As is the case among software firms, services providers with demonstrated industry-specific competencies have been the preferred acquisition targets. Web developer iXL Enterprises recently announced an agreement to acquire Tessera Enterprise Systems, a provider of web-based CRM integration and consulting services to the financial services, telecommunications, and direct marketing industries. The transaction was valued at approximately $120 million, over five times annualized revenues. Application outsourcing company Syntel acquired Metier, Inc., a privately held ESP specializing in the implementation of ERP and CRM applications for clients operating in the healthcare, financial services, and manufacturing markets.

We have highlighted several major transactions in the CRM and SCM spaces in Figure 13. Notably, we are not aware of

any IT ser-vices acquisition activity related to or motivated by EAI expertise. As this practice area develops, however, we fully expect that private firms with EAI capabilities will be highly valued as acquisition prospects. For example, Cherry Tree & Co. has surveyed many of the public web development companies who have repeatedly indicated that the skill sets they most require center around the ability to integrate web-based applications with legacy ERP systems.

Opportunities for Privately Held Firms

We believe the trends we have described above will continue to drive corporations to adopt the type of distributed applications architectures that we have dubbed as the extended enterprise. Although CRM and SCM are the two hottest extended enterprise application products at the moment, the evolution of EAI technologies will foster the growth of many other distributed application products - both packaged and custom designed. Whether the realization of the extended enterprise as we have depicted it becomes a reality for most companies over the next 2-4 years or over the next 5-10 years is yet to be seen. This time frame will no doubt hinge in part on the capability of the technologies we have described to deliver on the hype that is currently surrounding them.

Irrespective of the time frame, the direction is clear and so many IT services firms should consider positioning themselves to take advantage of this trend. We have identified several different strategies that

Figure 13: Selected IT Services M&A Transactions

Buyer	Seller	Functionality	Approximate Value	Revenue	P/Revenue
iXL	Tessera Enterprise Systems	CRM Integration and Consulting Services	120	11.5	5
CIBER	Waterstone	Management Consulting, CRM and SCM Services	31	15	2.1
CSC	ECS	Oracle, CRM, SCM, and Data Warehousing Services	N/D	18.5	n/a
Syntel	Metier	Oracle, CRM, and E-commerce Services	N/D	25	n/a
Metamor	PrimeSource	ERP and SCM Implementation Services	N/D	10	n/a
Interliant	Sales Technology	CRM and Groupware Implementation Services (UK)	N/D	1	n/a

Source: Cherry Tree & Co. Research

can be used and have summed them up as follows:

1. Partnering with CRM and SCM Vendors:
One suggestion is for firms to establish partnerships with vendors in the SCM and CRM markets, as listed in the appendices to this report. As we have described in our previous research, a good partnership with the right vendor can accelerate an emerging practice with in your organization, and certification as a major vendor's preferred partner may carry significant weight in winning new engagements.

2. Partnering with EAI Vendors:
Because this market is still in its infancy, private IT services firms that act quickly to develop EAI expertise will gain a significant "first mover" advantage over their competitors. We have compiled a very extensive listing of the public and private companies that have offerings in the traditional middleware and businessware categories and have included them in the appendices to this report. IT services firms seeking to differentiate themselves from their competitors should consider investigating partnership opportunities with these vendors.

For example, we recently spoke with Paul Auvil, Chief Financial Officer of businessware vendor Vitria Technology. Mr. Auvil indicated that Vitria's management is very open to the idea of partnering with private IT services firms, as they recognize the fact that many middle market and Internet-based "dot.com" clients prefer to work with niche-oriented services companies. Mr. Auvil indicated that Vitria is predominantly interested in selling product and that it will look towards its implementation partners for services. Although we haven't interviewed executives at all of the businessware vendors, we believe that the majority of these firms will focus predominantly on the technology sell — leaving the services opportunities to the ESPs.

3. Leveraging Vertical Industry and Business Process Expertise:
Another practical way to take advantage of these trends is to find ways to leverage vertical industry expertise with existing clients into a new practice area with a CRM, SCM, or EAI focus. All of these practice areas require business process expertise that comes from industry specialization. Leveraging business process expertise may be a better approach than seeking partnerships with vendors,

especially in the SCM and CRM areas, since most projects require the use of multiple vendors. In fact, knowing which vendors to use can be a major component of value that the IT consultant brings to the table.

The need for business process expertise is also extremely important for EAI projects. Consultants who can embed business process into the application integration infrastructure will develop reusable methodologies that can be transferred from client to client within the same vertical. Once developed, this capability will present a formidable competitive advantage. For those firms that only have marginal business process knowledge, perhaps a relationship with a business process oriented management consulting firm will facilitate the transition. As we described last summer in our Professional Consulting Spotlight Report, traditional management consulting and IT consulting are merging in a number of areas — nowhere is this more clear than in the context of CRM and SCM solutions.

4. Leveraging An Existing ERP Implementation Practice:

Firms with established ERP implementation practices should consider seeking out opportunities to use their brand recognition as enterprise software experts to build extended enterprise-oriented service offerings. In many cases, this strategy would not require a major realignment of vendor partnerships, as the Big Five ERP vendors are all migrating to the extended enterprise space and are thus providing implementation partners with the opportunity to adjust their offerings accordingly.

Several ERP implementation companies that we have spoken with have indicated that they have already been performing limited amounts of CRM and SCM based on the current offerings in those areas made available by the Big Five ERP firms. Recognizing those skill sets and then repackaging them as distinct practice areas will allow certain firms to draw attention to a set of consulting skills that might otherwise be buried within a stagnant ERP practice.

5. Leveraging Existing Middleware Expertise:

For those services firms with legacy and client/server integration capabilities using traditional middleware, migration to EAI represents a natural progression. Such a transition would most likely involve less custom coding but the process of embedding business processes into the EAI infrastructure will be a significant value-added that project-based firms will bring to the table. Execution of this strategy will require some re-tooling in general Internet and EAI technologies. We believe that traditional systems integrators who can manage this transition while maintaining recognition with their clients as integration experts will position themselves for success.

We also don't want to overlook the demand for point-to-point integration required for direct legacy-to-net connectivity. Firms with strong middleware capability should consider marketing themselves as the experts in the field of back-end plumbing required for e-commerce sites. While we have drawn a distinction between this type of integration and EAI, there currently is a tremendous

Chapter 2: How to Integrate CRM in your Business

demand for both skill sets as the pure-play Web developers such as Razorfish, Viant, and Scient are discovering that they can fall short in their integration efforts.

6. Utilizing EAI to Open Other Web Development Opportunities:

As we have discussed, the business case for a new web application is greatly enhanced if the new application can be integrated into an overall distributed application architecture. ESPs that already have a thriving Internet consulting practice will further advance their ability to win large projects once they can demonstrate their ability to use EAI to increase the ROI for new custom applications.

7. Partnering with an EAI Specialist:

Custom web application developers who have been inclined to avoid application integration issues may find that partnering with an EAI-focused services firm presents a significant opportunity to add value. As extended enterprise applications become pervasive, web developers will be under increasing pressure to demonstrate that they are able to integrate their offerings with an enterprise's existing systems. A partnership with an EAI specialist therefore represents a compelling addition to a web developer's value proposition.

Cherry Tree & Co. would like to thank IDC Analyst Ed Acly for his assistance with the EAI and businessware components of this report.

Biography: Presidents, CEOs and CFOs of IT services firms look to Cherry Tree & Co. as their leading provider of in-depth industry information and customized investment banking services. Cherry Tree & Co.'s Web site at www.cherrytreeco.com puts this timely insight at your fingertips, allowing you to make the most strategic and well-informed business decisions for your company. Cherry Tree exclusively focuses on offering customized service to emerging private IT services firms. Should you wish to discuss growth options or the sale of your business under confidential terms, please call us at 612-893-9012 or e-mail us at info@cherrytreeco.com.

Appendix 1
Cherry Tree Research — IT Services Universe by Subsectors

IT Consulting
Company	Ticker
CACI International	CACI
Diamond Tech. Partners	DTPI
META Group	METG
Superior Consultant Holdings	SUPC
American Management Systems	AMSY
The A Consulting Team	TACX
First Consulting Group	FCGI

Project-Based Service Providers
Company	Ticker
(1) App. & Systems Development	
Complete Business Solutions	CBSI
Affiliated Computer Services	ACS
Mastech. Corp	MAST
Tier Technologies	TIER
Whittman-Hart	WHIT
PSW Technologies	PSWT
Cambridge Technology Partners	CATP
Cognizant Tech. Solutions Corp.	CTSH
Intelligroup	ITIG
Metamor Worldwide	MMWW
Tenfold	TENF

(2) Implementation/Integration	
AnswerThink	ANSR
BrightStar	BTSR
Computer Task Group	TSK
Renaissance Worldwide	REGI
Technisource	TSRC
Technology Solutions Corp.	TSCC
Aztec Technology Partners Inc.	AZTC

(3) Network & Web Development
Sapient	SAPE
USWeb/CKS	USWB
Rare Medium	RRRR
Proxicom	PXCM
Razorfish	RAZF
AppNet	APNT
Scient	SCNT
iXL Enterprises	IIXL
Viant, Inc.*	VIAN

Value Added Resellers
Company	Ticker
Microage	MICA
Acxicom Corp.	ACXM
Alphanet Solutions	ALPH
Viasoft, Inc.	VIAS
Compucom Systems	CMPC
Comdisco, Inc.	CDO
Black Box Corp.	BBOX
Merisel, Inc.	MSEL
Inacom	ICO

Outsourcing
Company	Ticker
(1) Application Outsourcing	
IMRglobal	IMRS
Syntel	SYNT
Critical Path	CPTH
FutureLink	FTRL
Interliant	INIT
USinternetworking	USIX

(2) Information Utilities / Business Process Outsourcing	
Automatic Data Processing	AUD
BISYS Group	BSYS
Ceridian	CEN
Equifax	EFX
First Data	FDC
Fiserv	FISV

Sungard Data Systems	SDS
(3) Platform IT Outsourcing	
Computer Sciences	CSC
Electronic Data Systems	EDS
Perot Systems	PER
Sykes Enterprises	SYKE

Staff Augmentation

Company	*Ticker*
(1) Pure IT Staffing	
Analysts International	ANLY
Cotelligent	CGZ
Hall Kinion	HAKI
Metro Information Services	MISI
PRT Group	PRTG
Alternative Resources	ALRC
(2) Transitioning Firms	
Ciber, Inc.	CBR
Computer Horizons	CHRZ
Keane	KEA

(3) General Staffing	
Modis Professional Services	MPS
Romac International	ROMC
StaffMark	STAF
CDI Corp.	CDI
Comforce	CFS
Personnel Group America	PGA
Volt Information Sciences	VOL
RCM Technologies	RCMT

Education & Training

Company	*Ticker*
ARIS	ARSC
CBT Group	SMTF
Wave Technology International	WAVT
Computer Learning Centers	CLCX
Learning Tree International	LTRE

*Indicates companies tracked by Cherry Tree but not yet included in stock indices due to insufficient trading history.

Appendix 2
IT Services — Structural Perspective

While it is extremely difficult to place IT Services companies in specific subsectors, Cherry Tree & Co. has developed the following set of working definitions and categorizations for purposes of analyzing key trends and developments in the industry. We recognize that readers often have their own mental categorizations that may be slightly different than what we are suggesting. Although pure-play examples are hard to find, we have found the following structural perspective to be very useful in depicting critical developments within the IT Services industry:

Professional Consulting:
Firms that focus on corporate level business and strategic engagements; further divided into three sub-sectors:

▸ IT Consulting. Firms that predominately focus on high level consulting projects that are directed at strategic information technology engagements. Project scope often entails company-wide evaluation of client business needs and essential processes, existing platforms, available technologies, and solutions design. The effort to structure an IT initiative as an integral component of a strategic or business process design oriented endeavor is what separates these companies from their Project-Based service provider counterparts.

▸ Strategic Management Consulting. Firms that provide advice centering upon a client's overall corporate objectives and competitive position. Strategy should be thought of as the creation of a unique and valuable position for an enterprise that affords it a sustainable competitive advantage. Project scope involves such topics as market trend analysis, business and customer mix, marketing efforts, and capital structure.

▸ Business Process Consulting. Firms that provide consulting expertise relative to the maximization of the operational effectiveness of a corporation at either the functional or business unit level. Operational effectiveness includes practices and processes that allow a company to better utilize its resources to generate the highest level of output at a minimized cost.

Project-Based Service Providers:
Client projects within this sector have comparatively well defined tangible deliverables and scope. Contract designs range from a billable hours approach to fixed-price engagements for components and even entire projects. Companies typically focus around some type of vertical industry expertise, either in specific technologies or industry applications.

▸ Application and Systems Development. Companies that specialize in custom software development aimed at serving the specific needs of their clients, typically in proprietary systems settings. Deliverables can include targeted modules or components, upgrades to existing systems, as well as original application development.

▸ Implementation/Integration. Firms that specialize in the deployment of complex enterprise wide (ERP) software packages. As part of this implementation, these companies integrate the new software by ensuring that diverse hardware, network, and software components work together. Companies may also specialize primarily in integration technologies, interface development, database management, and other enabling technologies that allow disparate systems to share information.

▸ Network and Web Development. Firms that develop client/server and web-enabled technologies that link business units together via LAN and WAN facilities and various Internet-based client solutions. Projects may also entail vendor and supplier coordination, customer communications and overflow management, billing, and receivables, as well as various e-commerce initiatives.

Outsourcing:
Companies providing process automation services and facilities management and operations for clients desiring a variety of technical outsourcing solutions; divided into three subsectors:

▸ Platform IT Outsourcing. Firms offering a range of data center services, including hardware facilities management, onsite and offsite support services, server-vaults and data security, and disaster recovery capabilities. These relationships typically involve the transfer of IT facilities, staff, or hardware.

▸ Utilities or Business Process Outsourcing. Firms focus on economic and efficient outsourcing solutions for complex but

repetitive daily business processes. These processes could be as sophisticated as finance and accounting or be more repetitive processes, such as disbursements and payroll. The provider assumes all responsibilities associated with the entire business process or function.

▸ Application Outsourcing. Firms that manage and maintain software applications, with the provider assuming the responsibilities associated with the application. There are two subdivisions of the AO sector: Application Service Provider (ASP) remotely hosts and delivers a packaged application to the client from an off-site location. Application Maintenance Outsourcing providers manage a proprietary or package application from either the client's or the provider's site.

Staff Augmentation:
Companies that specialize in providing qualified IT professional staff on a temporary or long-term contract basis to clients in need of specific skill sets and project support for internal systems development projects.

▸ Pure IT Staff Augmentation. Firms that derive the vast majority of their revenues from their core IT staffing business. Company strategies are often defined by geographic concentrations, vertical expertise, or technology focus.

▸ Transitioning Firms. Companies that have traditionally been viewed as being in the IT staffing business but have recently attempted to redirect their growth towards higher value added and higher margin project-based services. Various combinations of merger and acquisition, divestiture, and internal growth facilitate this migration.

▸ General Staffing with IT. Firms that provide professionals with a wide array of skills including finance, accounting, etc., which also have an IT staffing division with significant revenues. Several companies in this category are rapidly building IT services divisions, through both internal growth and by acquisition, which may eventually reposition their business mix.

▸ Education and Training: Companies that provide training and help desk consulting for firms that have adopted custom designed or packaged software products. Engagements can include onsite or training center programs following new installations or for skills development and certain technical applications.

▸ Value Added Resellers: Solutions-oriented vendors providing integrated hardware and software systems, often including consulting, design, and implementation services. These companies have historically operated under specialty hardware and software distributor arrangements, though trends are towards broader vendor representation and increased consulting services.

Chapter 2: How to Integrate CRM in your Business

Appendix 3
Extended Enterprise Software Vendors

CRM Software Vendors / Marketing Automaton

Public Firms

Company	Ticker	Price as of 12/30/1999	Mkt. Cap.	TTM Revenue	TTM Net Income	P/E	P/Rev.	Web Address
Broadbase	BBSW	$105.13	1808.57	7.30	(20.84)	N/A	247.60	www.broadbase.com
E.piphany	EPNY	$211.38	5705.43	11.87	(19.67)	N/A	480.70	www.epiphany.com
Exchange Applications	EXAP	$52.13	606.89	37.53	0.90	473.86	16.20	www.exapps.com
Siebel Systems*	SEBL	$85.75	15984.14	616.94	97.07	161.79	25.90	www.siebel.com
Vantive Corp.*	VNTV	$18.13	489.38	183.71	(7.94)	N/A	2.70	www.vantive.com

| | | | | | Group Average: | 317.83 | 154.62 | |
| | | | | | Group Median: | 317.83 | 25.90 | |

Private Firms

Datasage	www.datasage.com
Knowledge Discovery One	www.kd1.com
MarketFirst Software	www.marketfirst.com
MarketSwitch Corp.	www.marketswitch.com
ON!contact	www.oncontact.com
Prime Response	www.primeresponse.com
Rubric	www.rubricsoft.com

* Indicates vendors whose software suites offer functionality across all three CRM segments

CRM Software Vendors / Sales Force Automaton

Public Firms

Company	Ticker	Price as of 12/30/1999	Mkt. Cap.	TTM Revenue	TTM Net Income	P/E	P/Rev.	Web Address
Calico Commerce	CLIC	$51.88	596.20	27.08	(19.89)	N/A	22.01	www.calicocommerce.com
FirstWave Technologies	FSTW	$3.50	19.86	12.13	(2.65)	N/A	1.60	www.firstwave.com
Onyx Software	ONXS	$38.50	665.43	51.36	(2.47)	N/A	13.00	www.onyx.com
Pivotal Corp	PVTL	$43.06	862.12	29.43	(2.63)	N/A	29.30	www.pivotal.com
SalesLogix Corp.	SLGX	$41.38	768.50	30.03	(6.62)	N/A	25.60	www.saleslogix
Siebel Systems*	SEBL	$85.75	15984.14	616.94	97.07	161.80	25.90	www.siebel.com
Vantive Corp.*	VNTV	$18.13	489.38	183.71	(7.94)	N/A	2.70	www.vantive.com

Group Average: 161.80 17.16
Group Median: 161.80 22.01

Private Firms

2order.com	www.2order.com
Actionware	www.actionware.com
Moss Software	www.mosssoftware.com
Saratoga Systems	www.saratogasystems.com
Trilogy	www.trilogy.com

Indicates vendors whose software suites offer functionality across all three CRM segments

CRM Software Vendors / Customer Service & Support

Public Firms

Company	Ticker	Price as of 12/30/1999	Mkt. Cap.	TTM Revenue	TTM Net Income	P/E	P/Rev.	Web Address
Astea International	ATEA	$4.28	59.64	32.44	5.90	10.11	1.84	www.astea.com
Clarify	CLFY	$123.00	2875.49	200.41	15.52	178.30	14.35	www.clarify.com
eGain Communications	EGAN	$36.69	974.40	2.41	(22.84)	N/A	404.32	www.egain.com
Kana Communications	KANA	$202.00	5510.36	7.99	(22.22)	N/A	689.66	www.kana.com
Pegasystems	PEGA	$11.50	331.18	68.67	(13.79)	N/A	4.82	www.pegasystems.com
Remedy	RMDY	$44.63	1384.27	206.39	23.58	53.80	6.71	www.remedy.com
Siebel Systems*	SEBL	$85.75	15984.14	616.94	97.07	161.80	25.91	www.siebel.com
Silknet Software	SILK	$165.50	2573.03	17.68	(10.46)	N/A	145.53	www.silknet.com
Vantive Corp.*	VNTV	$18.13	489.38	183.71	(7.94)	N/A	2.66	www.vantive.com

Group Average: 101.00 143.98
Group Median: 107.80 14.35

Private Firms

AIT (USA) Inc.	www.ait-us.com
Octane Software	www.octaneinc.com
Brightware	www.brightware.com

Indicates vendors whose software suites offer functionality across all three CRM segments

Chapter 2: How to Integrate CRM in your Business

SCM Software Vendors / Supply Chain Planning

Public Firms

Company	Ticker	Price as of 12/30/1999	Mkt. Cap.	TTM Revenue	TTM Net Income	P/E	P/Rev.	Web Address
12 Technologies	ITWO	$199.44	15202.56	508.56	16.84	867.12	29.90	www.i2.com
Logility	LGTY	$21.00	280.85	32.09	2.45	116.67	8.80	www.logility.com
Manugistics Group	MANU	$31.00	647.85	149.24	(79.05)	N/A	5.70	www.manugistics.com

Group Average: 491.90 14.80
Group Median: 491.90 8.80

Private Firms

Paragon Management	www.paragonms.com
SynQuest	www.synquest.com
The Lyte Group	www.lytegroup.com
LogicTools, Inc.	www.logictool.com
Distinction Software	www.distinction.com
Prescient Systems	www.prescientsystems.com

SCM Software Vendors / Supply Chain Execution

Public Firms

Company	Ticker	Price as of 12/30/1999	Mkt. Cap.	TTM Revenue	TTM Net Income	P/E	P/Rev.	Web Address
Agile Software	AGIL	$210.00	4157.79	22.58	(14.47)	N/A	184.10	www.agilesoft.com
Aspect Development	ASDV	$67.39	1924.75	86.99	9.26	224.64	22.10	www.aspectdv.com
Catalyst International	CLYS	$12.50	87.81	40.93	(2.42)	N/A	2.10	www.catalystwms.com
Descartes Systems Group	DSGX	$20.75	759.12	46.24	(22.86)	N/A	16.40	www.descartes.com
Industri-Matematik	IMIC	$5.56	175.81	75.10	(34.72)	N/A	2.30	www.im.com
Manhattan Associates	MANH	$7.06	169.81	78.06	1.96	88.29	2.20	www.manhattanassociates.com
OAD, Inc.	OADI	$8.28	250.28	233.74	(23.28)	N/A	1.10	www.qad.com
Robocom Systems Intl.	RIMS	$2.00	$6.94	6.78	(2.09)	N/A	1.00	www.robocom.com

Group Average: 156.47 28.91
Group Median: 156.47 2.25

Private Firms

EXE Technologies	www.exe.com
Global Technology Services	www.globaltechitd.com
HK Systems	www.hksystems.com
Marcam Solutions	www.marcam.com
McHugh Software	www.mchugh.com
Optum	www.optum.com
Vastera	www.vastera.com
Technology Advantage	www.tadv.com

EAI Software Vendors

Public Firms

Company	Ticker	Price as of 12/30/1999	Mkt. Cap.	TTM Revenue	TTM Net Income	P/E	P/Rev.	Web Address
Active Software	ASWX	$92.00	2,213.61	18.95	(10.73)	N/A	116.80	www.activesw.com
BEA Systems*	BEAS	$70.50	11,056.37	397.27	(9.95)	N/A	27.80	www.beasys.com
IBM*	IBM	$108.75	198,206.19	88,497.00	7,969.00	24.91	2.20	www.ibm.com
Intellicorp Inc.	INAI	$3.19	52.24	23.56	(5.10)	N/A	2.20	www.intellicorp.com
New Era of Networks*	NEON	$46.88	1,524.22	114.93	(36.45)	N/A	13.30	www.neonsoft.com
SAGA Systems	AGS	$19.94	606.77	231.16	23.83	25.24	2.60	www.sagasoftware.com
TIBCO Inc.*	TIBX	$153.75	9,280.50	96.44	(19.48)	N/A	96.20	www.tibco.com
TSO Software	TSFW	$54.75	1,389.23	82.48	(5.04)	N/A	16.80	www.tsisoft.com
Vitria Technology	VITR	$237.00	7,073.04	23.21	(13.03)	N/A	309.00	www.vitria.com

	Group Average:	25.08	63.19
	Group Median:	25.08	13.30

Private Firms

Company	Web Address
Aller Inc.	www.aller.com
Crossworlds Software	www.crossworlds.com
Cycle Software	www.livedata.com
Extricity Software	www.extricity.com
Mint Technologies	www.mintech.com
Muscato Corp.*	www.muscato.com
Oberon	www.oberon.com
OpenConnect Systems	www.openconnect.com
Software Technologies Corp.*	www.stc.com
ViewLocity	www.viewlocity.com
Visual Edge Software*	www.vedge.com

*Indicates vendors whose software offerings encompass functionality across multiple EAi/Middleware segments.

Chapter 2: How to Integrate CRM in your Business

Middleware Vendors / Legacyware

Public Firms

Company	Ticker	Price as of 12/30/1999	Mkt. Cap.	TTM Revenue	TTM Net Income	P/E	P/Rev.	Web Address
Ardent Software*	ARDT	$38.25	725.14	154.75	5.87	103.38	4.70	www.ardentsoftware.com
Carleton Corp.	CARL	$2.34	7.85	5.67	(9.33)	N/A	1.40	www.carleton.com
Computer Assoc Int'l	CA	$70.38	37,933.88	5,817.00	716.00	52.91	6.50	www.cai.com
Computer Network Technology	CMNT	$24.63	577.60	151.73	8.92	63.14	3.80	www.cnt.com
IBM*	IBM	$108.75	198,208.19	88,497.00	7,969.00	24.91	2.20	www.ibm.com
New Era of Networks	NEON	$46.88	1.534.22	114.93	(36.45)	N/A	13.30	www.neonsoft.com
Primix Solutions*	PMIX	$8.13	119.31	9.56	(5.67)	N/A	12.50	www.primix.com
Sterling Software*	SSW	$31.44	2,543.96	807.00	(10.76)	N/A	3.20	www.sterling.com
Unisys Corp.*	UIS	$31.88	9,878.22	7,633.50	504.90	19.20	1.30	www.vitria.com

Group Average: 52.71 5.43
Group Median: 52.91 3.80

Private Firms

Blue Lobster Software	www.bluelobster.com
CEL Corp.	www.celcorp.com
Clearview Software Int'l	www.clearview-software.com
Clientsoft Inc.	www.clientsoft.com
Connextions.net	www.connextions.com
Infospinner Inc.	www.infospinner.com
Macro 4	www.macro4.com
Metaserver Inc.	www.mserver.com
Mitem Corp.	www.mitem.com
MODCOMP Inc.	www.modcomp.com
Muscato Corp.*	www.muscato.com
Seagull Software	www.seagullsw.com
Software Technologies Corp.*	www.stc.com
Starquest Software	www.starquest.com
Translink Software	www.translink.com

* Indicates vendors whose software offerings encompass functionality across multiple EAi/Middleware segments.

Middleware Vendors / Data Access Middleware

Public Firms

Company	Ticker	Price as of 12/30/1999	Mkt. Cap.	TTM Revenue	TTM Net Income	P/E	P/Rev.	Web Address
Apple Computer	AAPL	$100.31	16,130.23	6,134.00	601.00	23.88	2.60	www.apple.com
Ardent Software*	ARDT	$38.25	725.14	154.75	5.87	103.38	4.70	www.ardentsoftware.com
BEA Systems*	BEAS	$70.50	11,056.37	397.27	(9.95)	N/A	27.80	www.beasys.com
Bull SA*	Paris Exchange	N/A	N/A	N/A	N/A	N/A	N/A	www.bull.com
Centura Software	CNTR	$5.00	176.99	50.61	(2.32)	N/A	3.50	www.centurasoft.com
Compaq Computer Corp.*	CPQ	$27.44	46,452.53	38,906.00	995.00	45.73	1.20	www.compaq.com
Hewlett-Packard Co.*	HWP	$115.25	117,425.46	42,370.00	3,491.00	37.66	2.80	www.hp.com
IBM*	IBM	$108.75	198,208.19	88,497.00	7,969.00	24.91	2.20	www.ibm.com
Inprise*	INPR	$11.81	682.34	277.47	64.01	9.84	2.50	www.inprise.com
International Software Group	SISG	$15.63	131.69	N/A	N/A	N/A	N/A	www.isgsoft.com
MERANT plc	MRNT	$30.75	916.00	371.50	11.70	78.29	2.47	www.merant.com
Neon Systems Inc.	NESY	$36.13	319.71	24.18	3.77	50.88	13.20	www.neonsys.com
Persistence Software*	PRSW	$24.13	459.53	13.24	(8.09)	N/A	34.70	www.persistence.com
Santa Cruz Operation Inc.	SCOC	$28.88	991.74	223.62	16.86	58.93	4.40	www.sco.com
Showcase Corp.	SHWC	$5.88	60.44	38.81	(1.04)	N/A	1.60	www.showcasecorp.com
Sterling Software*	SSW	$31.44	2,543.96	807.00	(10.76)	N/A	3.20	www.sterling.com
Sun Microsystems*	SUNW	$78.44	122,529.39	12,357.00	1,188.57	101.87	9.90	www.sun.com
Sybase Inc.	SYBS	$17.00	1,390.00	867.08	21.64	65.38	1.60	www.sybase.com
Symantec Corp.	SYMC	$57.44	3,310.61	662.662	89.48	36.12	5.00	www.symantec.com
Unisys*	UIS	$31.88	9,878.22	7,633.50	504.90	19.20	1.30	www.unisys.com

Group Average: 50.47 6.93
Group Median: 45.73 3.00

Private Firms

Attachmate Corp.	www.attachmate.com
Cornerstone Software*	www.corsoft.com
Cross Access Corp.	www.crossaccess.com
Dharma Systems	www.dharma.com
Easysoft Ltd.	www.easysoft.com
Enterworks Inc.	www.enterworks.com
Information Builders Inc.	www.ibi.com
Liant Software Corp.	www.liant.com
M.B. Foster Associates	www.mbfoster.com
NobleNet Inc.*	www.noblenet.com
Ontos	www.ontos.com
OpenLink	www.openlink.com
OpenPath Software	www.openpath.com
Promia*	www.promia.com
Secant Technologies	www.secant.com
Simba Technologies	www.simbatech.com
Solutions IQ	www.solutionsiq.com
The Object People	www.objectpeople.on.ca
Viaserv Inc.	www.viaserv.com

* Indicates vendors whose software offerings encompass functionality across multiple EAi/Middleware segments.

Chapter 2: How to Integrate CRM in your Business

Middleware Vendors / Message-Oriented Middleware

Public Firms

Company	Ticker	Price as of 12/30/1999	Mkt. Cap.	TTM Revenue	TTM Net Income	P/E	P/Rev.	Web Address
BEA Systems*	BEAS	$&70.50	11.056.37	397.27	(9.95)	N/A	27.80	www.beasys.com
Compaq Computer Corp.*	CPQ	$27.44	46,452.53	38,906.00	995.00	45.73	1.20	www.compaq.com
IBM*	IBM	$108.75	198,208.19	88,497.00	7,969.00	24.91	2.20	www.ibm.com
Level 8 Systems*	LVEL	$34.56	311.07	41.10	(28.22)	N/A	7.60	www.level8.com
New Era of Networks*	NEON	$46.88	1,534.22	114.93	(36.45)	N/A	13.30	www.neonsoft.com
Software AG	Frankfurt Exchange	N/A	N/A	N/A	N/A	N/A	N/A	www.softwareag.com
TIBCO Inc.*	TIBX	$153.75	9,280.50	96.44	(19.48)	N/A	96.20	www.tibco.com
Unisys Corp.*	UIS	$31.88	9.878.22	7,633.50	504.90	19.20	1.30	www.unisys.com

Group Average:	29.95	21.37
Group Median:	24.91	7.60

Private Firms

Allen Systems Group	www.asg.com
Candle Corp.	www.candle.com
Cornerstone Software*	www.corsoft.com
PeerLogic	www.peerlogic.com
Precise Software Solutions	www.precisesoft.com
Talarian Corp.	www.talarian.com
Tempest Software	www.tempest.com

Indicates vendors whose software offerings encompass functionality across multiple EAi/Middleware segments.

Middleware Vendors / Transaction Server Middleware

Public Firms

Company	Ticker	Price as of 12/30/1999	Mkt. Cap.	TTM Revenue	TTM Net Income	P/E	P/Rev.	Web Address
BEA Systems*	BEAS	$&70.50	11.056.37	397.27	(9.95)	N/A	27.80	www.beasys.com
Bull SA*	Paris Exchange	N/A	N/A	N/A	N/A	N/A	N/A	www.bull.com
Compaq Computer Corp.*	CPQ	$27.44	46,452.53	38,906.00	995.00	45.73	1.20	www.compaq.com
Hewlett-Packard Co.*	HWP	$115.25	117,452.53	42,370.00	3,941.00	37.66	2.80	www.hp.com
Iona*	IONA	$54.88	1,081.64	97.37	6.50	161.40	11.10	www.iona.com
Persistence Software*	PRSW	$24.13	459.53	13.24	(8.09)	N/A	34.70	www.persistence.com
Silverstream Software	SSSW	$116.50	1,978.05	17.07	(17.82)	N/A	115.90	www.silverstream.com
Unisys*	UIS	$31.88	9,878.22	7,633.50	504.90	19.20	1.30	www.unisys.com

	Group Average:	66.00	27.83
	Group Median:	41.70	11.10

Private Firms

Company	Web Address
Brokat Infosystems	w3.brokat.com
Chili !Soft	www.chilisoft.com
Constellar Corp.	www.constellar.com
GemStone Systems Inc.	www.gemstone.com
ObjectSwitch	www.objectswitch.com
Secant Technologies*	www.secant.com

Indicates vendors whose software offerings encompass functionality across multiple EAi/Middleware segments.

Chapter 2: How to Integrate CRM in your Business

Middleware Vendors / Object Middleware

Public Firms

Company	Ticker	Price as of 12/30/1999	Mkt. Cap.	TTM Revenue	TTM Net Income	P/E	P/Rev.	Web Address
Ardent Software*	ARDT	$38.25	725.14	154.75	5.87	103.38	4.70	www.ardentsoftware.com
BEA Systems*	BEAS	$&70.50	11.056.37	397.27	(9.95)	N/A	27.80	www.beasys.com
Compaq Computer Corp.*	CPQ	$27.44	46,452.53	38,906.00	995.00	45.73	1.20	www.compaq.com
Hewlett-Packard Co.*	HWP	$115.25	117,452.53	42,370.00	3,941.00	37.66	2.80	www.hp.com
IBM*	IBM	$108.75	198,208.19	88,497.00	7,969.00	24.91	2.20	www.ibm.com
Inprise*	INPR	$11.81	682.34	277.47	64.01	9.84	2.50	www.inprise.com
Iona*	IONA	$54.88	1,081.64	97.37	6.50	161.40	11.10	www.iona.com
Level 8 Systems*	LVEL	$34.56	311.07	41.10	(28.22)	N/A	7.60	www.level8.com
Primix Solutions *	PMIX	$8.13	119.31	9.56	(5.67)	N/A	12.50	www.primix.com
Rational Software	RATL	$48.25	4,213.82	479.77	73.06	56.76	8.80	www.rational.com
Sun Microsystems*	SUNW	$78.44	122,529.39	12,357.08	1,188.57	101.87	9.90	www.sun.com
TIBCO Inc.*	TIBX	$153.75	9,280.50	96.44	(19.48)	N/A	96.20	www.tibco.com

Group Average:	67.69	15.61
Group Median:	51.25	8.20

Private Firms

Black & White Software	www.blackwhite.com
Expersoft	www.expertsoft.com
I-Kinetics Inc.	www.i-kinetics.com
NobleNet Inc.*	www.noblenet.com
Objective Interface Systems	www.ois.com
Promia*	www.promia.com
Visual Edge Software Ltd.*	www.vedge.com

* Indicates vendors whose software offerings encompass functionality across multiple EAi/Middleware segments.

Appendix 4
Merger & Acquisition Review

1st Quarter, 1999

▸ JD Edwards (JDEC) announced the acquisition of The Premisys Corporation, a sales engineering automation software vendor. Privately held and based in Chicago, IL, Premisys was JD Edwards' first acquisition since 1997.

▸ AnswerThink (ANSR) acquired CRM vendor Quintus Corporation's (QNTS) Call Center Enterprises consulting organization. The group's 13 consultants were merged into AnswerThink's Customer Solutions practice, where they will continue to provide services related to Quintus' customer interaction software suite.

▸ Industri-Matematik (IMIC) announced its acquisition of Astea International's (ATEA) Abalon CRM software operations for $9.5 million. The Abalon operations, including 80 consultants and staff members, were integrated into Industri-Matematik's Advanced Supply Chain Execution Suite.

▸ TSI International Software Ltd. (TSFW) acquired Braid Group Ltd., a provider of EAI solutions to the financial services industry. Braid is privately held and based in London, England.

▸ New Era of Networks (NEON) acquired D&M Ltd., an IT services firm headquartered in Hong Kong. D&M specializes in designing, implementing, and managing enterprise applications, network infrastructures, and databases.

2nd Quarter, 1999

▸ JD Edwards (JDEC) announced the acquisition of Numetrix, a privately held Supply Chain Planning software vendor headquartered in Toronto, Canada. The transaction was valued at approximately $80 million.

▸ i2 Technologies (ITWO) announced an agreement to acquire SMART Technologies, a developer of Internet-based CRM software. SMART offers applications that facilitate e-commerce, customer care, and Internet billing. The all-stock transaction was valued at approximately $68 million, 9.4 times SMART's 1998 revenues of $7.2 million.

▸ SalesLogix (SLGX) announced an agreement to acquire Enact, Inc., a provider of sales configuration software. Enact's software manages marketing resources and product catalogs, and generates sales proposals and orders.

▸ SAGA Software (AGS) announced a definitive agreement to acquire Blue Lobster Software, Inc. for $12 million in cash. Blue Lobster, based in San Jose, CA, develops application integration software.

▸ NEON (NEON) announced two acquisitions this quarter. In early April the company acquired VIE Systems, Inc., a privately held provider of EAI software serving the travel, transportation, financial services, and retail markets. Later in April NEON announced the signing of an agreement to acquire SLI International AG, an implementation firm providing SAP implementation services. Headquartered in Zurich, Switzerland, SLI specializes in the following vertical markets: retail, electronics, manufacturing, chemicals,

Chapter 2: How to Integrate CRM in your Business

pharmaceuticals, and consumer goods. The $22 million transaction was composed of both cash and stock.

3rd Quarter, 1999

▸ Syntel (SYNT) completed two acquisitions this quarter. In August the company announced the acquisition of IMG, Inc., a consulting firm that provides services in areas such as e-business and web application development. Privately held, IMG reported 1998 revenues of $2 million. In September Syntel acquired Metier, Inc., a privately held firm based in Los Angeles, CA. Metier specializes in the design and implementation of e-commerce, CRM, and data warehousing solutions for middle market clients in the healthcare, manufacturing, and financial services industries, and reported trailing revenues of $25 million

▸ Interliant (INIT) acquired U.K.-based Sales Technology Ltd. in September. Sales Technology Ltd. specializes CRM implementation services and is an Onyx Software reseller and integration partner.

▸ Exchange Applications (EXAP) acquired GBI, a Seattle, WA-based marketing software vendor. GBI provides Web, email, and other customer interaction processing capabilities, primarily to "dot.com" firms. The all-stock transaction was valued at $24 million; GBI was privately held and employed 28 consultants and staff members.

▸ Clarify, Inc. (CLFY) announced its acquisition of Newtonian Software, a privately held developer of interactive selling/sales configuration software. The two companies had been marketing

partners since 1998. Clarify acquired Newtonian for a combination of cash and stock valued at $16.5 million.

▸ Remedy Corp. (RMDY) acquired Fortress Technologies, Inc., an IT services firm providing asset management consulting. Fortress is privately held and headquartered in Hinsdale, IL.

▸ NEON (NEON) announced two agreements this quarter. The first transaction to be announced was the agreement to acquire Convoy Corporation, a provider of application integration software for PeopleSoft ERP applications. Convoy is privately held and generated revenues of $10.4 million for their fiscal year ended March 31, 1999. NEON also agreed to acquire MicroScript, Inc., a vendor of application integration software for Windows NT based in the U.K. Privately held, MicroScript had 1998 revenues of approximately $8 million and has 62 employees.

▸ Metamor Worldwide (MMWW) acquired the assets of PrimeSource Technologies LLC, a Scottsdale, AZ services firm specializing in ERP and SCM implementation services. PrimeSource has projected 1999 revenues of approximately $10 million and employs 60 consultants.

▸ TSI International Software (TSFW) announced its intention to acquire Novera Software, Inc., a provider of web application integration software to the business-to-consumer market. Novera is privately held and headquartered in Burlington, MA.

4th Quarter, 1999

▸ PeopleSoft (PSFT) announced a definitive agreement to acquire The Vantive Corporation (VNTV). One of the leading vendors in the CRM space, Vantive provides an integrated customer management software suite. The all-stock transaction is valued at approximately $433 million, 2.4 times Vantive's trailing twelve-month revenues of $183.7 million. The acquisition is expected to close during the first quarter of 2000.

▸ Nortel Networks (NT) announced a definitive merger agreement with Clarify, Inc. (CLFY). Another top CRM vendor, Clarify's product offerings web-enable and automate customer service and support functions. Clarify has agreed to be acquired for approximately $2.1 billion, 10.5 times the company's trailing twelve-month revenues of $200.4 million.

▸ CIBER (CBR) announced the acquisition of Waterstone Consulting, Inc., for $31 million. Waterstone, a management consulting firm with CRM and SCM expertise, is based in Chicago, IL and employs 130 consultants and staff members. The purchase price is 2.1 times Waterstone's revenues of $15 million.

▸ iXL Enterprises (IIXL) announced a definitive agreement to acquire Tessera Enterprise Systems, a provider of CRM consulting and integration services to firms in the financial services, telecommunications, and direct marketing industries. Tessera agreed to be acquired for $120 million, 5.2 times annualized revenues.

▸ TIBCO Software (TIBX) acquired InConcert, Inc., a subsidiary of Xerox Corporation and a provider of infrastructure software for telecommunications firms.

▸ Calico Commerce (CLIC) entered into a definitive agreement to acquire ConnectInc.com (CNKT), a provider of technology and services designed to connect purchasing and selling companies via the Internet. The stock transaction is valued at approximately $90 million, 14.3 times trailing revenues.

▸ E.piphany, Inc. (EPNY) announced a definitive agreement to acquire RightPoint, a provider of real-time online marketing and personalization solutions. RightPoint is privately held and headquartered in San Meteo, CA.

▸ Onyx Software (ONXS) acquired Market Solutions, Ltd., a U.K.-based firm specializing in the development and implementation of CRM systems. The transaction consisted of $6 million in cash and stock, in addition to an $8 million earnout.

▸ Siebel Systems, Inc. (SEBL) agreed to acquire OnTarget, Inc., a provider of consulting and training services to sales and marketing organizations, and companies operating in the telecommunications and technology industries. The two firms have been partners since 1996. The stock transaction is valued at approximately $259 million, 6.5 times OnTarget's estimated 1999 revenues.

▸ Computer Sciences Corporation (CSC) acquired ECS Integrated Technology Solutions LLC, a provider of Oracle implementation and support services. ECS focuses on e-business, CRM, SCM,

Chapter 2: How to Integrate CRM in your Business

and data warehousing applications and reported trailing revenues of $18.5 million.

▸ Quintus Corp. (QNTS) acquired Acuity Corp., a provider of web-based customer interaction software with a focus on customer service and support. Acuity is based in Austin, TX.

▸ SilverStream Software (SSSW) announced that it will acquire two private firms, GemLogic and ObjectEra. GemLogic's product offering consists of an XML-based integration suite, and ObjectEra is a provider of distributed computing solutions using Java-based object request broker technology. The two firms were acquired for a total of $29 million in cash.

▸ Braun Consulting (BRNC) announced the acquisition of Emerging Technologies Consultants, Inc., a privately held services company specializing in CRM-related consulting. ETCI employs 40 consultants and was acquired for approximately $27 million in cash and stock.

▸ Broadbase Software Inc. (BBSW) entered into a definitive agreement to acquire Rubric, Inc., a provider of web-based Marketing Automation software to Fortune 500 and dot.com clients. Rubric is privately held and headquartered in San Mateo, CA.

Chapter 3: CRM in Practice

Customer - Brand Value

Title:	*Customer Brand Value*
Author:	*Targetbase*
Abstract:	*The customer-brand value approach provides a strategic framework for building and managing strong customer-brand relationships. As a strategic platform, it identifies and sizes opportunities for business-building and brand-building efforts. As a value metric, it provides a tool for determining the ROCI. As a segmentation scheme, it provides a structure for the continuous classification of customers into meaningful groups based on data retrieved from various customer contact points. Targetbase endorses the implementation of CRM strategies to improve the acquisition, retention, and maximization of high-value customers. Such strategies, however, require more than an investment in new technology. Successful CRM strategies require an approach to the market space that recognizes the differential value exchanged between customers and brands. Customer-Brand Value provides this approach.*

Preparing for Accountable Customer Relationship Management?

The concerns of top management with respect to customer care and communications expenditures are changing. As strategies for Customer Relationship Management (CRM) are being developed, the CEO and CFO are asking broader, more strategic questions regarding the return on investment (ROI) of finite corporate resources. CRM expenditures are competing with opportunities to build new factories, develop new products, or create new distribution systems. Fortunately, measurement and analysis techniques are becoming more available that allow ROI calculations to be performed on business-building activities like promotions and frequency programs. Even these techniques, however, ignore the longer-term, brand-building impact of many CRM efforts.

Competing successfully for scarce corporate resources requires objective measures of CRM activities that are comparable to those used to evaluate other investments. Since accounting systems still consider the only assets of a business to be those things with tangible value (i.e., cash, property, equipment, etc.), CRM investments must be measured through tangible returns. The most logical measure is the value of current and future income flows from the customers the business serves. By determining the expected revenue from customers and prospects to a brand or business, one can determine the amount that could and should be invested in these brands and/or customers. CRM investments can then be evaluated in the same manner in which other investments are evaluated—their economic return to the business.

Advances in technology and research methods now permit the tracking of the relevant behaviors used to calculate customer income flows. Customer databases, scanner panels, and survey research techniques all provide the necessary input to determine the performance of a behavioral audit for a brand and its competition. For many businesses, this information is already in-house. Mere measurement, however, falls short of taking full advantage of a focus on customer and brand value. CRM should be directed toward increasing the value of brands through the development of Customer-Brand Value.

What Is Customer-Brand Value (C-BV)?

C-BV is a proven assessment process for defining, evaluating, building, and monitoring brand strength by focusing on the relationship between the brand and its customers.

The assessment process is based on a model that assumes three fundamental principles of CRM:
▸ The strength of the brand is equal to the strength of the current and potential relationships between the brand and its customers.
▸ All of a brand's customers and prospects have a measurable current category value, brand value, and potential future brand value.
▸ The customer-brand relationship is defined and measured as a function of customer behavior and attitudes.

These principles provide the foundation for an approach to CRM that recognizes the need for accountability in the execution of CRM strategies and the expanded role of the "marketing" function in organizations that choose to pursue a CRM strategy. This paper will detail the C-BV process. First, however, a brief overview of the two

components involved in the relationship is in order.

Understanding the Customer

Today's marketers understand that the key to building brand value is to focus on building customer value. Unfortunately, most efforts to understand the customer fail to provide actionable insight. Some marketers focus on customer needs, while others choose to understand attitudes or life style. Still, others are satisfied with geo-demographic descriptions base on a customer's home address. Profiling the customer on all three dimensions is key to making the leap from strategy to implementation. Further, each dimension should be calibrated to behavioral measures of purchase that link to the estimation of customer income flows. In this manner, two forms of actionability are achieved. First, estimation of customer income flows link to ROI. Second, behavioral and environmental measures provide a link to targeting brand

Figure 1

Chapter 3: CRM in Practice

communications messages most effectively. In short, products that meet *customer* needs and are positioned well relative to the customer's *mindset* can only be successful if they can reach the customer's *environment*.

Needs:

What benefits are customers looking for in the category? Do these differ by occasion? The best place to begin understanding the needs of the customer is by listening to the "voice of the customer." Qualitative methods that identify primary, secondary, and teritary levels of customer needs are essential. Primary level needs are the global terms most customers use when describing the benefits they are seeking (i.e., quality, price, speed, etc.). Secondary level responses are those which serve to add more description to these terms. For example, the primary need of "quality" may be further described as "freshness" or "packaging" for a food product, or "reliability" and "ergonomics" for a personal computer.

Tertiary needs represent the level that can usually be acted upon because they are often the indicators of secondary level benefits (i.e., "color and consistency" are indicative of "freshness," "standard keyboards and large screens" indicate "good ergonomics"). A quantitative assessment of the importance of primary- and/or secondary-level needs can be obtained through direct ratings or through feature tradeoffs to more closely simulate actual behavioral choice. The tertiary level attributes can then be used to direct action relative to the most critical areas of improvement.

Mindset:

What attitudes, emotions, and motivations describe the manner in which the customer interacts with the category? This group of measurements is most similar to the traditional approach of segmenting markets. By understanding attitudes or mindsets, brands can be positioned to appeal to specific groups of targeted customers. For example, some customers have active information seeking styles, constantly looking for a "better deal." Others are more passive in their product choice requiring a "push" to another product or service rather than "jumping" in on their own.

It is important to understand the mindset that the customer brings to the category in order to direct brand communications to the customer or group of customers where they will have the most impact. Trumpeting the presence of a technology advantage may be lost on a customer who has little knowledge of the category. On the other hand, brand communications that emphasize the benefit of such advantages may be very well received among a less knowledgeable but information-seeking type customer. Strength of brand preferences, ability to differentiate offerings, and behavioral indications of variety seeking are additional examples of measures that provide insight into the mindset of the customer.

Environment:

What constraints and influences exist that determine the boundaries of purchase behavior? Demographics like income and household size obviously impact frequency, volume, and, in some categories, brand selection within the category. Many other factors relative to the customer environment will have an impact as well. In business-to-business categories, the complexity of a business's technology platform and decision process can have a major influence on the ability of a brand to communicate or even provide an advantage. As households become more "technologically sophisticated," access to media becomes an important differentiator of customer environments. Substantial research has also been done on the influence of children's preferences on household purchases. Even geography can play a role in determining access to, and influence of, particular distribution channels.

Survey research, syndicated panels, and customer databases are generally a good source for this type of information. This basic structure of the customer should be applied to each customer in the supply chain for the brand. Specifically, rigorous measurement is needed among end customers and intermediaries (i.e., retailer, wholesaler, sales reps, etc.). The methodology for this measurement system will vary depending on the specific market or distribution structure for the brand. Of course, the importance of various intermediaries will vary by category depending on the relative value that each plays in the delivery of a brand to its customers.

Understanding the Brand

Creating strategies to build brand value requires understanding the brand with respect to three key components of customer-brand loyalty. Without such understanding there is no clear path for leveraging strengths and eliminating weaknesses.

Product Advantage:
Does the product or service represented by the brand offer any true, objective advantage over the competition? Some product advantages can be assessed via "blind" tests performed among customers, including sensory or human factors measurements. Others (i.e., unique ingredients/nutritional value in packaged goods or "speeds and feeds" in technology products) can be gathered via competitive intelligence activities like comparing labels and/or laboratory tests of "off the shelf" competitive products. Finally, unique operational aspects of manufacturing or delivery may create distinct product advantages with respect to cost or availability.

Figure 2

Market Advantage:

Have past and current sales and marketing efforts given the brand a competitive edge in marketplace? Traditional assessments of distribution coverage and media plans, coupled with tracking measures of awareness, provide the basis for evaluating market advantage. In today's marketplace, however, simple awareness and availability of the brand are merely entry tickets to success. The brand must meaningfully interact with the customer and the channel to provide a level of value that can provide differentiation from competition. Mystery shopping studies and evaluations of direct selling programs and customer/channel support services via telephone or Internet are also essential to evaluating the presence or absence of true market advantage. Comprehension and management of C-BV, then, must extend through all levels of the supply chain.

Communication Advantage:

Is the brand perceived to possess an advantage over the competition among category buyers? Measures of preference versus relevant alternatives continue to be the best indication of true communication advantage. Behavioral data reflecting current customer loyalty (e.g., share of requirements and advocacy measures in the form of confirmed customer referrals) are excellent measures of preference. Such preference can, however, be assessed in many ways. Tracking performance ratings of the brand and its competitors relative to customer needs provides a measure of total preference, as well as valuable diagnostics to leverage strengths and improve weaknesses. Discrete choice models allow the simulation of purchase

behavior under various pricing scenarios to gauge intensity of preference. Finally, direct evaluations of multiple brands with respect to quality and price can provide an easily trended measure of communication advantage.

Linking Customer Profiles and Brand Advantages

Understanding actionable brand advantages, however, means going beyond a global inventory. Advantages must be identified at the customer or customer group level. This requires establishing a linkage between the brand and the customer. Product advantages can generally be leveraged relative to the needs and the mindset of customer targets. The leveraging product of benefits relative to customer needs must utilize information about the customer's mindset to be successful in achieving acceptance and persuasion. Likewise, market advantages can only be leveraged to the extent that they are matched with customer need and are compatible with the customer's purchasing environment. Attempting to leverage a global distribution advantage against a customer group that values convenience but is loyal to a particular channel would obviously be misguided. Finally, communication advantages can generally be leveraged relative to the mindset and environment of targeted customers. Imagery that is too "premium" would be a mismatch for a discriminating customer group that is facing budget constraints due to increasing household size.

Chapter 3: CRM in Practice

Figure 3: C-BV; Strategy Development Applications

Focus on...	Like...	If...
Product Strategies	Restages *Line Extensions* New Products	"Customer Opportunity" needs are incompatible with current brand value proposition
Communication Strategies	Competitive Contrast *Informative* Reward	"Customer Opportunities" are unfamiliar with brand benefits
Market Strategies	Targeted Media *Direct Distribution* Channel Optimization	"Customer Opportunity" behaviors are incompatible with retail channel

By properly sizing the market and capturing the appropriate customer and channel information, a view of the market that enables brands to set strategy based on customer and channel needs across the three advantages of market, product, and communications is complete.

The C-BV Assessment Process

The schematic below provides an overview of the C-BV assessment process. Each stage in the first major phase contributes to the strategies and tactics developed in the second. In the text that follows, details describing each step in the process are provided.

Figure 4

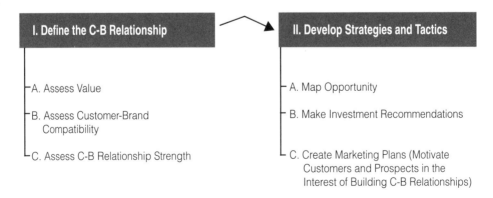

I. Define the C-B Relationship

- A. Assess Value
- B. Assess Customer-Brand Compatibility
- C. Assess C-B Relationship Strength

II. Develop Strategies and Tactics

- A. Map Opportunity
- B. Make Investment Recommendations
- C. Create Marketing Plans (Motivate Customers and Prospects in the Interest of Building C-B Relationships)

Figure 5: Strength of C-B Relationship

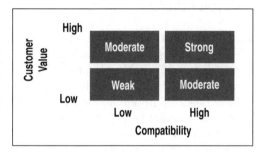

I. Define the Customer-Brand Relationship

The term "relationship" has slowly crept into the vocabulary of marketing professionals in virtually all industries including packaged goods, telecommunications, utilities, travel and entertainment, and high-tech. It is used to describe a number of activities (e.g., relationship marketing, CRM, etc.). And yet, we are hard-pressed to find a finite definition of the term "relationship" in a marketing context. The customer-brand relationship can be defined by the following simple formula:

Relationship Strength
=
f (Value, Compatibility)

There must be a mutual appeal (or interest) between two entities in order to have a strong relationship. Applying this concept to the CRM application, the value of the customer (in the brand's eyes) represents the brand's interest in the relationship. The ability of the brand to satisfy customer needs (i.e., compatibility) represents the customer's interest in the relationship. A C-B relationship is therefore strong when the following two conditions are met:

1. The customer represents relatively high current or potential value to the brand.
2. The customer perceives the brand to be compatible with the customer's needs, attitudes, and behavior.

A. Assess Value

Value refers to the current and future income flows to the brand. Some customers and prospects are better customers and prospects than others. The C-BV metric below illustrates how key purchase dynamics combine to determine value.

While the metric adequately represents the only possible way for a brand to derive financial value from a customer, multiple views of customer value are possible:

▸ Category Value—The total value ($) of a customer or prospect, determined by an individual's (or HH's) total current purchase activity in a particular category. An individual might spend $100 per year buying greeting cards; this person's category value is $100.

Figure 6: C-BV Metric

* Given data availibility, we can incorporate revenue or profit per unit to reach a $ value.

Chapter 3: CRM in Practice

▸ Brand Value—The amount of revenue (or $ profit) contributed to a particular brand. In the example described (above), this same individual might spend $40 per year on Hallmark greeting cards. The brand value of the customer (to Hallmark) is therefore $40.

▸ Growth Opportunity Value—Current category value less brand value. This amount is the level of revenue (or profit) the individual currently contributes to competitive brands. In our example, we would calculate this customer's current growth opportunity to be $60 ($100 - $40 = $60). Although it is possible Hallmark could capture all $60 of the growth opportunity next year, it is highly unlikely.

▸ Future Brand Value—The likely revenue or profit contribution to a particular brand in some future time frame. Assessor® (a proprietary model of Targetbase and The M/A/R/C® Group) forecasts future brand value given the projected impact of future marketing changes. By looking at changes in the way Hallmark markets to the customer in our example, we might anticipate the customer's future brand value to be $50 (next year) versus $40 (current brand value this year).

Calculating value measures at the customer/prospect level is a critical first step in the process. Without it there is no basis on which to determine current returns, growth opportunity, and future brand value in revenue/profit terms. Though the C-BV metric can be directly applied to most categories, the specific value metric used in a given category may differ depending on:

▸ Industry. While SOR as a measure of value is quite standard in packaged goods, for other categories it is meaningless unless marketing goals have been set around an industry-specific variation (e.g., "share-of-wallet" for credit cards, "share-of-communication expenditures" for telecom). Still other "all or nothing" categories (e.g., utilities and local phone service) will quite likely have little use for the concept. In these cases, SOR "drops out of the equation," leaving penetration and category buying rate as the key determinants of value.

▸ Data Availability. The value metric needs to be assigned on the individual customer level, preferably on an ongoing basis. The data may be recorded (transaction databases/behavioral panels), reported (surveys), or inferred (demographics). The important point is we need to calculate a value for each individual, and our approach can vary based on available data. Collecting the data through survey means is always an option. Obviously, this approach requires attention to modeling a link back to whatever internal databases the client owns or purchases. An audit of available data prior to determining the best value metric is a good first step.

Once individual level value has been determined, the next step is to create a classification scheme of customers and prospects into three or more discrete value

Figure 7: Example Customer Value Framework

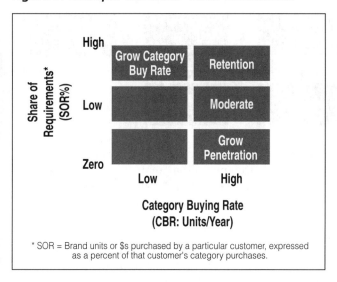

* SOR = Brand units or $s purchased by a particular customer, expressed as a percent of that customer's category purchases.

marketing strategies with each customer and prospect (e.g., applicable marketing strategies are noted in boxes).

For each group in the customer value framework example, the model calculates average category value, brand value, and growth opportunity on a per-customer basis. This is important information in determining appropriate investment levels. A customer's likely "future value" is also important to consider.

segments, based on their current revenue/profit value to the brand. The idea is to develop a framework that can be used to help simplify the view of the marketplace and serve as a basis for determining opportunities, allocating investments, and developing strategy.

Simple cross-tabs of the individual components of the C-BV metric (i.e., penetration, CBR, and/or SOR) using medians as breaks will generally suffice as first steps. A priori client definitions of value breaks or cluster analyses of value indicators are alternative options. The example customer value framework (below) is one way to classify individuals or households into value segments (consider it a "default" frame-work). Depending on industry and data availability, the framework utilized for a given client is likely to vary. One benefit of this approach is that it logically associates basic

Future income flows, at least in the short-term, are best measured attitudinally. The share-of-preference measure in Assessor (i.e., based on the evoked set and chip allocation) is a proven indicator of future share (given other marketing activities by the brand and its competition are accounted for). The Assessor measures that correspond with the C-BV metric are illustrated in figure 8.

Primary research that surveys both reported purchase behaviors and Assessor-based share of preference allows us to compute the short-term future value within each of the value segments. With current value segments serving as the "linking variable," these future values can be modeled back to transactional databases, independent panels, or trackers maintained by the client. This modeling may be attempted

Figure 8: Current and Future Value: Opportunity = (Future Value - Current Value)

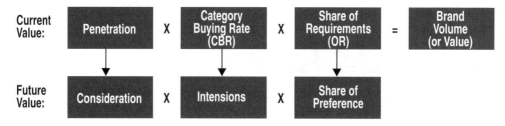

through demographics, transaction history, or even correlations with current value.

B. Assess Customer-Brand Compatibility

Compatibility refers to the "match" between a brand's value proposition (i.e., the brand's unique product, price, promotion, and placement) and the attitudes and behaviors of customers and prospects. The easiest way to determine this match is by trying to discriminate between a brand's very best customers (i.e., those who display a high category buying rate, are behaviorally loyal, and are also attitudinally loyal) and all other customers/prospects.

Using whatever additional attitudinal (e.g., importance ratings, brand perceptions, satisfaction ratings) and behavioral (e.g., usage habits, purchase habits, media habits) data is available, a profile of the brand's "best customers" is compared to the profile of all other individuals. Increasingly, a wealth of this kind of data is captured on an ongoing basis (e.g., panels and tracking studies for attitudes, transactions for behavior). A multivariate technique like discriminant analysis, CHAID, logistic regression, or cluster analysis (all available for large databases in the more recently developed "data

mining" packages) will generally accomplish the "matching" task. The individuals that "match" represent the most "compatible" prospects for relationship enhancement.

In some cases, a "best customer" group will not be available to model against (e.g., line extensions or new brands that are targeted to a completely different audience than is the parent brand). In these cases, a "brand delivery" profile can be constructed based on the brand's strategy or from concept testing research. This "hypothetical best customer" can then serve as the target against which prospect profiles are compared. The same methods and techniques apply.

The degree of accuracy that is required to call a customer/prospect a "good match" will, of course, depend on the data available and the reliability dictated by the goal. Most of these techniques will provide an individual level "probability of membership" in the "best customer" segment so the analyst can set the match criteria. More importantly, these techniques also provide diagnostics on the specific attitudes and behaviors that identify these compatible individuals. This way, a reduced set of critical indicators can be developed into a model that will classify new data (i.e., a customer database or additional event transactions recorded on the same individuals).

The results allow the business to produce three critical outputs:

1. Size the revenue/profit opportunity in each value segment that is compatible with the profile of the best customers. This sizing effectively identifies the "low hanging fruit" available in the market or on the customer database. Depending on the messages the brand sends, the positioning changes the brand makes, the targeting efforts put in place, and the communication/distribution channels utilized, some of the "full potential" value can be more easily realized than the rest. By assessing a customer's or prospect's compatibility with the brand, one can determine just how much of the full-potential growth opportunity can be considered

a "reasonable" brand goal.

2. Profile the differences that still exist between the "best customers" and the "low hanging fruit" for clues to potential barriers to relationship growth and thus, direct strategies toward these barriers.

3. Segment customers/prospects based on the indicators of compatibility and/or the remaining "barriers." Like the value segmentation, this step simplifies the view of the market by converting "ratings" to "groups." The examples (below) show how customer groups with high growth opportunity can be subsegmented to reflect potentially relevant attitudinal and behavioral data.

Figure 9: Nesting Frameworks - Alternative Data, Techniques, and Structures

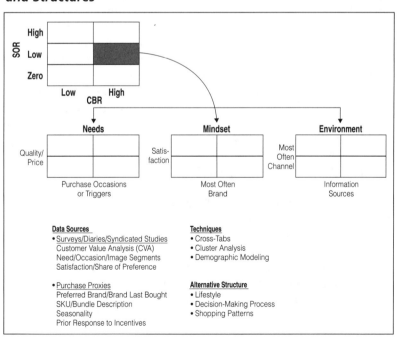

In these examples, "nested" frameworks based on customer needs, mindset, and environment have been created. Note that the actual frameworks created will depend on the data available— alternative data sources, techniques, and structures that might apply are listed. Experience suggests that, given five or six value segments, attitudinal and behavioral data will "correctly classify" about 60% of the individuals for whom data is available. Realize, however, that with five or six segments, one would expect only 17%-20% accuracy by chance. The increased accuracy represents quite an advantage when attempting to target prospects for relationship-building efforts. It should also be noted that choosing attitudes and behaviors that correctly identify high-value customers may be more important than classifying customers overall.

C. Assess C-B Relationship Strength

Relationship strength can now be quantified for each individual customer/ prospect based on the formula referenced earlier:

$$\textit{Strength of C-B Relationship}$$
$$=$$
$$\textit{wt v (Value) X wt c (Compatibility)}$$
$$\textit{Or}$$
$$\textit{wt v (Current + Future Income Flows) X}$$
$$\textit{wt c (Probability of "Best Customer"}$$
$$\textit{Match)}$$

The formula merely provides a method for creating a single metric that includes all the measures discussed. For example, consider the following data for two different customers:

	Customer A	Customer B
Current Value	50	50
Future Value	50	30
Probability of Match	.80	.60

Relationship strength for each of the customers is thus calculated to be:

Customer A = (50 + 50) x .80 = 80
Customer B = (50 + 30) x .60 = 48

In this scenario, the C-BV relationship is stronger with Customer A than it is with Customer B. The "weighting" components (i.e., wtv and wtc) are included in the formula to emphasize the fact that the importance placed on these components may differ depending on the business goals of the client. For example, for smaller brands, current value may carry a very small "weight." Acquisition strategies, and thus greater attention to compatibility, may be more important to drive consideration and trial. The weights are highly subjective and serve as a reminder that the process needs to involve a firm under-standing of the brand's objectives.

Figure 10: Strength of C-B Relationship: Stage

Chapter 3: CRM in Practice

II. Develop Strategies and Tactics

A. Map Opportunity $

Combining the original six value segments (assuming both current and future value have now been taken into account) with the two compatibility classifications, produce the following matrix of 12 relationship segments (see figure 10).

Segments 3, 4, 5, and 6 represent the worst relationship candidates for the brand to pursue. Both CBR and SOR are low. Therefore, even the compatible prospects may not be "worth the effort." Segments 2, 10, and 12 are the very best prospects for short-term, business-building efforts given their relatively high value and their compatibility with the brand. Segments 1, 9, and 11 represent opportunities for longer-term, brand-building efforts designed to extend the brand to customers and prospects that are currently "incompatible." Finally, Segments 7 and 8 represent the best

targets for retention strategies, with Segment 7 being the most "at risk."

The analysis can be simplified by returning to the 2 x 2 matrix in figure 11.

Obviously, the upper right quadrant represents the target for retention strategies and the lower left quadrant represents the least opportunity for return. The more interesting quad-rants are the two with "moderate relationship strength." The lower right quadrant

Figure 11: Strength of C-B Relationship

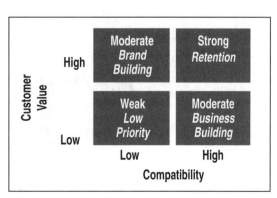

227

represents customers/prospects that are of lower current and future value to the brand, but highly compatible with the brand proposition. Short-term, business-building efforts like promotions and frequency programs will be most successful when targeted to this group.

The upper left quadrant represents the customers/prospects that have a high current and/or future value to the brand, but are incompatible with the brand proposition. Longer-term, brand-building efforts like line extensions, alternative channels of distribution, and "image" campaigns should offer the greatest return when directed toward this group.

B. Make Investment Recommendations

Once the quadrants have been constructed and the opportunity values have been calculated, strategies regarding investment levels and customer motivation can be developed. Though initially time consuming to collect, spending data is essential to calculating return on customer investment (ROCI). Collect the spending data in aggregate, then per-form a spending

allocation procedure to associate dollars spent with individual customer/prospects.

This process involves taking each spending type and determining the "share of investment" that should be assigned to each customer in data. In the case of advertising dollars, the media plan is input to a model that determines reach and frequency of media across various demographic profiles. Most advertising agencies and media buying firms employ such a model in determining targeted rating points (TRPs). This output is an algorithm and set of weights reflecting each customer's share of this spending.

Other spending is allocated based on the customer's purchase activity in certain distribution channels. For example, if a brand spent $1MM in the drugstore channel on signage, customers frequenting this channel are allocated a greater share of the total drug store dollars spent than are those customers who shop there less often. Using similar allocation processes for each spending type, one can eventually allocate all remaining marketing

Figure 12: Which Customers and Prospects Are Brand Spending $ Reaching?

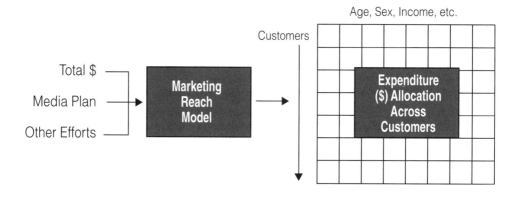

expenditures across customer/prospects in data.

The figure below illustrates the results for one client among the value segments (without the compatibility analysis performed). By comparing spending levels versus growth opportunities, this client chose to spend more on growing SOR among the "middle right" segment and less on promoting occasions to the "upper left" group. Using this model, recommendations relative to the absolute level of spending, the targeting of spending to various segments, and the mix of spending to achieve better efficiency (i.e., ensuring the expenditure reaches the target) are made.

Returning to the four quadrants (i.e., Value x Compatibility) this "opportunity to investment ratio" within quadrants

Figure 13: Marketing Investment Allocation Results (Specialty Retail Case Study)

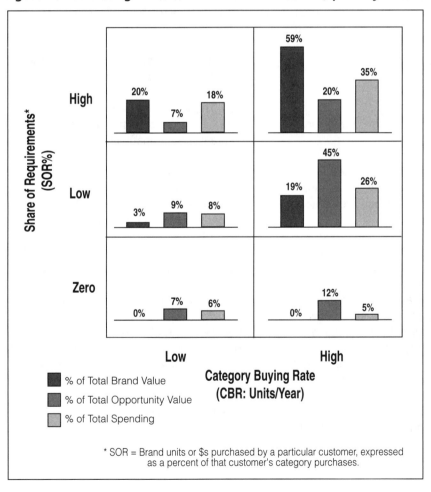

provides a straightforward method for determining how to spread marketing expenditures across broad strategic objectives like retention, business building, and brand building.

C. Create Marketing Plans: Motivating Customers and Prospects in the Interest of Building C-B Relationships

Developing product, communication, and market strategies to motivate stronger relationships with valuable customers and prospects is obviously much more of an "art" compared to the "science" previously described. The C-BV process bridges the science and art by providing specific insights to the creation and implementation of marketing communications.

The C-BV process provides three such insights:

1. An attitudinal/behavioral profile of the brand's best customers against which retention programs and messages can be developed.
2. An understanding of the differences in the profiles of a brand's best customers and their "lower value/compatible" counterparts. Specifically, purchase motivations that help determine the incentives that would lead a buyer to change his/her behavior (e.g., sampling programs, informational appeals, rewards, etc.). Strategies can then be devised that attempt to motivate customers and prospects with respect to these incentives.
3. An understanding of the differences in the profiles of a brand's best customers and their "higher value/incompatible"

counterparts. Specifically, higher level attitudes and behaviors (i.e., the ones we segmented on earlier) for clues as to how to close the "compatibility gap."

Gaps in the "needs" profile may suggest product strategies that lead to line extensions or new sub-brands. Gaps in the "mindset" profile may suggest communication strategies that inform and close knowledge gaps. Gaps in "environment" profiles like usage and purchase may suggest market strategies that lead to new channels or delivery systems.

The diagnostic profiles of the differences between the various segments provide the first steps in identifying and sizing these gaps. These profiles are generally an output from the analytic techniques used to create the compatibility measure. Additional custom research can help further quantify the product, communication, and market advantages that can be leveraged versus specific competitors within the opportunity segments.

Once these global, strategic gaps have been identified, specific customer groups can be targeted for further qualitative work. Focus groups, one-on-one interviews, and ethnographic research (i.e., observing the customer's interaction with the brand) can be used to delve deeper into the motivations that drive current choices and the barriers to future behavioral change.

Customer Focused Marketing - A Strategy for Success

Title: *Customer Focused Marketing. A Strategy for Success.*

Author: *Ron Brunt, International Computers Limited*

Abstract: *Ron Brunt describes how new decision support systems enable retailers to gain a more detailed understanding of their customer base*

"*Mass marketing, with its one price fits all approach, has been rendered obsolete by the sheer power of customer information - information which enables retailers to offer different price and benefit packages to their different customers and then measure its effectiveness in an easy, cost-effective way.*"
Brian P. Woolf

When the tools change, the rules change

Forward-looking retailers have always gained advantage by timely adoption of technology. Scanning and point of sale devices offered such an opportunity fifteen years ago. The new technology of data warehousing has opened the field once again. Early adopters have reaped rewards in the form of increased profits and reduced costs. Application of the technology is facilitating new approaches to marketing and merchandising. One of the most powerful is customer focused marketing.

Data warehousing gives retailers full access to detailed customer and transaction information previously not available. Analysis of this information has replaced retailing myths with hard facts that mandate and enable a transformation of retailers' core business strategies from product focused to customer focused marketing. This strategy increases profits by identifying the most profitable shoppers and those with a high profit potential; and then targeting them with customer specific rewards and incentives. It also cuts costs by focusing marketing spend where it will have the greatest impact.

All customers are not equal

When decision support technology was first applied to retailing data, it was discovered that in the course of a year the top 20% of a food retailer's customers spends 50 times the amount of its bottom 20%. Analysis further revealed that the common strategy of offering discounts to everyone is flawed. It rewards and encourages the least profitable group of shoppers - the cherry pickers who buy only the advertised specials - in the hope that they will convert to profitable, loyal customers. In fact, few do. What's more, retailers have been pursuing this strategy at the expense of their most profitable, loyal customers, who subsidise the special prices. Finally, to add insult to injury, the cherry pickers speed through express lanes, while the loyal shoppers wait in lines two and three deep!

Behaviour follows reward

Rewarding profitable buying behaviour stimulates repeat behaviour. We see this in our own experience with for example, frequent flyer miles; and it has been shown in studies. By rewarding profitable shopping behaviour, retailers will encourage more shoppers to be more loyal and more profitable, while removing reinforcements to unprofitable cherry picking.

The technology that revealed the shortcomings of "one price fits all" retailing has supplied a remedy. Retailers can pinpoint and reward loyal, profitable customers and encourage more shoppers to increase their loyalty, while letting the unprofitable convenience shopper pay full price.

"Customer specific marketing ... has exploded as a marketing practice because of the computer's ability to collect, process and analyse customer information. ... My observation over the past three years has been that the more a retailer moves away

from average pricing towards differentiated pricing, the more his profits increase. ... The more companies increase the degree of differentiation at [the] second level, the more their profits increase."
Brian P Woolf, Customer Specific Marketing

Customer focused marketing

Identifying customer segments and marketing to each one is known as customer focused marketing. It enables retailers to become as intimately familiar with their customer base and as responsive to the individual needs of their most profitable customers as a corner-shop owner. This knowledge is used to encourage and reinforce loyalty; and to modify shopping behaviour to realise the full profit potential of each customer relationship.

How do you know if a customer has profit potential? Compare their expected spend levels (from demographic data) with their actual spend, or look for gaps in their shopping patterns. You might note that a loyal customer never shops in your health and beauty department. So you might link a discount on a known favourite item with the purchase of a health and beauty item. And if the customer has a regular buying cycle for this favourite item, you can increase the attraction of the offer by mailing it just before the next purchase is due. This is accomplished by identifying the needs of small customer clusters, not by hand picking actual individuals.

Differentiated pricing

One way to encourage and reward loyalty is through differentiated pricing. Instead of wasting money on sales and special deals offered to all, retailers can make different offers to different customers at the checkout, depending on their shopping history. Item promotions can be structured to give different discounts for different levels of spend. Offers to encourage loyalty may be run concurrently. A grocer in the USA offered a free turkey to customers spending an average of $50 or more per week in the two months leading up to Thanksgiving. The number of households exceeding that threshold went up by 20% compared with the previous year.

A few guidelines have proven effective in customer focused marketing programmes. Setting self-qualifying thresholds; making rewards proportional to spending; and avoiding caps are all advised by those with experience in the field. The variety of incentives and rewards you can offer to make your programme unique is limited only by your imagination.

But how will customers react?

Retailers anxious about how customers would receive these new pricing strategies have been reassured by the positive response. Customers appreciate their loyalty being rewarded and see the reward as a fair exchange. Receiving offers tailored to their needs also makes them feel recognised as individuals. And it avoids antagonising customers with offers that are irrelevant to their needs.

The Way Forward

Transformation of your core business strategy is not achieved overnight. While a variety of routes can work in specific situations, we recommend the following path, which offers specific benefits at each step of the way.

1. Find an information systems partner

Make sure you have a technology partner who can work with you throughout your journey. ICL can handle the total solution, in whatever phases suit you. More importantly, as retail specialists, we understand how to use the technology to support your business strategy.

2. Introduce a loyalty programme

A good first step is to encourage customers to join a loyalty programme. The aim is to enrol as many as possible and gather data for analysis. Customers want something in return for giving you their data. A simple points system, redeemable as tender for purchases, has proven to be very effective, but other options, such as charity links, may be considered.

"Even discount merchandisers can benefit from customer-intimate approaches: No-one would argue that delivering more of what your customer wants than Wal-Mart is not a good tactic."
Seth Kranz and Jerry Love, RIS News, January 1996

Customers, especially loyal ones, want to feel valued and appreciated. Club membership gives you an opportunity to thank them for their business. A club newsletter can include offers for club members only.

Which type of programme is best?

There are two ways loyalty programmes can operate: batch and online. Batch programmes are simpler to run, but do not give the customer immediate rewards. Customer points are calculated and disbursed periodically, generally through the mail. Online systems solutions are more fully integrated with point of sales systems to offer immediate reward, redemption of points and other benefits. ICL offers both batch and online options.

3. Segment the customer base and offer differentiated pricing

Once you have gathered a reasonable amount of customer data, you can begin to harvest benefits from your database. You can analyse the Recency, Frequency and Monetary Value of customer visits, to begin segmenting and understanding your customer base. Now you can introduce differentiated pricing strategies and offers that further encourage and reward loyalty. You can also tailor some special offers that encourage purchase of higher margin goods, to increase the profitability of your customer base.

An excellent way to further increase loyalty at this phase, as well as to add variety to your programme, is to introduce continuity offers such as the 'Thanksgiving Turkey Offer'. These give a larger reward for a larger commitment over time.

4. Offer further incentives to top customers

Once spend from card holders has reached about 50% of total spend in a store, you may introduce further benefits limited to your most profitable group, such as a special checkout lane, parking privileges, or special offers. At this point, loyalty and profits will be up and your customers increasingly satisfied. Now is the time to capture the flow of data from the point of sales and take advantage of the sophisticated analysis available using a data warehouse based decision support system.

5. Introduce customer focused marketing

A decision support system enables you to gain a more detailed understanding of your customer base for skilled marketers to exploit. You can identify those customers with the highest profit potential and market to each of them differently, engaging the full potential of the loyalty programme to create a mass market of one. Information flowing into the warehouse will enable you to assess their effectiveness. At last, you can replace gut feel judgements with hard facts; and your marketers' creative skills can be applied, more appropriately, to devising attractive new incentives and programmes.

CRM. A Guide to Marketing, Sales, and Service Transformation

Title: CRM. A Guide to Marketing, Sales, and Service Transformation
Author: Deloitte Consulting
Abstract: The purpose of this report is to share some of the major trends occurring in the CRM marketplace. The document is divided into three sections. First, we deliver the results of a recent survey of 225 firms that engaged in the process over the past year. Next, we present a structured approach for how to manage your initiative to maximize your chances of success. In the final section, we profile seven firms that, by adopting the principles of CRM, are changing the way the game is played in their industries. By deciding to focus on your marketing, sales and service challenges, your organization is already headed in the right direction. The insights contained in this report will assist you in turning your efforts into successful action.

Biography: see end article

Chapter 3: CRM in Practice

Preface

Today, no single business topic commands more attention, yet generates more confusion, than transforming the way you market, sell, and service customers to build a competitive advantage – otherwise known as Customer Relationship Management (CRM). On one hand, some organizations that reengineer their CRM processes are reporting revenue increases of up to 51 percent, margin improvements of 2 percent, decreases in cost of sales of as much as 46 percent, reductions in sell cycle length of 25 percent, and increases in customer satisfaction ratings of 20 percent and more. On the other hand, we are still seeing claims that 50, 60 and even 70 percent of all CRM initiatives generate minimal gains or no improvement at all.

The truth surrounding CRM is elusive. Is the answer to all business challenges the transformation of marketing, sales, and customer service? Or will your efforts represent an enormous waste of time, effort, and money? Based on the CSO

Forum's review of over 1,400 CRM initiatives, and Deloitte Consulting's experience working side by side with clients in over 300 marketing, sales, and service transformation projects, worldwide, our conclusion is simple: Your success depends on the correct approach.

The difference between the success or failure of a CRM project lies in the knowledge and ability that an organization brings to its effort. Companies that know what problems they need to solve, how to sort through the hundreds of technology solutions available, and how to structure and manage their process reengineering efforts – these are the ones achieving breakthrough results through CRM. And as they succeed, they are setting the benchmark level for performance that all their competitors must meet.

Section 1 State of the Marketplace Review

Summary

Deloitte Consulting, a global leader in CRM consulting, prides itself on its track record of customer satisfaction. Our collaborative approach and focus on achieving sustainable business results quickly make us the choice of many clients to join them on their CRM journey. As part of the efforts to provide services of value to you, we have teamed with the CSO Forum, a leading authority on CRM benchmarking, to develop this guide to CRM transformation. We hope you find it of value.

Since 1993, the CSO Forum – a Boulder, Colorado-based research firm – has conducted an annual benchmark study to help track vital trends in the area once known as sales force automation (SFA), which has today evolved into Customer Relationship Management – a radical transformation of the ways companies market, sell, and service. To date, we have surveyed more than 1,400 such corporate initiatives.

In just six years, the CRM marketplace has changed in ways its pioneers could not even have envisioned. The sense of urgency surrounding projects has increased as companies look for new ways to remain competitive: increasing revenues, maintaining margins, shortening the sales cycle, increasing customer satisfaction. The scope of these initiatives, moreover, has broadened from a focus on the individual salesperson to include all touch points to the customer – sales, marketing, customer service, R&D, finance, management, channel partners, and even customers themselves. At the same time, the technical complexity of projects has increased as companies seek to integrate front office systems, back office systems, and the Internet, giving timely information access to every appropriate user within the enterprise.

To learn where the market is currently headed, in early 1999 we completed a review of an additional 202 CRM initiatives. We surveyed the executive management, marketing, sales, service, and information systems professionals ultimately responsible for these projects. Through this effort, we uncovered a wealth of insights into the critical success factors that generate meaningful results from reengineering investments. The following summary of our research outlines the major trends now transforming the CRM marketplace. By delineating these trends, we aim to help companies better align their business and technology strategies to deal with the marketing, sales, and service challenges they currently face.

Research Project Background

The 202 companies surveyed were divided into two, nearly-equal groups. The first group included those firms in the implementation process. Under this definition, we included organizations just starting to review their operations and technology, all the way up to firms in the actual pilot phase of their CRM initiative. The second group included companies that had already implemented a project – that is to say, organizations that had rolled out their system into full production. Of these

202 companies, 47 percent were manufacturing firms, 39 percent service organizations, 7 percent distributors, 5 percent retail firms, and 2 percent other (government agencies, charitable organizations, etc.).

In gathering preliminary information for this research project, we asked participants to complete a survey form. Where projects had already been rolled out, we conducted phone interviews to gain a more detailed perspective on the organization's project experiences. In cases where companies had hard performance numbers for their projects, we conducted onsite meetings. (Individual project results were kept in strict confidence and used only to create a summary analysis.)

Customer Relationship Management Project Trends

To begin, we explored the business objectives of each firm in the survey. What was driving them to undertake the project? The answers, as seen in Figure 1, reflect two interesting shifts from prior surveys. Six years ago, when this research project was first conducted, most firms were primarily focusing on issues associated with efficiency: increasing selling time, decreasing paper work, reducing administrative burdens, etc. Now companies are focusing on increasing selling effectiveness as well.

Organizations are realizing that in order to achieve their business objectives, increasing efficiency alone is not enough. "If I only make my sales reps more efficient, that just means my average rep can now make

Chapter 3: CRM in Practice

Figure 1: CRM project Goals

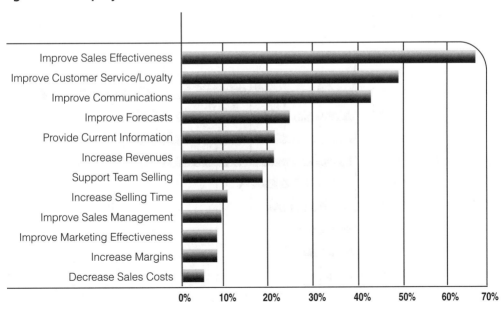

more average sales calls," said the vice president of sales for a manufacturing firm. "What I need is to have my average rep make world-classsales calls." The issue is effectiveness . CRM leadership teams are exploring how they can bolster the abilities of their people rather than just automating what they do.

The second shift in project goals is an increased focus on improving customer satisfaction and loyalty. Few companies reported that they had a dominant product advantage in their marketplace. Instead, many stated it was not what they sell, but how they sell to and service customers that helped them establish long-term business partnerships. They are therefore expanding their CRM efforts by exploring ways to improve the vendor/customer relationship.

The survey participants were next asked to describe where in the company they were targeting their initiatives. As organizations go beyond sales and service efficiency and concentrate on customer satisfaction and sales effectiveness, they are expanding the scope of their project as well. It is now common for departments such as marketing, service, and telebusiness to take an active role in CRM projects, as is shown in Figure 2. The goal is to share knowledge across the enterprise, providing access to the information wherever it is needed.

Another project trend is worth noting: Companies are expanding the areas in which they use CRM systems. Early CRM systems were designed to help sales or service personnel place or follow up on a call when they were at headquarters. The trend now is to allow access to CRM capabilities when working from remote locations, or on the road, as seen in Figure 3.

Figure 2: Targeted Users

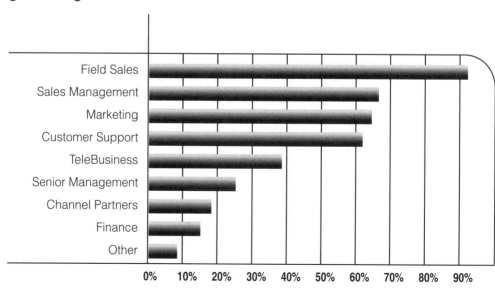

Figure 3: Planned System Usage

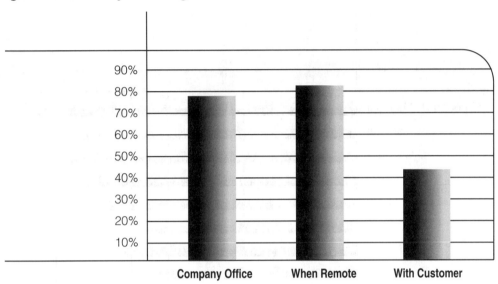

| | Company Office | When Remote | With Customer |

In the past year, sales and service reps have expressed a desire to have more knowledge and information at their fingertips while dealing directly with the customer. The reps surveyed said that during a sales call, they would like to be able to: conduct presentations (71.6 percent), conduct needs analysis (65.1 percent), generate proposals (46.7 percent), answer customer questions (56.3 percent), and perform product configurations (20.9 percent).

Customer Relationship Management Technology Trends

The technology choices companies are making mirror these project goals, as the inclusion of CRM tools and systems that address effectiveness and service objectives are on the rise. We continue to see a transition from simple systems to more complex applications that address a variety of functions across the enterprise. An increasing number of projects include applications such as opportunity managers, marketing encyclopedias, proposal generators and configurators as part of their CRM system. The importance of leveraging the Internet and e-Business as a platform for sales and service has also skyrocketed. Figure 4 shows the variety of technologies that companies are integrating into their CRM solution.

Many more companies are planning to link front office and back office systems. Over 18 percent of the companies surveyed stated they planned on integrating their CRM and ERP systems as part of their initial rollout. Nearly twice as many intend to do so at a later project phase.

When we asked CRM project teams to review the specific products they were

Figure 4: CRM Planned Functionality

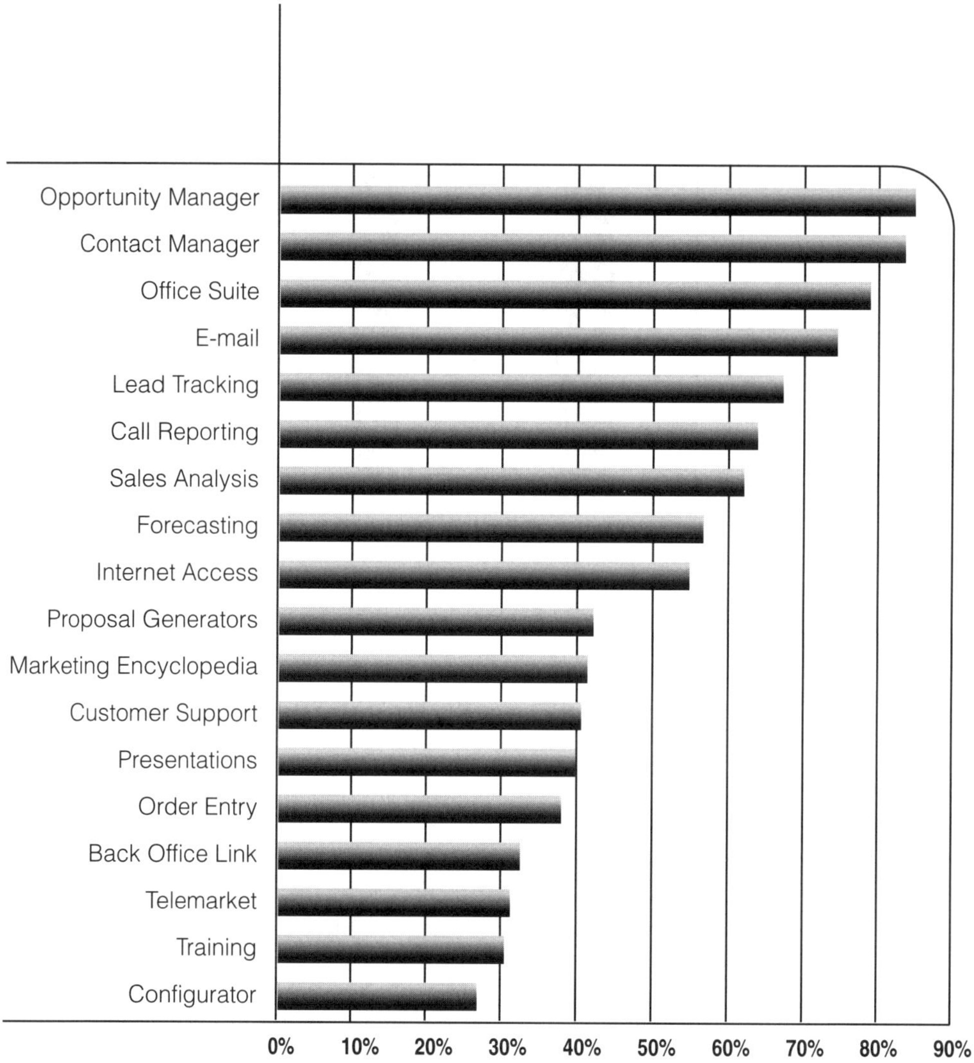

Functionality	Percentage
Opportunity Manager	~84%
Contact Manager	~84%
Office Suite	~80%
E-mail	~75%
Lead Tracking	~67%
Call Reporting	~63%
Sales Analysis	~61%
Forecasting	~56%
Internet Access	~54%
Proposal Generators	~42%
Marketing Encyclopedia	~41%
Customer Support	~40%
Presentations	~40%
Order Entry	~37%
Back Office Link	~32%
Telemarket	~30%
Training	~30%
Configurator	~26%

evaluating and purchasing, a significant market trend emerged: a shakeout of front office vendors appears to be at hand. Today, there are over 500 sales and service automation tool developers, with new Internet-based players still entering the market. Two years ago, no real market leaders existed. But in the course of our recent interviews, a dozen CRM players were mentioned far more often than the rest.

As the market matures, we expect two developments. First, the general CRM market will continue to be dominated by fewer and fewer larger players. The smaller companies will be forced to change their business focus in order to survive. They will either need to select a market niche to focus on – as some players are already doing in vertical segments like pharmaceutical, insurance, and advertising – or they will look to be acquired by back office system vendors looking to broaden their product line. Firms who fail to respond to this market shift could easily fail. Second, the number of CRM industry players could start to decline as early as 2000.

With the vast number of product choices available, many CRM project teams reported that wading through the offerings – and really understanding the differences between vendors – was difficult. But the technology evaluation process can be made easier. Figure 5 highlights the sources that CRM teams recommended for reliable information on product alternatives.

Overall word-of-mouth was rated as the best source of reliable information on vendors and product offerings. This included getting insights from consulting firms on their experiences implementing various systems, reading product reviews and user stories in technical and business publications, and talking directly to users of systems at other companies. The Internet has also given people access to a wealth of information. Vendor sites and user group sites were the two most commonly mentioned places to search on the Web.

Using the above sources can help reduce the number of potential vendors from 500 to 5 rather quickly, but making your final choice still requires a lot of work. Companies that completed their technology selection process reported that understanding what tasks a product performs is not enough; you also need to have a complete understanding of how the product operates. We asked these firms to rate the value of various techniques they used to compare solutions. Using a 1 to 5 scale, with 5 being most valuable, Figure 6 ranks the evaluation steps mentioned.

Chapter 3: CRM in Practice

Figure 5: Best Resources for Reliable Vendor Information

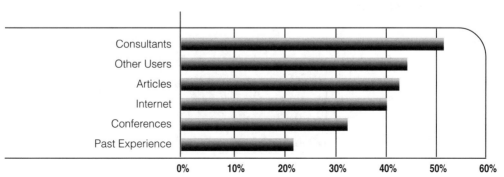

Figure 6: Best Evaluation Steps

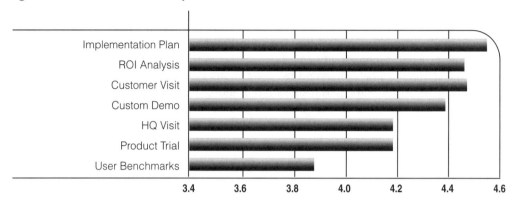

Tap into a vendor's project experiences. Ask them to develop an implementation plan and an ROI analysis along with their proposal. Spend a day with existing users of products. Meet with the development, support and management teams of the vendor firms. All are valuable tactics to help separate myth from reality in understanding competitive offerings.

We also asked these firms to describe how they made their final technology choices. Figure 7 overviews the top 5 decision criteria mentioned. Ease of use and functionality fit were cited as key – you need to ensure that your users will support the systems.

Customizability was also highlighted – few of the products purchased were useable right out of the box. Due to the specific ways that a company sells to and supports customers, changes to the systems almost always need to be made.

A final technology-related trend emerged when we surveyed firms on their investments. The cost of implementing a CRM solution has been falling steadily. We asked companies who had fully deployed their systems to calculate how much they spent on hardware, software, system customization, training and support. For the first time in five years that number decreased from the previous year. The new

Figure 7: Decision Criteria

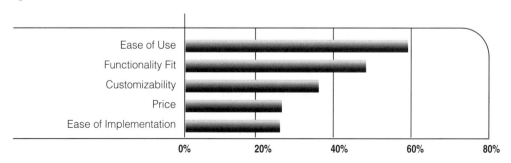

Figure 8: CRM Project Cost Breakdown

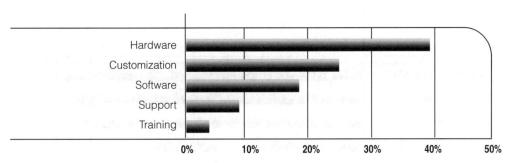

average investment per rep came in at $9,864,versus $10, 385 in 1998, and $13,039 in 1997. A cost breakdown is shown in Figure 8.

The major cost changes from the 1997 survey occurred in two areas. The first was the cost of the marketing, sales, and service automation software. The competitive nature of the CRM market has resulted in software costs falling this year to $1,875 per seat from $3,800 two years ago, as some vendors use price as a way to win deals. The costs may continue to notch down as the vendor shakeout continues.

Customization costs also declined. The leading edge vendors continue to significantly enhance the robustness of their systems, thereby reducing the need for major customization. In addition, they are also providing new development tools to assist in streamlining the implementation process. This has helped reduce the cost of customization from $3,800 per seat in 1997 to just under $2,560, a trend that should continue into 2000.

It should be noted that these figures represent the average investments companies are making in their systems. Specific project costs varied greatly, from a low of $2,200 to a high of $32,550 per user. The CRM initiatives generating the best results have a significantly higher price tag than the average. As companies integrate some of the more complex marketing, sales, and service tools into their CRM systems, and invest in additional training on new business processes, the investments can easily come in at approximately $16,840 per rep.

Customer Relationship Management Project Implementation Trends
While selecting the right technology to support a CRM initiative is an important task, other issues need to be confronted. When asked to rate the top three challenges that they encountered during their project, organizations that had fully deployed their Customer Relationship Management systems cited a number of additional critical problems, as seen in Figure 9.

Figure 9: Toughest Challenges

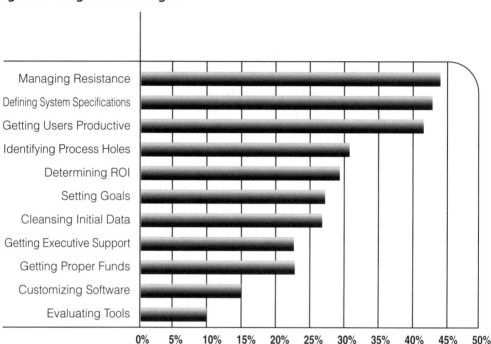

Several process-related obstacles must be overcome when embarking on a CRM project. The overall project goals have to be clearly identified and agreed upon and executive sponsorship is key . Weaknesses in the existing marketing, sales, and service processes must be identified. Well-defined specifications must be developed to map how technology needs to be designed to enable change. Failing to perform any of these tasks competently can jeopardize a project's chances for success.

Even more important are people-related issues. The best processes in the world, supported by the latest technology, can still result in a failed project if the people involved are not behind the effort.

Ensuring that you have executive support, providing the right level of training and support to get new users comfortable using the new systems, and managing the potential resistance to change were listed as critical people-related challenges that CRM teams frequently have to deal with.

While transformation efforts still require a great deal of time, effort, and money, they are starting to produce solid and measurable results. Past projections from industry groups and analysts have shown failure rates as high as 80 percent. But organizations are now starting to crack the code on how to successfully reengineer their marketing, sales, and service operations, as reflected in Figure 10.

Figure 10: Project Results vs. Expectations

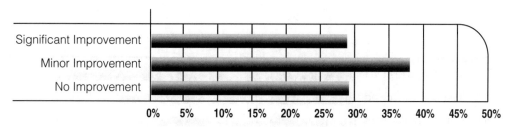

For the first time, a majority of projects surveyed said that they were achieving at least some improvement.

The most successful CRM initiatives are generating significant returns on investment. A few examples include the following:

Combining the capabilities of an opportunity management system and a configurator, a $2.5 billion manufacturing firm cut the time for generating a custom bid from 10 days to a matter of hours. This helped cut the sales cycle length by 25 percent.

A $1.7 billion medical products distribution firm implemented a mobile computing-based marketing encyclopedia that allowed their sales reps to access information on the 30,000 products they sold. New product introduction close rates increased 400 percent and revenues increased 30 percent per rep within 120 days of system rollout.

A communications firm implemented an Internet-based needs analysis system that allows customers to determine on their own what products or services they need.

They are now generating over $3.5 million in sales per day with this system.

Results like these can change the competitive balance in a market, giving one firm a significant advantage over other companies offering similar products or services. But success is still not guaranteed. The above numbers still show that nearly one-third of all CRM projects still generate no meaningful results. We asked the firms who had been through the process to share their recommendations for how organizations just starting (or restarting) a transformation project should structure their initiative. Their top 10 suggestions are seen in Figure 11.

Chapter 3: CRM in Practice

Figure 11: Recommendations

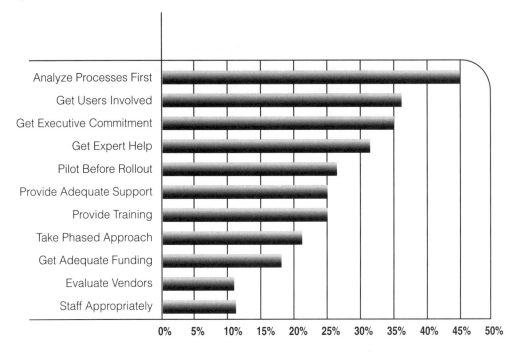

In projects that fell short of meeting all expectations, at least one of the above items was missing from each project. The most critical of these items is the need to analyze your processes prior to focusing on technology. The most successful projects took the time to look at how they are marketing, selling, and servicing, as well as how their customers are buying. In doing so, they identified the specific problems they needed to address, and focused their CRM project on dealing with those challenges. Having established a specific goal made the rest of the job much easier.

We hope that the insights shared by other companies dealing with marketing, sales, and service challenges are helpful to your organization. In the next section, we discuss, in more depth, the critical factors that contribute to generating CRM wins.

Chapter 3: CRM in Practice

Section 2 Critical Success Factors

Why is there such a wide disparity in the results generated by CRM initiatives? To begin answering that question, our research efforts focused on the 21 percent of marketing, sales, and service organizations whose projects met or exceeded expectations. We searched for common trends and discovered seven critical success factors. We encourage organizations embarking on a transformation program to examine what they share with these success stories.

Executive Sponsorship

Universally, successful CRM initiatives have an executive project champion. Who is the project champion? Individual titles may be vice president of sales, general manager, vice president of marketing, president, or partner. They are the individuals ultimately responsible for ensuring that their company or business unit is able to compete effectively in today's increasingly complex marketplaces. In a business environment where product or pricing advantages are short-lived, and quality is a given, this is the person assigned the challenge of transforming the way a company markets, sells, and services to sustain a competitive advantage.

This executive oversees the initiative, ensures the project stays on track, and breaks down any barriers that get in the way of success. They have enough authority to make changes happen, and they also clearly understand that if they continue to sell and service in the late 1990s the way they did in the '70s, '80s,

and early '90s, they may not make it past the turn of the century.

The role of project champion can be broken into three parts. They serve as a visionary, a motivator, and a leg breaker. As a visionary, they set specific targets for the transformation project: increase sales by 20 percent, improve margins by a percentage point, shorten the sell cycle by a third, double new product introduction close rates. They give the project team a specific goal to achieve.

As the motivator, they realize that while goals come from the top down, solutions need to come from the bottom up. They provide the transformation team with the time, money, and resources to develop solutions for achieving the objectives that have been set. They then fight for the investments that need to be made to implement sound reengineering strategies.

Finally, as a leg breaker, they continually ensure that the organization realizes that success of the transformation initiative is imperative to the firm's future survival. When problems do occur during the project, they focus their people on working through the issues rather than dwelling on them.

How important is a project champion to a company embarking on a transformation project? In organizations absent a project champion, studies may get completed, some sub-processes may be redesigned, and technology may be purchased – but the chances of meaningful change occurring are low. CRM is not as much about marketing, sales, or service automation, as it is about marketing, sales, and service process optimization. Since CRM processes span multiple functional areas within a firm, an executive champion is required if enterprise-wide improvement is to take place.

Commitment to Process
Some project teams make the mistake of immediately focusing their attention on technology. However, the best CRM initiatives first focus on process. These teams understand that technology is an enabler, not a solution by itself. They therefore invest the time to illuminate and correct flaws in their marketing, sales, and service strategies prior to doing anything else.

To identify these flaws, project teams conduct an up-front analysis of how their company is marketing, selling, and servicing – and just as important, how and when their customers are buying. They start by interviewing marketing, sales, and service personnel to find out what they do, how they do it, and what information they rely on to do their work. Next, they focus on determining what users see as the barriers to their own success: difficulty in getting hold of product experts, inability to access current information, difficulty in generating error-free configurations.

Project teams often go through the same process with their customers, reviewing their prospects' buy cycle steps: what they do to evaluate competitive offerings, select the right vendor, and cost-justify the expense. Again, they look to identify process flaws where it becomes difficult for the prospect to buy, such as taking too

long to respond to customer inquires, delivering incomplete proposals, or providing poor post-sales support.

Next, having determined the flaws in the process, CRM teams assess the causes. They determine why it takes several days to get a lead to the field, why it takes a week to get a custom bid signed off on internally, why salespeople do not have access to key customer support information. And they determine the costs for letting that problem continue.

By doing some initial homework, CRM teams discover the most important problems they need to target for solution, and they create a baseline of performance that they can use for comparison after the new systems are installed. This process makes the rest of the project flow much easier.

Intelligent Use of Technology
When reviewing the best CRM projects, project teams' technology choices are directly tied to solving specific business challenges. If reps are having difficulties communicating between headquarters and the field, they may have selected an opportunity manager. If they are experiencing a high rate of errors in processing orders, they may have turned to a configurator.
If sales management is trying to reduce the time it takes to get new salespeople productive, they may have selected a marketing encyclopedia. The bottom line is that they select technology that supports their processes, versus expecting their processes to change to accommodate technology.

While they may take a tactical approach of starting with a single department, such as marketing, field sales, or customer service, successful CRM projects ensure that the technology foundation they use is flexible enough to meet future expansion needs. They understand that they will want to connect all the users across the enterprise into a single system, allowing everyone to have access to the customer information they need to do their job. This holistic approach to selecting the technology foundation means that they select a more comprehensive software system than they need initially, so that they have the ability to grow in the future.

When evaluating CRM tools, they do not just focus on what a product does, but how it does it. They do their homework to fully understand the system architecture around which vendors are building their programs. They select the solutions that best fit their own internal information system strategies, versus attempting to change their technology plans to accommodate a vendor.

Assemble the Right Team

The best CRM initiatives ensure their project team has competencies in four areas. The first of these is reengineering. CRM is not about doing everything 5 percent better. It is about doing a few things an order of magnitude better. This requires an organization to be willing to transform critical components of their business. The key to making this work is to have representatives on the project team who have no vested interest in the status quo: You need people who will ask why

things are done a certain way, and challenge the group to change.

The second competency area is system customization. Regardless of what CRM solution the companies surveyed selected, some degree of customization was always required. As this is a fairly young industry, most of the products have been developed using the latest technologies. Successfully modifying these CRM tools to fit the workflow of a company is critical to gaining end user acceptance, and therefore is typically assigned to developers who are skilled in programming environments in which the tools are written. Dealing with system integration issues is equally important, especially if a company plans to support mobile users. This third competency requirement necessitates that an IT organization successfully size the network correctly, support the application with adequate power on the user's desktop or laptop workstations, and adequately design a data synchronization strategy.

System rollout support is the final area companies need to ensure they have covered. Implementing CRM systems normally requires users to change the way they work. Having change management skill sets on the CRM project team and providing adequate help desk support coverage is necessary to assist users make the transition to the new way of doing business.

The most successful CRM project teams assess their skill levels in all four of these areas. When they discover an area that they are weak in, they involve outsiders to fill that role. They may add representatives from sister divisions, or outside consultants, but they ensure their team has members experienced in successfully implementing complex projects.

Take People into Consideration

The human side of reengineering is often neglected in project planning, but not because the teams don't think it is important. More often it is because they do not know how they should approach the issue. Organizations that reported exceptionally high end user buy-in for their projects shared a number of strategies for how to manage the people part of the CRM equation. Some examples are as follows:

The first sale your CRM system should make is an internal sale. To start to build end user support for their CRM initiative, a paper manufacturer invited one of their suppliers' salespeople to show their sales force how he sold. This parts supplier had rolled out a very successful project the year before. When their sales rep did a day-in-my-life demonstration of their system at the paper manufacturer's annual sales meeting, he got a standing ovation. Having a peer present the potential for CRM helped the project team win the support of the sales force early in the process.

An often mentioned strategy is to actively involve users in the project. A semiconductor manufacturer chose the region that would be the pilot for their system very early in the project, and involved those nine salespeople at each major milestone in the process. The field reps initially identified the problems they saw existing in the way they sold to and serviced customers. They took part in the half-day meetings with the top four CRM vendors. They reviewed and signed off on the ROI plan for the project. They took part in full-day joint application design sessions with information systems to work on the screen layouts and workflow diagrams for the system. The end result was that by the time they were asked to start pilot testing the system, they had already accepted responsibility for the success of the project; it had become their project as well.

Another idea was shared by the leader of a consulting firm who wanted to demonstrate to his sales force that the management team was committed to the success of the CRM project. To do this, instead of having the company's training group handle educating the reps on the use of the system, he placed that responsibility on the sales managers. The sales managers attended a train-the-trainer class, and then they were required to conduct the classes for the salespeople. Seeing their managers become proficient at using the new sales tools created a sense of importance for the project.

Finally, when a manufacturing firm surveyed their salespeople, they found that only 23 percent of them had previous exposure to PCs. So, early in the project they decided to budget extra resources for follow-up training on an as-needed basis, after the kickoff session. Several of their reps struggled with learning how to use computers, let alone complex interactive selling tools. But instead of allowing them to become increasingly frustrated, they made trainers available starting on the first day of in-field usage to help them become proficient with the tools. The end result was that every salesperson was successfully using the system within 60 days.

In each of the above cases, taking the time to look at the personal aspect of reengineering contributed to the overall project success. The best process in the world, supported by the latest and greatest technology available, can still yield poor results if the people who will ultimately use the systems are not committed to the project. The most successful CRM initiatives ensure that the human side of reengineering gets as much attention as technology and process, thereby significantly reducing the problems they encounter.

Realize Less is More

While they have a long-term vision of where they want to be in three, four, or five years, CRM initiatives that excel tend to break that vision into manageable phases. Introducing massive changes all at once overwhelms an organization. Through their process analysis, they may identify many areas of their business that could benefit from reengineering, but establish priorities and tackle only a few at a time.

For example, a computer firm documented their existing order-generation process. The resulting flowchart, using miniature print, was eight feet long. In reviewing the process flow, the CRM team identified 42 different process steps that could be streamlined. But instead of trying to do them all at once, they picked the three steps that represented the greatest potential payback, and reengineered those sub-processes first.

By scaling back on the initial scope of the project, they were able to get phase one of the CRM tools into the hands of the users in only a few months. Using the new system and revised procedures, the sales force was able to reduce the sales cycle length by 25 percent within four months of rollout. The ROI from this improvement alone covered the costs of the hardware, software, and customization for the phases going forward.

Build from a Solid Foundation

The final trait common to successful projects is in how they put all the pieces together. Figure 12 shows our presentation of the approach CRM teams often take to building successful projects. As we discussed earlier, they first analyze their processes and then use that input to develop their technological system architecture definition. After those steps, it is how they assemble their systems that makes a key difference in the results a project achieves.

Experience has shown that, in order to ensure that they have support for the project, CRM teams are best served by solving end user problems first. The initial focus should be on marketing, sales, and service process problems that are causing users to be frustrated, as opposed to management or enterprise-wide issues. If their users are not yet computer literate, CRM project teams should begin by focusing on personal efficiency. This is a safe starting point, as it leverages the more mature parts of CRM systems, and allows users to become familiar with computer and networking operations.

Figure 12: CRM Pyramid

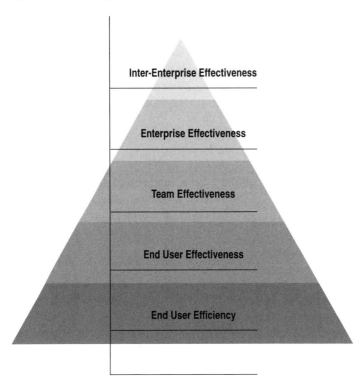

reps. Not only did they become familiar with the technology, they also had evidence that it relieved them of busywork. The stage was set for future project phases.

If users are already comfortable with technology, they can then be given some of the more sophisticated tools, such as proposal generators, marketing encyclopedias, and configurators. These systems help increase end user effectiveness. Take, for example, an investment firm that provided its salespeople with a PC-based system for doing an asset allocation analysis. What used to take three or four calls to complete manually could now be done in a single client meeting. The firm reported an 85 percent close rate when using the system with first-time prospects.

For example, as part of their first steps into CRM, a sporting goods firm provided their salespeople with laptops, a contact manager, and some software agent technology to automate many of the internal and external correspondence tasks the reps complained were taking too long to accomplish. When salespeople took the time to input their customer profiles into the system, they were pleasantly surprised: The system took over the task of generating dozens of memos to manufacturing, sales management, marketing, and the customer. The project team scored a quick win in the eyes of the

Once users experience how these tools are designed to help them do their jobs more competently, they will voluntarily put accurate information into the systems. When this occurs, team selling effectiveness tools such as opportunity managers that allow all members of the sales/service force to communicate with each other, as well as management to do accurate pipeline and forecast management, can be introduced. Organizations that reach this level of the pyramid then find that moving the next step, to enterprise effectiveness, is easier. At this level, they link front office and back office systems together, so that everyone is informed about customer-related issues. They can also feed information from these systems into data warehouses, in order to conduct sales and marketing trend analyses that previously were not possible.

Finally, once all their internal users are integrated, an organization can move beyond their own walls to involve other groups who are part of the process – such as suppliers, channel partners, and even customers themselves. Recall, a communications firm reported that they gave customers access to an Internet-based configurator which is now generating $3 million a day in sales from clients completing their own needs analysis and placing their own follow-on orders.

The key to effectively using the CRM pyramid concept is to accurately assess where your organization is today, and start building from there. You cannot focus on running until you have taught your people to walk. Get users comfortable with the systems and show them early how the tools and new processes benefit them personally, and they will support the initiatives. Once information is shared freely across the organization, the rest of the project will run much more smoothly. The insights shared in this section will help you identify any weaknesses in your CRM strategies early in the process. The key feedback from these successful

organizations was that CRM initiatives can have a profound impact on a firm's future, if they are managed correctly. In the following section we will review some of these successes in detail.

Section 3 Case Studies

Company Profile
Cable TV Firm
2 Million Subscribers
North America-based Operations

Business Challenge
In the past two years the business climate for this cable service provider had changed dramatically. The exclusive hold they had on their marketplace was being challenged by not only competing cable companies but also new services such a satellite delivery. Realizing that this new competition would start to attract users from their customer base overtime, the company knew they had to start doing things differently to minimize their loss of market share. The question though was "what"?

The company brought in a new CEO to help define the business strategies for maximizing their performance in this new competitive world. One of the first actions he took was to focus on letting customers determine what changes the firm should make. He formed a transformation team to initially survey what their subscribers valued in terms of product or service. Based on those insights, the team sought to develop the systems and plans to improve customer relations, minimize market share erosion, and generate more revenue per subscriber.

Project Milestones
Process Analysis
Phase one of the project was a customer demographics analysis. The project team surveyed 3,000 existing customers to determine who they were, what they

valued, how they made cable services decisions, what other services they wanted, etc. Through this research, six clear customer segments emerged, each with its own set of preferences and needs. With this new understanding of their customer base, the team developed a series of innovative marketing strategies designed specifically for the needs of each segment.

Technology Application
The next objective of the project was to assign each of the 2 million current customers to their appropriate market segment. The cable firm had an existing 18.data warehouse containing information on each of their subscribers. To make that data more useful, they needed to compare each of their existing customers against the demographics models and place them in the correct category. They then needed to make that information available to the customer service representatives in the call center so they could more effectively market the new service offerings.

Program Development
Using the data from the 3,000 customers initially surveyed, the transformation team developed a set of algorithms to determine in which market segment a customer should be placed. After conducting a number of sample runs against that database, they were able to modify the algorithms so that they correctly assigned a customer to the right category with a extremely high rate of reliability. They then ran those metrics against the full database and created the new marketplace data warehouse.

System Rollout

The system and the new marketing strategies are currently being integrated into the call center operations. When a customer or prospect now calls in, the call center system will determine the market segment they are in and present the customer service representative with the options that best fit the customer's needs. Increased flexibility has been built into the system so that the customer has much more choice in picking the specific shows they would like access to, increasing the attractiveness of the cable firm's offerings.

CRM Benefits

By going through this process, the cable firm uncovered a number of insights that helped them more clearly define their marketplace strategies. For example, when they surveyed customer preferences, they determined that programming content was the Number 1 priority. The firm had been assuming that service issues, such as fast installation, were key to keeping customers, and had been planning to make significant investments to further improve their service response times. After discovering that service was not a key issue, they redirected those budgeted funds into what customers valued most. Taking the time to build the data warehouse on all their customers has now positioned the firm to be much more effective at marketing new services. The cable firm is now in the position to be more agile in their sales and service. By accessing the data warehouse, the call center representatives will be able to do a more effective job of segment marketing, offering individuals a set of services more tailored to their unique needs.

Recommendations

Many companies state that they are customer-driven, yet they never invest the resources to really understand what their users want and value. As a result of this transformation effort, this cable service provider's view of their market place is much clearer. Their advice to other CRM teams is:

- Survey, survey, survey. Take the time to regularly ask customers and prospects what they think is important, rather than assume you know.
- Build flexibility into your offerings.
- If you do not have the right levels of expertise internally, supplement your team with outside resources, and then bring the project in house.
- Expect your human resources model to change dramatically, and offer people the training needed to develop new skill sets.

Company Profile
Retail Store Chain
$20+ Billion in Revenues
1,400+ Locations

Business Challenge
The introduction of 15,000 to 20,000 new products into the marketplace each year represented a major opportunity and challenge for this nationwide retail chain. The opportunity was provided in the form of a variety of incentives manufacturers offered to motivate retailers to stock new items. But, as with any retail operation, the firm had a finite amount of shelf space. So the challenge came in first trying to decide which of these new products to carry, and then deciding which existing product to discontinue to free up display room.

The company realized they needed to become much more effective at making stocking decisions to maximize their profitability and customer service. To do that, they needed better insight into what customers really wanted and valued. To achieve this, they formed a transformation task force and chartered them with the task of designing new business methods that would enable their product managers to become experts at category management. The goal was to streamline the product mix within a given category – cake mixes, detergent, wine – to meet customer expectations while optimizing inventory.

Project Milestones
Process Analysis
The project started with a review of sales at the category level. The firm found that in many cases, 10 percent of the products

generated up to 90 percent of sales in a given category. Therefore, an unnecessary duplication of products was taking up valuable shelf space. This study also uncovered that the most desired products were often out of stock because they were not allocated enough shelf space. When these findings were shared with the product managers, they reported that the processes and systems they used did not allow them to easily determine these trends. To move to true category management, they would need to reinvent the role of the product manager.

Technology Application
It became apparent that the product managers needed to have access to two types of new applications. The first was a data mining system that would allow them to easily analyze buying trends – what customers expected in variety, packaging and price. In addition, they needed the ability to review products from a competitive perspective, to see what was available at other stores in a geographical area. The product managers also needed a group of analytical templates to guide them through the process of working with this data in order to make better product choices. The goal was set to deliver these two systems as a single toolkit for product managers to combine data and conduct analysis.

Program Development
A data warehouse was created that combined consumer buying information with third-party competitive data into a single category management database. The analytical templates were then designed to allow product managers to do

multidimensional analysis to determine the optimum product mix, by product type and location, to meet the needs of consumers while minimizing inventory.

System Rollout
The category management system was introduced in parallel with a series of organizational changes and new job training. The training focused not just on system usage, but also dealt with other issues such as strategies for getting non-profitable products off the shelves. Within months, the product managers had made the shift to category management.

CRM Benefits
With the ability to conduct detailed market basket and competitive analysis, the firm started dramatically streamlining operations. For example, in the wine category, even though the number of brands carried fell from 600 to less than 150, wine sales increased significantly. Customers reported that they actually felt the product selection had increased, because the wines they wanted now had enough shelf space to remain in stock.

The company was also able to work much more effectively with their suppliers, since they could now generate quantitative results on the sales of each brand of a product they carried. This increased their ability to negotiate better deals for future purchases. The performance of the product managers now has a significant impact on maximizing profitability.

Recommendations
In retrospect, this retailer made a significant shift in their business model in a short amount of time. Looking back on their progress, the following lessons should be noted by other CRM teams:

▸ True transformation needs to start with the customer. You need to understand what they want and value first.
▸ Data warehousing represents a powerful tool for sales and marketing, but it is totally dependent on good information. Do not underestimate the challenge of data clean-up.
▸ Ultimately, you need to give users tools that help them use data, as opposed to just playing with it. The analytical templates made the system much more valuable.
▸ Make sure you provide adequate training. Reengineering of this type requires users to make fundamental changes in how they work. They need solid support to make the transition to these new business models.

Chapter 3: CRM in Practice

Company Profile
Telecommunications Supplier
$10+ Billion in Revenues
200+ Customer Support Representatives
4 Call Centers

Business Challenge
When the new senior vice president took over the sales operations of this telecommunications firm in late 1996, he was concerned about a trend in the industry of using price discounts as a way to attract customers from other service providers. This practice provided a short-lived competitive edge, but did nothing to build long-term customer loyalty. Having built value-focused sales organizations previously, the new SVP set about transforming the sales operations at his new firm. The challenge he presented to his CRM team was to develop a consultative sales process that accomplished three objectives. First, it had to enable salespeople to be well informed about industry facts, issues, and trends, and to stay attuned to the goals and inner workings of their customers. Second, it needed to help formulate communications solutions that precisely met customer needs. And finally, it had to capture strategic marketing data on customers.

Project Milestones
Process Analysis
Through a series of focus groups conducted with end users and management, the project team identified the core challenge. Salespeople required better information about customers and their business challenges in order to make a successful consultative sell. Two process teams were then formed to address this

need. The first focused on developing knowledge databases for each of the 28 industries the sales force was targeting. These knowledge bases included such information as industry trends, key performance metrics, benchmarks, and specifications the customer could take to improve their business operations. The second team's charter was to build a knowledge base that included the full spectrum of the firms' products and services, including features, pricing, and inventories.

Technology Application
To allow these knowledge bases to be utilized interactively during a sales call, the CRM team determined that they would need to develop an Interactive Selling System (ISS). The ISS would utilize an artificial intelligence (AI) engine to help sales reps identify weaknesses in the client's operations by comparing them against industry benchmarks and best practices. Next, the ISS would formulate solutions to these problems, based on an analysis of the 3,000+ universal service order code options. Ease of use and system performance would be key to winning end user support for using this system when working directly with clients.

Program Development
The two process teams, and a third technology team focused on the AI-based engine, worked concurrently to develop and integrate the industry knowledge database, the products/services database, and the rules-based ISS. Utilizing the insights that resulted from the internal focus groups and leveraging the experience of external experts in ISS development,

these projects were completed in 24 weeks.

System Rollout
In October 1997, the system was ready for deployment. To thoroughly assess how the ISS performed in real-life sales situations, the CRM team opted for a pilot with a sample of existing customers. The feedback from usage in actual sales calls allowed the CRM team to tune the system to help their salespeople take on a true consultative role in qualifying the business needs of a prospect, proposing custom solutions, and closing business.

CRM Benefits
Having benchmarked the ISS usage at other companies, the firm's business case was built on improving four areas. With the new ISS, the company expected to increase sales productivity by helping reps handle more customers more effectively in less time; increase revenues by presenting robust solutions; increase margins by shifting the decision point from price to value; and increase customer retention by becoming a true business partner. The company's field test supported each of these goals, plus an additional one. Using the ISS, the credibility of the salespeople increased: They were able to demonstrate knowledge about the customer's industry that in many cases the client did not even have. As a result of using the new tools, the morale of the sales force increased.

Recommendations
The company is now poised for full system rollout of a new sales process that can fundamentally change how business is done in their industry. Based on the

insights gained from this project, their recommendations to new users are:

▸ Ensure you have senior executive sponsorship, someone that challenges and supports the project team throughout the initiative.
▸ Take the time to conduct focus groups to involve users early on in the project, and emphasize that the goal of the initiative is to make them more effective.
▸ Pilot before you deploy. Real customer feedback is priceless in ensuring that you are providing them with real value.
▸ Realize that the real goal of transformation projects needs to focus on creating long-term customer loyalty. You will no longer simply be selling products or features – you will be turning the sales force into a true consultative sales organization.

Company Profile
Computer Firm
$10+ Billion in Sales
Worldwide Sales & Service Operations
3,000+ Salespeople

Business Challenge
As the complexity and breadth of their product increased in the early 90s, this computer firm noticed a significant increase in order problems. It was taking salespeople days to prepare a quote for a client, and even then the proposal was often inaccurate – prices were being misquoted, configuration errors occurred, and promised delivery dates were incorrect. This problem reached crisis level as the company found they were spending more than 3 percent of total sales for service allowances or gratis parts to correct these errors.

The firm assigned a sales transformation team to deal with this problem. They knew a quick solution would be to develop and offer a set of pre-certified configurations, but that alternative would not meet marketplace requirements long-term. Customers were demanding more customized solutions to fit their specific needs. Therefore, the team was challenged to come up with a method for allowing salespeople to develop custom configurations – right features, right price, right delivery dates – in minutes, not days. Further, the salesperson needed to deliver the figures while working interactively with the customer.

Project Milestones
Process Analysis
As the project was launched, the CRM team began analyzing the existing order process. They found that across the firm there was not one, but more than 100 processes in place to generate an order. In addition, the information technology groups within the company were maintaining 12 internally developed software tools to support these processes, none of which were integrated. The project team first focused on obtaining agreement on a single process that everyone would follow. They then took six weeks to define the architecture requirements for a single configuration system to support this process.

Technology Application
The team evaluated the capabilities of their existing tools, as well as commercially available products. Based on the significant investment they would have to make to support an internally developed system, they decided not to develop their own configurator. They opted to do a boardroom pilot of a software vendor's product and were able to prove to themselves that the commercial tool could handle the task.

Program Development
After the core technology decision was made, the team then took three months to define the business case and functional requirements for the project. This was followed by a six-month intensive development effort. A major aspect of the development phase included a functionality usage audit to ensure the system supported the new process, and to surface

and correct any usability issues prior to introduction to the salespeople.

System Rollout
When the system was formally introduced to the sales force, initial adoption of the new configurator was slow. However, once the project team started conducting presentations at sales field offices on the new capabilities, the groundswell for the project picked up significant momentum. The delivery of multimedia-based training tools also helped facilitate increased system usage.

CRM Benefits
The CRM initiative business plan estimated the six-year project costs would be over $30 million (excluding the hardware costs for laptops and servers, which had been previously budgeted to support the sales operations). For the 3,000 users involved in the project, this represented a per-salesperson expense of $10,000. Based on the sales force's ability to generate accurate customized configurations in only a few minutes, projected annual benefits were targeted at $250 million per year, based on the following improvements:

▸ Significant reduction of service allowances and gratis parts write-offs for orders generated by the new system.
▸ Elimination of the information systems expense of supporting 12 internally developed tools.
▸ Increased win rates due to the ability to respond much more quickly to customers with solutions.
▸ Improved customer satisfaction due to the reduction of service problems caused by incorrect configurations.

▸ Improved morale of sales force, who were now able to sell more effectively and professionally.

Recommendations
Based on their experiences, the CRM team's recommendations to other firms attempting to deal with this type of business challenge include:

▸ Obtain executive sponsorship early on. This type of effort will undoubtedly span multiple functional areas with a firm.
▸ If you do not have the right levels of expertise internally, supplement your team with outside resources who have successfully implemented these types of projects before.
▸ Conduct a usage audit prior to introducing the system to the sales force to ensure that the workflow aspects of the system meet their needs.
▸ Over-invest in training. New users need to be proficient and productive as soon as possible.

Company Profile

Investment Firm
4+ Million Investors, $300+ Billion in Assets
Worldwide Sales and Service Operations
4,000+ Account Representatives

Business Challenge

While many companies struggle with the problem of not having enough prospects, this investment firm's challenge was that they had too many. As their business grew, they found their lead flow increasing from hundreds to thousands per day. Even with an aggressive hiring plan, they still were unable to respond to all inquiries. And when they did contact a prospect, all too often they presented only a fraction of the offerings in which a client might be interested, due to the expanded breadth of the product line.

In the early 1990s, the company tried twice to boost the abilities of the sales force through enhanced technology. Both attempts failed. The first project tried to accomplish too much, as they attempted to reengineer everything all at once. In the second effort, the technology itself presented roadblocks. So a new team set out to avoid past mistakes, and designed a new CRM system that would allow account representatives to prioritize their prospects, spending time with high-yield accounts first, and more effectively presenting the entire product line.

Project Milestones

Process Analysis
Having learned from their past failures, a vice president was assigned to be the project sponsor. For real change to occur, executive support was crucial. The CRM team also evaluated the skill levels of their internal resources, and brought in outside consultants to supplement areas where they were weak. Instead of trying to master the project by themselves, the project team significantly increased the participation of the users. Forty individuals from the functional departments involved were included in the project from day one, and assisted in conducting the problem analysis and requirements definition phases. The training department was also involved in the project at the onset, so that they would be better prepared for the system rollout when it occurred.

Technology Application
Having defined the system requirements to meet the users' needs, the team then looked at the technology required to support the project. Their key concerns were how easily the system could be customized to support their processes, and whether the technology was scaleable enough to eventually support 4,000+ users. They narrowed down their list to two vendors. Each was then asked to prove, through a series of technical review sessions and prototyping examples, that their products could meet the challenge. This intensive review helped them select the technology and business partner that clearly met their needs.

Program Development
The detailed advance work proved worthwhile. Once the technology choice had been made, the team was able to have a system ready for pilot within four months. From that point on, the project adopted a "go slowly, to move fast" attitude. They took an additional three

months to fully field test the system. While no major problems were found in the design, several usage annoyances emerged. The CRM team decided to take the additional time to fix those problems prior to the rollout.

System Rollout

Once the pilot issues were resolved, the project was ready for introduction to the sales force. The time invested in dealing with the usability issues paid off, as user acceptance was very high. Since the training department had been involved in the project from the start, it was able to provide the necessary education to get users productive quickly. Over the next few months, 2000 users were brought onto the system.

CRM Benefits

The original project business case was built around improvements in three areas. They projected a 20 percent minimum increase in sales activities, a 5 percent minimum increase in conversion rates, and a higher close rate of key prospects due to better targeting. After several months of usage in the field, the firm found they were achieving a different, but very beneficial set of results. As opposed to increasing the quantity of their calls, they found that using the new CRM system, their salespeople were improving the quality of those calls. They were able to target high potential individuals much more easily for fast response. They were then able to access information on their full product line and tailor solutions to customer needs. While they did not see a noticeable increase in their close rates, the profitability of accounts showed a significant improvement.

Recommendations

Having learned not just from this success, but from their two previous miscues, the CRM team felt there were four factors that contributed significantly to their success. Their recommendations to other firms are:

- Involve a senior executive actively throughout the project.
- Develop your functional requirements from working directly with the users who will ultimately be using the system.
- During the design phase, you cannot anticipate all the problems that may occur. Conduct a detailed pilot and fix any problems prior to rollout.
- Realize that you cannot spend too much on training.

Chapter 3: CRM in Practice

Company Profile
Municipal Utility Firm
Unionized Workforce
100+ Customer Service Representatives

Business Challenge
As deregulation of the utilities industry loomed, this municipal utility company was concerned that their customer service levels were not meeting the demands of the marketplace. Compared to industry benchmarks, customers calling their service center encountered busy signals twice as often as the norm. When their calls did go through, they were answered three times slower than the industry average. This was even more disturbing when the firm saw that their customer service reps (CSRs) were fielding 33 percent fewer calls per day than their counterparts in other organizations.

Initially, the performance problems were thought to be due to the CSRs' reliance on outdated mainframe-based legacy applications. The information technology (IT) group was therefore chartered to update the call center systems. But as the IT team began the project, it became clear that process and people problems were also contributing to these low service levels. This prompted the firm to expand the scope of the project to transform the call center. They established a CRM team to develop a plan to improve customer care, increase operational efficiency, and improve employee morale.

Project Milestones
Process Analysis
The CRM team launched the project by conducting a detailed analysis of the existing environment. This effort identified weaknesses in both the systems and processes the CSRs were using. In addition, it brought to light other issues contributing to a serious morale problem. The CSRs felt stagnant in their jobs, and believed that the rest of the company perceived their value as low. Consequently, they lacked the motivation to do a good job.

The results of this analysis were shared with the executive management team during a one-day visioning session. After reviewing the existing operational and people-related problems, and learning what technology could and could not do to help, the executives were asked to discuss and agree upon a set of critical success factors (CSFs) for customer service going forward. These CSFs clearly established a consistent set of goals for the organization to achieve.

With the CSFs defined, two teams were formed to attack the problem. The first team focused on operational workflow. Working with the client groups, they broke down the call center operations into six major customer support processes. They then spent six weeks further analyzing each process, surfacing operational flaws, and establishing baseline metrics for improvement. The second team focused on the human side of the CRM equation.

Working with human resources, call center personnel and change management experts, they analyzed the role of the CSRs and their supervisors. The roles of the group were redefined, and the procedures for how they would work with customers were modified to reflect a process everyone could support.

Technology Application
By dealing with the workflow and people problems first, the utility avoided making a common mistake encountered by some CRM projects – applying technology to flawed operations. The technology selection process that is currently under way is targeted toward supporting the new work procedures versus perpetuating past problems.

CRM Benefits
While the new application development project is still underway, improvements are already occurring. The personnel related changes within the customer service department have been implemented and a noticeable increase in employee morale has resulted. In addition, a solid foundation of support for the upcoming automation project has been laid, which will make the introduction of the new call center information systems run more smoothly.

Recommendations
Through their transformation efforts to date, this utility company has learned that CRM projects need to focus on people and process as well as technology. Their advice to other organizations is:

▸ Do not expect technology to be the answer to all your operational problems; success will ultimately be dependent on your people.

▸ Take the time to establish agreement on a common set of goals before you dive into the project.
▸ Involve cross-functional teams in analyzing problems and developing solutions.
▸ Since CRM efforts often require people to significantly alter how they work, involve change management experts to make that transition run as smoothly as possible.
▸ Do not underestimate the complexity of the technology side of the project.

Chapter 3: CRM in Practice

Company Profile

Health Maintenance Organization (HMO)
Division of Nationwide Firm
$7 Billion in Revenues, 1.5 Million
Members
400 Customer Support Representatives

Business Challenge

As the competitiveness of the health care industry increased in the mid '90s, this HMO faced, for the first time, the loss of market share. A review of their operations showed that the processes they were relying upon were creating a severe customer service problem. After a client signed up for their health care program, they were not officially enrolled until they had been billed and their payment posted. This process involved multiple departments, contracts, billing, and customer service. The process took up to 60 days to complete.

The HMO was planning some very aggressive marketing campaigns to attract new members. It was, therefore, imperative that they correct this operational problem. With a large number of leads being generated and the company unable to process them promptly, a fiasco was in the making. The CRM team was chartered to reengineer the enrollment process, to reduce the time to complete an enrollment to less than a day, and modernize their call centers to handle the projected increase in lead flow.

Project Milestones

Process Analysis
The sales transformation team first conducted a business process reengineering (BPR) analysis. The current process required new customers to fill out a five-page, 100+ question form as part of the medical review. The information for accepted members was then forwarded to multiple departments where it was manually entered into each functional area's systems. This resulted in extensive data entry duplication. The process was redesigned and streamlined so that the information requirements were reduced to a single page with fewer than 20 questions. The team also defined the functional requirements for a system to automate the cross-functional information sharing process.

Technology Application
It was determined that the CRM system to support the new procedures needed to include the following five modules: automated medical application review, contact management, lead generation, marketing encyclopedia, and billing. Due to the unique requirements of the company, each of these ended up being a customized application. The goal was to implement a system that would require data to be entered once, with the appropriate information routed electronically to the other functional areas as needed to complete the enrollment process.

Program Development
Because of the critical need to eliminate the new member application backlog, and to prepare to support the increase in lead flow resulting from the new marketing programs, the medical review system was developed first. Thanks to the definition work conducted during the BPR phase, the task was completed in just 90 days. A

parallel project was started to complete the other four modules. These were finished within six months.

System Rollout
The implementation plan called for the system to be rolled out in a single region first, then made available to other parts of the firm. The rollout was split into two phases, each with a pilot prior to full release. The medical review module was introduced first, with the second phase of modules coming 90 days later. The CRM team compiled a process deployment model to help the other regions assess their readiness to implement the system and new processes.

CRM Benefits
The first benefit noted was a dramatic drop in the amount of time it took to process each new client application – a decrease from 28 days to less than one. There was also a noticeable reduction in the overall enrollment time, as the billing and the posting of payments processes were also streamlined. The HMO also experienced cost reductions from elimination of duplicate data entry and increased customer satisfaction with the overall enrollment experience.

The most significant improvement was the HMO's ability to handle the increased lead flow resulting from the marketing campaign. The firm exceeded their new member target by 45 percent. This would have been impossible if they had been processing enrollments using the old procedures. The new system's ability to integrate the efforts of marketing and

telesales resulted in the firm signing 300,000 new members last year.

Recommendations
While the pressure was on the HMO to make changes quickly, they never panicked and tried to cut corners. The lessons that they felt served them well were:

- Take the time to fix your existing processes first. Automating fundamentally faulty business procedures will not fix the problem.
- Take a phased approach; you need to walk before you can run. Work on the biggest problems first, and then move to the next set of issues.
- Pilot your system first and then scale up. You need time to analyze the systems in production before you roll them out to everyone.
- Develop deployment assessment guides to help users surface the pitfalls that can impact their system implementation.

In Conclusion

We hope this executive white paper has been helpful to you as you consider your customer relationship management challenges. We've highlighted some of the basic issues you should address. And we've provided recommendations on helping clients solve these issues on a global scale. If you have any questions or you'd like additional information about any of the topics covered in this white paper, please contact the CRM practice at Deloitte Consulting and the CSO Forum:

Bo Manning
Deloitte Consulting
(312) 374-3073
bmanning@dttus.com

Steve Pratt
Deloitte Consulting
(415) 783-4007
stpratt@dttus.com

Jim Dickie
CSO Forum
(303) 530-6930
jimdickie@csoforum.com

Biography: Deloitte Consulting is one of the world's top management consulting firms, providing services to transform your entire enterprise -- your strategy, processes, information technology, and people. Deloitte Consulting offers its clients a very different approach, because of a highly respectful, flexible, and collaborative working style that allows an unmatched ability to transfer knowledge and skills and generate employee buy-in. In addition, Deloitte Consulting focuses on the realization that changing business processes is necessary to achieve the promised returns from strategy and technology. This approach enables the delivery of very different results – results clients can build on because Deloitte Consulting helps make organizations more robust and adaptable to future shifts in the environment. Deloitte Consulting is an integral part of Deloitte Touche Tohmatsu, one of the world's leading professional services firms, delivering world-class assurance and advisory, tax, and consulting services. More than 82,000 people in over 130 countries serve nearly one-fifth of the world's largest companies as well as large national enterprises, public institutions, and successful fast-growing companies. Our internationally experienced professionals deliver seamless, consistent services wherever our clients operate. Our mission is to help our clients and our people excel.

CRM Measurement: Measure up... or shut up!

Title: CRM Measurement: Measure up... or shut up!
Author: Professor Robert Shaw, Business Intelligence
Abstract: For years customer service enthusiasts have been preaching that customers
                 create value. That gives everyone a nice warm feeling, but nothing happens.
                 Prove that customers create value, and the prestige of professional service
                 management will rise as surely as night follows day. It is time to measure
                 up... or shut up.

Biography: Dr Robert Shaw is founder of the consulting and education firm, CRM Best Practice, and visiting Professor of
Strategic Marketing at Cranfield School of Management, editor of the Journal of Targeting, Measurement and Analysis and
author of Measuring and Valuing Customer Relationships (Business Intelligence).
Professor Robert Shaw
Tel: +44 (0)208 995 0008, Fax: +44 (0)208 994 3792
Mobile: +44 (0)7940 526833
Email: shaw@MarketingBestPractice.com

Why creating customer value involves more than a wish list

Creating customer value is rather like a bandwagon: for most managers itÕs an entertaining side-show, some will want to jump aboard, and few will stand in its way. Heads nod vigorously up and down when chairmen say, as they are wont to do, that customers are their principal assets. Sadly, practice does not always match theory. Somehow in the rough and tumble of business life, decisions are taken which favour short-term profits over long-term building of customer value. Customer service is run as a highly discretionary cost, subject to cutting and slashing, where quality and value are compromised, and systems maintenance consumes valuable cash earmarked for more constructive developments.

The time has come to redirect the customer service bandwagon. Its momentum is undeniable, the cost of maintaining its speed is tremendous, but only for a minority of exceptional companies is it heading in the right direction. Why? Because in setting the customer bandwagon on its tracks, we have been guided by wish-lists, half-truths and overblown expectations about satisfaction, loyalty, quality. Many misconceived customer investments are draining our profits, rather than boosting them.

Customer investments do not necessarily pay dividends. Aspects make profits, others waste money. As Professor Merlin Stone noted in his perceptive article "Second-Rate Customer Service" in the May 1998 issue, first-rate customer service does not always pay.

Why is this? Some say that the blame is lack of middle management training. I am sure they are right. Others advocate benchmarking, the discipline of rigorously calibrating best-practice and matching or exceeding it. They too make out a good case. Others see the solution in new organisational structures, multi-disciplinary teams replacing elitist functions.

While I think all these proposals deserve serious consideration, I myself would look further upstream for the elusive key. I would seek it in company boardrooms. Corporate conviction and commitment offers the key to customer value creation, and these are things that can originate only at the highest level within a business, otherwise like a thinly rooted plant, good practice will be washed away by the first winter storm.

How many top executives regard customer project budgets as a source of profit assurance against times when the market is hard, a hidden part of the shareholder dividend reserve? More than a few, I suspect.

The new strategic performance measurement agenda

What gets measured gets done, goes an old saying. For many Boards, this creed is not just affecting financial measurements any more. There is a new corporate agenda at work.

The Boards of some enlightened companies are beginning to demonstrate their unswerving commitment to long-term prosperity, and customer lifetime value, by introducing new non-financial performance measures.

By producing annual reports which give prominence to status reports on customer satisfaction, quality or loyalty, and by talking to the City and to financial editors, fund managers and analysts about their customers as an opening topic, not an

after thought, Boards are demonstrating their commitment to creating value through customers. Investors too are also demanding more and better disclosure of customer statistics.

By demanding from their management teams long-term plans that link financial and customer measures, and regular, objective measurement of progress against specific objectives and, most important, backing these plans when short-term considerations tempt them to do otherwise, they are using measurement to change the rules of the customer game.

A passion for measurement is gripping the Boards of many major corporations. Books such as The Balanced Scorecard, Managing Customer Value, and Keeping Score are best sellers. Conferences are full to overflowing on Strategic Performance Measurement, Marketing Accountability, and Customer Profitability Measurement. Customers are central to these new developments.

Measurement is neither academic nor purely financial. Project teams are actively implementing new customer measurement frameworks in over half the major corporations of the US and Europe, according to a recent survey of measurement practices that I carried out for Business Intelligence.

Transforming service-artfulness into customer-science

While the idea of customer measurement is good in theory, many Boards are sceptical. Many believe that customer measurement is more art than science and even the art is a work of fiction. And unfortunately this scepticism is often justified.

"The simple principle is that the company exists to serve its customers long into the future. Business leaders that act on this, and persuade all their people to believe in it, can transform ordinary companies into world beaters" says Sir Colin Marshall, chairman of British Airways, adding the note that "If you go around and ask chairmen and chief executives, they will say they are very good with customers, but only a handful of businesses measure up"

"You can't begin to compete until you know precisely what your customers want. Knowing that, you can then design a product that sells itself. Branded goods manufacturers live by this credo already, but every type of business should take it to heart. It's the critical element." says Sir George Bull, former Chairman of Grand Metropolitan, and shortly to become Chairman of J. Sainsbury.

When it comes to practical implementation of these measurement principles, our delegates at Cranfield School of Management, and also clients of Shaw Consulting regularly ask three questions:
▸ How do we make sure that we are using the best methods to measure customers. We abound with charts and tables with titles like "Quality Improvements" or "Satisfaction" or "Loyal Customers", but why are they not credible with top management?
▸ How can we link general business performance measures, such as shareholder value, to service input measures (e.g. quality) and associated customer behaviour measures (e.g. satisfaction and loyalty)?
▸ Different strategies imply different key performance drivers - so how do we determine what the critical things to measure are for our particular circumstances, and so ensure our measures are not just a wish list?

Take a clean sweep of tired old measures

To provide clients with answers all three questions, I have worked my way through over 500 journal articles and books, both scholarly and practitioner. I have canvassed the opinions of over 100 experts, on both sides of the Atlantic. I have studied the practices of 50 leading companies in detail, and surveyed the state-of-the-art in a sample of 200.

Findings from this research have so far been published in a 250 page Financial Times report. The Economist Books will be publishing more in the Autumn, and Business Intelligence are also publishing the most comprehensive report of all, Customer Relationship Management - Strategic Performance Measures and Knowledge Tools, also in the Autumn.

What has emerged from these studies is that the majority of firms do not measure

Chapter 3: CRM in Practice

the right factors to understand the customer. Worse still, many of the measurement practices and analysis methods are outdated, or flawed, or both, and lead management to take dubious decisions. It is no wonder that they have little credibility with senior colleagues.

What is also emerging from new research, published in my own Journal of Targeting, Measurement and Analysis, and in the American Journal of Customer Satisfaction, Dissatisfaction and Complaining Behaviour, is the realisation that many myths of customer relationship management - myths about loyalty, quality and so forth - are being blown away by hard evidence.

Satisfaction is being measured by the majority of businesses today, but it's hardly ever producing credible statistics. Often the reason for the poor measurements is cost cutting. We know of one major corporation whose top management didn't get their satisfaction-bonus, because they had assigned some spotty eighteen year old student intern the task of measuring satisfaction, and he screwed up.

Can't get no satisfaction:
Are satisfaction scores always closely bunched together, or do big differences show up in some satisfaction surveys? Why do scores tend to bunch together in many satisfaction surveys, and what does this imply for those who intend to spend millions improving their scores?

Skewed measurement sometimes offers momentary optimism for management. Thus Centrica's Board tells its shareholders in their 1997 annual report that "Our most important priority is to deliver excellent customer service and we have made significant progress, the externally monitored "Customer Satisfaction Index" places British Gas Home Energy service within the "good to excellent" category." Yet how credible do Centrica's shareholders find their "good to excellent" index, when they know British Gas is receiving a barrage of bad press over the hundreds of thousands of customer complaints they receive annually. Coloured measures will give rise only to misplaced optimism.

Choose an integrated measurement system

Intuitively, the management of many businesses believe that high quality leads to high satisfaction and that in turn results in high profitability. Yet what links the measures together? Should companies be striving for an integrated measurement framework?

The ideal customer service operation will link service to the bottom line in a similar way to the one illustrated below. Reading from right to left: financial outputs would be measured in terms of profitability. Super-profits would result from loyal customer behaviour. Loyalty would come about from customers thinking satisfied thoughts and feeling satisfied feelings. Satisfaction would be created by exceptional service quality.

Figure 1

SERVICE INPUTS	>>	CUSTOMER THOUGHTS & FEELINGS	>>	CUSTOMER ACTIONS & BEHAVIOUR	>>	FINANCIAL OUTPUT
Quality measures		Satisfaction measures		Loyalty measures		Profit measures

"Start by measuring and meeting existing needs. Then drive up quality standards and cost effectiveness by continuous improvement. Standards of customer satisfaction, targeted and measurable, are the bedrock on which to create long-term wealth" argues Sir John Egan, Chairman of BAA.

Quality and satisfaction:
Quality and satisfaction are often discussed as if synonymous. Yet a purchaser of the Rolls Royce is much more likely to be very dissatisfied by a minor scratch on the paintwork, yet still attribute high quality to the Rolls, whilst a purchaser of a second-hand Ford Fiesta with scratched paintwork is likely to score it higher on satisfaction but low on quality. Are quality and satisfaction unrelated, or if not, how are they related?

Care must be taken when integrating the measures. Quality measures frequently have failings resulting from their heavy reliance on one or other widely accepted definitions of quality, whether single-stimulus such as 6s, or multi-factor such as

SERVQUAL. Consumer perceptions of quality tend not to fit preconceived management notions.

In a novel study of consumer perceptions of service quality in the airline industry, Ozment and Morash found that consumer quality judgements were sensitive to the level of advertising expenditure. Heavily advertised airlines were perceived to be higher in quality. Consumers were also sensitive to the level of congestion (percentage of plane seating capacity filled). Yet no widely adopted measure of quality in the airline industry was related to these two variables.

Airlines were widely found measuring quality in terms of on-time arrivals, problem-free baggage handling, and minimal flight cancellations. Underlying this definition was a conflict. Consumers desire less passenger congestion, but management desires full loads. Since management have an over-riding say in defining quality, no wonder load-factor is not reported as a quality dimension, even though it is greatly desired by customers.

> **Bad attitude:**
> A client is reluctant to sponsor a survey of customer attitudes because he says that attitudes fail to predict action. Is he right? Are there some ways of measuring attitudes that are better predictors of customer behaviour than others?

Tailor the framework to your business context

Sir Clive Thompson, who transformed Rentokil from a low-profile pest control and wood preservative specialist into a service leader, that has earned him a large fan club in the City, commented to me that "measurement is totally important. I cannot over emphasise its importance. I believe strongly that you don't expect but inspect. The key question is what is essential to measure, because it can become difficult if you handle too many things."
No single set of measures can apply to all firms, but the process for putting together a set for any particular firm is straightforward to implement, albeit requiring hard work and experience.

Step 1 is to define which groups are important and therefore have to be tracked. We start by recalling that customer value comes from whatever lies between the ears of the key players in the marketplace: consumers, channels, influencers (journalists for example) and our own staff.

Step 2 is to recall that we cannot directly measure customer value. We proceed indirectly in two ways: what is implied by behaviour (complaints, repeat purchases, trial purchases, advocacy), and what is implied by intermediate psychological measures of thoughts and feelings (attitudes, beliefs, feelings). The measurement team, i.e. all those including marketing and finance who will be affected by measurements, should list all those proxy measures that they think are relevant.

Step 3 is to find out what other firms are measuring. This can be done by benchmarking studies. It can also be done by holding workshops for the measurement team. Here you add to the list from step 2. You will probably end up with 40-50 measures. In practice many such measures are linked. Do you need repeat purchases by volume and value for example? Some are couples that you might prefer to uncouple. This is an empirical question. Do the measures vary together or move differently?

Step 4 is to reduce them to a manageable number to track. Tracking is expensive and no managers can comprehend more than a few measures together. You may need advice or help to assess the best-practice arrangement.

Step 5 is to add the measures to your corporate data warehouse. This will facilitate the job of comparing measures, and presenting results. EIS software can help enormously, as can analysis tools. Packages such as SAS are obvious candidates for this task. Don't underestimate the sheer human effort and cost of such an undertaking.

Step 6 is to use the system and revise it. All science works that way, no less so customer science. First we can see which measures behave over time in a similar way. For example, do market share and repeat-purchase always correlate? There is no point in tracking both if they tell us the same thing. We need to see which measures are static and which volatile. For example, average satisfaction may be too coarse a measure for short-term control. We need measures that are sensitive, but not too sensitive.

> **A Matter of Loyalty:**
> Is there such a thing as loyalty? Does it differ significantly from brand to brand? Is loyalty predictable? Are highly loyal customers worth having?

Gather the data and see what really happens in your type of business. When you have the crucial data, stick with it. Track it over time, and follow the trends. With learning, some changes will need to be made over three year time horizons, so that year to year comparisons are never lost. The individual metrics matter little. The change is what counts.

Conclusion

My position then is that world-class customer service will not become commonplace unless and until company

Boards commit themselves and their organisations to set real customer targets and measure themselves against them. If you accept this hypothesis, the question we must then ask becomes "Who will measure customers and the value they create?" Senior customer service managers and directors must be called upon. They are perfectly placed to start the revolution. Why are they so bashful? Do they find it difficult to measure customers and the value they create? Even the financial community is urging them on.

> **Paradoxical brain drain:**
> It has been reported recently that many accountants are taking an interest in customer service and are switching professions. Some wag quipped in the press recently that this brain drain will lower the average IQ in both service and accounting. How is this paradox possible?

Analytical Customer Relationship Management

Title: Analytical Customer Relationship Management
Author: Frank Teklitz and Robert L. McCarthy, Sybase, Inc.

Abstract: This paper examines a new approach to implementing a Business Intelligence
                solution focused on the analytical aspects of CRM. This approach will help
                businesses better analyze their target markets. From there, they will gain the
                insight needed to formulate profitable strategies and tactics to reach their
                customers more effectively. It will provide an insight on how a customer-
                focused data warehouse can be implemented faster with fewer resources at
                the same time as it delivers reduced risk.

Biography: see end article

Introduction

The need to find new sources of revenue is a fundamental requirement for business growth. Typically it means reaching current customers and prospects in ways that will encourage them to do more business with you. From your customer's perspective, there are so many choices in products, services, delivery, and packaging that your efforts to sell them more products can result in an onslaught of information — often confusing information. And from your business's perspective, there are so many "touch points" where information is exchanged between you and your prospective or current customers such as customer support centers, direct mail, telesales, direct sales, e-commerce, and the Web, that it is difficult to determine which methods deliver the best results.

Over the last 30 years, we have moved from a mass-market culture of relatively few products with a limited number of options to a dynamic market where many products may be easily customized to fit the specific requirements of an individual customer. For example, not that long ago, banking customers had relatively few product choices —savings accounts, checking, CDs, and fixed rate mortgages. Today, every bank provides a variety of investment choices, loan types with fixed and variable interest rates, direct deposit accounts, electronic banking options, leases, credit cards, and more. Banks even offer insurance and brokerage services.

Prospective and current customers are, at times, overwhelmed with invitations from their existing suppliers to increase their use of products and services. At the same time, they are repeatedly courted (and provided incentives) by their supplier's competition to move their business for a "better deal." In the past, many organizations depended on personalized service to develop and maintain the loyalty of their customers. As the customers' relationship with their supplier has become more electronic, the traditional source of customer loyalty — personal service —has been impacted. The one-to-one contact with an organization now occurs most often by telephone or on the Internet.

Customers order products by fax, e-mail, over the Internet, and computer to computer via electronic data interchange. They also interact with a telesales operator or sometimes even an automated attendant. Customer service is quite often conducted by Internet, e-mail, or by telephone. The only constant in the relationship contact is the customer. While this may facilitate the process and make the sales and service aspects of doing business more cost-effective, it can lead to a more impersonal relationship between the customer and the organization. This adversely affects the relationship from both the customer's and the supplier's point of view.

First of all, if you're the customer, you want to be remembered! Doesn't everyone? Remembering your purchase patterns to remind you when it's time to restock is important. So is monitoring them for aberrations to detect and uncover fraud. You want your recent contacts with the supplier recalled so you don't have to repeat your interests over and over to each new contact. Many of us have experienced this kind of "remembering" in dealing with Internet-based firms like those who sell books. By knowing your buying pattern, the supplier can make reasonable recommendations on new books for you to purchase. And by "remembering" your delivery and billing information, you facilitate and expedite the placement of an order.

Today's consumers are both educated and demanding. They demand that any interaction with their suppliers be quick and efficient. With the increasing impact of the Internet and telesales operations, customers can shop for alternatives without leaving their chairs.

> "*Companies are realizing that the keys to long-term, sustainable revenues and profits are identifying, acquiring, and retaining profitable customers. Unfortunately, most companies don't know which customers are profitable and which are not. They also don't know which customers are likely to defect and which are likely to respond to particular offers and products. Most importantly, few companies can identify those customers or prospects that have the greatest potential to become profitable customers over time, given the right marketing investment.*"
>
> — Wayne W. Eckerson Senior consultant/analyst Information Assets Patricia Seybold Group

Think of your own buying decisions. Have you ever made a purchase because:

▸ One supplier had the item in stock and another did not?
▸ One supplier could meet your specific needs promptly with just what you wanted?
▸ One supplier was more responsive to your inquiries and "remembered" previous contacts?

And this "memory" concerning customers is important to suppliers as well. Many organizations have recognized this opportunity already. They have implemented operational customer relationship management (CRM) software such as call center technology for customer care or sales automation technology to improve their sales process. If used properly, these tools can personalize the process of sales and support more, addressing the customer's needs in the "touch points" of sales and service. The supplier wants to leverage these tools to deepen their customer relationships — especially with those customers whom they regard as low-risk and highly profitable.

CRM has too often been used as an opportunity for one-way communication. Put more crudely, cleverly targeted mailings and sophisticated profiling techniques may have helped the direct marketers increase their response rates. But, used in isolation, they will not, and cannot, deliver true customer relationship management. "The real benefits of CRM are located in the customization of service, not literature," says Sean Kelly, Vice President, European Operations for Sybase, Inc., and author of the first authoritative text on data warehousing, Data Warehousing —the route to mass customization.

"Far too many organizations are focusing on CRM simply to up-sell or cross-sell their products and services without giving enough thought to how they will enhance their customer care strategy. By focusing exclusively on the sales opportunities that CRM presents, they ignore other forms of interaction such as the analysis of customer consumption patterns, levels of customer contact (including complaint procedures), and more effective analysis of customer profitability."

So how does a business in today's world begin to understand who its low-risk, high-profit customers are? And even if it establishes who its best customers are, how can it leverage this to determine how to reach and keep customers whose demands are changing and whose attentions easily shift from one company to another within the marketplace?

The early adopters of data warehousing understood the power of customer information — and the benefits to be gained from the business intelligence solutions needed to deliver that information. The data warehouse technology provides the location where data may be centralized, integrated, stored, and accessed. But without business intelligence, it may not be exploited. Organizations that have had the expertise and the resources to implement a customer-focused data warehouse now are reaping the rewards of true CRM — simply by understanding what their customers want from them.

This paper examines a new approach to implementing a Business Intelligence solution focused on the analytical aspects of CRM. This approach will help businesses better analyze their target markets. From there, they will gain the insight needed to formulate profitable strategies and tactics to reach their customers more effectively. It will provide an insight on how a customer-focused data warehouse can be implemented faster with fewer resources at the same time as it delivers reduced risk. Implemented effectively, Business Intelligence com-bines technology with business strategy to give your customers the services and products they want, thus better protecting them from being taken away by your competition. At the same time, Business Intelligence allows you to grow your business with new customers who share the profitable characteristics of your current customer base.

Challenges for Customer-Oriented and Market-Oriented Companies

Currently, many customer-oriented and market-oriented companies evaluate their customers along demographic (age, sex, geography), lifestyle (buying habits, activities, and affiliations), and family (household) groupings. With these database-marketing techniques, marketers use traditional methods such as direct mail to "touch" potential customers for new business. For example, it is common to do mailings by specific groupings or segments for, let's say, "all prospects 55 or older who play golf." This kind of modeling yields virtually no insight regarding the profit potential of this group or even if these prospects respond to direct mail. In fact, many questions are left unresolved by these kinds of traditional database marketing techniques. Among the questions are:

▸ Increased Acquisition Costs. How do we reduce the cost of gaining a new customer, which often exceeds the profit that can be generated from that customer?

▸ Increased Customer Service Costs. How do we move customers toward more cost-effective service channels like the Web?

▸ Inadequate Knowledge of the Customer. What are the customer's service needs, profit performance, and lifestyle choices?

▸ Complex Customer Profitability Models. What are the right combinations of products, services, sales, and marketing support needed to drive profitable business?

▸ Increased Account Churn. How can we retain customers and build loyalty?

The New Approach for Business Intelligence

Today, with the advent of Business Intelligence applications and integrated supporting data models, it is possible to deliver fine-tuned analyses of the needs of individual customers, based on buying habits, preferred marketing interactions, and lifestyle choices. This helps create more profitable and more personal business relationships that can drive every "touch point" in your organization, including customer service, telesales, direct sales, e-commerce, Web marketing, and business operations.

For example, a business analyst can use the customer's buying needs and preferences to deliver a specifically designed service package that addresses the customer's business needs directly. This builds a stronger business relationship with that customer and provides the company with new revenue opportunities. At the same time, the marketing department not only can evaluate direct marketing programs, but also can determine the optimal follow-up activities for every customer based on the relevant customer segmentation combinations. Ideally, all this new customer intelligence enables you to direct your most profitable customers to your most experienced customer service or sales representatives.

Analytical CRM Defined

Analytical CRM is the focused analysis of data created by the operational side of CRM and legacy applications for the purpose of business performance management. Analytical CRM is necessarily dependent on the existence of a data warehouse infrastructure that integrates CRM data and facilitates access to it. Analytical CRM, therefore, enables organizations to identify and balance needs, patterns, opportunities, risks, and costs associated with existing and potential customers to maximize the overall enterprise value.

An integrated Analytical CRM solution addresses all of the following:

▸ Customer Profiling (segmentation, risk, propensity)
▸ Campaign Management (analysis of campaign effectiveness)
▸ Customer Care (analysis of customer contacts and service)
▸ Customer Loyalty (persistency, retention, churn)
▸ Sales Analysis and Prospecting (sales by product, category, store, channel, customer acquisition, cross-sell, up-sell).

A Recipe for Closed-Loop Business Intelligence

The key to success for developing a sophisticated and functional Business Intelligence system begins with understanding the business problem to be solved and a realistic assessment of the data needed and available. From there, it is possible to develop an end-to-end solution to deliver a Business Intelligence system that:

▸ Performs customer analysis
▸ Applies market segmentation information to that analysis
▸ Analyzes ongoing target marketing activities
▸ Models various ways of predicting customer behavior

In addition, an analytical CRM solution should allow all the accumulated knowledge and activity to be reapplied to a new customer analysis. This is often called a "closed-loop" system. Figure 1 illustrates the system's primary functions within the Business Intelligence model.

Customer Analysis

The key to any information system is quality information. Customer Analysis not only requires quality information, but lots of it, and from a variety of data sources. This information must be integrated and placed into a customer data warehouse in a way that enables both standard reporting and ad-hoc analysis, provides the means for segmentation, and enables data mining. With a well-constructed customer data warehouse, it is possible to answer such questions as:

Figure 1: Closed-Loop Business Intelligence

Before any analysis can begin, it is essential to know the information available, the quality of that information, and the level of integration and cleaning (extraction and transformation) needed to deliver a functional data warehouse. The emphasis here is on "functional" rather than "complete" because with any decision support system, including Business Intelligence systems, new sources of information are constantly being identified, cleaned, and added. Also, older information should continually be evaluated for relevance in light of current business and market demands.

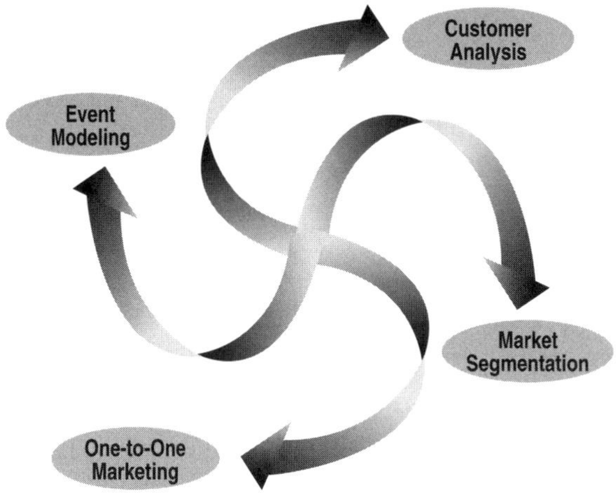

▸ Are newly acquired customers more profitable than current customers?
▸ What is the lifetime value of your top customers?
▸ Are customers under 35 years of age profitable?
▸ Is the Internet helping your business grow and, if so, how?
▸ Government statistics tell us people are saving more. Are you attracting your customers' increased savings dollars or do they take their discretionary money elsewhere?

Getting the Right Information—A Customer Analysis Example

The information needed for customer analysis typically represents key "touch points" for customers (customer service, World Wide Web, automated teller machines), key revenue points (point of sales, e-commerce, order entry), and external data (demographics, lifestyle, householding).

The key information often associated with the customer analysis phase includes customer service history, customer marketing history, sales and revenue by customer, and customer demographic and lifestyle data.

These numerous sources of information must be integrated to create a complete view of the customer in the data warehouse. Once customer information is integrated to reflect product purchases, revenue, service history, demographics, and lifestyle information, it is now possible to rank customer behavior and profitability, and to develop scoring models that begin to predict future behavior. By maintaining a complete history of each customer's revenue, cost, and utilization, it is possible to:

- Determine customer profitability
- Score customer receptiveness to different forms of marketing
- Determine the number and type of products in use
- Measure customer retention and determine degree of loyalty
- Assess customer self-service patterns based on their activities recorded on your Web site.

Market Segmentation

With a customer data warehouse in place, it is possible to perform sophisticated customer segmentations to analyze and target both strengths and weaknesses in your customer and prospect base. Some common market segmentation questions include:

- Which customers buy product A but not product B?
- Which customers respond directly to particular marketing programs?
- Who are the most profitable customers?
- Does our customer profitability vary according to geographic or demographic characteristics?

A Market Segmentation Example

Ad-hoc analysis and data mining may be used to evaluate permutations and combinations of variables, allowing you to discover new ways to segment the customer base. For example, your data-mining tool of choice may discover that customers whose primary hobby is sailing have a high interest in vanity VISA cards. The data warehouse may also reveal that not only do these customers like vanity VISA cards, they also use the cards frequently. By doing ad-hoc queries against

this customer group, you may discover that many of these sailing customers do not currently have boating loans with your bank. With additional analysis, you might discover that customers who did obtain loans responded well to direct telesales calls, but not to direct mail campaigns. Finally, you may determine whether your current sailing customers are "low maintenance"— i.e., they use the Web for self-service needs.

This example illustrates the value of developing an integrated customer data warehouse for Analytical CRM. With the right tools and information, it becomes possible to discover market segmentations that would not be visible with conventional data analysis techniques.

One-to-One Marketing

Having discovered a number of potentially profitable market segments, it is now possible to deliver tailored marketing campaigns for every "touch point" in the organization, from telemarketing to customer service designed for the specific needs of the customer segment. These end-to-end programs are often called "treatment strategies," not unlike the treatment strategies of a medical doctor who uses "best practices" to deliver the most optimal, efficient, and complete patient care.

A Treatment Strategy Example

Continuing with the boating customer example, imagine that you develop a treatment strategy for your sailing customers to promote a new line of boat loans. As an incentive for this promotion, you have decided to include a "no fee" direct deposit and VISA account for one year, using vanity cards in a choice of four nautical themes. Not only do you develop a telemarketing plan to reach customers with an interest in sailing, but you also create special Web pages and appropriate customer service scripts.

Through this kind of detail-level analysis, you can put together similar treatment strategies designed around the relationship needs of golfers, triathletes, and Home Network shoppers. Through your use of targeted marketing and execution, your company can make a significant and lucrative transition. Where you once promoted your products to customers who may not have wanted them, you now can become a builder of specific customer relationship programs designed around the needs of your high-potential, high-profit customers.

Event Modeling

Event modeling enables business organizations to deliver more accurate and successful marketing campaigns and treatment strategies. Event modeling takes advantage of statistical tools to build models that "explain" the behavior of customers and predict the response of customers and prospects to future marketing promotions. Event modeling enables you to understand which events in a customer's life —birthdays, purchase of a new car or house, birth of a child—can lead to opportunities that add value with your products and services. These events, which can be ascribed to market segments, are also powerful tools to evaluate customer and prospect profitability. Event modeling seeks ways to reduce the number

of promotions, manage the costs of business strategies, and increase the percentage response rates to promotions— all of which ultimately boost profits.

Some typical questions addressed with predictive event modeling are:

▸ Which customers by age segmentation are most likely to respond to a reduced price promotion?
▸ How long after buying a new car (securing a car loan) are customers likely to pursue a home mortgage?
▸ Who is likely to buy only if contacted in person?
▸ Is our marketing strategy for high-profit customers impacting profitability and retention as predicted?

The objective is to learn which of the possible variables most effectively predict customer response. You then can identify customers or prospects with similar characteristics to target. In many cases, you can use the newfound knowledge about buyer characteristics to test alternative treatment strategies. With further refinement, your treatment strategies can produce greater customer satisfaction with your message, service, and products— leading to a higher response rate.

An Event Modeling Example
Returns and Early Predictions
To continue with our boating example, imagine you are now three months into the boat loan promotion. Your telesales campaign reached 10,000 customers and prospects, and generated a whopping 8% response rate of which 50% closed—that is, you acquire 400 new boat loans. The

close rate was well within expectations, but the number of loans rejected was high. Of the 800 prospects who responded, 300 were rejected mostly because of credit risk. Your next step might be to model the sailing customers using a variety of modeling techniques—including regression, chaos classifiers, and neural networks—to determine what variables best predict the propensity for credit risk. These models would consider group and individual risk factors such as family income, home value, type of dwelling, age, number of children, and geography.

Now, imagine your team has determined that the 300 rejected prospects had a high propensity to live in an apartment (30% of population), with an annual income under $35,000 and an average age of less than 27 years. The average size of the loan this segment requested was $23,000. On the other hand, your team determined that those prospects who did obtain a loan generally own a home (66% of population), earn $72,000 annually, and on average are 34 years old. The average loan approved for this segment was $37,000.

Refining Treatment Strategies
Your next step is to do some quick ad-hoc analysis and, behold, you find that 70% of the rejected loans were for a first-time boat owner. This leads to a special treatment strategy that includes loans for used boats. You modify your Web site to include a Web search window for used boats being sold in the area. You also include a boat loan calculator to help first-time boaters determine the size of loan for which they can qualify.

You also can explore the key characteristics of those customers who qualified for loans greater than $50,000, $70,000, and $100,000. This leads to a three-segment treatment strategy. For medium-risk customers who make less than $35,000, you provide new and used boat loans. For customers making $35,000 to $100,000, the treatment strategy described earlier will be used. And for those prospects who make more than $100,000, you team up with a boat insurance company to offer $1,000 in free merchandise if they qualify for a loan and also purchase boat insurance. As part of the treatment strategy for your high-end prospects, you feed your prospect leads into the new sales force automation system. Your campaign management system then could automatically generate an e-mail to the field representative for all top-level prospects who respond to the telesales campaign. It would include all appropriate customer information (name, address, birth date, secondary interests, and hobbies) needed to help close the deal.

These refinements in the strategy lead to increased response and close rates for the most lucrative customers and increased profitability of the low-end segments as well.

The Ultimate Refinement: Your Bottom Line
Effective Analytical CRM will allow you to see your customers in new ways that increase revenues and profits from your installed base. You can gain a better working knowledge of how, when, where, and what your best customers respond to —and this knowledge allows you to improve your prospecting strategies.

Ultimately, an analytical CRM solution designed for Closed-Loop Business Intelligence that allows you to explore your interactions with your customers and prospects becomes the hub of your corporate information systems. This approach gives you the means to convert knowledge obtained from your sales, marketing, and operational systems into strategies that yield significant competitive advantages.

Challenges in Delivering Analytical CRM

Today, conventional large-scale data warehouse development projects typically cost up to several million dollars. They may require many months and often years in development time. To gain the benefits of Business Intelligence solutions focused on Analytical CRM, the following challenges must be addressed:

▸ Source data for Analytical CRM comes from multiple and disparate systems within an organization and frequently from outside the organization as well. Therefore, information must be captured from multiple systems, integrated, cleansed, modeled and presented in a way that reflects how you do business with your customers. Users need analysis capabilities to devise marketing strategies that will effectively drive your operational systems.
▸ Information must be easily queried and analyzed to determine the success of business and marketing decisions. Successful Analytical CRM solutions— including on-time and on-budget

delivery—require the right applications, data models, meta data management, Extract/Transform/Load (ETL) tools, and database technology. With this necessary infrastructure, you can integrate relevant data from operational systems and deliver a productive, effective environment for business users.
▸ Analytical CRM solutions require quick, flexible access to business information— potentially by a large number of business users. An abundance of technology exists for storing data. But few of these technology choices enable the flexible analysis needed to support all the various users of your system.
▸ Current operational systems are built to manage product and service delivery— not to manage customer relationships. And those operational systems typically were developed and implemented independently, resulting in "stovepipes" of information. To build an Analytical CRM solution, information from those operational systems dispersed throughout an enterprise must be integrated. This allows a comprehensive view of the customer's relationship with your company, enabling an integrated view of this relationship as well as a closed-loop business analysis.

Typical Data Warehouse Project Development

Building a data warehouse has historically been a long and often risky proposition. Industry analysts estimate the failure rate to be as high as 60% to 70%. In many cases, the failure rate was driven by trying to apply traditional project development and data modeling techniques to the design of the data warehouse. Projects were often staffed with resources that had little to no experience in developing and implementing data warehouses. As well, they often used tools acquired from different vendors to build the warehouse, resulting in integration problems.

The key project tasks associated with designing and implementing data warehouses are identified in Figure 2.

▸ *Gather Requirements* refers to the process of identifying the business needs and defining the key elements and relationships important in solving the business problem.
▸ *Understand the Line of Business* is necessary so that the data and relationships identified may be validated as representing the business process or logical model and providing the infrastructure to respond to the business need.

▸ *Design Schemas* refer to the physical implementation of the data models. This is critical since you may design a very elegant business model that meets all requirements, but if it is implemented ineffectively from a physical perspective, it can lead to queries that take hours or days to finish, if they get completed at all.
▸ *Create ETL Templates* refers to the process of developing and implementing the transformation/loading scripts. These define the source to target mapping and transformation rules that must be applied as data is extracted from their source locations and as the target data warehouse is populated.
▸ The project also must develop and *Build Queries for Analysis* that provide examples of how to access and use the models effectively. These queries are typically designed to address a set of key questions that will assist the user of the data warehouse in understanding the

Figure 2: Typical Data Warehouse Project Tasks

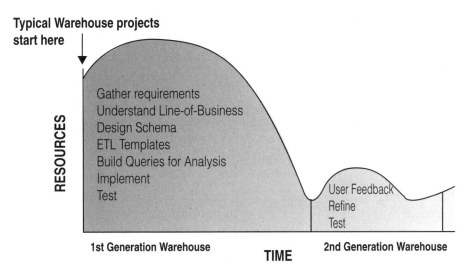

Typical Warehouse projects start here

RESOURCES

Gather requirements
Understand Line-of-Business
Design Schema
ETL Templates
Build Queries for Analysis
Implement
Test

User Feedback
Refine
Test

1st Generation Warehouse   2nd Generation Warehouse

TIME

value of the data available. They are meant to position the decision maker for creative exploration of an information domain, rather than the more predefined, static user interface generally associated with packaged operational applications.

▸ Finally, the project must *Implement and Test* the data warehouse before it can be critiqued via *User Feedback,* then *Refined* or customized to more accurately meet the customer needs, and then *Test* again. This process associated with building and maintaining a data warehouse is usually referred to as the Iterative Development process.

Benefits of Using a Packaged Data Warehouse Infrastructure

As the data warehousing market matures, it also undergoes substantial changes. Most significantly, it appears that the data warehouse market is moving from a "build" to a "buy" market. That is, rather than conceive and build their data warehouses starting from a "blank page", today's data warehouse implementers prefer to buy a packaged data warehouse infrastructure designed as "solutions" to address specific business problems or opportunities in their industries. By using these "packaged data warehouse infrastructures" and customizing them as necessary on implementation, the entire process of data warehouse implementation may be speeded up considerably. As a result, the customer can realize the benefits of access to the data warehouse information sooner.

The key components of a packaged data warehouse infrastructure include:

▸ *Predefined business models* that define the key elements and relationships important in solving the industry-specific business problems.

▸ *Predetermined database structures* that define the physical implementation of the data models. This is critical since you may design a very elegant business model that meets all requirements. But if it is implemented ineffectively from a physical perspective, it can lead to queries that take hours or days to finish, if they get completed at all.

▸ *Predeveloped meta data definitions* that serve as the documentation that describes the data in the data warehouse in terms of what it is, where it came from, when it was last updated, and more. As the number of users of a data warehouse increases in the future, this will become increasingly more important. Extensive documentation of the data warehouse in the form of meta data in technical and business terms will be considered a valuable asset.

▸ *Transformation/loading scripts* that define the source to target mapping and transformation rules that must be applied as data are extracted from their source locations and as the target data warehouse is populated.

▸ *Reporting templates* that in the implementation of a packaged data warehouse solution show ways to use data. The 80/20 rule shows it is more important to deliver reporting templates that provide examples of how to access and use the data warehouse models most effectively.

Figure 3: Benefits of Using a Packaged Data Warehouse Infrastructure

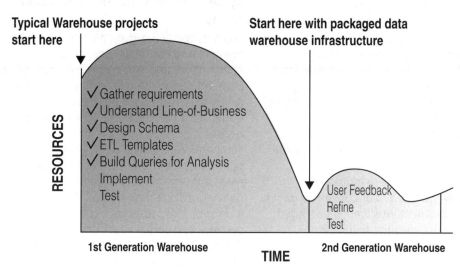

Figure 3 illustrates the specific steps in which using a packaged data warehouse infrastructure speeds the project development process. The most time-consuming steps associated with the startup design and initial implementation of a data warehouse are greatly reduced by choosing to use a solution based on a packaged data warehouse infrastructure.

The packaged data warehouse infrastructure solution delivers the following key benefits:

▸ Implementation of the data warehouse is accomplished at a much lower cost and with the requirement for far fewer resources than traditional development methods.
▸ It enables earlier access to and use of the data warehouse by the end user.

▸ It reduces the risk normally associated with building a data warehouse.

Introducing the Sybase Industry Warehouse Studio

Vendors such as Sybase have gained significant experience through numerous engagements that dealt with the development and implementation of data warehouses and their associated Business Intelligence or analytical applications. At Sybase, we have studied our implementation with the objective of understanding what makes developing analytical applications based on a data warehouse such a lengthy process, involving high costs and great risk. At the same time, through our experience we discovered that within specific industries, there are common treatments of workflow, measurements, reporting requirements, terminology, and data types.

The result of these efforts has been the development of a series of customer-focused, industry-oriented packaged data warehouse models and accompanying analytic applications. They take the risk out of delivering Business Intelligence capabilities while reducing the costs involved and optimizing application value.

By implementing Sybase Industry Warehouse Studio™, our customers gain a complete business intelligence packaged solution containing the following components:

▸ Industry data model
▸ Packaged application reports
▸ Database design tool suite
▸ Meta data repository and Web client
▸ Database independence: integration with standard databases such as IBM, Informix, Microsoft, Oracle, and Sybase
▸ Methodology and project plans optimized for industry-specific implementation

By providing a detailed analytical template mapped to defined applications that have a proven business benefit in a specific vertical industry, each Business Intelligence packaged application takes the risk out of data warehousing, reduces the costs involved, and optimizes application value. And because it is designed to meet the requirements of a targeted industry, these customer-focused, vertical solutions provide benefits faster and more consistently within the targeted industry compared with a technology-based decision support implementation.

Sybase Delivers the Right Solution Today

Business today is a dynamic environment of mergers and consolidations, global competition, and encroachment from other business sectors. In this environment, the ability to analyze your business to understand the impact of your business decisions on sales revenue, market competition, financial costs, and operational effectiveness becomes even more important. Every decision you make not only affects the way your business works, but also how your customers perceive you versus your competition. Across every major industry, firms look at new ways to discover business opportunities by better understanding customer needs, analyzing profitable market segments, providing specific products their profitable customers demand, and measuring how well their organizations are executing these demands. Sybase Business Intelligence delivers industry-leading applications and technology through partner-ships with the Sybase Professional Services team and our network of system integrators and solution providers to enable business success.

Industry-Focused Warehouse Studios

Today, conventional large-scale data warehouse development projects typically cost several million dollars and require many months—and often years —of development time. Sybase recognizes that data warehousing and Business Intelligence solutions are rapidly evolving toward packaged vertical applications. Sybase, today, provides proven industry applications for Business Intelligence. These applications, combined with Warehouse Studio, form the basis of Sybase's new Business Intelligence offerings.

The Industry Warehouse Studios function as an integrated application infrastructure that addresses the different, but related, aspects of customer behavior, customer value, and customer potential. The component-based approach, which has been used to construct the solutions, facilitates an incremental deployment strategy that ensures the seamless integration of the entire data architecture. The richness, flexibility, and performance of the database design unlock the key to application capabilities that truly facilitate the development of real sustainable customer relationships.

Industry Warehouse Studio Packaged Application Reports

The Analytical CRM focus of the Industry Warehouse Studio is delivered through the following cross-industry application areas:

▸ Campaign Analysis
▸ Customer Profile Analysis
▸ Sales Analysis
▸ Customer Loyalty
▸ Customer Care Analysis

Each application area is delivered with several packaged reports designed to exploit the accompanying data models and provide the information to address and answer key business questions related to the application domain.

The reports described in this paper are those defined for the initial delivery of the Industry Warehouse Studios. Since

additional reports are being developed on a regular basis, please check with your Sybase representative for the most updated list of available reports.

Campaign Analysis

Accurately targeting customers in campaigns and promotions as well as analyzing their responses to promotion episodes is a key part of the learning process that enables the transition from mass marketing to mass customization. Most organizations launch many different kinds of promotional campaigns for many different products using many different media. This application enhances the organization's understanding of the entire process—from selecting customers to be targeted to analyzing how they responded. It is clearly an analytical application and a prerequisite for any operational software package to manage the campaign episode itself.

The Campaign Analysis application supports an analysis of campaigns by both households and individual customers. It includes an analysis of customers who are highly responsive to campaigns. It compares the characteristics of customers who are highly unresponsive with the characteristics of customers who have opted to be excluded from campaigns. As well, it provides the ability to measure the effectiveness of individual campaigns and the effectiveness of different media, and has the ability to conduct several cost-benefit analyses of campaigns.

Chapter 3: CRM in Practice

Campaign Analysis—Sample Packaged Application Reports

▸ POSITIVE RESPONSE PROFILE ANALYSIS BY HOUSEHOLD Establishes the characteristics of households that have had a historical pattern of responding positively to promotions and campaigns. Identifies the attributes of customers who respond positively to a campaign, then identifies all customers who share the same attributes.

▸ NEGATIVE RESPONSE PROFILE ANALYSIS BY HOUSEHOLD Establishes the characteristics of households that have had a historical pattern of responding negatively to promotions and campaigns. Identifies the attributes of customers who respond negatively, then identifies all customers who share the same attributes.

▸ PROMOTION CAMPAIGN EPISODE ANALYSIS BY CUSTOMER Analyzes the response to a particular campaign or promotion and identifies the characteristics of customers who responded to that specific campaign episode. In addition, identifies those customers who did not respond (but who share the characteristics of those who did) for the purposes of remailing information only to those identified.

▸ COST/BENEFIT ANALYSIS OF PROMOTION CAMPAIGNS Analyzes the relative costs and revenues of similar campaigns that have been executed.

▸ PROMOTION CAMPAIGN EFFECTIVENESS ANALYSIS Analyzes the efficiency and effectiveness of campaigns by comparing outcomes, media, channels, and regions to compare and contrast the effectiveness of one campaign episode with others.

> "By providing a common technology base for different industries, Sybase offers a unique advantage by making it possible to integrate information across industry sectors. For example, if an insurance company acquires a healthcare firm, then the information for both segments can be integrated because the technology framework is common to both."
>
> —Michael Burwen, President Consortium for Business Intelligence and Data Warehousing Research.

Customer Profile Analysis

This application allows organizations to distinguish, among the mass of customers, the many microsegments that make up the whole. Increasingly, customer segmentation forms an essential element of marketing strategy as markets become more fragmented and customer segments exhibit distinct and different characteristics. This application helps build genuine customer relationships in the era of one-to-one marketing.

The Customer Profile Analysis application includes an analysis of both households and individual customers. The analysis features profiling by product use and frequency, by product holding pattern, by demographic characteristics, by psychographic characteristics, and by geographic characteristics.

Customer Profile Analysis—Sample Packaged Application Reports

▸ HOUSEHOLD PRODUCT UTILIZATION ANALYSIS Profiles households on the basis of the product mix and product consumption. The purpose of the report is to facilitate segmentation based on the product dimension.

▸ HOUSEHOLD BEHAVIOR ANALYSIS Identifies the value of households based on purchase history. The purpose of the report is to facilitate household segmentation based on value.

▸ HOUSEHOLD PROFILE ANALYSIS Profiles households on the basis of household attributes. This report facilitates segmentation based on demographics, geography, and profession.

▸ CUSTOMER PRODUCT UTILIZATION ANALYSIS Profiles individual customers on the basis of the product mix and product consumption. This report facilitates segmentation based on the product dimension.

▸ CUSTOMER BEHAVIOR ANALYSIS Identifies the value of individual customers based on purchase history. This report facilitates household segmentation based on value.

▸ CUSTOMER PROFILE ANALYSIS Profiles individual customers on the basis of customer attributes. This report facilitates segmentation based on the customer's demographics, psychographics, geography, and profession.

Sales Analysis
The Sales Analysis application provides an analysis of sales presented from a variety of viewpoints, such as sales by channel, outlet, or organizational unit; sales by product, product category, or product group; sales by region; and sales by season.

This application gives the organization an integrated perspective on sales results and enables sales managers to understand the underlying trends and patterns in their sales data.

Sales Analysis —Sample Packaged Application Reports

▸ SUMMARY SALES ANALYSIS Provides a consolidated summary of sales by product over time and identifies the organizational unit responsible for the sales.

▸ SALES/CUSTOMER ANALYSIS Describes any relationships that exist between customer categories and product preferences.

▸ SALES/SATISFACTION ANALYSIS Analyzes the relationship between sales and cancellation events with customer satisfaction. Customer satisfaction is measured with reference to resolved and unresolved contact events during the proceeding 12-month period.

▸ CUSTOMER LOYALTY ANALYSIS
Identifies product usage and frequency by customer over time and any relationship that exists between usage patterns and the number of products held by a customer or the mix of products held by a customer.

▸ CUSTOMER LATENCY ANALYSIS
Identifies the attributes of customers who have more than "n" products and identifies those customers with the same attributes who have fewer than "n" products in ascending order. This analysis identifies customers with few products who share the same profile as customers with many products.

▸ SALES/ORGANIZATION PERFORMANCE
ANALYSIS Identifies the high-performing and low-performing organization units and channels in the enterprise.

Loyalty Analysis

One of the keys to profitability in any enterprise is customer loyalty. Yet so few organizations measure customer loyalty in a structured way or seek to understand the underlying causes of customer attrition. This application is designed to do just that.

The Loyalty Analysis application measures customer loyalty with reference to the duration of the customer relationship; the range of services and products consumed by the customer; and the demographic, psychographic, and geographic influences on customer attrition.

By itself, the Loyalty Analysis application measures and monitors customer loyalty and facilitates the development of customer retention programs. When combined with the other applications in the full IWS suite, the customer loyalty can be assessed in the context of their value, their contact history, the segments they belong to, and individual transaction events that may influence their loyalty.

Loyalty Analysis —Sample Packaged Application Reports

▸ CUSTOMER FREQUENCY ANALYSIS
Identifies the number of purchase events by customer, by region, and by product during the past 12 months, and calculates the average frequency.

▸ CUSTOMER RELATIONSHIP DURATION
ANALYSIS Identifies the duration of the customer relationship and orders by product, region, demographics, and psychographics for the longest duration of customers.

▸ CUSTOMER PRODUCT RANGE ANALYSIS
Identifies the relationship between the number of products held by the customer and the duration of the relationship.

▸ CUSTOMER REVENUE ANALYSIS
Identifies the relationship between the revenue generated by customers and the duration of the relationship.

▸ ATTRITION ANALYSIS Identifies customers who have cancelled a product or service, along with the product, region, demographics, and psychographics involved.

▸ RETENTION ANALYSIS Identifies customers who share the same demographic or geographic attributes as customers who have cancelled a product in the past 12 months.

Customer Care Analysis

Customers interact with organizations in many ways using different "touch points" to initiate inquiries, make complaints, give compliments, provide feedback, report faults, or make suggestions. This information provides valuable insight into the behavior of customers and the track records of the organizations servicing customers. The likely level of satisfaction or dissatisfaction of a customer can be determined by their customer contact history.

Analyzing customer contacts is essential in maintaining and nurturing customer relationships and preserving the loyalty of customers into the future. The application enables users to analyze the customer contact history of individual customers; resolved and unresolved complaints; the number of positive and negative contacts; the time taken to resolve customer complaints; and inquiries and the response of customers to these interactions.

Customer Care Analysis—Sample Packaged Application Reports

▸ CUSTOMER COMPLAINT ANALYSIS Identifies customer complaints by complaint type, product, day, time of day, time taken to resolve complaint, sales person, and region for the past 12 months. It also identifies complaints that were resolved successfully and those not resolved successfully.

▸ CUSTOMER INQUIRY ANALYSIS Identifies customer inquiries by product, organizational unit, day, time taken to resolve inquiry, and region for the past 12 months. It also identifies those that were resolved successfully and those not resolved successfully.

▸ CUSTOMER FAULT REPORT ANALYSIS Identifies customer fault reports by product, organizational unit, day, time of day, time taken to clear the fault, and region for the past 12 months. It also identifies those that were resolved successfully and those not resolved successfully.

▸ CUSTOMER SUGGESTION ANALYSIS Identifies customer suggestions by product, organizational unit, and region for the past 12 months. It also identifies those that were implemented and those not implemented.

▸ CONTACT CONTENTION ANALYSIS Identifies the number of unsolicited contacts made to the customer during the past 12 months by organization unit, product, and week. It also identifies if the customer received more than one communication in any week from more than one organizational unit.

▸ CUSTOMER SATISFACTION ANALYSIS Identifies the customer satisfaction rating of the top 20% of customers and the bottom 20% of customers, as well as their orders by product, region, and demographics.

Getting Results Today

At Sybase, we've built Business Intelligence technology that focuses exclusively on the information needs of your business. Our dedicated staff of sales, support, marketing, partner relations, product development, consulting services, and technical experts provide high-yield solutions to your problems.

Through our network of partners and system integrators, we can provide the services you need—from project management, to full-scale development, to business collaboration. We know your industry. We're here to help.

Business Intelligence is a sophisticated and powerful way to retain and engage your customers. Now, Sybase customers enjoy stronger revenue growth, better market penetration, and reduced cost of customer acquisition and service while improving customer satisfaction and retention. For more information on Sybase's capabilities and product offerings for data warehousing and Customer Relationship Management, visit us on the Web at http://www.sybase.com/bi, or call us at 1-800-8-SYBASE.

Appendix A: Sybase Industry Warehouse Studio Components

In the past five years, Sybase has examined the processes surrounding the development of analytical applications — taking care to catalog all factors that typically contribute to high costs and lengthy development and implementation cycles.

Industry Data Models (Included with IWS)
Our Business Intelligence applications minimize design and implementation risk through proven, detailed data models that map to your specific business analysis needs. Our data models and business applications have grown and evolved through five years of successful implementations at large-scale installations throughout the world. With our data models and methodology, we have provided significant value to our customers by:

▶ Reducing risk of failure, design costs, and implementation time
▶ Ensuring scalability, data integration, and enterprisewide scope
▶ Providing extensibility that allows you to add information critical to your business
▶ Exploiting proven designs that "future-proof " the database while reducing disk space requirements
▶ Reducing the complexity of application development and enabling graceful change management
▶ Offering integrated models with conformed dimensions to provide a consistent "snapshot" of information across multiple areas

Packaged Application Reports (Included with IWS)

Each Industry Warehouse Studio application module comes with a set of packaged application reports or "report templates" in the form of SQL that provide a starting point for customizing the applications to meet the specific customer needs. These reports answer key business questions related to the application area. Sample reports for each of the core Analytical CRM applications are described elsewhere in this document. Partners such as Cognos, Business Objects, and others will be developing sample applications using the SQL templates that will highlight their own product strengths in providing "view access" to the IWS models.

Warehouse Architect (Included with IWS)

It starts with the design. Warehouse Studio gives you PowerDesigner® WarehouseArchitect™ so you can graphically design exactly what you want. WarehouseArchitect then creates scripts to load the warehouse and even delivers information to business applications so users can interact with the warehouse immediately. With support for relational, star, and aggregated multidimensional schemas, WarehouseArchitect gives you the tools to build your warehouse, no matter how complex your business requirements.

A full range of reporting capabilities ensures the documentation and availability of warehouse-specific objects like external tables and columns, facts, dimensions, attributes, matrices, and source mappings. You can share this information throughout your organization.

Warehouse Control Center® (Included with IWS)

Whether you're in the initial stages of developing a data warehouse or you have multiple data marts, you need to manage your investment. The key is meta data. Meta data provides descriptions and attributes of warehouse contents in terms a business user can understand. From warehouse design through delivery, Warehouse Studio's Warehouse Control Center lets you capture, synchronize, manage, and use logical, physical, and contextual meta data throughout your data warehouse, while storing it in a central repository. You also can synchronize the meta data with query tools so users can immediately access data using meaningful business terminology rather than complex database nomenclature. And users can easily navigate through and search the data using the Warehouse Control Center's Meta Data Browser.

Methodology and Project Plans (Included with IWS)

The IWS methodology has evolved as a full life cycle methodology to help design, develop, and administer data warehouses and data marts. The methodology is broken into four phases and is composed of nine separate steps or tasks. It provides a description of each task and includes a task summary table that guides the consultant through the task.

The summary table refers to each of the following components of a task:

- Purpose—identifies the benefit of performing this task.
- Deliverable(s)—describes what is to be delivered from each task and indicates how that deliverable is to be used.
- Dependencies—shows which tasks must be completed before another task may start and which tasks run concurrently.
- Participants—identifies the different participants in the data warehouse project that need to be involved in the task. Any special responsibilities are defined in this section.
- Activities—describes a set of activities that may be used to complete the task. These are suggestions based on the author's experiences and should be modified to fit the unique characteristics of each project.
- Techniques and tools—represents a means of completing the task, and where one or more options exist, how to select the optimum tool or technique. It is assumed that the project has a standard office suite (word processor, spreadsheet, etc.) and a project management tool.
- Estimating and project management guidelines—estimates how much effort should be involved (in elapsed calendar days and in labor) in the completion of a task on a typical project; estimates the guidelines that indicate the factors that may cause the task completion to take more or less time.
- Quality assurance guidelines—discusses measures for the success of each task or the content of each deliverable.

Project management tasks are incorporated in the methodology steps. Some important activities such as status reporting and change control are required throughout the project, and are not specifically addressed in the work breakdown.

Database Independence (Standard feature of IWS)

To guarantee the success of our application-driven approach, Sybase delivers database-independent solutions that support all the major database platforms including IBM, Informix, Microsoft, Oracle, and Sybase. The IWS applications also run on Sybase's analytic engines, exclusively designed for Business Intelligence: Adaptive Server® IQ12 and Adaptive Server IQ12 —Multiplex.

PowerStage™ (Optional feature of IWS)

Designing your warehouse is just the beginning. You need to populate that warehouse with information, and that process involves more than simply dumping in bits of data. Data must be extracted from a variety of sources and transformed into information that makes sense to the business user. Warehouse Studio's PowerStage™ provides an easy-to-use, component-based solution for just that — automating the extraction, transformation, and cleansing of data from multiple operational sources.

Using PowerStage's graphical drag-and-drop environment, developers easily design the data integration process from the source through transformation to the target warehouse. PowerStage breaks the process into a series of easy-to-understand, discrete steps that can be scheduled for execution or performed on demand. And PowerStage's component-based architecture increases productivity by

allowing you to build components that
reflect specific needs and then package
and reuse those components.

*Biography: Sybase, Inc. is one of the largest global
independent software companies. Sybase helps businesses
integrate, manage and deliver applications, content and data
anywhere they are needed. With a commitment to
distributed, open, and end-to-end computing, Sybase, Inc. is
helping companies build advanced data warehouse solutions.
The company is also leveraging core enterprise product
strengths to capitalize on the emerging enterprise information
portal market to provide dependable solutions that deliver on
the promise of e-Business.
http://www.sybase.com/bi*

Successful Customer Relationship Management: Why, ERP, Data Warehousing, Decision Support, and Metadata Matter

Title:	*Successful Customer Relationship Management: Why, ERP, Data Warehousing, Decision Support, and Metadata Matter.*
Author:	*Jim Davis and Ellen Joyner, SAS Institute*
Abstract:	*A CRM system is only as successful as the quality of data and data-management processes supporting it. Organizations planning wisely beyond the next millennium are thinking beyond process automation and are focused on getting better acquainted with customers to increase revenues and profits. Maintaining a sound metadata strategy – as well as understanding the roles of ERP, decision support, and data warehousing systems – is crucial for attaining this higher level of understanding.*

The year 2000, then what? Many companies aren't thinking past the new millennium. But smart organizations are considering initiatives and strategies to increase profits and revenues. Many have invested heavily in enterprise resource planning (ERP) and supply chain (SC) systems to automate the back office and cut costs through more efficient and streamlined financial, inventory management, and order-entry systems. Cutting costs alone is a tried-and-true route to return on investment. But why not increase revenue while also reducing costs? While many of these ERP and SC systems improve external processes, such as distribution, these initiatives remain largely internally focused. Yet addressing external issues and pressures have the greatest impact on corporate profitability. That is why so many smart businesses have turned their attention to customer relationship management (CRM) strategies.

CRM recognizes that customers are at the core of the business, and the company's success depends on effectively managing relationships with them. To correctly manage those relationships, the company must first know who its customers are, not just as groups or segments of customers, but each individual customer. Is this customer a good customer? Is he or she profitable? Why does he or she do business with me? What does this person like about my business? Does this person also do business with my competitor?

Data warehousing technology makes one-to-one interactions with customers possible because they sit at the core to consolidate information and turn data about customers into customer intelligence. Smart organizations know that they have to think beyond automating processes and figure out how to better understand their customer base to increase revenues and profits. Information technology plays a crucial role in ensuring that the data and metadata associated with these various systems is kept clean, accurate, and valid. There is an increasing realization that a metadata strategy is central to an organization's future. The demand for readily accessible and reliable information to support strategic and tactical decision making has grown steadily in recent years. As a result, organizations have dedicated substantial resources (in some cases massive resources) to building data warehouses and data marts.

The case for CRM

A high level of customer knowledge is crucial to organizations today because of competition in shrinking markets. Deregulation, diversification, and globalization have stimulated a dramatic rise in competitiveness, making it more imperative than ever to better manage customer relationships at every point of contact, and to acquire and build loyalty among those customers deemed most profitable. This has focused intense scrutiny on front-office applications, where the company interacts most often with the customer directly or indirectly via such outlets as branch offices, kiosks, call centers, sales representatives, marketing, the Web, email, and order entry. Customers are defined in many different ways. For example, the customer can be the direct consumer or an organization, such as a business partner, distributor, or shareholder. The point is, today's customers have many choices, and it is up to the company to make sure profitable customers remain loyal and new prospects grow in loyalty and profitability.

Customer satisfaction and customer loyalty: not the same thing

Monitoring and capturing customer satisfaction information isn't new. But is this information really telling companies what they need to know about their customers? Is satisfaction alone good enough? Not according to a recent survey from the Meta Group:

"Fifty percent of your company's satisfied customers will do business with your competitors. Twenty-five percent of your company's VERY satisfied customers will do business with your competitors."

Percentages like that mean companies need to discover much more about their customers than their satisfaction level. Building loyalty among customers involves understanding the various ways that they are different and using that knowledge to tailor appropriate behaviors towards those customers. To be customer focused and customer centric, the company must continuously learn from interactions with each individual customer and be prepared to dynamically respond to information and knowledge gained from those interactions. The company must be well equipped with the information and knowledge to engage proactively with the customer versus reactive. Proactive customer engagement and interaction involves much collaboration throughout the organization. CRM is a concept, and it is also a process because a company has to organize itself such that all information coming from customer touch points and other customer related information is consolidated to facilitate a learning process. Bestselling author, Dr.

Fred Wiersema speaks of five essential steps to help organizations reach their customer oriented potential. Step 5 involves establishing trust as the key to building stronger, lasting relationships with customers. "First, you have to communicate clearly what you are and what you are not going to do for that customer-and follow through. Second, customers must know that you are trying to understand what is important to them-the critical aspects of their business and their life. And third, in many cases, companies hold large amounts of very personal information about customers. They must trust that you will protect their privacy. Ultimately, if you develop trust, you should be able to get a customer to outsource part of their decision-making to you." This involves support from many lines of business units and information technology.

Marketplace pains...CRM remedies

The issues that motivate organizations to seek a CRM solution can take many forms, and the needs originate from many functional areas of the business. The following scenarios indicate the need for an overhaul of an organization's customer management strategy:

▸ No real understanding of who the customers are, which are the most profitable, or what their lifetime value is.
▸ Communications efforts with customers are not effective enough. Customers often receive conflicting messages from the company's different business units,

and the sales and marketing cycle is too long.
▸ Inability to get a handle on the market in general, and in particular, what customers need or want.

The best CRM solutions allow a company to bring together the most complete repository of information about customers and competitors—including market research data from both internal and external sources—within a single, customer-centric data warehouse. Exploiting such a repository leads to a solid understanding of market trends and competitive marketing activities. With this understanding, a company is in a good position to develop new products or reposition or abandon existing ones to satisfy customer demands and gain competitive advantage in the marketplace.

The best CRM processes also incorporate newfound knowledge into existing customer-related operational systems and analyze the results of previous actions to predict which customer segments are more likely to respond to which type of campaign or product offering. They also use multidimensional data analysis and data mining techniques to understand what drives profitability by identifying the most profitable current customers and predicting future customer profitability. Finally, the best CRM solutions manage and store all customer-related data, from every point of customer contact, in a single data warehouse. This information is surfaced to every customer contact point through Web-enabled dynamic reporting systems and executive information systems. This provides business managers with timely reports on any aspect of customer relations, allowing them to refine resource allocation to maximize profits. For example, marketing managers can manage campaign efficiency (profitability, impact, percentage of respondents to a given offer) as well as sales activities (average sales cycle length, cost of sales, sales profitability).

The role of metadata

Until very recently, a surefire way to provoke an embarrassed silence at any meeting between business and IT people was to mention the word metadata. Even if they knew what you were talking about, business peoples' eyes would glaze over. IT people might think, "Someone ought to do something about metadata, but please, not me!"

Organizing all customer data into an integrated warehouse environment is one of the biggest challenges faced by information technicians. However, an equally important challenge is to create an integrated environment for telling everyone what data is available and how it can be exploited. Without data about data (metadata) the organization will, at best, fail to get the full return on its investment in data warehousing. At worst, there is the risk that as the amount of data in the data-warehousing infrastructure rises exponentially, business users will despair at the time it takes to find useful information. Other trends are also contributing to the need for a tighter inventory of information resources. For example:

▸ Changes in the business environment create constantly evolving business definitions.
▸ Data marts are proliferating, often without central planning.
▸ Business units and teams create their own terms for similar data elements.
▸ Trans- and multinational ventures create language difficulties.
▸ Increasing staff turnover means a constant outflow of undocumented business knowledge.
▸ Valuable but unstructured external information (such as Web-based) is adding to data volumes.

Develop a methodology early

One of the great advantages of a data warehouse is that it provides a repository of data, independent of operational systems, that is centered around the business users' needs. But inevitably, when these users begin accessing the information within a warehouse, certain questions arise:

▸ What information is available in the warehouse?
▸ What do the definitions mean (for example, exactly how is a customer defined)?
▸ Is the data current and can I trust it?

From the enterprise level, most likely the level at which the success of the data warehouse ultimately will be judged, metadata is designed to help answer these sorts of questions. These questions usually can be answered relatively easily early in the life of a data warehouse initiative.

However, the role of metadata becomes more complex as the enterprise information matures and users' demands increase. Consequently organizations can save themselves a lot of trouble if they structure a complete environment for metadata management and approach the issue methodically from day one.

The functions of metadata

Metadata serves several functions for both technical and business users. Technical metadata describes or documents data and information items, providing details such as what an object is named; when, how, and by whom it was created; its type and size; its sources; and transformations. It also provides an integral record in data quality management practices -- establishing naming and other standards, documenting source-to-target transformations, and measuring and reporting compliance to systems of record. The true value of metadata emerges when it is used to guide information update and access processes.

Additionally, metadata can be used to enforce security on the data in a data warehouse. Although it may be desirable to allow broad access to all the data elements in a warehouse, special-purpose data marts and operational data details may require restrictions. Moreover, security of access to the data stores may be necessary to minimize redundancy.

For business users, metadata is essential to the management, organization, and exploitation activities that occur throughout the evolution of a truly active

information environment. Things change quickly in the business world. It is very helpful for business users to be able to see, for instance, how the profit variable was calculated, or that perhaps sales territories were divided differently prior to a certain date, or even just when the data was last updated. This type of metadata, such as documented business rules, helps extend the value of data warehouse information. People feel that they can trust it.

Given the complexity of the relationship between operational and information delivery/decision support systems within increasingly close-knit enterprise information systems, metadata should document all data elements from data source to data exploitation as completely as possible. And, as more and more data warehouses and data marts are created, an integrated, effective metadata management strategy is key to avoiding confusion and chaos later. Inheriting data warehouses and data marts without metadata would be worse than just a surprise for IT technicians. It would be a real pain.

Think big and plan for more

Getting data warehouse projects off the ground with the impetus needed to deliver an early return on investment invariably involves overcoming skepticism and raising expectations. A methodology that emphasizes the benefits of starting small and building the warehouse iteratively is highly recommended. That way, people see an early reward for their efforts and trust. Metadata represents the key element on the other side of the equation. When planning a metadata environment, it is advisable to think big and build an environment that allows for never-ending evolution.

Organizations need to realize that ERP vendors know OLTP technology and that transaction processing is their core competency. And although ERP vendors' data warehousing solutions will offer the appeal of easy integration with their own ERP modules, it's less obvious that their toolsets will be as sophisticated as competing data warehousing and decision support solutions from integrated data warehousing/decision support vendors. ERP vendors are good at managing and maintaining OLTP systems and delivering static reports. However, ERP vendors are just beginning to offer first-generation solutions to their customers' data warehousing needs. The point is, there's a fundamental disconnect between OLTP and DSS systems.

As organizations continue to develop enterprise-wide information delivery mechanisms to support decision support via databases, data marts and data warehouses, the next logical step is to extend these information stores from ERP system and other legacy links to data exploitation. Organizations must maintain their legacy systems to evaluate past data to make better business decisions (many of these legacy systems are still active and gathering new information). The challenge remains in tying legacy data into a complete information architecture.

Begin by developing an enterprise decision support architecture that contains metadata and integrates ERP environments. Managing metadata is not only a key component of a well architected IT infrastructure, it also represents a valuable road map that can provide an organization's decision support users with a strong competitive advantage. It requires a customizable solution that offers a single point of control, making it easier to respond to the ever-changing needs of the business community.

Is a data warehouse the same as a decision-support system (DSS)?

A data warehouse is best used to enable analytical information processing. Since this analytical information processing is performed "online" and interactively (though not necessarily over the Internet), the discipline is called Online Analytical Processing (OLAP). OLAP is an analytical processing technology, which creates business information through a robust set of business transformations and calculations upon existing data. For a DSS to supply valuable information, it has to represent the information the way the users perceive it in real life. Users look at the information in the form of business events and the different ways the events are analyzed.

How does a data warehouse feed a DSS?

The suite of products that could be called DSS products consists of: OLAP, query and reporting, data visualization, data analysis, data mining, executive information systems (EIS), and business solutions, including financial consolidation and reporting, human resources, and Web enablement.

A data warehouse designed for DSS armed with the appropriate OLAP software tools can give users easy and intuitive access to their data for analysis—making users self sufficient and getting developers out of the report writing business. Users should be able to combine their data in any order they desire, at any level of aggregation and over several time periods. Users should be able to analyze the data by clicking on the dimensions and the data itself.

ERP vs. DSS?

Enterprise Resource Planning (ERP) software is a set of applications that automates finance and human resources departments and helps manufacturers handle jobs such as order processing and production scheduling. The main mission of ERP systems is integrating the processes of an organization. ERP systems involve processes that in most organizations that have evolved over the years, so are notoriously complex to install and maintain. A data warehouse, on the other hand, has an "information out" mission. The major mission of a data warehouse is to enable the users to "take out the data" for analysis.

Data warehouses have different design criteria and need to be judged by different performance monitoring criteria than OLTP databases. The fundamental assumptions of data warehouse design are that data is stored so as to be readily accessible in ways that are of interest to users and that the design of the data model is driven by usage. In general (and this can drive a traditional DBA crazy), data redundancy is favored over data model complexity. Because a simple model is favored over a complex model, most standard relational database modeling tools, without modifications for data warehouse usage, are of little use in deriving a data warehouse design. Unfortunately, most cost-based database optimizers aren't well suited for data warehouse queries.

There is a fundamental disconnect between OLTP and DSS systems. Although ERP customers can take advantage of those systems' built-in reports, they often discover how hard it is to get a "global," unified view of all their data which may be distributed across multiple ERP servers vendors. The functionality of ERP systems is not easily transferable to decision support.

ERP systems, generally haven't been built to integrate data from external sources, or even integrate legacy data on an ongoing basis. They weren't designed to support and manage data marts or data warehouses for DSS applications. They weren't designed with a data transformation engine to store the types of complex data transformation rules often associated with populating and freshening data warehouse data. They weren't built with tools to let data architects design and model data warehouses and marts. ERP systems didn't ship with OLAP viewers that let end users slice and dice. Therefore, bridging the gap between that front office and the back office ERP systems through and integrated DSS approach is crucial for a successful CRM solution. But there's one other element.

Collaboration of Customer Knowledge

Collaboration of this customer intelligence and customer knowledge becomes another key issue for organizations as they expand the customer channels. How can customer knowledge be shared in such a way that each customer touch point has the most accurate and up-to-date customer information independent of which channel that customer chooses to interact with?

Collaborative Business Intelligence (CBI) allows companies to unlock the power of their data stores by creating collaborative, contextual information environments. Analysts who traditionally use business-intelligence tools to look for important business factors can now save their findings into a knowledge repository, making it easily accessible to the rest of the organization over the Web. Decision makers become more engaged in the knowledge-building process as they add to the thread, and everyone can search for similar projects and re-use ideas that have worked in the past.

Linking structured and unstructured information

Creating CBI environments will allow organizations to expand the way they are already doing business by knowledge enabling their existing and future business processes. Organizations will be able to link structured data – the reports, and graphics created by business-intelligence tools, for example – with unstructured information, the documents, email, and on-line discussions that support structured data. By surfacing this linked information through a Web browser, everyone in the organization can benefit from the capture, organization, and re-use of corporate knowledge. As a result, knowledge remains available regardless of employee availability or mobility, and current systems are better utilized.

CBI takes that customer information, stores it in a common knowledge repository, and allows anyone with proper Web clearance to locate information quickly, dynamically use linked business intelligence tools, and contribute their own ideas. Users can set up subscriptions to be notified of additions to the knowledge repository and can email directly into the repository.

CRM in action: First Union
Building enterprise-wide 1:1 customers relationships

First Union Corporation, the nation's sixth-largest bank, started considering customized marketing in 1996. Since then, it has been methodically implementing the strategy and refining what it means to do

1:1 marketing. While the vision is broad and encompasses many interrelated goals, the knowledge-based marketing strategy follows two guiding principles. The first is to develop profitable and long lasting customer relationships through access to and insightful analysis of customer information. The second is to provide the company's internal business partners consistent marketing services and flawless execution.

First Union has assembled a sophisticated combination of front-office technology, including innovative proprietary systems for CRM, data warehousing, and a marketing data-mart. Using data mining and extrapolation tools from SAS Institute, the bank's knowledge-based marketing division has developed a process which evaluates every customer relationship and matches each customer, statistically speaking, with the next financial products or services that they are likely to acquire. It delivers highly segmented, individual customer profiles to the sales person who can then speak to customers about very specific services that they most likely to buy next. On the customer service side, agents can conduct the same quality of conversations with their customers. When a customer calls into the bank to check a balance, for instance, "opportunities," appear on the agent's screen that suggest services directly relevant to the calling customer. The results generate solid product sales utilizing customer-centric data.

First Union also uses the technology to develop customer segmentation leads. For example, First Union identifies customers by their value to the bank and what group each customer falls into. These are customers who have a strong history with the bank, carry high balances, and are working with the bank in a variety of ways. The customer segmentation list, along with individual customer profile information, gives each sales rep an intelligent framework to launch into a business conversation with the objective of deepening, broadening or retaining the customer relationship.

Building the Business Case Blues or Business Case Blues

Title: Building the Business Case Blues or Business Case Blues
Author: Michael Meltzer, Computer Sciences Corporations

Abstract: *This article introduces some of the ways you can go about creating you own set of inputs to your very own and unique business case. I will introduce a range of approaches for you to consider: Political, Analytical, Economic, Cost Reduction and Strategic. The idea of a CRM is to provide you with a competitive set of processes and tools – how you justify survival is an interesting task – good luck few find the journey to creating a business case pleasant – this paper might lighten the load.*

Biography: see end article

If you understand the need to introduce positive change in the way you interact and deliver products and services to your customers, then you are taking the first step towards becoming more competitive. You understand the concepts of life time value, customer retention and acquisition costing as part of the relationship management process and you want to implement them. Customer Relationship Management is seen as one of the most important ways for a company to survive and thrive today yet it still remains difficult to justify the costs and the changes required to make it happen. Given the need to E-Business everything you do makes the need to justify expenditures on new technologies and business practices even more important. Few companies will make that leap of faith without some thought to actual outcomes. To introduce these concepts as operational realities you need to introduce new technology, processes and ways of thinking about the customer - you must invest in change.

The journey towards introducing the knowledge repository (data warehouse), that will create the base infrastructure for a customer relationship management system is really part of that process that is currently changing business forever. This article addresses the overall dimensions of the business case as it relates to a knowledge repository (KR), Customer Relationship Management (CRM) and the conceptual consequences as a means of creating sustainable competitive advantage.

You want to choose the right customers to serve, retain and develop. You want to understand customer's preferences, their profitability and exactly who the right people are to mailshot with your hot new service and or product. But you don't have the right information to act. The information exists in disparate systems, in different formats, on different computers that are likely to be geographically distributed.

Your need is to bring together the relevant data and turn it into actionable information in your quest for CRM. You know that there is a way forward and that is through the introduction of a new conceptual approach and a technology called a data warehouse. This is merely one of the first steps you can take to realise your vision. Some will argue that you could of course introduce a sales force automation system and that is CRM too up to a point. But without a sound base of valid and trusted information about your customers - garbage in garbage out (GIGO still lives).

There are people who can help you make the right technology decisions in your own organisation and they are usually part of, or linked to your information services group. Together you must move towards introducing the solution that will enable you to take advantage of the opportunities on offer. But before you can go forward you must prove that what you want to introduce will have demonstrable benefits. This is where you need a business case. There are many opportunities to use specific technology to increase your organisation's competitive position in the market. To enable you to successfully introduce the new technology and the changes it will bring, you must think carefully about the way in which your organisation makes investments decisions. A major help in some case has been the Information services team when seen as partners. As was the case at Signet Banking Corp, Richmond Virginia which saw the Data Warehouse as a major part of their information based CRM and decision support system.

"We took it on faith that it would generate value, " says David Knelliger the architect of Signet's business systems. "Management was committed to taking the risk even without a guaranteed return." And according to Knelliger, the management really didn't know what the bottom-line impact would be, only believing they would show a return. They just knew that if they could get a better understanding of their marketing campaigns, actual customer profitability whilst also enjoying improved operational efficiency, they would make money.

The Political Approach

Signet's approach and thinking demonstrates quite well the concept of a bank willing to take risks in pursuit of differential and early competitive advantage (they took the plunge in 1994 before the term CRM was mainstream). Part of the reason they could push the project through was the heavyweight support given by senior management and the specificity of the initial investment. For a visual representation of an organisational impact model of investment decision making see figures 1. and 2. In figure 1 you can see that this organisation believes strongly in understanding the business case for any major investment decision. In figure 2 the emphasis is on senior decision makers willing to take risks with little analysis.

Using the figures above we tackle each element in a clockwise direction. Work on the analytical aspects of investment decision making is lengthy whilst the other,

Figure 1

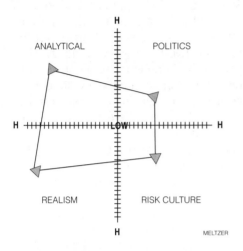

Figure 2

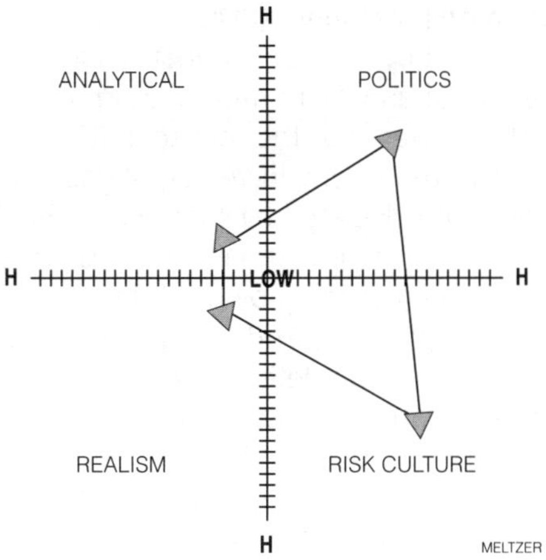

softer aspects of an organisation move us towards strategic studies, social psychology, anthropology and organisational ecology. Perception is reality in organisational life and what you perceive in your organisation is probably what you get. I will only discuss briefly the softer aspects, but they can make or break even the most well-crafted analytical business case.

Analytical Approaches

Analytical (economic man) approaches to decision making have all the hall marks of the rational business manager guided by logic, a calculator and strategic insight. Studies in this arena have been extensive, with articles written and companies being formed around the concept of building the better and more efficacious business case. The term "business case" itself is often misunderstood. As M J Schimdt of Solution Matrix Ltd puts it, "a request for a business case is similar in some ways to a request for your personal resume: you have a lot of freedom to design the structure and select the content: whether or not the result is effective depends on your ability to tell a convincing story with compelling logic and facts." A basic premise of any business case is that an investment will have an impact and payback that spans a particular time line which can spread across months or years. Inputs in terms of costs and outcomes used should be made up of incremental or total costs related specifically to the investment decision. Some assumptions and even arbitrary judgements will have to be made to accommodate the complexities that can be involved. Few of the techniques used are clear cut and many overlap, but until someone invents a better method.....! Some approaches used are: Economic, cost reduction, and strategic.

Economic approaches

Return on Investment (ROI) -

Often used by financial analysts as a measure of an organisation's return on assets invested. For the manager, ROI means return or any incremental gain. The measure is calculated by subtracting the total cost of the investment from the total benefits then dividing by the total cost and then multiplying by 100. The result is then compared to a predetermined internal hurdle rate, and the result of this comparison results in either a "yes" or a "no". IDC has carried out research using standard investment formulas which showed that a three year ROI for all types of data warehouses was 401%. A quarter of the 62 participants in this study showed returns in excess of 600% with a payback on initial investments within 2.3 years. (Brian McWilliams) As a subtext to the ROI approach you have to consider the more sophisticated financial metrics your own organisation uses. These could consist of:

Net Present Value (NPV) -

This looks at today's value of a set of future payments, discounted by a specific rate. This method can also be referred to as the Discounted cash flow (DCF) technique. When an investment achieves an NPV equal to or greater than zero then it will achieve the minimum rate-of-return. These measures are usually used when the time horizon stretches over two or more years, and when investments are being compared that have differing cash flow profiles.

Internal Rate of Return (IRR) -

Similar to the NPV approach but utilises an internal hurdle rate rather than an external rate as the base measure. This approach takes an investment view as money will be paid out to bring in monetary benefits. The higher the hurdle rate the investments achieve the better. This approach can be quite misleading if there is no large initial cash outflows.

This can occur when you are building that prototype customer information file or where you are outsourcing the effort.

Often the simplest approach is the "break even/payback" method, a state achieved when the cumulative flow of income/ benefits exceeds the cumulative flow of costs. Clearly, the shorter the payback the better the opportunity. This approach is simple and clear but cannot really deal with any decision that has a more strategic flavour as it does not recognise the time value of money. It is, however, the way many simple purchase decisions are justified. Often, all the above are presented in one business case, although one is given primacy depending time factors and risk.

The problem with attempts at quantification is that some things "even when we try hard" are not quantifiable. Given we are talking about moving your business case forward for change, then you have to consider the problems that IS executives have to deal with and some of the comments they have made. The point about different applications or uses of IT is that they differ in purpose, nature, certainty and risk. These differences are often expressed in practice by statements such as these:

a) 'You can't prove competitive advantage through discounted cash flow';
b) 'To get strategic IT applications approved, we have to circumvent appraisal procedures';
c) 'We didn't know the real benefits until after we experimented with and installed the system'; and
d) 'To get the project started, I had to tear up the formal appraisal'." (M.J. Earl Management Strategies For Information Technologies)

Cost reduction approaches

Cost Displacement/Cost Avoidance -
This has been the most direct way of justifying the introduction of new information systems. You simply compare the cost of the new system against the one you are displacing or avoiding. Lower costs are substituted for higher on the assumption that the new system's benefits are equal to or better than the existing system. If a company is automating a function, task or process and/or reducing or avoiding costs by re-engineering, then this tends to be the method used. This approach can also be used if there is some certainty in the cost reductions you can achieve in a particular project. However, to quote Paul A. Strassman, "asking for a direct tie-in between increased funding for computers and a commitment to deliver provable savings is an invitation to prepare figmental projections that demean both those who produce them as well as those that accept them". This reality was seen first hand in his work at Xerox, General Foods, Kraft Corporation and the Department of Defence in the US where he

was their chief information officer (CIO).*

* Paul A Strassman The Value of Computers, Information and Knowledge

Yet there are situations where you can prove that others have achieved results and if you follow in their footsteps you too can prove cost reductions. What if you could purchase a system that could help you reduce the costs of your direct mail campaigns through effective target marketing? Customers are more likely to respond to direct mail and buy whenever a product offer is directed to the customer - all due to a more timely and relevant contact. Following a switch in a campaign to a more focused database marketing approach, one bank generated a 3% to 4% converted response with a far smaller mailshot. Similarly, when making guaranteed offers of a debit card, a bank was able to generate responses between 20% and 25%, compared to previous bests of around 8%. The project champion had strong evidence that he could displace the cost of postage to the extent that the investment would save the bank money. He also used a simple payback model as the return was expected within an eighteen month period. With these kinds of results proving a pay back through cost savings alone, better customer conversion rates and additional incomes flows were a bonus. However cost reduction alone as a continuos strategy without investment in innovation is not the recipe for corporate longevity.

Work value Analysis -
The base assumption is that there is more work to be done than the company can

accomplish, or alternatively, business opportunities are not being seized due to lack of time. This investment can be recognised in the automation of the cheque clearing process. If cheques were cleared manually you would need more employees than are currently in the working population of many countries. This approach is also used in re-engineering efforts: IT has the ability to restructure work patterns so that efficiency is improved (doing the same work faster, better, and cheaper), and increase effectiveness (doing more higher value work versus lower value work). The approach also requires extensive work pattern measurement so that the introduction of new technology will enable managers to perform managerial and professional activities. The idea is to automate the administrative, clerical and other 'non-productive' tasks. The idea of a decision support system could be introduced here, but often the very lack of systemic support in the past makes it difficult to identify the so-called work patterns that would benefit from IT support. And what is the specific value in terms of effectiveness and efficiency of better decisions, anyway!?

Strategic Approaches

Any investment decision regarding information technology must take a view on the future. The decision is part of a strategic alignment of IT with business needs. It is an attempt to proactively manage uncertainty. Any one decision is one of a number that could be made given the information available. The strategic

arena is both a path to high politics and risk taking. Although strategy is often thought of as being crafted by the smartest people the company has, it often becomes the plaything of powerful individuals with their own agendas. You can break the ties that bind strategy and risk taking together through an explicit and calculated understanding of your own organisation and power base. Very clearly you must understand "what works here" and the concepts relating to "that's the way we do it here" to be successful in getting your projects approved. If you appreciate that the environment you face accepts risk and is highly political, with low emphasis on realistic payback or analytical rigour then; then you need to find a champion at the highest level who will support your ideas and is willing to take risks, seems like the best way to ensure success.

However there have been attempts to bring rigour to the political domain by trying to evaluate alternative decisions in light of their strategic import. To evaluate each possible decision, values are placed on each decision as 'option values' for the future. "An advantage of this approach is the explicit recognition that not investing leaves the firm in a weakened competitive position for the future—a recognition that is often ignored, at their peril, by executive committees." (Meredith and Hill) The danger in not looking at the strategic implications of an investment opportunity in IT is the failure to undertake projects perceived to be risky although they may be viewed as strategically vital (or even politically important). Economic approaches would rule out many important opportunities as they cannot demonstrate a clear break even or return in financial terms.

The option value approach (Real Options?)- This requires a value to be placed on each of the possible options in any given investment. Then a judgement must be made on the environment and circumstances within which each option may be exercised. The option's aggregate value must then be considered, weighing it against any shortfall in the project's cash flow value. Assigning a value to the options may be difficult but this very act, based upon the organisation's competitive position, is an important part of the decision making process. The managers that want the investment can, even in an uncertain environment, assign a value to the project. If you asked them how much extra revenue would this project bring in they might balk at answering, especially if it is in the area of quality, customer service, brand image or customer satisfaction. However if you ask them for a judgement that might bundle many aspects of their business together and say 'will it bring in one Euro they say oh yes!' Is it worth five million Euro's they say no. And so the questions go, to get closer to a consensus. (Glazer) This then becomes the potential value of the option based on input from those that are going to make the actual project successful.

From the cover of M Amram and N Kulatilka's Real Options book "....this innovative approach brings a financial market discipline to the evaluation of a company's opportunities. Using real options theory, managers can more effectively

target crucial opportunities to redeploy, delay, modify, or even abandon capital intensive projects as events unfold. "

Technical Importance

Some projects have technical importance -- you can't have one without the other, but one is more difficult to quantify although the strategic imperative is obvious. Before you can manage data at a granular level so that it can become actionable information you have to have a knowledge repository. Yet to quantify even in terms of an option the KR is very difficult. To get to KR you could push the direct mail project where you can assign some hard numbers to the outcome. You then move towards you main goal: total relationship management that would include at a minimum an understanding of your customers' actions to enable you retain, develop and grow the right customers.

It is accepted that you must tie IT investments to business needs. Many studies now emphasise the need for systems to support management decision making. "If 'business alignment' is a prerequisite of 'systems alignment' and if the firms information systems are not well aligned with the business strategies of the firm, IS can only help the organisation move in the wrong direction" (Meyer and Boone) Studies like these can very beneficial to your quest for support for that project you set your heart on and recognise as having strategic value.

Senior management have become aware that hard analytical measures are not enough, but the other approaches described above makes many uncomfortable. The list of potential complimentary measures goes on and the more there are, the less comfortable some get. See figure 3.

Accounting approaches are often rear facing rather than strategic in focus and cannot measure what might be beyond initial financial measures. Success however depends on the ability to continually create and recreate sources of tomorrow's revenue, such as customer retention, service quality, speed to market and product/service innovations that anticipate customer needs.

The Balanced Scorecard

Another approach that attempts to use the concepts outlined by Kaplan and Norton in their seminal paper on 'The Balanced scorecard - Measures That Drive Performance'* is the business value profile. This tackles the political elements of the organisation by including the major influencers and decision makers within senior management in the process (through dialogue and interviews) and the strategic through competitive positioning, customer value analysis and business alignment. The business value initiative uses a range of techniques that includes rather than excludes financial and strategic measures. This also enables a more objective dialogue to take place between senior management, who approve funding,

Figure 3

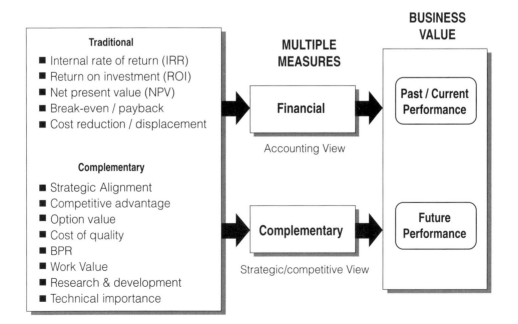

and the junior managers who are often responsible for developing and implementing the business initiative. By taking in analysis across a number of dimensions then expressing them graphically it is easier to see the value of the IT investment you want to make. You look at areas that are important to the success of your organisation and the strategies that can make that success a reality. Couple the strategies with market forces analysis and a dose of financial rigour and you can produce a diagrammatic approach to understanding

your business initiative as shown in figure 4.

* Robert S. Kaplan and David P. Norton HBR and their book The Balanced Scorecard

The business value approach -
This attempts to overcome some of the major faults of both the classical accounting techniques and the more recent, potentially less rigorous approaches by producing a range of technology profiles. The axis on the diagram will vary by organization because their future business drivers are unique to themselves

Figure 4: Business Value Profiling

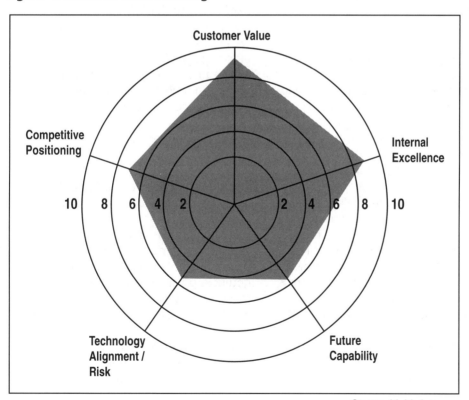

Source: M. McAreavey

Chapter 3: CRM in Practice

Chapter 3: CRM in Practice

and they move from a baseline perspective to one that is initiative based. The BVP approach treats each organisation differently as each has its own set of unique capabilities and strategic imperatives. A non exclusive list of methods that can be included in a profiling exercise are: financial modelling, business contribution profiling, process mapping, activity based costing methodologies, and the cost of quality. It is an all encompassing approach that attempts to overcome the problems associated with real world organisations by producing outcomes that reflect real world dilemmas. BVP is another view on the organisational impact model of investment decision making (see figure 1.)

Even More Approaches !

There are many approaches to producing a better business case and all of them vary in complexity and real world applicability. They are part of the question that still vexes managers: "what is the value of information?" And how can we really place a value on what might be? These questions are often at the heart of the internal procedures and policy manuals that some organisations regularly produce and many managers try to avoid using. The strength of the political culture can distort any plans. Managing information systems is primarily a matter of organisational politics and only secondarily a matter of using strategic technology for obvious business benefits.

The softer side of the organisation in terms of its risk culture is often an element of senior management style over the analysts' substance. Analysis and realism often go together. The less realism in the organisation regarding the use of numbers to help run the business, and the need for rigour in strategic thought leads to confusion and decline. IDC see the data warehouse as "the management foundation of the next century" and many systems and business managers are plunged into purchases by suspending their streaks of realism.

Times have changed and there are many business sources today that can provide hard evidence that relationship management systems backed by data warehouses can improve operational efficiencies and make you more competitive. Many still find it difficult to understand the benefits of strategic initiatives and maybe that is one of the defining characteristics of a project that will have significant impact on your business.

The above has been an exploration of the many and varied ways you can build a business case. In some organisations the rule book prevails. In others the champions can still win through. Where does your organisation fit? If you do progress to getting a go ahead for your knowledge repository you could take into account the words of the father of direct marketing: "You are what you know - data is an expense - knowledge is a bargain. Collect only data that can become information, which in turn, can become knowledge. Only knowledge can build success and minimise failure. A company is no better than what it knows." Lester Wunderman*

* Lester Wundermann in Being Direct

Once you get your knowledge repository you could perhaps consider looking more closely at customer buying patterns, their individual segments, usage of channels or maybe when, where and how the uptake of a singular product can be encouraged. If these questions intrigue you then the application of analytical data modelling should be of interest. These techniques cover neural networks, decision trees, confirmatory or exploratory analysis and more. Data mining is covered in an paper I wrote to dispel some of the hype and mythology that now surrounds this very valuable tool set.

Biography: Michael Meltzer has over 20 years experience in Financial Services and Information Technology. He has authored many articles on banking and computing using the customer focused approach, and is a frequent speaker at industry conferences. With a Bachelor's degree in Marketing and a Master's degree in Business Administration, Michael is a valued member of CSC's global consultancy practice. He specialises across CRM in three related areas: Profitability management, Customer relationship management and Risk management. mmeltzer@csc.com

Chapter 3: CRM in Practice

Customer Profitability - Information just isn't enough

Title: Customer Profitability - Information just isn't enough
Author: Michael Meltzer, Computer Sciences Corporations

Abstract: Customer relationship management demands that you understand which
                customers create profits and those that destroy it. However this is just not
                enough if you want stay in business in the long term. This paper explores
                how customer management solutions based on a scaleable data warehouse
                and a strategy to couple profitability measurements with predictive modeling
                can create sustained competitive advantage. Historic profitability measures
                just don't measure profitability - financial accounting systems fail the test.
                You need something to replace them that can actually support the business
                and the business decisions that must be made.

Customer Profitability just isn't enough

Every Financial Services Provider (FSP) wants to know if they are profitable or not and financial reporting systems tell them this. But they also want to know who and what makes that so and here the financial accounting systems fail them. What also makes sense is to know who are the customers are that create and destroy your profits so you can identify who you don't want to keep or those you really want to attract. So more and more FSP's are asking questions about just what makes up individual customer profitability. Initially managers have asked simple questions that reflect simple needs as who they are? Simple because few managers have been able to do very much with highly aggregated and untrustworthy profitability information even when they could actually tease it out of their financial accounting systems. Yet the question of customer profitability is one of the most important questions that any FSP can ask. They are beginning to ask the more important questions: If I know who the customers are, can someone tell me why they are profitable, can then identify or profile others that could become profitable and then tell me how I can do all this?

Information is an asset

This article continues my theme regarding the need to manage information as a valuable asset and the application of currently available technologies to improve customer relationships and the real litmus test, actual profitability! The first part will describe some of the difficulties and history of getting at customer profitability whilst in the second part I will discuss how to apply and extend its use. In other articles I have argued the case for using customer profitability information as a means of segmenting your customer base and choosing the customers to serve, these arguments are still valid. However I will extend these views with some insights into the need for behavioural information added to profitability measures to make any real solutions actionable.

Customer Relationship Management (CRM)

Today the term Customer Relationship Management (CRM) is banded about by consultants and the press as if the mere chanting of the term can change the way organisations have done business for decades. The term is misused for sales purposes by those marketing call centres, sales automation software, Enterprise Resource Planning systems (ERP's) and other systems that will change the way business is to be carried out "tomorrow" - yes well!? Claims made by vendors, sales people and consultants are sometimes true but the success of CRM rests on both technology and organisational change. This change should start with understanding the profitability of each customer at a granular level and then actions can be planned to make use of the other wondrous technologies and change management practices available. CRM is a vision founded upon customer profitability as its centrepiece. By taking an enterprise-wide focus CRM identifies the customer as the driver of all the FSP's business.

CRM is Holistic

The power of the CRM vision is that it pervades the whole of the enterprise and is founded on the concept of a strategic information repository a scaleable data warehouse (SDW). Information soft and hard is captured from all points of contact: phone, branch, retail counter, call-centre, internet, personal adviser, ATM and kiosk. This information is assimilated into "one version of the truth" that enables decision makers and customer service representatives to make the right decisions and take the right actions that build relationships and enhance profits. One of the major reasons for this drive to undertake the CRM journey is that it is good for profits and survival. In other articles I have stressed the benefits to be derived from the move from simplistic data-base marketing to critical event driven marketing as a move from FSP push tactics to a customer pull strategy. The foundation however of any strategy is an understanding of what drives customer profitability and as an exercise in addition what actually drives an FSP's overall profitability.

Can you use the Profitability System?

There is also a problem facing many institutions in how to actually use the profitability system once implemented. It is not just a financial or management accounting system it is an input for creating a more profitable business. And as such must be planned for across business units with a clear vision that it has a multiplicity of uses. It will be a FSP wide solution that supports many business units and this in itself will require a plan for change management that will be supported by senior management. Profitability solutions must be implemented that incorporate multi-dimensional views that see the profits of the organisation as a whole, it's products, channel, business groups, and specifically customers.

The History of Measuring Profitability

Historically the ways of finding out customer profitability have been very difficult the task often hindered by the very accountants (who are there to help?) that were supposed to understand how to derive the magic numbers! This has much to do with the history of accounting practices and the lack of acceptable number crunching technologies that were understandable and trustworthy. From about 1825 to 1925 huge and successful industrial conglomerates emerged and there were a host of innovative management accounting practices. Many of the largest companies were unlikely to have survived without those robust management accounting systems that could provide insights into the efficiency and effectiveness of their decentralized operations. However between 1925 and 1985 there was little innovation in management accounting techniques and practices. Criticism of management accounting techniques came to a head in the 1980's. Robert Kaplan in a number of Harvard Business Review articles questioned the relevance of the then current management accounting practices. He then co-authored a book with Thomas Johnson called "Relevance Lost: The Rise And Fall of Management Accounting." This seminal work created a watershed in the development of management accounting leading to a number of new techniques and application of new technologies.

Criticisms of Management Accounting

The principal criticisms of management accounting could be summed up:

1. Current management accounting practices do not meet the needs of today's industries, manufacturing or service!
2. Product costing systems provide misleading information that can lead to the wrong decisions being taken!
3. Financial accounting requirements make management accounting subservient to external reporting needs!
4. There is too much focus on internal activities with little attention given to the what exists externally and effects the way a firm operates!

Proxies instead of Actual Costs

With the above as a backdrop to attempts by FSP's trying to understand customer profitability it is easy to see why many have attempted to use proxies instead of untrustworthy "actual" costs as a basis. These proxies were often based on personal bias and inadequate information:

▸ Account balances: The higher the account balance the more valuable the customer is. There is a need however to measure the customers usage of other FSP services to really see whether they are profitable or not. This also goes for those customers that have large loans outstanding.
▸ Multiple account and product relationships: The more accounts the

customer has and or the more products the customer has means they are more profitable than those with few accounts and products. More accounts and products does not lead automatically to increased profits if their the wrong products and the accounts incur high costs.

▸ Particular products used: the belief is that if the customer uses specific high value services such as private banking or investment facilities then by default they must be valuable customers. Once again it all depends on the overall cost incurred in servicing the relationship.

▸ Socio-demographics: Where the customer lives, occupation, income, and so on are used as predictors of potential or actual customer profitability. However it all depends on the customers cost to serve and the way the customers makes use of FSPs services obvious and hidden. The obvious costs relate to actual chargeable services used whilst the hidden are often the soft services not recorded like branch visits or telephone queries direct to a bank branch or insurance broker.

▸ Use of facilities(channel usage and transaction volumes) : the more the staff of an FSP has contact with the customer or they carry out numerous transactions implies that they must be more valuable than the customer that is invisible. The reverse is often the case. The cost of face-to-face interaction is high and their high transaction volumes may in fact be destroying profits.

The above then are not satisfactory measures or predictors of customer profitability. What those proxies state

clearly is that the FSP's just didn't have the right data to turn into useful information or metrics in evaluating one customer from another. What is needed is a set of principles that will enable a consistent approach to profitability measurement. For many this means finding ways of allocating costs to individual customers that are both realistic and cost effective in application.

The Road to Customer Profitability

On the road to customer profitability many institutions began by attempting to carry out product profitability. Initially we could see this attempt at product profitability and hence better costing as a manifestation of FSP's fixation on being product driven as opposed to customer focused. However even this approach was difficult to implement as a product's profitability was often managed only vertically, from development through sales, with no measurement of costs borne horizontally through an institution's administrative and back-officeexpenses. Manufacturing had overcome this problem but the FSP's found it difficult because of the many attributes their products had. A television may have many working parts but it performs one function and does not have a range of service or risk elements attached to it. A current account actually has many functions acquiring and dispenses many costs and charges along the way. The fixation by many FSP's on being product driven created product aligned organisations. Systems were developed for the needs of particular products that could not communicate with systems from other parts of the organisation. The other considerations centre on the concepts of cost allocation and cost attribution.

Existing Costing Systems

To determine customer profitability you would normally look to your existing costing systems. These systems which are invariably based on the standard accounting rules which only look at profits for the current year. These accounting systems take no account of the potential profits or losses attached to individuals, customer segments or the range of products they take. Revenue is normally the one thing you can get at. There are mechanisms to track charges made for services and products used. This revenue is collated at many levels of aggregation but rarely is there enough detail to clearly see the total revenue and cost picture for the individual customer. It is worth remembering that in most FSP's their tend to be failure to charge at least one per cent of the time. This is often referred to as "leakage." Charges for providing the services and products internally are normally passed down to the actual group providing the service to the customer by simple allocation methodologies. Often traditional top-down methods of measuring customer profit, product profit data was simply allocated using few customer characteristics such as balance, rates and product types and is most often applied to customer segments (e.g., small business, private banking, etc). Yet the charges and revenue captured must be built up from actual charges made and there is this problem of leakage! Few FSP's talk about this however.

Attributing Costs

Cost attribution is focused on cost/profit centre profit and loss that eventually rolls up to the institutions overall profit and loss statement. The accounting system is not focused on customers or FSP performance but on cost allocation. In age of steam it was easy material costs and direct labour were the largest proportion of total costs in a manufacturer's world and the rest was overhead. In the new world of service-dominated economies the old accounting methods distort profitability. Almost every activity can be seen as undifferentiated overhead. The whole process is top down as there was no granularity to the actual customer transactions. In the past the technology was just not available to enable an FSP to see the trees for the wood!

The General Ledger

Many FSB's initially believed that the numbers shown in the General Ledger (GL) were a true reflection of reality. But it soon became apparent that something was missing. While the general ledger system contained the FSP's financial accounting data, it carried very little transaction or volume related information. FSPs needed volume information from FSP application systems (account based systems, savings systems, payments systems, ATM's, loan systems, etc.) to calculate percentages and to drive the cost-allocation process. Staff had to collect the missing information manually and then input it into memo accounts on the general ledger.

Activity Based Costing (ABC)

To overcome this we must view another allocation methodology called Activity Based Costing (ABC), the use of funds transfer pricing and capital allocation methodologies to really reflect the reality of the financial services organisations. To actually benefit from the accounting activities an FSP must also build a transaction based system to get at granular level detail (a SDW), implement predictive modelling and use customer lifetime value as key ingredients in any CRM solution. The bottom line to this is that allocation of shared costs among business units, products, customer accounts and channels of distribution is required to make good profitability decisions.

Understanding the Behaviour of Costs

ABC emphasises the need to understand the behaviour of overhead costs and how they relate to products and services. ABC is a costing system that breaks down departmental costs into distinguishable activities. Activities (account openings, payments, system development and so on) in the FSP create the need for the services provided that cause costs and the products/services provided to customers create the demand for the activities. Activities are linked to products/services by the assignment of costs to those products/services based on their actual consumption or demand for those activities. The design of an ABC system for an FSP can involve the following steps:

1. Identifying the major activities that take place in the FSP;
2. Creating a cost pool/cost centre for each activity in the FSP;
3. Identifying the direct cost categories for the product;
4. Identifying the indirect cost pools and develop a rate to allocate these costs associated with the product;
5. Determining the cost driver for each major activity;
6. Assigning the cost activities to products/services according to the products/services demand for activities.

The use of ABC goes much further than enabling more accurate customer profitability profiles. There is an opportunity to begin to understand what drives costs and then be in a better position to make both macro and micro decisions. These can be related to cost to serve individual customer types. To the extent of identifying optimum staffing in a bank branch or brokers office dependant on the costs incurred and the profits to be made by handling customers in different ways. At the micro level, FSP management could consider alternative workflow processes for a given activity that would reduce the overall cost of that activity.

Funds Transfer Pricing

The financial services business is about borrowing money (from depositors) at one rate and lending it to others (borrowers) at a higher rate. The difference between the cost of borrowing and the interest income received from lending is the operating income of the FSP from which business expenses are paid and operating profits/losses created. The more competitive the market for deposits and loans, the less margin is available to the FSP.

The Treasury Function

The Treasury function inside the FSP conceptually "buys" the deposits from the deposit gatherers and "sells" those funds to the lenders (and they manage the "float" in between). In this way, the deposit taking function can be treated as a profit centre based upon the revenue it generates from the marked up sale of its funds to Treasury. The loans products are treated similarly.

Techniques

Funds transfer pricing is a technique aimed at improving the way internal costs are determined and allocated across an FSP. The FSP creates the pretence that its deposits are sold in the open market at the going rate. In the same way, the FSP continues the pretence that the lending group is borrowing its funds at the price the FSP could get for those funds in the open market. In this way, the arbitrary allocation of costs for purposes of determining product and service profitability is replaced by a more rigorous pricing method based on the "pretence" that funds are placed in the open market. While the resultant profit is necessarily a book entry type of profit, the approach does provide management with a better methodology from which to approach product and service pricing in general.

For purposes of a modern profitability system, a robust funds transfer pricing capability allows individual product pricing to be determined for individual customers based upon that customer's current and expected future behaviours. This leads us nicely into the topic of predictive behaviours that I will cover later in this article. Customers grouped upon behaviours which drive funds transfer pricing does not necessarily match up to how the FSP's customer base is or will be segmented by other groups (e.g. marketing) within an FSP.

Capital Allocation/Risk Provisioning

The capital allocation methodology is to take the capital of the FSP and apportion it to the individual products and services as a function of the risk associated with them and the requirement for capital to be "held in reserve" in support of current and future risks. By then levying a charge for the capital (a rate of return –referred to as the "hurdle rate of return") and deducting that charge (the "risk-adjusted cost of capital") from the net income of the product or service they gets a truer picture of performance. Capital allocation theory allows FSP's management to ask the question: What is the value of a service or product set after paying "rent" for the capital it requires? This approach allows for an equivalent comparison of performance across widely differing parts of the business.

Individual Customer Level

A more sophisticated and useful approach when getting at customer profitability is to repeat the above process down to the individual customer level for a given product or service. By understanding individual customer behaviour, a risk factor can be assigned to that customer, capital allocated as a function of that particular risk and a capital charge levied against the net income generated from that customer. The sum total of individual customer allocated capital equals the total amount of capital allocated to the products and services provided.

In all there are five measures that make the difference (figure 1): Net interest revenue, Other revenue, direct expense and risk provision - the other element that is an input to the others is funds transfer pricing. To make a profitability system part of an overall CRM there is a need to approach the subject in a different way from the traditional methodologies that were forced to be top down. Systems of record were designed to carry aggregates

Figure 1

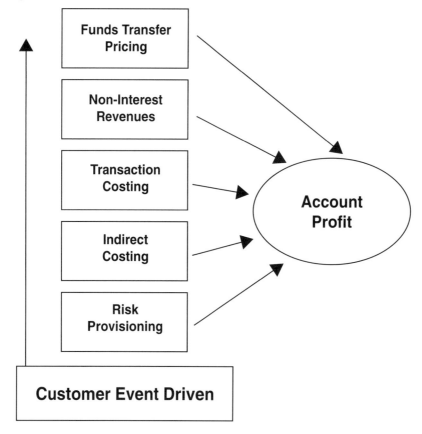

to enable the financial reporting systems to function correctly in support of investors, creditors, regulators, and tax authorities .

Three Accounting Systems?

Today many FSP's have seen the need for multiple accounting systems as Robert Kaplan and Robin Cooper states in Cost and Effect:.

▸ A traditional, but well-functioning financial system that performs basic accounting and transactions-capturing functions, and prepares monthly or quarterly financial statements for external users, using conventional methods for allocating periodic production costs to cost-of-goods sold and inventory accounts.
▸ One or more activity-based cost systems that take data from the "official" financial system, as well as from other information and operating systems, to measure accurately the costs of activities, processes, products, services, customers, and organizational units
▸ Operational feedback systems that provide operators and all front-line employees with timely, accurate information, both financial and non financial, on the efficiency, quality, and cycle times of business processes.

There is an addition to this a system, a further wrinkle that enables an organization to be able to look at the profitability of the customer that actually creates the future streams of profit. Accounting is more than reporting historical costs it is also about supporting

the business in providing guidance for business decisions. A new approach is required that starts from the basics. The basics for an FSP is a customer transaction. From understanding what drives the costs and the revenues, the FSP can gain a clearer picture of multi-dimensional profitability in support of future revenue and profit generation. The implementation of a scaleable data warehouse based cost allocation system gives the flexibility to view the organisation in any way together with an ability to access detailed account level information.

Approach Profitability Bottom Up

By approaching the topic of customer profitability bottom up (see figure 2) we can measures in detail the components of income and expense at the account level, based on account characteristics such as transaction behaviour, term, risk probability, and fee revenue generated. The customer drives account profitability based on actual transaction activities that roll up to a total account profit or loss. From this base of data, any number of aggregations can be performed – across customer, channel, product and organisation. This approach means that profitability measurement and analysis could now be driven by customer behaviour not product averages. This ensures that the true cost and income drivers of the organisation can been understood at the most detailed level. By designing a flexible system a number of dimensions of profitability can be looked at: pricing relationship, distribution channel, individual account

Figure 2

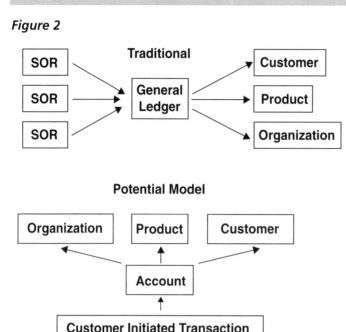

Traditional

Potential Model

However if you just use profitability information as it stands mistakes regarding the value of a customer over time can be made. Profitability is not static. A good summing up of just looking at current and historic information is summed up by Peter Carrol and Madhu Tadikonda of Oliver, Wymen & Co.

"In fact, three drawbacks undercut the utility of customer profitability data for operational decision-making:

manager portfolio, customer segment, or geographical region and so on.

Event Driven Marginal Costs

Innovative and sound, this methodology focuses profit measures at the account level, using event driven marginal costing methods or other allocation methods that the FSP feels is right for them. The techniques used measure each account's profit contribution in five dimensions: net interest revenue, non-interest revenue, direct expense, indirect expense and risk provision. This approach is designed to reconcile with the General Ledger and allows for consistent analyses of customers, products and channels historical profita-bility. A revolutionary step for FSP's today.

▶ Descriptive, not predictive. Profitability figures broadly indicate which customers have been economically valuable over a given period. It may not suggest how that customer will behave in the future, especially in the context of the sales/service action under consideration.
▶ Myopic. Virtually all retail financial services products have a specific life cycle. With certain types of loans, for example, customers may have a negative profit contribution in the early years and become more profitable later on. As a result, profitability recorded in a given performance period may incompletely describe the value of a particular relationship.
▶ Retrospective. Historical profit data is a lagging metric. It does not adequately reflect anticipated changes in customer

holdings or changes in usage patterns. Furthermore, a retrospective metric may incorporate specific market conditions (e.g. interest rate environment, competitive intensity) which no longer exist."

Consider Time

To bring customer profitability alive and to dovetail it into the CRM vision we need to consider the customer over time. Some major lifecycle events that affect customer's product needs and potential profitability include graduation from school, marriage, first home purchase, birth of a child, children leaving home, retirement and to finally prospective death. So we must also introduce other methodologies to predict customer behaviours. Once this information is integrated with predictive capabilities what was static although useful, becomes a valuable weapon in the FSP's armoury.

Lifetime/Long term Value (LTV)

The concept identifies that a customer normally has a relationship of sorts with the FFSP that spans a particular period of time. There isn't any customer relationship management if there is no relationship to speak of. By taking into consideration a customer's age, the anticipated length of his financial relationship with the FSP, his lifestyle stage, demographics and potential future financial holdings a set of cash flows are assumed to occur stretching into the future. To bring the cash back to today a

discounting techniques such as net present value (NPV) are used.

Assumptions

In order to calculate the future value of a customer's tenure, assumptions have to be made. Assumptions regarding the length of time a customer is likely to remain with you could include information relating to their age, their lifestyle, occupation, geographic location and income. From this information certain predictions have to be made regarding the types of products he is likely to purchase; the income that will be derived from those products; and the costs associated with marketing and providing those products. Based on analysis of existing customers using particular products predictions are made for similar looking customers. Current customer relationship characteristics, such as average length of the relationship, average account balances, and default or prepayment rates, are compared to other customer attributes representative of relationship behaviour, including age, income, education, credit history, and life stage. Based on this analysis, longevity predictions are made about customers relationship tenure, account balances, payments tendency, and other inputs that will affect future profitability. A quote form Bottom Line Banking by McCoy, Frieder and Hedges puts it all in context: "*The ultimate competitive advantage does not lie with technology or economies of scale but with superior knowledge of the consumer, a corresponding business (profit) model and the ability to keep both up-to-date*"

Using the information

One of the first major benefits of looking at lifetime values as an added dimension to profitability and a customers predicted behaviour is an FSP's ability to begin micro-segmenting it's customer base based on value over time. The FSP can segment customers into tiers or by combining data use a multi-dimensional approach based on factors that are unique to the FSP and it's customers.

In addition a start can be made in identifying for each customer, what actions or dynamics have the potential to change his or her value to the FSP. Product development and pricing strategies, including channel migration strategies, cross-sell activities, up-sell and fee structures, can positively or negatively impact the customer's value, as can customer service and retention treatments. Profitability measures coupled with LTV numbers enable an FSP to better profile their the potentially profitable customers and to identify look-alikes amongst it's prospective customers.An FSP can use the information it has pulled together in it's CRM system to enable it to retain customers, develop customers and to acquire new customers.

Retention

By identifying the customers that the FSP must retain because it has identified just how profitable these customers really are the FSP can undertake specific customer retention treatments. These customer groups can then receive special services, be given personal bankers and whatever else is required to keep their business. By knowing who your current and potentially profitable customers are enables the FSPO to alter its treatments to the less profitable customers.

Cross sell, Up-Sell

To increase their share of the customers wallet many FSP's believe that a depth of products taken means profit. As demonstrated above this may not be the case. However armed with profitability and LTV information an FSP can now cross-sell other products or up-sell more valuable services and products in the knowledge that they are contributing towards the bottom line. There is also the opportunity to move that marginally profitable customer into profit if understand the customer dynamics involved. For every decision or action, there is a likely pattern of behaviour, cash flow and risk outcomes that can be anticipated. Any cross-sell action includes estimates of all cash flows associated with the actual marketing decision. Costs would include up-front acquisition expense, ongoing account maintenance and servicing, and potential risk weightings. Revenues would include potential LTV from fees and interest spreads. With an understanding what components make up a customer's profitability, banks can analyse the potential impact of various cross-sell initiatives on individuals, segments, and down to the segment of one profitability.

Data Mining

Using the predictive information that the FSP has gleaned from both it intuitive and machine based data mining, cross-selling can be far more effective . Customers with the likelihood to purchase will be targeted rather than those unlikely to respond. As a result, the cost of acquisition can be reduced while the profitability on each campaign increases. When the FSP moves to a customer event driven ca[ability campaigns as they are used now become less frequent. What takes over are micro-campaigns based on individual customer needs as predicted by the CRM system and valued by the bottom up profitability metrics.

Acquisition

An integrated SDW solution that incorporates the CRM vision enables an FSP to carry out numerous customer centric activities. Yet one of it's most powerful capabilities comes into play when an FSP wants to acquire new customers that look just like it's own already profitable customers. Given sufficient size and depth to it's historic base of data it can build predictive models that will identify the attributes of customers it would like to have within the universe prospective customers. Taking direct mailing as an initial example we could create a PVC score for the customers we intend to mail internally and externally. What we want to do is optimise our return on investment in the marketing campaigns we undertake. The algorithm uses each customer's propensity to purchase the product (P), the value of the purchase over time (V) and the cost of the contact (C). By its construction the score takes account of relevance (propensity) and profit (product value and communication cost), and the best type of contact for an individual. It means that the ones with the highest score per offer is contacted for that offer first. This goes against the grain of mass mailing but is just one of the effective new ways of marketing a well planned CRM solution offers when profitability metrics are an integral part.

Customer Treatments

Because an FSP can work at the individual customer level although apply treatments at group level decisions can be made regarding customer charges. Customer service personnel can respond on a customer by customer basis to requests regarding special services, interest rates and fee waivers.

Armed with information on customers enable the FSP to differentiate according to value to the organisation. Some customers that are marginal may be guided towards facilities that are less costly and thereby improve that customers profit margins. Some unprofitable customers could be guide to a competitor or reduced level of service that matches their contribution.

Chapter 3: CRM in Practice

Putting it all together

To build a CRM capability is not a simple task, see figure 3. It is a journey that starts with senior management sponsorship and commitment. For some FSP's total vision of CRM is far in the distance and simpler quickly implemented solutions to current problems must be considered. However with a good architectural plan and the right technology even speedy solutions can grow into a full blown CRM system. A major question any organisation must ask when it invests in the future is: " if we invest in this, what does it do for us and will it value - when?" When making investment decisions, managers must consider their main options and then build

customised analyses to support their deliberations. However in many cases you cannot prove to a disbelieving management that the figures you come up with are real. Therefore it is always good to have a senior champion in your corner. Some try to be very analytic in their approach to making decisions as it seems the right thing to do. Yet today many FSP's have trod the path of implementing SDW and started on a CRM that the "truth is out there".

To effectively support your business you need to take the journey towards the customer relationship management vision. This leads to FSP differentiation and profit if implemented effectively and with insight

Figure 3

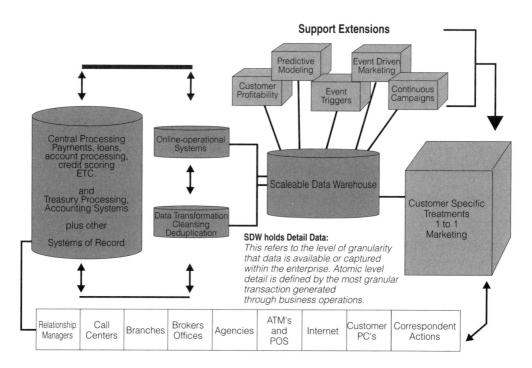

Support Extensions

Predictive Modeling

Event Driven Marketing

Customer Profitability

Event Triggers

Continuous Campaigns

Central Processing Payments, loans, account processing, credit scoring ETC.

and Treasury Processing, Accounting Systems

plus other

Systems of Record

Online-operational Systems

Data Transformation Cleansing Deduplication

Scaleable Data Warehouse

Customer Specific Treatments 1 to 1 Marketing

SDW holds Detail Data:
This refers to the level of granularity that data is available or captured within the enterprise. Atomic level detail is defined by the most granular transaction generated through business operations.

Relationship Managers	Call Centers	Branches	Brokers Offices	Agencies	ATM's and POS	Internet	Customer PC's	Correspondent Actions

into just why you are on this journey but
this is another story.

*Biography: Michael Meltzer has over 20 years experience in
Financial Services and Information Technology. He has
authored many articles on banking and computing using the
customer focused approach, and is a frequent speaker at
industry conferences. With a Bachelor's degree in Marketing
and a Master's degree in Business Administration, Michael is a
valued member of CSC's global consultancy practice. He
specialises across CRM in three related areas: Profitability
management, Customer relationship management and Risk
management. mmeltzer@csc.com*

Building profitable customer relationships with data mining

Title:	*Building profitable customer relationships with data mining*
Author:	*Herb Edelstein, President Two Crows Corporation*
Abstract:	*This white paper describes the various aspects of analytic CRM and shows how it is used to manage the customer life cycle more cost effectively. Note that the case histories of these fictional companies are composites of real-life data mining applications.*

Copyright: SPSS Inc. 2000
Biography: Herbert Edelstein is an internationally recognized expert in data mining, data warehousing and client-server computing and is a founder of the Data Warehousing Institute. He currently is president of Tow Crows Corporation.

You've built your customer information and marketing data warehouse – now how do you make good use of the data it contains?

Customer relationship management (CRM) helps companies improve the profitability of their interactions with customers, while at the same time, makes the interactions appear friendlier through individualization. To succeed with CRM, companies need to match products and campaigns to prospects and customers – in other words, to intelligently manage the customer life cycle.

Until recently, most CRM software focused on simplifying the organization and management of customer information. Such software, called operational CRM, focuses on creating a customer database that presents a consistent picture of the customer's relationship with the company and providing that information in specific applications. These include sales force automation and customer service applications, in which the company "touches" the customer.

However, the sheer volume of customer information and increasingly complex interactions with customers have propelled data mining to the forefront of making customer relationships profitable. Data mining is a process that uses a variety of data analysis and modeling techniques to discover patterns and relationships in data that are used to understand what your customers want and predict what they will do. Data mining can help you select the right prospects on whom to focus, offer the right additional products to your existing customers and identify good customers who may be about to leave. This results in improved revenue because of a greatly improved ability to respond to each individual contact in the best way and reduced costs due to properly allocated resources. CRM applications that use data mining are called analytic CRM.

Data mining

The first and simplest analytical step in data mining is to describe the data. For example, you can summarize data's statistical attributes (such as means and standard deviations), visually review data using charts and graphs and look at the distribution of field values in your data.

But data description alone cannot provide an action plan. You must build a predictive model based on patterns determined from known results and then test that model on results outside the original sample. A good model should never be confused with reality (you know a road map isn't a perfect representation of the actual road), but it can be a useful guide to understanding your business.

Data mining can be used for both classification and regression problems. In classification problems you're predicting what category something falls into – for example, whether or not a person is a good credit risk or which of several offers someone is most likely to accept. In regression problems, you're predicting a number, such as the probability that a person will respond to an offer.
In CRM, data mining is frequently used to assign a score to a particular customer or prospect indicating the likelihood that the individual behaves the way you want. For example, a score could measure the propensity to respond to a particular offer or to switch to a competitor's product. It is also frequently used to identify a set of characteristics (called a profile) that segments customers into groups with similar behaviors, such as buying a particular product.

A special type of classification can recommend items based on similar interests held by groups of customers. This is sometimes called collaborative filtering.

The data mining technology used for solving classification, regression and collaborative filtering problems is briefly described in the appendix at the end of this paper.

Defining CRM

Customer relationship management in its broadest sense simply means managing all customer interactions. In practice, this requires using information about your customers and prospects to more effectively interact with your customers in all stages of your relationship with them. We refer to these stages as the customer life cycle.

The customer life cycle has three stages:

▸ Acquiring customers
▸ Increasing the value of customers
▸ Retaining good customers

Data mining can improve your profitability in each of these stages when you integrate it with operational CRM systems or implement it as independent applications.

Chapter 3: CRM in Practice

Acquiring new customers via data mining

The first step in CRM is to identify prospects and convert them to customers. Let's look at how data mining can help manage the costs and improve the effectiveness of a customer acquisition campaign.

Big Bank and Credit Card Company (BB&CC) annually conducts 25 direct mail campaigns, each of which offers one million people the opportunity to apply for a credit card. The conversion rate measures the proportion of people who become credit card customers, which is about one percent per campaign for BB&CC.

Getting people to fill out an application for the credit card is only the first step. Then, BB&CC must decide if the applicant is a good risk and accept them as a customer or decline the application. Not surprisingly, poor credit risks are more likely to accept the offer than are good credit risks. So while six percent of the people on the mailing list respond with an application, only about 16 percent of those are suitable credit risks; approximately one percent of the people on the mailing list become customers.

BB&CC's six percent response rate means that only 60,000 people out of one million names respond to the solicitation. Unless BB&CC changes the nature of the solicitation – using different mailing lists, reaching customers in different ways, altering the terms of the offer – it is not going to receive more than 60,000 responses. And of those 60,000 responses,

only 10,000 are good enough risks to become customers. The challenge BB&CC faces is reaching those 10,000 people most efficiently.

BB&CC spends about $1.00 per piece, for a total cost of $1,000,000, to mail the solicitation. Over the next couple of years, the customers gained through this solicitation generate approximately $1,250,000 in profit for the bank (or about $125 each), for a net return of $250,000 from the mailing.

Data mining can improve this return. Although data mining won't precisely identify the 10,000 eventual credit card customers, data mining helps focus marketing efforts much more cost effectively.

First, BB&CC sent a test mailing of 50,000 prospects and carefully analyzed the results, building a predictive model showing who would respond (using a decision tree) and a credit scoring model (using a neural net). BB&CC then combined these two models to find the people who were both good credit risks and were most likely to respond to the offer.

BB&CC applied the model to the remaining 950,000 people in the mailing list, from which 700,000 people were selected for the mailing. The result? From the 750,000 pieces mailed (including the test mailing), BB&CC received 9,000 acceptable applications for credit cards. In other words, the response rate rose from one percent to 1.2 percent, a 20 percent increase. While the targeted mailing only

reaches 9,000 of the 10,000 prospects –
no model is perfect – reaching the
remaining 1,000 prospects is not
profitable. Had they mailed the other
250,000 people on the mailing list, the
cost of $250,000 would have resulted in
another $125,000 of gross profit for a net
loss of $125,000.

The table 1 summarizes the results.
Notice that the net profit from the mailing
increased $125,000. Even when you
include the $40,000 cost of the data
mining software and the computer and
employee resources used for this modeling
effort, the net profit increased $85,000.
This translates to a return on investment
(ROI) for modeling of over 200 percent,
which far exceeds BB&CC's ROI
requirements for a project.

Increasing the value of your existing customers: cross-selling via data mining

Cannons and Carnations (C&C) is a
company that specializes in selling antique
mortars and cannons as outdoor flower
pots. It also offers a line of indoor flower
pots made from large-caliber antique
pistols and a collection of muskets that
have been converted to unique holders of
long-stemmed flowers. The C&C catalog is
sent to about 12 million homes.

When a customer calls C&C to place an
order, C&C identifies the caller using caller
ID when possible; otherwise the C&C
representative asks for a phone number or
customer number from the catalog mailing
label. Next, the representative looks up the
customer in the database and then
proceeds to take the order.
C&C has an excellent chance of cross-

Table 1

	Old	New	Difference
Number of pieces mailed	1,000,000	750,000	(250,000)
Cost of mailing	$1,000,000	$750,000	($250,000)
Number of responses	10,000	9,000	(1,000)
Gross profit per response	$125	$125	$0
Gross profit	$1,250,000	$1,125,000	($125,000)
Net profit	$250,000	$375,000	$125,000
Cost of model	0	40,000	$40,000
Final profit	$250,000	$335,000	$85,000

selling, or selling the caller something additional. But C&C discovered that if the first suggestion fails and the representative suggests a second item, the customer might get irritated and hang up without ordering anything. And, there are some customers who resent any cross-selling attempts.

Before implementing data mining, C&C was reluctant to cross-sell. Without a model, the odds of making the right recommendation were one in three. And, because making any recommendation is unacceptable for some customers, C&C wanted to be extremely sure that it never makes a recommendation when it should not. In a trial campaign, C&C had less than a one percent sales rate and received a substantial number of complaints. C&C was reluctant to continue cross-selling for such a small gain.

The situation changed dramatically once C&C used data mining. Now the data mining model operates on the data. Using the customer information in the database and the new order, it tells the customer service representative what to recommend. C&C successfully sold an additional product to two percent of the customers and experienced virtually no complaints.

Developing this capability involved a process similar to what was used to solve the credit card customer acquisition problem. As with that situation, two models were needed.

The first model predicted if someone would be offended by additional product recommendations. C&C learned how its

customers reacted by conducting a very short telephone survey. To be conservative, C&C counted anyone who declined to participate in the survey as someone who would find recommendations intrusive. Later on, to verify this assumption, C&C made recommendations to a small but statistically significant subset of those who had refused to answer the survey questions. To C&C's surprise, it discovered that the assumption was not warranted. This enabled C&C to make more recommendations and further increase profits. The second model predicted which offer would be most acceptable.

In summary, data mining helped C&C better understand its customers' needs. When the data mining models were incorporated in a typical cross-selling CRM campaign, the models helped C&C increase its profitability by two percent.

Increasing the value of your existing customers: personalization via data mining

Big Sam's Clothing (motto: "Rugged outdoor gear for city dwellers") developed a Web site to supplement its catalog. Whenever you enter Big Sam's site, the site greets you by displaying "Howdy Pardner!" However, once you have ordered or registered with Big Sam's, you are greeted by name. If you have a Big Sam's ordering record, Big Sam's will also tell you about any new products that might be of particular interest to you. When you look at a particular product, such as a waterproof parka, Big Sam's suggests other items that might supplement such a purchase.

When Big Sam's first launched its site, there was no personalization. The site was just an online version of its catalog – nicely and efficiently done but it didn't take advantage of the sales opportunities the Web presents.

Data mining greatly increased Big Sam's Web site sales. Catalogs frequently group products by type to simplify the user's task of selecting products. In an online store, however, the product groups may be quite different, often based on complementing the item under consideration. In particular, the site can take into account not only the item you're looking at, but what is in your shopping cart as well, thus leading to even more customized recommendations.

First, Big Sam's used clustering to discover which products grouped together naturally. Some of the clusters were obvious, such as shirts and pants. Others were surprising, such as books about desert hiking and snakebite kits. They used these groupings to make recommendations whenever someone looked at a product.

Big Sam's then built a customer profile to help identify customers who would be interested in the new products that were frequently added to the catalog. Big Sam's learned that steering people to these selected products not only resulted in significant incremental sales, but also solidified its customer relationships. Surveys established that Big Sam's was viewed as a trusted advisor for clothing and gear.

To extend its reach further, Big Sam's implemented a program through which customers could elect to receive e-mail about new products that the data mining models predicted would interest them. While the customers viewed this as another example of proactive customer service, Big Sam's discovered it was a program of profit improvement.

The personalization effort paid off for Big Sam's, which experienced significant, measurable increases in repeat sales, average number of sales per customer and average size of sales.

Retaining good customers via data mining

For almost every company, the cost of acquiring a new customer exceeds the cost of keeping good customers. This was the challenge facing KnowService, an Internet Service Provider (ISP) who experiences the industry-average attrition rate, eight percent per month. Since KnowService has one million customers, this means 80,000 customers leave each month. The cost to replace these customers is $200 each or $16,000,000 – plenty of incentive to start an attrition management program.

The first thing KnowService needed to do was prepare the data used to predict which customers would leave. KnowService needed to select the variables from its customer database and, perhaps, transform them. The bulk of KnowService's users are dial-in clients (as opposed to clients who are always connected through a T1 or DSL line) so KnowService knows how long each user was connected to the Web. KnowService also knows the volume of data transferred to and from a user's computer, the number of e-mail accounts a user has, the number of e-mail messages sent and received along with the customer's service and billing history. In addition, KnowService has demographic data that customers provided at sign-up.

Next, KnowService needed to identify who were "good" customers. This is not a data mining question but a business definition (such as profitability or lifetime value) followed by a calculation. KnowService built a model to profile its profitable customers and unprofitable customers. KnowService used this model not only for customer retention but to identify customers who were not yet profitable but might become so in the future.

KnowService then built a model to predict which of its profitable customers would leave. As in most data mining problems, determining what data to use and how to combine existing data is much of the challenge in model development. For example, KnowService needed to look at time-series data such as the monthly usage. Rather than using the raw time-series data, it smoothed the data by taking rolling three-month averages. KnowService also calculated the change in the three-month average and tried that as a predictor. Some of the factors that were good predictors, such as declining usage, were symptoms rather than causes that could be directly addressed. Other predictors, such as the average number of service calls and the change in the average number of service calls, were indicative of customer satisfaction problems worth investigating.

Predicting who would churn, however, wasn't enough. Based on the results of the modeling, KnowService identified some potential programs and offers that it believed would entice people to stay. For example, some churners were exceeding even the largest amount of usage available for a fixed fee and were paying substantial incremental usage fees. KnowService offered these users a higher-fee service that included more bundled time. Some users were offered more free disk space to store personal Web pages. KnowService then built models that would predict which would be the most effective offer for a particular user.

To summarize, the churn project made use of three models. One model identified likely churners, the next model picked the profitable potential churners worth keeping and the third model matched the potential churners with the most appropriate offer. The net result was a reduction in KnowService's churn rate from eight percent to 7.5 percent, which allowed KnowService to save $1,000,000 per month in customer acquisition costs.

KnowService discovered that its data mining investment paid off – it improved customer relationships and dramatically increased its profitability.

Applying data mining to CRM

In order to build good models for your CRM system, there are a number of steps you must follow. The Two Crows data mining process model described below is similar to other process models such as the CRISP-DM model, differing mostly in the emphasis it places on the different steps.

Keep in mind that while the steps appear in a list, the data mining process is not linear – you will inevitably need to loop back to previous steps. For example, what you learn in the "explore data" step (step 3) may require you to add new data to the data mining database. The initial models you build may provide insights that lead you to create new variables.

The basic steps of data mining for effective CRM are:

1. Define business problem
2. Build marketing database
3. Explore data
4. Prepare data for modeling
5. Build model
6. Evaluate model
7. Deploy model and results

Let's go through these steps to better understand the process.

1. Define the business problem.

Each CRM application has one or more business objective for which you need to build the appropriate model. Depending on your specific goal, such as "increasing the response rate" or "increasing the value of a response," you build a very different model. An effective statement of the problem includes a way to measure the results of your CRM project.

2.Build a marketing database.

Steps two through four constitute the core of the data preparation. Together, they take more time and effort than all the other steps combined. There may be repeated iterations of the data preparation and model building steps as you learn something from the model that suggests you modify the data. These data preparation steps may take anywhere from 50 to 90 percent of the time and effort for the entire data mining process.

You will need to build a marketing database because your operational databases and corporate data warehouse often don't contain the data you need in the form you need it. Furthermore, your CRM applications may interfere with the speedy and effective execution of these systems.

When you build your marketing database you need to clean it up – if you want good models you must have clean data. The data you need may reside in multiple databases such as the customer database, product database and transaction databases. This means you need to integrate and consolidate the data into a single marketing database and reconcile differences in data values from the various sources. Improperly reconciled data is a major source of quality problems. There are often large differences in the way data is defined and used in different databases. Some inconsistencies may be easy to uncover, such as different addresses for the same customer. However, these problems are often subtle. For example, the same customer may have different names or, worse, multiple customer identification numbers.

3. Explore the data.

Before you can build good predictive models, you must understand your data. Start by gathering a variety of numerical summaries (including descriptive statistics such as averages, standard deviations and so forth) and looking at the distribution of the data. You may want to produce cross tabulations (pivot tables) for multi-dimensional data.

Graphing and visualization tools are a vital aid in data preparation and their importance for effective data analysis can't be overemphasized. Data visualization most often provides the "Aha!" that leads to new insights and success. Some common and very useful graphical data displays are histograms or box plots which display distributions of values. You may also want to look at scatter plots in two or three dimensions of different pairs of variables. The ability to add a third, overlay variable greatly increases the usefulness of some types of graphs.

4. Prepare data for modeling.

This is the final data preparation step before building models and the step where the most "art" comes in. There are four main parts to this step:

First, you want to select the variables on which to build the model. Ideally, you take all the variables you have, feed them to the data mining tool and let the data mining tool find those that are the best predictors. In practice, this is very involved. One reason is that the time it takes to build a model increases with the number of variables. Another reason is that blindly including extraneous columns can lead to

models with less, rather than more, predictive power.

The next step is to construct new predictors derived from the raw data. For example, forecasting credit risk using a debt-to-income ratio rather than just debt and income as predictor variables may yield more accurate results and are also easier to understand.

Next, you may decide to select a subset or sample of your data on which to build models. If you have a lot of data, however, using all your data may take too long or require buying a bigger computer than you'd like. Working with a properly selected random sample usually results in no loss of information for most CRM problems. Given a choice of either investigating a few models built on all the data or investigating more models built on a sample, the latter approach usually helps you develop a more accurate and robust model of the problem.

Last, you need to transform variables in accordance with the requirements of the algorithm you choose to build your model.

5. Data mining model building.

The most important thing to remember about model building is that it is an iterative process. You need to explore alternative models to find the one that is most useful in solving your business problem. What you learn when searching for a good model may lead you to go back and make some changes to the data you are using or even modify your problem statement.

Most CRM applications are based on a protocol called supervised learning. You start with customer information for which the desired outcome is already known. For example, you may have historical data from a previous mailing list that is very similar to the one you are currently using. Or, you may have to conduct a test mailing to determine how people will respond to an offer. You then split this data into two groups. On the first group, you train or estimate your model. You then test it on the remainder of the data. A model is built when the cycle of training and testing is completed.

6. Evaluate your results.

Perhaps the most overrated metric for evaluating your results is accuracy. Suppose you have an offer to which only one percent of the people respond. A model that predicts "nobody will respond" is 99 percent accurate and 100 percent useless. Another measure that is frequently used is lift. Lift measures the improvement achieved by a predictive model. However, lift does not take into account cost and revenue so it is often preferable to look at profit or ROI. Depending on whether you choose to maximize lift, profit or ROI, you choose a different percentage of your mailing list to whom you send solicitations.

7. Incorporating data mining in your CRM solution.

In building a CRM application, data mining is often a small, albeit critical, part of the final product. For example, predictive patterns through data mining may be combined with the knowledge of domain experts and incorporated in a large application used by many different kinds of people.

The way data mining is actually built into the application is determined by the nature of your customer interaction. There are two main ways you interact with your customers: they contact you (inbound) or you contact them (outbound). The deployment requirements are quite different.

Outbound interactions are characterized by your company, which originates the contact, such as through a direct mail campaign. Thus, you select people to contact by applying the model to your customer database. Another type of outbound campaign is an advertising campaign. In this case, you match the profiles of good prospects shown by your model to the profile of the people your advertisement would reach.

For inbound transactions, such as a telephone order, an Internet order or a customer service call, the application must respond in real time. Therefore, the data mining model is embedded in the application and actively recommends an action.

In either case, one key issue you must deal with in applying a model to new data is the transformations you used in building the model. Thus if the input data (whether from a transaction or a database) contains age, income and gender fields, but the model requires the age-to-income ratio and gender has been changed into two binary variables, you must transform your input data accordingly. The ease with which you can embed these transformations becomes one of the most important productivity factors when you want to rapidly deploy many models.

Conclusion

Customer relationship management is essential to compete effectively in today's marketplace. The more effectively you can use information about your customers to meet their needs, the more profitable you will be. (This paper doesn't address meeting customer needs. What are their needs? Did we ask them? Or are we simply suggesting products based on past behavior?) Operational CRM needs analytical CRM with predictive data mining models at its core. The route to a successful business requires that you understand your customers and their requirements, and data mining is the essential guide.

Appendix: data mining technology

Decision trees

Decision trees are a way of representing a series of rules that lead to a class or value. For example, you may wish to offer a prospective customer a particular product. The figure shows a simple decision tree that solves this problem while illustrating all the basic components of a decision tree: the decision node, branches and leaves.

A simple classification tree

The first component is the top decision node or root node, which specifies a test to be carried out. Each branch will lead either to another decision node or to the bottom of the tree, called a leaf node. By navigating the decision tree, you can assign a value or class to a case by deciding which branch to take, starting at the root node and moving to each subsequent node until a leaf node is reached. Each node uses the data from the case to choose the appropriate branch.

Decision trees models are commonly used in data mining to examine the data and induce a tree and its rules that will be used to make predictions. A number of different algorithms may be used for building decision trees including CHAID (Chi-squared Automatic Interaction Detection), CART (Classification And Regression Trees), Quest and C5.0.

Neural networks

Neural networks are of particular interest because they offer a means of efficiently modeling large and complex problems in which there may be hundreds of predictor variables that have many interactions. (Actual biological neural networks are incomparably more complex.) Neural nets are most commonly used for regressions but may also be used in classification problems.

A neural network starts with an input layer, where each node corresponds to a predictor variable. These input nodes are connected to a number of nodes in a hidden layer. Each input node is connected to every node in the hidden layer. The nodes in the hidden layer may be connected to nodes in another hidden layer or to an output layer. The output layer consists of one or more response variables.

A neural network with one hidden layer

After the input layer, each node takes in a set of inputs, multiplies them by a connection weight, adds them together, applies a function (called the activation or squashing function) to them and passes the output to the node(s) in the next layer. For example, the node below has five inputs (x0 through x4) each of which is multiplied by a weight and then added together resulting in a sum I:

I = .3X1+.7X2-.2X3+.4X4-.5X5= .3-.7-.2+.4+.5=.3

This output y is then the sum that has been transformed by the non-linear activation function, in this case to a value of .57.

The goal of training the neural net is to estimate the connection weights so that the output of the neural net accurately predicts the test value for a given input set of values. The most common training method is back propagation. Each training method has a set of parameters that control various aspects of training such as avoiding local optima or adjusting the speed of conversion.

Neural networks differ in philosophy from many statistical methods in several ways. First, a neural network usually has more parameters than does a typical statistical model. For example, a neural network with 100 inputs and 50 hidden nodes will have over 5,000 parameters. Because they are so numerous and because so many combinations of parameters result in similar predictions, the parameters become uninterpretable and the network serves as a "black box" predictor. However, this is acceptable in CRM applications. A bank may assign the probability of bankruptcy to

an account and may not care what the causes are.

One myth of neural networks is that data of any quality can be used to provide reasonable predictions and they will sift through data to find the truth. However, neural networks require as much data preparation as any other method, which is to say they require a lot of data preparation. The most successful implementations of neural networks (or decision trees or logistic regression or any other method) involve very careful data cleansing, selection, preparation and pre-processing. For instance, neural nets require that all variables be numeric. Therefore, categorical data such as "state" is usually broken up into multiple dichotomous variables (e.g., "California," "New York"), each with a "1" (yes) or "0" (no) value. The resulting increase in variables is called the categorical explosion.

Clustering
Clustering divides a database into different groups. The goal of clustering is to find groups that are very different from each other and whose members are very similar to each other. Unlike classification, you don't know what the clusters will be when you start or by which attributes the data will be clustered. Consequently, someone who is knowledgeable in the business must interpret the clusters. After you have found clusters that reasonably segment your database, these clusters may then be used to classify new data. Some of the common algorithms used to perform clustering include Kohonen feature maps and K-means.

Don't confuse clustering with segmentation. Segmentation refers to the general problem of identifying groups that have common characteristics. Clustering is a way to segment data into groups that are not previously defined, whereas classification is a way to segment data by assigning it to groups that are already defined.

Data mining makes the difference

SPSS Inc. provides solutions that discover what customers want and predict what they will do. The company delivers solutions at the intersection of customer relationship management and business intelligence that enable its customers to interact with their customers more profitably. SPSS' solutions integrate and analyze marketing, customer and operational data in key vertical markets worldwide including: telecommunications, health care, banking, finance, insurance, manufacturing, retail, consumer packaged goods, market research and the public sector. Headquartered in Chicago, SPSS has more than 40 offices. For more information, visit www.spss.com.

Chapter 3: CRM in Practice

CRM Application Service Providers - Risks and Rewards

Title: CRM Application Service Providers - Risks and Rewards
Author: Paul Sweeney, Sweeney Group
Abstract: Application Service Providers (ASP's) are here and changing the Customer
                Relationship Management (CRM) landscape. If you haven't heard about ASP's
                yet, don't worry, you will. Also known as application hosting, this is a new
                model of selling software on a "pay as you go" basis -- made possible by the
                marriage of the Web and conventional Customer Relationship Management
                (CRM) products.

Biography: Paul Sweeney is founder and president of Sweeney Group, Inc., a Customer Relationship Management (CRM)
consulting firm. Paul offers over 20 years of sales, marketing, and financial systems experience.

Virtually every CRM and Sales Force Automation (SFA) vendor is in the process of developing web-based versions of their products that can be "rented" on a per user, per month basis. No software is installed on the end-users' PC's. Rather, access to these Web-based CRM applications is provided over the Internet (or Intranet) using standard Web browsers (i.e. Netscape Navigator or Internet Explorer).

Although many CRM vendors now offer the ASP software model, they do not consider themselves ASP's. However, by definition, if a vendor offers software "for rent" over a network, they can be considered an Application Service Provider, or ASP.

Expect to see this software model pushed aggressively by the software industry due to the ease at which CRM licenses can be sold; provide a credit card number and you can be "up and running" in just a few minutes. This allows hosted CRM applications to enter the enterprise through the "back-door", just as PC's running VisiCalc did in the early 1980's -- essentially cutting IT out of the software purchase and installation role.

Although this may seem to be an attractive option for small sales or marketing groups, there are risks that should be understood. First and foremost, corporate data is at risk. Currently, an ASP or "hosted solution" assumes that data will physically reside with the ASP vendor. Therefore, research your data security requirements. Questions might include:

▸ How is data kept secure and protected from unauthorized uses?
▸ How often is data backed up?
▸ What backup methods are used?
▸ Has the vendor recently attempted (successfully) to restore data from a back-up source?

Next, it is critical to assess the vendor's stability and reliability. Questions to ask might include:

- Is "uptime" guaranteed?
- What procedures are in place to support a vendor's claim of reliability (fault tolerance, system redundancy, etc.)?
- What systems infrastructure and business procedures are in place to ensure reliability during the vendor's high-growth phase?
- Does the vendor provide adequate technical and application support?
- What disaster contingency plans are in place in case of fire, power loss, or other catastrophic events that may affect the ASP?

Other points to ponder when considering a hosted CRM solution include:

- What options are available for integration with legacy systems?
- Is the ASP's attitude and culture a good match?
- How do you terminate the agreement (and get your data back)?
- How is the CRM system administered (adding/deleting users, adding/deleting fields and records, bug fixes, installation of upgrades, etc.)?
- Is the ASP financially secure?

Benefits

To summarize, data security and reliability are two significant issues to consider when evaluating a hosted CRM solution from an ASP. With these concerns aside, let's briefly explore the benefits of the ASP model.

Rapid Deployment

As previously stated, end-users can be installed and running in just a few minutes with Web-based CRM applications provided (or hosted) by an ASP. Assuming web browsers are in place, little additional work is usually required. The most difficult part of the process may be deciding how to arrange for payment to the vendor. Of course, any legacy systems integration or conversions will require additional systems development work.

No Software Ownership

Unlike traditional client-server CRM applications, there is virtually no software to own. Consequently, there can be a substantial reduction in software management tasks and related costs. Again, the CRM application is accessed over the web with the ASP vendor maintaining (hosting) both the application and the database for a monthly per-user fee. This can reduce both software and system administration costs while providing clear cost of ownership data.

Virtual Network

Web-based CRM applications offer the ability to instantly network sales and marketing groups. By definition, these applications are accessed over the Internet or through a firm's own Intranet. For companies lacking network assets and other systems resources, this option offers a compelling reason to employ web-based applications via ASP's.

Reduced Management

The ASP model can substantially reduce many of the tasks associated with maintaining traditional client-server applications. Generally, the application vendor will handle all system maintenance tasks, including back-up and recovery, upgrades, network management, and user additions and deletions.

Tradeoffs

Depending upon your point of view, many of the benefits mentioned may also be viewed as some of the tradeoffs. Three related and somewhat obvious tradeoffs exist: Control, Network Dependence, and Ownership.

Clearly, giving control to an ASP is a double-edged sword. Although an ASP will generally manage all systems related tasks, loss of control and management oversight is assumed. You are trusting the ASP to follow good systems procedures for disaster recovery, user support, system upgrades, bug resolution, version control, and data security.

Network dependence is another tradeoff. Unless the web-based application can operate in a "disconnected mode" (not connected to the Internet or Intranet), then all users are dependent upon the their connection to the network. This raises concerns about network reliability, privacy, uptime, and connection speeds.
Lastly, not owning the application could indeed be a tradeoff for some firms. Ownership provides control, and control

can provide comfort. By definition then, application hosting implies some loss of control. However, as the application hosting market matures, confidence and comfort levels will follow. In the meantime, ask your ASP vendor to clearly document how they intend to address your concerns. In particular, what guarantees can be provided that your data will be secure and that the application will perform reliably over the Internet?

Summary

In short, look for service level agreements, documented disaster recovery procedures, data security statements and descriptions, scalability benchmarks and proven technical support. Just as important, ensure the ASP you are considering is financially fit so that your data will not be held hostage in the event of a bankruptcy or other catastrophic failure.

A Realistic View on Customer Relations

Title: *A Realistic View on Customer Relations*
Author: *Xander De Bruine, editor of Telebusiness Magazine*

Abstract: *The attention that CRM attracts at this moment leads to an equal amount of questions and answers in the service industry. In the US the market responds with Internet sites and communities with a focus on knowledge sharing regarding CRM. Bob Thompson, also member of the board of directors of the Northern Californian CRM Association, is one of them. He initiated an Internet site with news discussions and success stories. Interview of Bob Thompson by Xander De Bruine*

Can you explain the exact definition of, and difference between, CRM and Extended Enterprise CRM. And what is their current status of implementation in the market?
CRM is the process of targeting and acquiring new customers, convincing customers to buy your products or services, and then taking care of them after the sale so they come back again and again! Traditionally these functions are called marketing, sales, and service. Together they form a lifecycle of Customer Relationship Management. Note that none of the above necessarily has to include technology. CRM is a process with a goal to have the most profitable relationships possible. To reach this goal, marketing, sales and service must work more as a team and share information. Computerized CRM applications help make this possible.

Extended Enterprise CRM, usually called Partner Relationship Management, simply means including your indirect sales and service channels in this CRM process. Although the CRM software industry is quite large now -- estimated to reach $2Billion in 1999 -- and is growing about 50% per year, partners have generally not been included. Why? Until Internet-based systems became more common, it simply wasn't practical to include resellers, agents, integrators, and other partners. Client/Server technology is a poor fit in the extended enterprise due to complexity and cost. Now with Web-based applications, many designed specifically for indirect sales channels, it's practical to include partners in CRM systems. This PRM market is emerging in 1999, and is poised for very rapid growth, fueled by venture capital investments and real needs in the market.

What do managers often forget in aligning business and IT environment?
Business managers sometimes forget they must clearly define the business problems to be solved before installing IT systems. IT managers can contribute to this by focusing just on getting the application up and running, thinking that success is defined as "on time, on budget." Business goals and strategies should drive IT

investments. Ideally success should be defined up as meeting business goals -- such as revenue productivity, customer satisfaction and loyalty, high profitability per customer, etc.

What are important factors for Customer Facing Applications and communication technologies that interact?

The most important communications technology is of course the Internet -- no surprise there! A low-cost, universal communications platform solves a lot of problems. I think wireless will become increasingly important as the technology improves and the workforce becomes more and more mobile.

What are important factors for Datawarehouse architecture?

I'm not a data warehouse expert, so I can't comment on architectures. I do feel that data warehouses, data marts, and analysis tools are critical to CRM -- especially in the marketing process. After all, if you don't target the right customers with the right products, offers, etc., you can end up with a lot of unprofitable sales. Many of the larger CRM vendors are building data marts into their Marketing Automation modules for just this reason. And Marketing Automation is a hot new segment.

What do customers expect from CRM software and how are their expectations changing?

I think expectations are slowly changing from "CRM is sales automation" to a more complex and realistic view. It's not enough just to sell faster. You have to smarter

about the customers to find and keep, and build "raving fans" that will be loyal to you even when your performance slips a little.

What problems could be solved by CRM and what are the main added values for customers/partners?

In marketing -- targeting the right prospects, customers, and partners and then effectively developing and running marketing campaigns. This has enormous leverage and I think is overlooked by many companies that think CRM is just about selling faster.

In sales -- reduce sales cycle time, higher sales productivity per rep, faster new rep ramp up time, and improved account management are typical goals. Sales Automation can help, but you'd better apply it to the prospects and customers with the best potential!

In service -- lower cost, higher customer satisfaction, faster response. Good service is strategic because it can lead to loyal customers that tend to be more profitable over the long term. Unfortunately many businesses still see it as a cost center -- "yes, we know service is important, but how can we save money?" Web-based self-service applications are all the rage now because they reduces costs and free up skilled service personnel (which are always in short supply) to work on more complex issues.

Chapter 3: CRM in Practice

What does it take to get an organizational change and cultural mindset for CRM, or what are important learning factors for potential CRM-companies?

I think it has to start with the CEO setting the tone that "we are a customer-focused company." This is easy and popular to say, and hard to do in practice. Focusing on service excellence is one tangible way of showing that a company really believes it.

Could you give a reaction on Customer lifetime value and the importance for investment in CRM?

CLV is a great idea. Some industries, most notably financial services, have done a lot of work to determine customer acquisition cost and profitability over time. The key point is that you have to keep customers to make money! It seems obvious, but most companies have no idea what it costs to acquire a new customer, and don't worry much when they leave. "Let's go get another new account," is the usual reaction, and sales people are unwitting accomplices because they are usually paid on new sales, not on profitable long-term relationships. Calculating CLV can raise awareness of the critical importance of customer retention. I see it as an important pre-cursor to implementing a CRM system, or perhaps as part of the marketing process when decisions are made to target certain customer or prospects.

Can you tell us about some CRM failures and their learning aspects?

The CRM failure rate has been widely reported and debated the past few years. Results are improving from a failure rate of up to 80% about 3 years ago. Still, about 50% of CRM projects have significant problems today. Some of the big issues are:

▸ Failure to identify and focus on specific business problems
▸ Lack of active senior management (non-IT) sponsorship.
▸ Poor user acceptance, which can occur for a variety of reasons such as unclear benefits (i.e. CRM is a tool for management, but doesn't help a rep sell more effectively) and usability issues.
▸ Trying to automate a poorly defined process

Could you describe the top- and mid-market of CRM vendors?

The CRM market is large, diverse and dynamic. It's hard to keep up with all of the established companies, much less the new firms! That said, the companies that consistently stand out in the large enterprise market are Siebel Systems, Vantive, Clarify, and Baan. IBM also has great potential. Oracle and SAP have ambitious goals but haven't executed very well yet.

In the mid-market, it's getting very interesting. Some of the top companies include Pivotal, ONYX, and SalesLogix. However there are a host of other excellent companies, many offering new web-based solutions. Some of the large enterprise companies (including Siebel) are targeting the mid-market, but I'm skeptical that they will have much success.

There are plenty of other exciting companies focused on niches, such as Epiphany for marketing analysis, Silknet for web-based self service, Wisdomware for knowledge-enabled selling, Trilogy for configuration tools, etc. And new Partner Relationship Management solutions from startups like Webridge and ChannelWave.

Could you say something about the Web based Collaboration and renting vs. buying applications (the possibility of Application Service Providers)?

Web-based collaboration and broadcasting is a huge opportunity. Although not usually thought of as a CRM application, I say it is! Why? Because it helps companies market to, sell to, and support their customers more effectively and at lower cost. The technology is improving rapidly and I believe should be in the plans of every company planning a CRM project. I think we'll see web collaboration technology increasingly integrated into CRM systems.

ASPs are "catching fire" here in the U.S., with new announcements seemingly every day. I am very enthusiastic about the prospects for ASP-based CRM systems, especially for smaller to mid-market customers. Why install something when you can plug in and start using it immediately? CRM skills are in short supply, and time to deployment (and benefits) is paramount. ASPs make good business sense and will grow rapidly as customers get comfortable entrusting customer information to a third-party service provider.

How big is the importance of standards between CRM vendors and market potential of exchanging sales, marketing and service data with third parties?

I think standards will become more important in the next year or two as partners get involved in CRM processes. Just like email must span multiple systems, CRM data should flow easily between different companies. For example, standards are needed for the exchange of customer contact info, leads, forecasts, service incidents, etc. If large manufacturer chooses to use Siebel, and a channel partner is using GoldMine, why should either party have to rekey information?

Third parties could fill this need in the interim, serving as clearing houses to translate CRM information from one company and deliver it to another. Before email standards emerged, a few services helped bridge the gap between proprietary email systems. But when standards developed, these services because unnecessary. I think we'll see a similar evolution in the CRM industry, and it will be driven by the growth of Partner Relationship Management systems. RosettaNet is one organization working on some of these issues in the computer industry.

You mentioned in a newsletter the risk of Microsoft Outlook Encroachment. Can you explain the risk?

Microsoft Outlook is a great low-end contact manager. For a few hundred contacts it does a fine job and integrates well with Microsoft's email and browser products. It doesn't seem too great a leap to me for Microsoft to extend Outlook into a more full-featured contact manager, which would threaten products like ACT!, GoldMine, and Maximizer. However I don't know of any plans in this area. I do see GoldMine and Maximizer increasing being positioned for workgroups and even mid-sized CRM projects, which should keep them out of the Microsoft "crosshairs."

Could you give a short reaction on other CRM vendors?

HP is an interesting one. It remains to be seen how successful companies like HP (and IBM/Corepoint) will be with CRM applications. I like IBM's chances a little better because of its strong focus on E-business and services. Note that both companies have large, loyal customer bases and could do quite well by adding CRM capabilities to existing products and bringing new CRM solutions to current accounts.

Chapter 4: CRM in Callcenters

CRM Success: Call Center Improvement

Title: CRM Success: Call Center Improvement
Author: Hyperion
Abstract: *In this paper Hyperion applies the CRM lifecycle to a common business problem: call center improvement. The three stages of the CRM lifecycle will be applied to the business problem and the solutions will demonstrate how essential CRM analytics are to customer success.*

The Business Problem

An outbound call center, providing customer service support to commercial banking clients, wants to expand its services. The bank wants to take advantage of cross selling and up selling opportunities that arise during customer service calls. Studies indicate that customers increasingly want "one stop shopping," and the current call center's inability to sell products and services is leaving money on the table.

However, implementing a service + sales program would increase the call center's operational expenses. Extensive sales and product training would be required for CSR's and average call lengths would generally increase, as CSR's spent more time with each customer. Greater average call lengths would require even more CSR's in order to maintain current service levels. Accordingly, the bank has decided to implement a selective service + sales program.

The bank knows that their top 15% most profitable customers (their premium customers) generate approximately 75% of profits. Accordingly, they've chosen to selectively route calls from premium customers to a specially trained team of CSR's providing service + sales support. All other customers will route to the regular CSR team and receive customer service support as they always have.

This plan promises a higher level of service and relationship building for premium customers, while taking advantage of opportunities to cross sell and up sell within this very profitable customer segment. Less profitable customers, who are less likely to cross sell and up sell, will still receive quality customer service, but without increasing the costs of service delivery.

The Solution: Required Integration

▸ A CTI system integrated with customer data determines whether the incoming call is from a premium or regular customer, based on caller ID.
▸ An integrated ACD system routes the call to the appropriate CSR based on customer type.
▸ Via screen pops, a complete view of the customer's sales history and service request history is presented to the CSR as they receive the call.
▸ Customer profiling suggests possible cross sell and up sell products that have sold successfully to other customers with similar characteristics.
▸ Integrated scripting utilities guide the CSR through the call, where questions are dynamically generated based on answers to previous questions.

The Solution: Required Analysis

The key to solving this call center problem is knowing whether a potential solution is cost effective. If a sales +support offering to premium customers fails to generate sufficient additional revenue to offset the added expense of the program, then the solution is not a success.

A number of measures need to be carefully monitored, both initially to determine the effectiveness of the solution, as well as ongoing to ensure adequate call center quality and profitability over time. Standard call center quality measures typically focus on service level, but other important quality measures include: average call length, number of rings until answer,

average hold time, abandon rate, first call/first handle and average response time. These measures must be analyzed across a number of different call center dimensions. This helps to identify causal factors for both high quality and low quality trends. For instance, an analysis of average hold times across the dimensions time of day, day of week, customer service representative, customer type and product/service class might indicate disproportionate hold times for premium customers on Friday afternoons. Further research might show that after normal branch hours on Fridays, premium customers tend to call in with more complex requests. These take longer to resolve; thus tying up CSR's and increasing hold times for subsequent calls.

Call center profitability analysis would measure the increase of sales revenue through the service +sales program and the degree of cross selling and up selling. It would also be important to measure program costs (due to CSR staffing, training and increased call lengths) relative to increased sales revenue to determine the ongoing profitability of the program.

The Solution: Required Business Actions

The bank should compare call center metrics against both internal and external quality benchmarks over time. Internal benchmarks measure call center quality improvement, while external benchmarks score the bank's call center quality relative to peer groups and competitors. Following the performance management adage, "you can't manage what you can't measure, "this provides the bank a quantifiable view of their sales + service program success.

The bank needs to develop a method of measuring customer satisfaction across different customer segments. Good benchmark statistics don't guarantee that a customer is happy, but rather provide a baseline for comparative analysis and focus improvement initiatives on customer interaction activities. A customer 's satisfaction is a highly subjective measurement, which tends to be more personal and less easily quantified, but is critical to strengthening customer relationships.

CSR's moving towards a service +sales role need intensive coaching and management support as they learn how to uncover customer needs. CSR's need to understand bank products and services, and the potential value they hold for different customer segments.

An incentive program should be developed to recognize and reward successful CSR's, based on customer satisfaction, call quality and attainment of sales goals. Best practice reviews of successful CSR's and CSR groups help others to learn and improve.

The bank needs to evaluate the profitability of the program, relative to the increase in customer satisfaction over a period of time. Based on the results, they may chose to extend the program downwards to include more of the less profitable customers or even upwards to serve fewer more profitable customers. This allows the bank to balance profitability and satisfaction across the most appropriate customer population.

Call Center Terminology

Outbound	-A call center that makes outgoing calls (i.e., for telemarketing).
Inbound	-A call center that receives incoming calls (i.e., customer service).
CSR	-Customer Service Representative.
ACD	-Automatic Call Distribution. A system that can route incoming calls to specific individuals or CSR groups based on call characteristics.
CTI	-Computer Telephony Integration. The ability to integrate voice call information with business applications. CTI systems frequently use "screen pops" or application pop-up windows to deliver customer-specific application data, based on the caller ID number of the incoming phone call.
IVR	-Interactive Voice Response. A system handles routine customer servicing through a series

of interactive pre-recorded menus. IVR's are customer self-service systems that help reduce CSR labor expenses.

Service Bureau -A company that provides outsourced call center services, either full-time or in call overflow situations.

Service Level -Answering X% of calls within Y seconds. Common averages are 80/20 - 80%of calls within 20 secs. This is based on average call time, call volume and the number of CSR's.

Average Abandonment Time
-The average time in seconds a caller waited before abandoning a call.

Percent Abandonment
-The percentage of all calls received by the call center that are abandoned before reaching a CSR.

Average Handle Time
-The average of the sums of talk time and after-call work time.

Calls per Hour -The average number of calls each agent handles per hour. It's the total number of calls handled per agent in one working

shift divided by the number of hours in the shift.

Percent Agent Utilization
-The percentage of an agent's time spent working with customers. It's the total talk time and hold time (in minutes)for an agent's calls in a shift divided by the length of the shift in minutes.

"*The real payback from the customer call center is that it allows us to get to know more about the customer ...*"

"*...Analysis is essential in order to understand what [the customer] is trying to tell us...*"

"*...Decision makers are really hungry for quantifiable analysis. And without it, quite frankly, they don't tend to listen to the customer.*"

-Dr.Jon Anton, Purdue University Center for Customer Driven Quality

Integrating the Call-Center with Customer Information

Title:	Integrating the Call-Center with Customer Information
Author:	Michael Meltzer, Computer Sciences Corporations
Abstract::	This article looks at how a call-centers can be integrated as part of a multi-channel contact and touch-point management within a Customer Relationship Management (CRM) solution based on a Scaleable Data Warehouse (SDW) as the infrastructure for competitive advantage.
	This paper explores how the CRM philosophy coupled with a clear vision of how a Scaleable Data Warehouse (SDW) can be effectively integrated and implemented can lead to success. There is also a need for clear marketing strategies that can be applied to web enabled call centers. This is to support customer retention, cross-selling and up-selling opportunities, improve direct/continuous marketing campaigns, marketing to that segment of one and to put the organisation on the road to marketing one to one!

Aren't all customers fickle? They seem to move their business to another financial service provider even though your financial services provider (FSP) has the best services and prices available. Yet there are at least two questions you have to ask yourself: have you really, really communicated with your customer recently and are you that certain you have the best deal? Whereas we may leave the second question at this time for Competitive Intelligence Analysis, the first question is based on the need for relationship management and a true dialogue, an that's the basis of this article. This time, I look at Call Centers, and although Call-centers are often used as customer service touch points and as a means of tele-selling to non customers many banks, telecommunication companies and retailers use them to retain and increase their share of their current customers wallet rather than just acquire new customers. The call center has become part of the CRM (customer relationship management mythology). What was part of providing quality customer service and a means of creating dialogue with the customer has now been re-badged as being CRM spelt in bold loud letters.

Although CRM does include customer call and contact management many of the call contact/contact management software vendors have managed to convince many unwary purchasers that all they need do is install their 'solution' and all their prays will be answered well…..? This article will look at the evolution of the call contact and its integration with the data warehouse (information on customer contact, billing, segmentation and so on) to serve as a focal point for the customer centric approach to CRM. We will also consider the reasons for this new approach that responds to customers' needs by providing high quality support, a dynamic marketing channel and a means of gathering soft data. "Organisations are frankly frantic about providing more customer service", says Carter Lesher, VP and research director at Gartner Group. "In many cases, it's what they're competing on: Products have become commoditised, and customer service is one way to differentiate themselves."

RETENTION

Customers are more expensive to replace than to retain; some put the cost of acquiring a customer as high as 5 - 10 times more than to retain one. Customers have been educated to expect a high level of service and a wide range of competitive products. Some non-banks that offer a narrow range of products specifically targeting consumer segments that have special service requirements have been successful (credit cards, insurance, home loans etc.,) but it all depends on what your customers expect from you. Failure to live up to their value expectations increase the risk of defection to a bank that meets their perceived value needs. Studies by Reichheld and Sasser (HBR 1990) demonstrated that: "As a customer relationship with a company lengthens, profits rise. And not just a little. Companies can boost profits by 100% by retaining just 5% more of their customers." Call Centers have become a critical element in a

company's armoury to retain customers by providing high quality service, creating a dialogue with their customers and providing an opportunity to initiate proactive marketing. Yet their evolution into a mission critical financial services tool has been far quicker in the US than anywhere else, as has the move to integrate the data warehouse to better target and respond to customer needs, which is still in its infancy elsewhere. The call center enables a personal touch to be reintroduced if handled carefully. It is an opportunity to introduce high technology balanced by information and humanity. For a reiteration of the differences between acquisition and retention look at fig.1.

VOICE RESPONSE IS NOT ENOUGH

Okay, so the 'enquirer' got through to your fully automated 'help desk' that has the latest integrated voice response (IVR) system, which in itself was seven levels deep, but they gave up after the fourth level having been annoyed or frustrated and then tried unsuccessfully to get through several times before giving up!

Figure 1: Source: J M McIntyre

Retention	Acquisition
Nurturing Relationships	Acquiring potential relationships
Internal analysis	External research
Demographics and transactional history	Demographic profiles
Actual needs driven	Projected needs driven
Contacts must be personal	Contacts can be less personal
Accuracy required	Inaccuracy tolerated
Offer relationship driven	Offer driven
Offers must be integrated	Offers can be events
Supports reactivating	Supports assimilation
Synergistic with acquisition	Synergistic with retention

Were you aware who they were or even that anyone had tried to get through at all? When you upgraded from the complaints desk did you move to a customer focused approach or was it an exercise in cost reduction moving the customer away from the teller to some form of automaton? Did you 'merely' replace humans with technology?

A number of major company's made this initial error when moving over to what we now know as 'call centers', but the move today is to use technology to support integrated marketing and provide quality customer services efforts. The call center is now viewed as one of the channels available to interact directly with the customer. Oh! and many companys' have gone back to using 'humans' as part of the equation to better serve the customer's and the company's needs.

The call center has gained in importance as the use of telephones has spread and is set to gain momentum as countries deregulate their telecommunications industry and competition flourishes. The US, where deregulation occurred some time ago and where the telephone is ubiquitous, is believed to be some 12- 24 months ahead of Europe in its use of the telephone for: call centers, computer telephonic integration and of course the Internet. A simple definition of a call center is any grouping of operatives and or automated voice response units(VRUs) that support customer contact functions over a telephone. We can add today that the addition of computer support is also a prerequisite for any support unit to function adequately. Another definition of the call center is a physical location (although there are some implementations of virtual call centers) where calls are placed or received in volume to enable sales, marketing, customer service, telemarketing, technical support or other specialised business activity.

HISTORY

Although helpdesks and call centers have been with us for a long time, historically their only connection between the voice processing systems (PBX/ACD) and the data processing systems used by the services support operatives were the operative themselves! It was in the late 80s when CTI (computer telephonic integration) became commercially available, enabling linkage of the PBX/ACD to a mainframe. Screen popups and the ability to pass information and commands across this link became the latest technology boon to call centers. With the introduction of open systems, the client server environments adoption rate has quickened. But adoption rates have not been uniform, and this is so even in the US where it is estimated that there are some 60,000 call centers in total, with banks alone accounting for over 1,300 (Metis). Culture, geographies and available technologies have affected adoption rates:

1. The need for an ISDN (Integrated Switched Digital Network) network facilities to pass needed originating and dialled number information.
2. The complexity of implementing the needed systems to create an integrated customer interaction site.

3. The cultural differences in doing business over the telephone and
4. Simply the number and robustness of telephones and infrastructure available to the general populace.

SERVICE LEADERSHIP

Providing quality services to your customers is prerequisite to stay in the game today. Bad or inappropriate service in a highly competitive environment where the customer demands high quality anytime, anyplace support, will see your customers move to a competitor. The base line for enhanced customer relationships rests on timely and accurate responses to inquiries and requests. Many customers also expect personal attention and often dislike voice response alone. The whole point of any call-center today is to help retain the customer, and where appropriate expand the relationship. Before you can get into all the other opportunities a fully integrated call center offers you must provide the customer with the support and care they believe they deserve. ", advises Joe O'Leary of Arthur Andersen. "Together, these drive satisfaction--which drive loyalty, which drives profits. When customers wield the power of choice, providers respond". Although price-based marketing is a short-term method to attract customers, over the long haul customer care will build the loyalty necessary to ongoing success. Service alone can be a differentiator but as so many banks are striving to provide world class services it is difficult to see how this will be achieved. To illustrate: since Sanwa Bank of California put in branch call centers, calls to its toll-free 800 number

have shot up, from 6 million in 1995 to 18 million. Sanwa is tying together databases on mortgage loans, credit cards, and regular accounts, enabling one call-center teller to handle most of a customer's inquiries and "making him feel like the only person in the world," says David Minor, a VP at Sanwa bank.

Further, a study by the Strategic Planning Institute has found that:

Service Leaders.....

▸ Charge on average 9 to 10 percent more for their basic products and services.
▸ Grow twice as fast as their low-service competition.
▸ Improve market share on average by 6 percent per year. By contrast, low flyers lose market share by as much as 2 percent annually.
▸ Have an average return on sales of 12 percent compared to 1 percent for bottom feeders.

SALES AND CHANNELS

From service support and care the call center has grown into a cost effective sales and distribution channel. This has lead to the need for more sophisticated applications and even tighter integration between telephony and the organisation's computing systems. However, the latest findings from the Henley Center (UK) would indicate a wholesale decline in customers' perceptions of service by the telephone. In centralising operations and closing branches, many banks have lost that local, friendly feel that is all-important when developing relationships with customers. The actionable information the SDW provides, integrated with the latest computer integrated telephony (CIT) can make the difference between success and failure when centralising support call centers. The data warehouse supports this tight coupling and goes on to supply much of the needed information to support the call center. At the same time, it also provides a means to take in the soft data (potential complaints and potential leads etc.) that the call center accumulates on an on-going basis.

The information to provide operational support is customer based and must be available real-time. This is achieved by using a Data Mart (The DM being a subset of the data warehouse). The data mart is particularly tuned to work as part of a real time operational environment, but the reason there is a need for the DM and SDW is based on the need to understand who your customers are. All customers are not equal and a simple understanding of their value to a bank proves this. Should you therefore treat all customers equally when some are more valuable than others? By knowing the value and potential value of customers to a bank enables the bank (to be perceived) to sell and provide services one customer at a time. Even in countries where organisations are not allowed by privacy initiatives to use some of the data in their SDW they can look at customer profitability. To look seriously at the way the data warehouse is now essential for the success of a proactive customer centric call center lets peek at a current scenario that incorporates use of the Internet.

A SCENARIO

This scenario focuses on a bank but could easily be extended to any other organisation that are willing to invest in the vision, technology and cultural changes needed.

You call your bank from home to initiate some simple payments and to enquire about your balance. The bank's telephone system identifies you by the number you dialed in from, and your call is directed to a specific operative (you are in a particular segment and are treated accordingly) who answers the call and greets you by name. Your usage profile and account balance has popped up on the workstation (you normally ask for your balance) plus a flashing prompt to inform the operative that there is a potential sales message to deliver. The operative has a single comprehensive view of you as an important customer of the bank. You proceed to make your payments and get your account balance. The operative puts their cursor on the prompt key and a dialogue appears. Your car loan will expire in three months and there is a special pre-approved loan on offer if you wanted to consider another. You would like some details quickly and you ask if they can be E-Mailed or faxed. The operative says which would you like -you answer e-mail as that would be quicker tonight. You are about to tell the operative your e-mail address, but you are informed they already have it and the information is on its way to you. You are also informed that you could have someone call you to talk you through the information or you could elicit a phone call by responding to the e-mail or even look further at the various summer offers on the bank's web site. If there is anything further of interest on the web site all you have to do is type in your phone number and a specialist tele-consultant will call back.

THE FOCUS IS THE CUSTOMER

The information held in the SDW can help identify the right customers to provide special services to and can profile customers' particular needs. Without this information drawn from the SDW and placed in the operational data mart (DM) for real time on-line support, much of the above would be difficult to accomplish. Without the customer there is no business and it is this focus on the customer that drives the need for detailed information. The information the organisation has on its customers is its unique advantage in the marketplace. Information that can be bought in, can be purchased by any organisation, its value only becomes apparent when you integrate it with your own information. This integration of external data with the company's own creates a unique differentiated set of information to be queried and mined. However, your ability to understand your own customers is hidden in that data you accumulate about their activities, and their likes and dislikes - not external inputs.

TORONTO DOMINION

To get at this data and turn it into actionable information and deliver it to the points of customer contact, many banks rely on their SDW. They also use it to make customer information available bank-wide for both branch and call-center customer contact and for future detailed marketing analysis. An example of the need for different types of information can be gauged from the work Toronto Dominion (TD) is doing in Canada: ``The telephone's emergence and rising popularity as a primary banking tool is a progressive result of the move towards greater convenience and increasing automation in every facet of our lives,'' says Mr. Baillie of TD. ``Our customers have expressed their need for easy-to-use telephone banking services,'' adds Frank Van Nie, Director of Telephone Banking, at TD. ``We are answering their call with an expert team of Banking Agents who can now help them arrange mortgages and loans, contribute to RRSPs, (savings plans) buy GICs, (Guaranteed Investment Certificates) open an account, answer their financial questions, in addition to paying bills, transferring funds, and checking their account balance. Service is available in English, French, Cantonese and Mandarin.''

US WEST

Described by Drury Jenkins as a closed loop CRM system US West enhances it's marketing effectiveness and cross-selling by integrating data from many sources and then supporting their outbound channel with scripts and offers that are pertinent to their customer base. John Barac (Marketing Decision Support Systems Director) said that in this SDW "..... we have all kinds of data from all our different lines of business. We know the customers' behaviour and history. We also have external data, demographics, what kind of area they live in and the average income in that area. We have all the contact information....." yet one of the most important uses of this integrated approach is in the area of inbound calls. Many have found that if you can satisfy customer problems on the inbound call you are more likely to sell more to a very receptive customer! "On an inbound channel, if we get information, we try to capture that information for future use and we try to adjust our offer". They use the information they capture as part of their knowledge base so they can learn their customers needs and alter their future responses based on their understanding of the customer.

THE CHALLENGE

The challenge that faces all organisations is how do you get all the required information together to support the customer centric approach? In the early days some talked about clever middleware (interfacing and extraction software). This was only a small part of the answer. Information about the customer comes from many systems, divisions and channels. The information has to be available and trusted by its users. The SDW and the real-time operational DM enables the banker to gain a holistic view of the customer. As the SDW is the one version of the truth that can be trusted it is the resource that can unleash the power of the call-center to create new higher levels of service. It also enables the organisations to create the perception of unique segment of one relationships. However the reasons why a SDW is an important part of an integrated and effective call-center becomes obvious when the banks tries to answer a range of questions:

‣ What is the real value of my customer base - what is the difference between profitable and unprofitable customers?
‣ How do I segment my customers appropriately?
‣ How do I increase my share of their wallet and what are the best ways to cross-sell?
‣ What are their preferences and can I use this knowledge to create unique segment-of-one offerings?
‣ Can I make predictions regarding their future purchases and then use that information to drive customer dialogue?
‣ How can I retain the right customers?
‣ What is the most effective delivery channel by particular service/product?
‣ Who is amenable to tele-consultative selling?

THE REAL VALUE OF CUSTOMERS

If you know the value of a customer you can decide the sort of customer care and sort of relationship you need to have with them to maintain or grow their profitability. This decision will impact their treatment as a customer in the call center. To do this you need to look to at least at two measures of customer value: their actual long-term value to the bank and the potential value

Chapter 4: CRM in Callcenters

the bank could capture. To begin this process of understanding the real value of a customer you need to look at estimated customer lifetime value (LTV). To start you must identify the sales of each product or service by some or all of the following: customer or number of accounts held or tenure. Finding out the frequency of customer defection and likelihood of switching will enable you to better understand the cost to you in future revenue streams. By analysing the information you have about the customer tenure you will be able to predict the length of time a customer is likely to stay with you (this equates to the lifetime in the equation). You would then measure the future incomes, net of transaction costs and discounted by a rate you choose to get at their net present value. The equation can of course get more complex as more factors such as propensity to defect are introduced at a macro level, or as cost models are altered over time. You could of course decide to assign a rank order to your customer base, based on the LTV as an approximation of true value. The idea is to identify those tiers of customers that are worth allocating resources to support and those that require different treatments. For example, by being able to identify those tiers that are marginal (borderline profitability) you can allocate those specific resources to move them into profit. Note that without a good measure of real customer profitability LTV remains merely another approximation of customer value.

HOW CUSTOMERS CAN SEGMENT THEMSELVES

Customers and prospects tend to look for different things in any relationship they have with a vendor of any services or products. They also buy in different ways dependent on their knowledge, lifestyles and education. The idea is to understand your customers and what does and does not work for them. Much of the information about customer preferences can be gathered from the SDW and enriched from external sources. Once you know the way they like to be treated and their value to the bank you can provide the right level of quality services based on solid business reasoning. A good summary of how customers can be split in to buying segments appeared in 'Customer-Centred Growth' by R. Whiteley and D. Hessan:

1. The Transactional Buy: Little need for information or relationship (use of Automated banking machines PC based services are a boon to these customers).
2. The Relational Buy: High relationship needs based on their need for personal emotional support throughout the purchase. (Purchase of complex insurance products and investments).
3. The Information Buy: They want information but no relationship as they know what they want but want information and an education (buying a mortgage, or discount brokerage services).
4. The Partnership Buy: They want a relationship and they want information as they have high affiliation needs and the desire to trust and partner with whoever they buy from (The purchase of

Personal Equity Plan, Mutual Funds and Endowment policies).

USAGE PROFILES

By knowing what products a customer takes, by default you know what products they don't have. By modelling the ideal customer portfolio you can identify the range of products that would bring you the most profit. You can also identify the ideal service and product usage pattern and once again profile customers against this. Are some more amenable to using telephone banking or billing enquiries rather than branches or shop fronts- who are they and what are they worth? You will then have a profile to test your customer base against and you also have the basis on which to plan marketing campaigns. The campaigns will be designed to improve the company's share of wallet and each customer's profitability (including LTV). This technique, coupled with demographic and psychographic data, can also form the basis of your segmentation rules. By using knowledge discovery (see Data Mining Dispelling The Myths another white paper in this series) you can begin to predict behaviours and make use of life triggers as part of your sales messages and outbound tele-marketing campaigns.

CHANNEL MANAGEMENT

An integrated multi-channel SDW provides the means of knowing what channels your customers use and prefer. The SDW collects all the transactional data from all the delivery channels and touchpoints.

Once you know what channels your customers are using, you can look at their usage patterns. The patterns will quickly show whether a customer prefers certain channels to others. For a bank some may want to use the bank branch, some use only the call center's telephone banking service and ATMs or even their new WAP Portable. Yet another transacts all their business at a branch or set of ATMs in another part of the country, away from the branch that holds her current or chequeing account. You could also collect information about the frequency of use by channel, by product, by value and so on. An understanding of preferences will also help you when considering structural changes to your network, larger and more centralised call centers new self service terminals, Internet portals, refurbishment, or a radical alteration or closure of a branch, etc. By choosing certain channels rather than others (e.g. Internet broking, home banking and ATMs) customers themselves will map directly to a bank's desire to lower the cost of delivery by their use of these channels. The whole process of understanding the customer is in pursuit of managing the customer relationship for greater profit.

RELATIONSHIP MANAGEMENT

But customer relationship management is not dependent on just understanding the customer better but is about providing effective services and products that meet their perceived values. The delivery channels that meet their needs have to be fast, convenient, flexible and cost-effective. A significant subset of the customer information that is available to your knowledge workers must be available for use by customer facing staff, call center workstations, voice response Units, ATMs, screen phones, decision support systems, WAP, the internet portals and home banking applications for PCs or interactive television. Your understanding of the customer's value to an organisation and their preferences enables you to devise treatments that will meet the customer's needs as well as the firm's need for continued profitable growth. Organisations rich in transactional data (telcos, banks and retailers) must capitalise on their unique informational advantage quickly. The faster they can get new services up and running to attract new customers, or cross-sell products to retain customers, whether through store fronts or in the E-Space the better their competitive advantage. This means the customer information and the technology infrastructure needed for product and service delivery have to be available today.

A SUMMARY

In summary the reasons that the SDW, call-center and E-Business are being integrated rests on the needs of an organisations need to: Increase revenue generation - by having customer insight and understanding of dynamics of the cross-sell/up-sell opportunities. The idea is to increase revenue per customer contact by selling higher margin products through the call center. Then to further leverage the call center capabilities as a direct sales channel using where appropriate consultative sales personnel. Each marketing campaign can

be carried out at many levels, utilising direct mail, customer response advertisements, web site offers, WAP and direct tele-selling. Each element however can be tied back to call-center, touch point, Internet support and usage. The SDW has for many years been used as the base (trusted view of the customer) to guide and manage such marketing efforts. It is the SDW's integrative capabilities that make it the ideal support mechanism for a dynamic multi-channel management that includes that customer centric call-center. Many believed the cost of building integrated an effective call-center can be a barrier to entry. The potential benefits and profits easily outweigh the costs.

Increase customer satisfaction - by improving the ability of the organisation to provide quick and accurate answers with the personalised attention customers have come to expect. The SDW enables the call-center operatives to recognise the high value customers and provide them with a set of associated service levels. By better understanding the customers changing needs the call-center can build a relationship perception with each individual customer. When interacting with each customer, new customer information can be gathered that will enrich the underlying base data and improve the next interaction with that customer. This enrichment is useful in helping the bank respond to customer needs/values/motivations and thereby develop the new products and services the customers will want.

Strengthen competitive advantage - by unlocking the power of detailed customer information and applying that power directly to the points of customer contact. This means providing the team players that come into contact with the customers the same kind of information that the call-center, the web, stores or branches uses so that customers perceive an enterprise wide approach to their relationship with the firm. The idea is to increase the company's share of the customer's wallet and the only way to do that is to know enough about the customers to provide them with the right services/products at the right time. By gathering information whenever there is a customer interaction, the company has the opportunity to gauge the success of its service levels and benchmark customer satisfaction.

The competitive environment is heating up for all types of company – now is not the time to do little and hope the waves of change will pass you by. In every country where the telephonic infrastructure is improving, the use of the Internet and call-centers grow up. Additionally the financial, telecommunication and retail services community cannot ignore the need for improved service levels and the need to retain/develop and acquire the right customers. The holistic approach to this is the use of the SDW to fully integrate the disparate information systems that exist and the multiplicity of channels to and from the market. The call-center is one of those channels as is the Internet that benefits from a tight coupling with the firms' knowledge repository the data warehouse.

CRM, Customer Service and Workflow in the Call Centre

Title: CRM, Customer Service and Workflow in the Call Centre
Author: Bill Sproul, Managing Director, Eastman Software UK
Abstract: The combination of customer service and marketing functions into a CRM call
                    centre has clear advantages. Customer service benefits from a more holistic
                    view of the total customer relationship and can effectively gather important
                    sales and intelligence. Managing the type and variety of work that operators
                    are handling can make a critical contribution to their productivity, quality and
                    job satisfaction. Yet there remain challenges. Although effective solutions are
                    being delivered on the platform of workflow and work management
                    technology, preparatory analysis of the dynamics of each company's particular
                    types of customer relationship is critical to effective specification of the
                    software functions required.

Datamonitor's latest figures show web-enabled UK call centres growing tenfold in the next four years. The UK online consumer community is predicted to reach 8.7 million over the same period (current estimates of connected households vary between 1 and 2 million). Responsive advertising and customer communications is also growing on a similar scale. The result is not only an increasing total volume of calls handled by call centres, but also a widening variety of responses and queries which the call centre and its supporting systems is expected to handle and successfully conclude.

Figure 1: The Growth of Direct Marketing in the UK

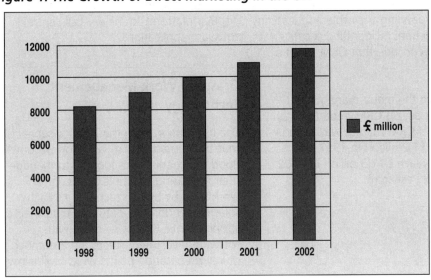

Eastman Software's own research programme recently asked the UK's top 1000 companies what they saw as the most critical factors in successful Customer Relationship Management. Proactive Customer Service came top, closely followed by Product Quality, and a strong third was A Single Telephone Number and Web Address for all Enquiries.

The Onset of CRM

This, then, is the practical reality which faces call centre management directly as a result of our current burning enthusiasm for Customer Relationship Management or CRM. There remains, by the way, heated debate about what CRM encompasses in terms of method and of technological support. Let it suffice to say here, that the idea of managing the ongoing relationship with customers covers two main functions – sales and service – and that senior customer service professionals are either on a CRM steering committee, or are frequently expanding their role and leading the CRM function. Incidentally, sceptics will now have to concede that CRM is not a passing fad.

Not only have the major management consultancies set up CRM departments, but the global CRM market was already worth some $1.2 billion in 1997 and is predicted to reach $11.5 billion in 2002 (source: AMR Research).

Varied Workflows for the Call Centre

The traditional bugbear of the volume call centre has been handling peaks and troughs of response. However, with the introduction of a greater variety of queries, often arriving over telephone, e-mail, fax, and post, the new CRM-style call centre is moving much closer to the customer service or helpdesk model, where query routing, resolution monitoring, and so on, are fundamental factors in ensuring call handling quality. A recent survey by software developer Noetica, conducted amongst the UK's top 300 call centres, found that whilst the greatest current concern today was seen as staff skills and staff retention (48.5%), development of the call centre's activities over the next two years would be mainly reliant on systems developments (50%). The fundamental technology underpinning this emerging, complex CRM-style call centre, is workflow or work management, elements of which are embedded into Windows NT, the most popular platform for newer call centre software applications.

Grasping Work Management Technology

The implication from the Noetica survey is that the current stream will soon become a flood of organisations looking to manage their increasingly complex call centre workflows by buying technology. Each solution vendor will, naturally, plug their strong points. But, as so often with software investment, there are a number of key preparation points which will allow the purchaser to prepare a demanding, yet realistic, set of business goals which the solution must support.

From Satisfaction to Profit

First we need to look at the supposed relationship between customer satisfaction and customer loyalty, a connection now being challenged by leading commentators. It is well proven that good customer service leads to increased customer satisfaction. Equally, the now historic report by Bain & Co. has made legendary Frederick Reichheld's research which indicated a 5% upturn in customer retention can increase lifetime value by as much as 75%. However, in his latest report for Business Intelligence Dr Robert Shaw, visiting Professor of Marketing at Cranfield University, challenges the widely held assumption that increased customer satisfaction leads to increased customer loyalty. In this report, he points out that, "real data on satisfaction often serves to contradict the assumption of a sequential impact on loyalty".

So why is this so important to work management systems in the call centre? The answer is twofold.

The Cost of Satisfaction

First, in a time when the mantra of customer satisfaction has become an end in its own right, many organisations are making the mistake of delivering superb levels of satisfaction either at unacceptable cost or to little effect. The latest book by Cambridge University's Dr. Andy Neely, which examines the latest state of play in Business Performance Measurement methods, raises an early warning flag on precisely this point.

He quotes the horror story of a cross channel ferry operator which was initially delighted to find their customer relationship management centre were hitting target by satisfactorily responding to all customer complaints within five working days, until the company realised that they were only doing so by issuing full refunds to everyone who wrote in.

Investing in work management technology in the call centre is often seen as an effective route towards dealing with customer queries in a more efficient, effective and measurable way. However, it is worth stressing that the automatic routing of queries, information access and retrieval, escalation triggers, and so on, which work management systems enable, are only as effective and the business rules governing them.

Much of Dr Keely's arguments centre around the need to judge what customers themselves perceive as good service, and then make sure that those service levels are delivered, but are not overdelivered. Work management solutions allow the call centre to regularly capture ongoing data on customers' perceptions of the service they are receiving, and thereby regularly re-appraise the service standards which should be delivered. So an appropriate call centre workflow management system can provide the key to customer service effectiveness and cost-efficiency.

The Effect of Satisfaction

Secondly, each organisation needs to identify whether, and precisely where, there is a correlation between customer satisfaction and increased likelihood of repurchase or further purchase. Initially, this needs to be a stand-alone exercise based on historical detail. Repeat purchasers or extended purchasing needs first to be identified, and then the motivations behind their behaviour analysed. There are many consumer and business market tools with which to achieve this goal, ranging from geodemographics, to lifestyle, to psychographic profiling systems. Once the key factors have been identified, however, the work management system will help capture, monitor and measure the on-going validity of those key factors. Moreover, returning to the theme of only delivering the level of service which delivers a commercial return, it is also straightforward to introduce test workflows which allow variations from the current rules to be evaluated on a small sample of customers, offering an ongoing champion-challenger yardstick.

Available Data

The CRM-style call centre is also only as good as the information its operators can access. A survey conducted by Saratoga Systems in 1998 of 4,700 sales and marketing directors found that two fifths of the respondents' organisations had no centralised procedure for sharing customer information gathered by the service staff and the salesforce. Another research

project from KPMG found that, whilst almost 90% of firms valued customer information as vital to business success, nearly half could not identify the cause of customer churn. Although these figures seem a terrible indictment of the slovenly attitude of businesses towards their customers, this is precisely the failing that CRM-style call centres are designed to alleviate.

A Case Study

Take the example of a high-value hi-fi retailer who is an example of best practise. The company relied heavily on direct response advertising to attract its niche audience, much of it delivered through direct mail. Response was encouraged by telephone, fax and e-mail. The company's website acted as an important avenue for customers to obtain information and make further queries. Its average customer only replaced their main system every five years, but the value of accessories, add-ons and associated services over this period could amount to as much as 50% of the system purchase price. Customers tended to be very demanding and by no means backward in complaining when they felt so inclined. Customer attrition rates were running at some 30% per annum, mostly defections to the two major competitors.

It was decided to merge all advertising response, information queries and complaints handling into the one European call centre supported by a work management solution. It soon emerged that one of the principal causes of customer dissatisfaction was the receipt of a standardised marketing offer within two weeks of making a complaint or query. Regardless of whether their query had been satisfied, customers felt let down that marketing offers were not personalised at least broadly to their areas of interest. Another point of dissatisfaction came from customers buying tailored systems who were not kept informed of progress as their system was being built. It was estimated that the cost of losing these customers was about three or four times the average long-term customer value.

An exclusion routine was built into the call centre system so that enquirers (customers or prospects) being mailed within two months of their query had to receive a tailored content. Triggers in the system meant that high-value tailored system customers received a call every week to report on order progress, the information coming from a link to the factory's electronic library of authorisation documents. And finally, a smiley face graphic on each operator's front screen showed them visually, through its expression, the customer's current state of satisfaction/dissatisfaction so that they could instantly use the right tone of voice during the call.

The result during the first year of operation has been a twenty percent drop in customer attrition rates, but each of those customers retained has been worth 150% of average customer value. From the operators' point of view, they feel more confident in their call handling and have their work 'blended' to include mixed work on call handling, e-mail replies and fax

processing. Call centre staff are now half as likely to leave their job.

Customer Relationship Management in the Internet Age

Title: Customer Relationship Management in the Internet Age
Author: Stephen Kowarsky, EVP, CosmoCom
Abstract: *Much of business today is conducted between people who have never met before and are likely never to meet again, and who experience each other only as disembodied telephone voices. Beginning with the development of Interactive Voice Response systems and specialized kiosks (mainly ATMs) as a means of self-service, and continuing now with the tremendous growth of Web-based self-service, there is a movement toward business without any live personal communication at all. What does the phrase "customer relationship" mean in this kind of a world?*

DEFINING THE TERMS

Let's define the customer relationship as the sum total of a customer's experience and interaction within the new customer contact zone, which today is becoming more virtual than physical.

The three main elements of this new, virtual customer contact zone are:

▸ The customer care applications which provide the repository of information about a customer, and allow the business to perform transactions with that customer.

▸ The Call Center provides the means to create live, real-time connections between customers and the customer service representatives who use the customer care applications.

▸ The Web provides a whole new zone of customer contact, and increasingly, options for self-service business transactions.

Figure 1: Elements of the Customer Contact Zone

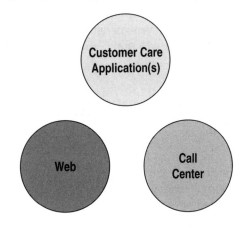

Figure 2: The Ideal Customer Contact Zone

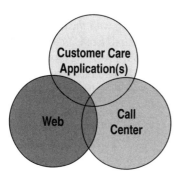

It is immediately clear that, ideally, these three elements should create an integrated whole that offers the customer a consistent, positive experience. It's easy to say, and it's easy to draw. But it's not at all an easy thing to do.

TODAY'S BEST CASE IS NOT THE IDEAL

If we look at the customer care situation today, the best implementations have achieved only a portion of this ideal integration.

Using IVR and CTI Middleware, some companies can now provide personalized call routing and even offer call-answering by CSRs who already know who is calling, and in some cases, why. But this remains a relatively rare and pleasantly surprising experience for the customer.

We can all testify that it's much more common for the CSR to ask you who you are, even if you've already entered your account number when the recorded message asked you for it.

There is also a tremendous amount of system development activity linking Web sites with customer care applications to allow Web site visitors to view personal information such as account balances, billing detail, service options, etc., as well as engage in actual transactions. These links are accomplished via a wide range of CGI techniques and Web to back-end interface products.

But looking at this picture, we can see two important things:

First, any business that has achieved all of this has probably done so by investing tremendous amounts of time, effort, and expense with half a dozen suppliers or more, plus a system integrator or two putting it all together. Second, there is still

Figure 3: The Best Customer Contact Zone Available Today

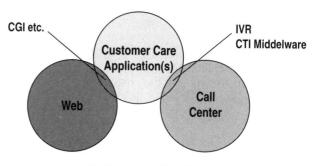

- Half a Dozen Suppliers
- Systems Integrator
- Web is Self-Service Only

no link between the Web and the live personal interaction provided by the Call Center.

THE COMPLETE SOLUTION

CosmoCall provides a real alternative to this situation. The CosmoCall Center is an open, computer-based, software oriented alternative to traditional call center technology. One of the advantages of this new technology is its ability to integrate with the two other computer-based elements we have been discussing as illustrated in the diagram below.

For systems integrators, CosmoCall is a technology that both reduces the cost and risk of solution development and implementation, and increases the value of the solution delivered.

For developers of customer care applications, who are increasingly providing their own, integrated Web front-ends,

Figure 4: The Customer Contact Zone CosmoCall Alternative

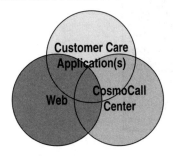

- Fewer & More Compatible Vendors
- Simpler Integration
- All Computer Technology

CosmoCall provides the missing piece that can make possible a complete computer-based solution with out-of-the-box integration.

COMPUTER ASSOCIATES EXAMPLE

One example of such a partnership is the relationship between CosmoCom and Computer Associates. CA and CosmoCom have integrated CA's flagship customer care application for help desks -- Paradigm, (a/k/a the Advanced Help Desk option of Unicenter), and CosmoCall.

As the diagram at the right shows, the CA application provides the main functions of many Customer Care applications:

1. Call tracking, with caller history and other relevant customer information.

2. Knowledge-base management, support problem-solving.

In addition, CA provides a very complete web access capability, both for customers and for CSRs. Thus, the CA software contributes two of the three elements we have identified in the modern customer contact zone.

In the past, that third element, the call center, was left to telephone system providers and their system integrators, whose best efforts only achieved part of what CosmoCall provides. As you have seen, CosmoCall provides the heart of any call center, the telephone ACD, along with a fully integrated IVR capability. The

IVR/ACD integration is the functional equivalent of a CTI Middleware package.

In addition to these capabilities -- equivalent to the best of today's call centers, CosmoCall provides live access from the web, and automatic distribution of messages (AMD) as well as calls.

The result of this integration is a total solution that fully achieves the ideal state pictured on the previous page with just two explicitly partnering vendors. It is an integration that is built into both products and works out-of-the-box -- without costly CTI investments. Instead of "computer-telephone integration," we have an all-computer technology base that solves the same problems traditionally addressed by telephone call center technology, and much more besides.

Figure 5: Computer Associates Example

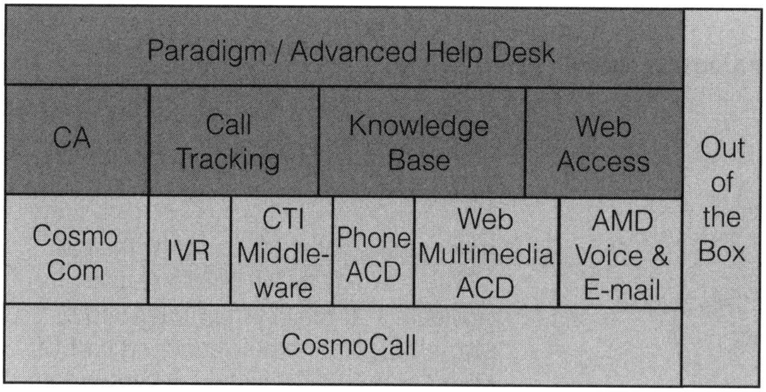

Paradigm / Advanced Help Desk					
CA	Call Tracking	Knowledge Base	Web Access		Out of the Box
Cosmo Com	IVR	CTI Middle-ware	Phone ACD	Web Multimedia ACD	AMD Voice & E-mail
CosmoCall					

- Two Partnering Vendors
- Out-of-the-Box Integration
- All Computer Technology

The Users Speak: Trends in Call Centers and Web-Based Customer Care

Title: *The Users Speak: Trends in Call Centers and Web-Based Customer Care*

Author: *The Yankee Group*

Abstract: *The Yankee Group researches the growth of call centers. Will it continue? What is the future of call centers? And what about the development of Web-based call centers? These questions will all be answered in this Yankee Group survey.*

I. Introduction

Over the past five years, call centers have moved to the heart of European customer service and sales operations, resulting in high growth in both minutes and equipment sales. For an increasing number of customers, call centers are the main or the only point of contact between customer and business. So it's not surprising that call center budgets are increasing much faster than mainstream corporate telecommunications budgets.

Will that growth continue? Industry Cassandras say that the market is becoming saturated. Moreover, call centers may ultimately be replaced or scaled down as dot-com companies create Web-based customer care solutions that are much cheaper and complement Web-based e-commerce.

However, our first survey of European call center managers suggests that strong growth in conventional call centers will continue for the time being. Call centers are handling more calls, and more complex calls using a variety of number types (see figure 1). Far from threatening the future

Figure 1: Main system used for incoming calls

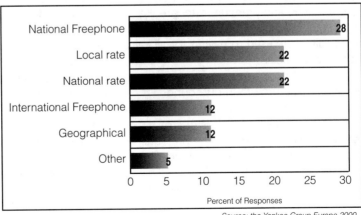

Source: the Yankee Group Europe 2000

Chapter 4: CRM in Callcenters

of call centers, the development of Web-based call centers is still immature compared to the United States, with only limited interaction between the Web site and the call center.

Nevertheless, an understanding of the importance of the Web to the call center is growing: Web sites are becoming more widely seen as a vital complementary technology. Together, the Web site and the call center can help companies make the transition (and bridge the gap) between ".bam" and ".com" activities. Almost four out of ten call center managers said they expected to have a Web-based customer care solution in place within one year of the survey. Today the Web site complements the call center; in the future the call center may come to complement the Web site, and the most Web-oriented consumer sales operations are already moving in this direction.

The survey also found that there is a wider divergence of number types used by call centers for incoming calls in Europe than in the United States. While freephone is important, other number types, such as local, national, and premium rate, are growing in popularity in an environment where callers are used to paying for all calls (including local calls).

Meanwhile, the growth in outbound calling by call centers has been much stronger than expected. This is one of several trends that increases the pressure on agents, especially where "call blending" (i.e., combining both inbound and outbound calling) is used. The job of the call center agent is becoming more

complex, and there is a greater understanding of the importance of the agent as the representative—often the sole customer-facing representative—of the organization. It takes longer to train agents, and competition among call centers is putting upward pressure on wages and leading to a stronger emphasis on job satisfaction.

In this environment, call center managers are required to find the right technologies and ensure that higher-value agents are as efficiently served as possible. In this environment of increasing value and growth, telecommunications service providers and vendors that can offer the right solutions combining appropriate technology with Web hosting capabilities stand to prosper.

In the second half of 1999, the Yankee Group Europe conducted its first-ever survey of European call center managers, focusing on 100 large companies, mostly multinational in scope. Figure 2 shows that most of the surveyed companies had more than one call center site. The survey also concentrated on sectors where call centers are most widely used. Just under 60% of the respondents came from three key sectors: finance, information technology, and telecommunications. These sectors are also important in assessing the speed of the migration to Web-based solutions.

The survey confirmed our own intuition and anecdotal opinion that the European call center market continues to be among the continent's warmer sectors for growth—though not as hot as some. The best evidence for this is in Figure 3. Call

Figure 2: Number of callcenters per organization

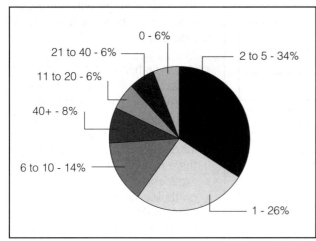

Source: the Yankee Group Europe 2000

II. Calling Patterns

It isn't enough for service providers and vendors to know that the market is growing.
What exactly is driving that growth? Two things especially stand out from our survey:

▸ Calls are getting longer, and
▸ More importantly, more calls are being made to call centers.

center budgets are showing surprising growth especially when compared to general telecom budgets of large corporates in Europe, which are almost flat. Overall, fewer call centers are indicating a decrease in budgets, while there are significantly more call centers indicating substantial budget growth (i.e., greater than 10%). The dichotomy between general corporate telecom expenditure and call center budgets shows the increasing importance and relevance of call centers within the corporate networking environment, and indicates that call center managers and marketing managers can convince budget holders to release increased funding for the call center.

An understanding of trends in calling patterns is an essential element of call center management. Many of the technological changes within call centers, such as the implementation of interactive voice response (IVR), computer-telephony integration (CTI), and automatic call

Figure 3: Growth in callcenter budgets

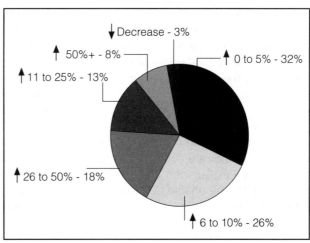

Source: the Yankee Group Europe 2000

Chapter 4: CRM in Callcenters

Figure 4: Average length of a call

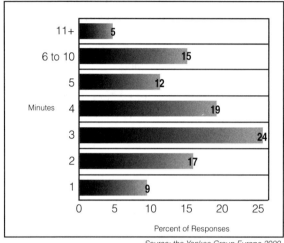

Percent of Responses

Source: the Yankee Group Europe 2000

About half of respondents said that calls were getting shorter, or were about the same length (see Figure 5).

However, half said that call length is increasing. This is often a result of the launch of new products and services, or it may be a result of high agent turnover and inexperienced staff; in addition, there may be a limited pool of experienced agents able to pass on their experience. This may suggest that more resources must be spent on agent training before new products are introduced.

distribution (ACD), as well as agent training, are affected by calling patterns. Call centers need to allocate resources, in particular staff, and to understand the complexities of calls. Changes in the length of calls may have an impact on productivity, as does the number of calls.

Figure 4 outlines the average length of calls. Most calls are within three to four minutes, and are used for relatively simple functions such as ordering and giving out information. Anecdotal evidence suggests that many of the shortest calls are crank or nuisance calls.

However, a significant proportion of calls (i.e., 32%) are over five minutes in length. While this may indicate complex calls that require lengthy explanation, the corollary is that agents may be unable to answer queries effectively.

While the average call length may not be increasing that much (about 5% on average), the number of calls received is continuing to rise sharply (see Figure 6). Half of all call center managers report that the number is rising by over 20%.

One reason may be that a lot of inquiries are not satisfied the first time around. The survey found that 43% of inquiries take more than one call to resolve, and quite a few take two or more calls to resolve. The inability to resolve the inquiry during the first call shows a failure within the organization. The failure may be insufficient training, inadequate information-retrieval capabilities, or the inability of departments within the organization to interact effectively. Anecdotal evidence suggests that there is inadequate flow of information between marketing departments and the call center. Often the call center is regarded as incidental to the marketing process and is

Figure 5: Change in length of calls in the past year

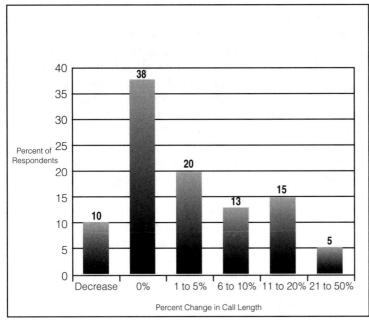

Percent of Respondents

Percent Change in Call Length

Source: the Yankee Group Europe 2000

Figure 6: Change in number of calls received the past year

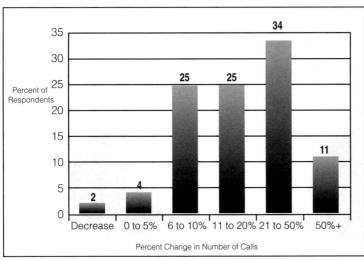

Percent of Respondents

Percent Change in Number of Calls

Source: the Yankee Group Europe 2000

informed only when decisions have been made. As we shall note later, technology can sometimes help fix these problems by directing calls more effectively.

Incoming Calls: Systems and Patterns
Figure 1 showed the range of number types that are used for incoming calls. Unlike in the United States, where freephone is universally used, with perhaps 90% penetration for call centers, in Europe it is used for about 40% of calls (this aggregates both domestic freephone and international freephone). Freephone numbers are free to the caller with the cost borne by the recipient, in this case the call center. In the United States local

calls are free and there is an expectation that customer service calls, whether for orders or information, should also be free. In Europe, phone users pay for almost every call. There is an increasing realization that call centers need not adopt freephone numbers.

A surprisingly high proportion of call center managers reported that they would never use freephone numbers (see Figure 7). Though some respondents operate internal call centers, it still shows the level of relative hostility to using freephone numbers and potentially the greater popularity of local- and national-rate calls.

Local-rate and national-rate tariff calls are almost equally used right now. The "other" category includes premium rate, which is expected to increase in use in the next few years. However, the use of premium rate increases customer expectations in terms of the level of service. Here the customer is not only

paying for the call, but at a significantly higher rate.

The use of different number sets with differing charging bands enables call centers to segment customers, with high-spending loyal customers offered freephone access and lower-spending customers using local rate or national rate (British Airways uses this method to segment its Executive Club members). There is an increasing awareness of the value of maintaining high-spending customers. The corollary of the availability of a multiplicity of number types is the potential to confuse the customer. There is already some uncertainty; call centers and telcos should ensure that they endeavor to educate the end customer to minimize such confusion.

For the call center, the prevalence of various number types may create management difficulties. The same agent may take calls from different customer

Figure 7: When will you use freephone numbers?

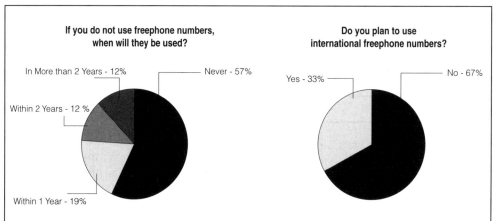

Source: the Yankee Group Europe 2000

Figure 8: Function of outbound calling

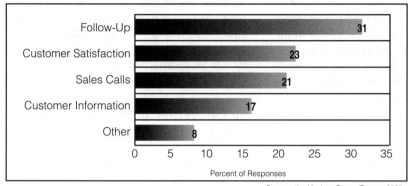

Source: the Yankee Group Europe 2000

types, and scripting and CTI must be adjusted to take account of their diverse spending and needs.

For telcos that provide services, there is clear demand for such number translation services that offer additional and growing revenue streams. However, a number of hurdles may emerge. Foremost are the inherent difficulties of revenue collection. For example, a premium rate call may be routed to a call center in another country and the call center should be able to receive those revenues from the originating carrier. Some carriers have indicated their willingness to act as a go-between; MCI WorldCom is one example. Most call center managers have insufficient resources to obtain payments from diverse carriers across Europe. We believe this will become a more important issue in the future as the use of premium rate services by call centers increases.

Outbound Calling: The Next Growth Area?
Outbound calling is more widespread at call centers than commonly assumed. Two

thirds of respondents' call centers make outbound calls, and of the remainder two thirds will make them within two years. This contrasts sharply with a 1997 Yankee Group Europe estimate that less than 5% of call center activity was outbound. Growth in outbound calling has been much stronger than many had anticipated at the time. One reason is that outbound calling can be a key aspect of marketing and customer care. A number of call center operators—most notably BT, which operates the largest call center network of its kind in Europe—have realized the potential of outbound calling as a marketing tool. There is a trend toward call blending (i.e., mixing both incoming and outbound calls in the same call center and using the same agents to conduct a multiplicity of tasks). However, a closer investigation of the types of calls made suggests some deep-seated call center inefficiencies.

Figure 8 shows what the survey respondents saw as the main function of outbound calling: that almost one third of all calls made are to follow up inbound calls. This suggests that they are unplanned and consequently unnecessary. The inquiry or problem could not be resolved during the initial call perhaps because of a lack of information. Not only does this waste agent time, but it may lead to lower levels of customer satisfaction.

The other calling functions include customer satisfaction, sales calls, and customer information, although the boundary lines between these types of calls are often blurred.

The growing trend toward the adoption of customer relationship management (CRM) applications, particularly by the banking-and-finance and telecom sectors, especially mobile operators, will result in an increase in outbound calling.

For carriers there are a number of implications here, not least the opportunity to bundle inbound and outbound calling services. We believe that carriers have failed to take full advantage of this trend, largely because their organizational structure makes inbound and outbound service integration difficult.

III. Call Center Technologies: Future Trends

As the foregoing discussion suggests, call centers are handling more complex calls in more complex ways, and technology, properly deployed as a part of the solution, can help deal with this complexity.

Figure 9 shows that ACDs, voice mail, and call management tools are already almost universally used. However, this technology may be dated and incompatible with new hardware and software. Older ACDs may be ineffective with a number of CTI applications, and it's likely that some of this

Figure 9: Technologies used in callcenters

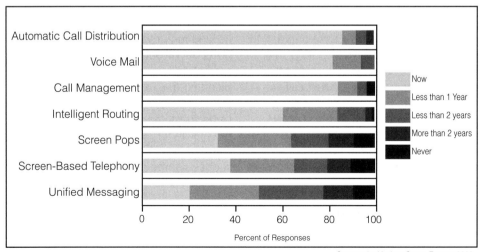

Source: the Yankee Group Europe 2000

legacy equipment will be replaced as managers move to more sophisticated solutions.

Among technologies expected to penetrate more deeply, IVR is perhaps the most important. The survey found that 44% used it today. A significant proportion uses IVR to ensure there is no agent interaction. However, this application of IVR can only be used when the information required is simple and callers are satisfied with an automated response. Often, callers still require confirmation from an agent. Nevertheless, the use of IVR requiring no agent interaction is expected by respondents to increase strongly in the next few years, not least because it allows agents to concentrate their time on more complex inquiries.

The main application for IVR technology is as the initial interface between the caller and the agent. Two thirds of those who use IVR for this purpose utilize the system for a significant proportion of their incoming calls. Such use allows the call center to focus its resources on providing a high-quality service either by deflecting calls that can be answered by the automated response or by letting the customer choose the correct department.

The major challenge of IVR is to ensure that the customer does not become frustrated listening to numerous menus and continually moving from one set of menus to another. The widespread hostility to complex IVR menus—voice mail hell— suggests that technology can sometimes create more problems than it resolves. As always, appropriate use is the key to happy customers.

Computer-Telephony Integration

A more helpful technology for users, though one with some privacy problems, is computer-telephony integration and associated screen pops. CTI with screen pops allows a much more rapid response to customers, more efficient use of agent times, and happier customers. Our last call center Report in 1997 suggested that fewer than 10% of call centers were CTI-enabled. Today that figure has risen to 44%; within one year it will rise to over 60% and in two years to over 80%.

Screen pops are the most common CTI application: a window appears on the agent's desktop containing caller information. Details of the caller, obtained through the use of calling line identification (CLI), are matched with customer records maintained in databases. CLI use allows the agent to offer a personalized response to the caller and more importantly get immediate access to the caller's history.

CLI is now available in most European countries and is generally only usable for calls from homes rather than businesses. However, this availability is the major determinant for CTI implementation, and the fact that callers can block their CLI when making initial calls to call centers could turn into a major problem. Domestic users in the United States frequently block their CLIs, and this could become a growing trend in Europe as public awareness grows.

Skills-Based Routing

Another way to improve call handling is skills-based routing, and although it is not as widely used or anticipated as CLI, it will be implemented in a majority of call centers within two years, respondents said (see Figure10).

Skills-based routing enables incoming calls to be directed to the most appropriate and available agent based on a number of criteria that can be changed to include the skill set of each individual agent (e.g., languages, and product and service knowledge). Used in conjunction with IVR and CLI, skills-based routing allows the call center to present a personalized response as well as to have the most appropriate agent dealing with the call.

The indicated growth in skills-based routing suggests increased resources must be dedicated to agent training as their responsibilities and specializations increase. That is not, of course, primarily a technology issue, and the next section considers some of the non-technical issues in call centers and their potential impact.

IV. The Human Dimension

A number of issues related to agents have already been raised. Most of the focus to date has been on increasing productivity in terms of the number of calls answered. However, this focus appears to be changing, with a stronger emphasis on delivering a high level of customer service; productivity is still an issue, but must be

Figure 10: Use of skills-based routing

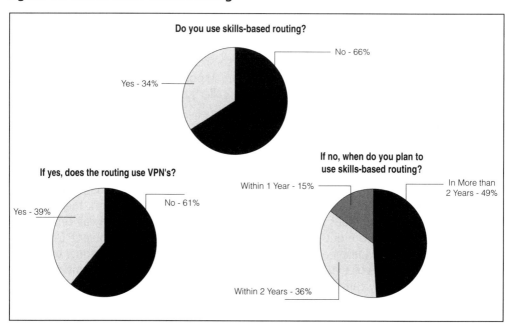

Do you use skills-based routing?

No - 66%

Yes - 34%

If yes, does the routing use VPN's?

No - 61%

Yes - 39%

If no, when do you plan to use skills-based routing?

Within 1 Year - 15%

In More than 2 Years - 49%

Within 2 Years - 36%

Source: the Yankee Group Europe 2000

The Users Speak: Trends in Call Centers and Web-Based Customer Care

Figure 11: Agent training periods

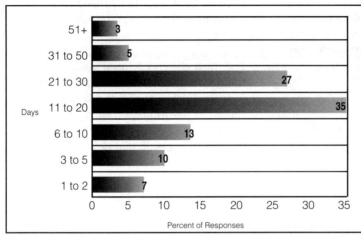

Days

Days	Percent
51+	3
31 to 50	5
21 to 30	27
11 to 20	35
6 to 10	13
3 to 5	10
1 to 2	7

Percent of Responses

Source: the Yankee Group Europe 2000

▸ The shortage of suitably educated potential agents.

Some parts of Europe are experiencing shortages of qualified agents. Most notably, these are in regions of strong pan-European call center activity—in particular, the Netherlands, Belgium, and Ireland. There is increasing poaching of agents and movement between call centers. As call centers grow, particularly nationally, these shortages are expected to increase. In response, managers will seek to increase wages and encourage stronger agent loyalty. Greater priority is given to working conditions and less to measurement of activity solely by numbers of calls answered or made. Staff shortages may spark a shift toward outsourcing, and a number of operators have developed call center "hotels" to encourage the trend.

The increasing value of agents is corroborated by the increased time spent training them. Most agents get more than 10 days of initial training, and many get more than 20 (see Figure11). In addition, average training periods for new agents are increasing, with 65% reporting that it takes longer to train agents.

balanced by the need to deliver the right service or information. Measuring call volume alone does not indicate the quality of the response received.

Initially, agents were seen as replacements for various jobs such as bank clerks or shop assistants. Within the last year, there has been a shift in the perception of call center agents from mere factory workers to skilled company representatives.

This reappraisal of the role of agents has occurred because of:

▸ The complexity of the technologies used,
▸ Multitasking (i.e., conducting both incoming and outbound calls),
▸ The realization that the agent is often the only customer interface,
▸ Combining both voice and other media (e.g., e-mail, text chat), and (increasingly)

The increasing complexity of calls received is also a factor in agent training. As Figure 12 shows, over 60% of calls are either moderately or very complex. The greater the complexity, the more resources must be placed in agent training to ensure that calls are answered effectively.

With such high levels of investment, it's clearly vital both that agents are efficiently used and supported by technology, and that efforts are made to improve job satisfaction and reduce churn.

V. Web-Based Call Centers: The Holy Grail, but When?

Given the range of pressing day-to-day issues revealed by the survey so far, it is no surprise that the considerable hype about the potential for Web-enabled call centers is not matched by today's reality.

The results obtained in the survey present a conflicting view of priorities. Figure 13 appears to show that many managers are ready to move to Web-based solutions. Yet in Figure 14, when we asked about specific capabilities of Web-based solutions, it became clear that many managers are lukewarm about the Web, now and in the future.

The most commonly used Web technology today is the capability to submit problems over the Web. Other technologies will spread in the future, including a request to make a return call, request for an e-mail, request to speak in real time, and interactive text-based "chat."

Yet the responses in Figure 14 suggest that almost 75% of call centers will not have Web-based capabilities even in two years. This indicates either an unwillingness to accept the importance of Web-based solutions, or a belief that most customers will prefer to resolve problems and make inquiries via a phone call. This is surprising considering that almost all respondents reported having a Web site, though it may reflect the relative immaturity of the Internet in Europe as a whole, with household penetration hovering around 15%.

Figure 12: Complexity of calls received

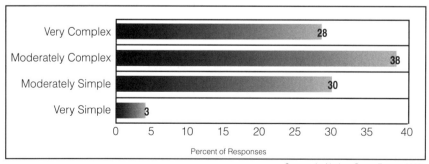

Source: the Yankee Group Europe 2000

Figure 13: When will you build a web-based customer care solution?

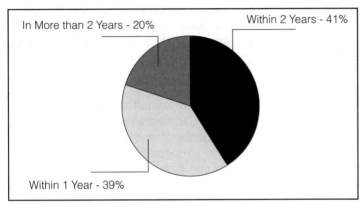

Source: the Yankee Group Europe 2000

In More than 2 Years - 20%

Within 2 Years - 41%

Within 1 Year - 39%

Technological uncertainty is also a factor. Combining text and voice capabilities will require significant re-engineering of the call center and, as noted earlier, will require wider skills among agents—not least in helping clients with Web-oriented technical inquiries. The main challenge will be to integrate a multiplicity of contact types without limiting the customer to one medium. A customer may maintain a voice contact while sending e-mail to confirm details, but the e-mail records may need to be updated immediately.

Dealing with a myriad of technologies presents difficulties even for Internet-savvy companies. It requires new rules on agent behavior, and not all companies implement them—one reason why response to e-mail is often slow, with many replies taking two weeks or more, and often no replies sent at all.

However, the Web may precipitate growth in phone call volume, for the greatest impact of Web-based technology will come from voice-based capabilities. Respondents believe that speaking in real time to an agent and requesting a return call will achieve the greatest impact of any Web

Figure 14: Use of web technologies

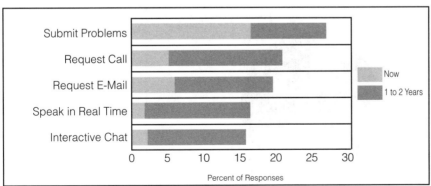

Source: the Yankee Group Europe 2000

technology (see Figure 15). Consequently, many customers, while seeking information on the Web and using self-service mechanisms, will continue to demand direct voice contact to confirm orders or product details, and to become more complex in the future as well as more onerous. In sum, the growth of the Web will create greater demand for call centers in the future—not a diminution, as was believed.

Though this survey indicates that many have still not appreciated the impact of the Internet on their business, we expect that will change as highly publicized ".com" companies spread into almost every sector. Pure Internet companies such as Amazon.com and the UK Internet bank Smile will be quick to exploit the available technologies. Yet we should note that many companies are taking a hybrid approach to customer care: Smile prominently advertises its call center numbers on all of its Web literature, and it sees the call center as a vital part of its banking operation.

VI. Conclusions

In a rapidly evolving growth market, how should carriers adapt themselves to meet the needs of call centers? Among the most important solutions, we believe carriers should:

▸ Offer more consulting services, including training, to help agents. This should also include the offer of outsourced call centers, especially as recruiting of agents becomes more difficult.
▸ Develop more bundled packages to include both outbound and inbound calling. To date this appears untapped, with different divisions in the carrier offering separate services to the call center.
▸ Focus more on the services deliverable to the customer and not on the technology, especially as more non-technical personnel, in the form of marketing managers, will play a stronger role in the operation of the call center, and in the development of the Web and

Figure 15: Web technology that achieves the greatest impact

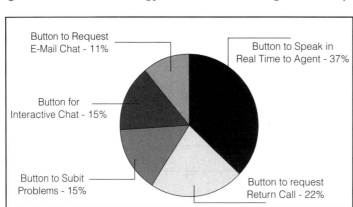

Source: the Yankee Group Europe 2000

customer relationship management
strategies.

▸ Help the call center managers
understand that the development of
Web-based call centers will not threaten
the existence of the call centers but will
strengthen them. This will emerge as the
key challenge in the next 12–18
months, and carriers able to
demonstrate strong skill sets in both
Web-hosting and call center technology
will be in a good position to exploit the
inevitable integration of customer-facing
Web activities and call centers over the
next two to three years.

HOTT-Guides – Hands On HOTT Topics

SCN Education B.V. (Ed.)

Customer Relationship Management

The Ultimate Guide to the Efficient Use of CRM

2001. 406 pp. with 121 figs. DM 98,00   ISBN 3-528-05752-1

Introduction to CRM - How to integrate CRM in your business - CRM in practise - CRM in callcenters

SCN Education B.V. (Ed.)

Data Warehousing

The Ultimate Guide to Building Corporate Business Intelligence

2001. 336 pp. Softc. DM 98,00   ISBN 3-528-05753-X

Introduction to Data Warehousing - How to integrate Data Warehousing in your business - Strategical considerations - Data-mining

SCN Education B.V. (Ed.)

Electronic Banking

The Ultimate Guide to Business and Technology of Online Banking

2001. 204 pp. with 48 figs. Hardc. DM 98,00   ISBN 3-528-05754-8

Introduction to Electronic Banking - Electronic Banking in practice - Secure Banking - Internet Banking Products

Abraham-Lincoln-Straße 46
65189 Wiesbaden
Fax 0611.7878-400
www.vieweg.de

vieweg

HOTT-Guides – Hands On HOTT Topics

SCN Education B.V. (Ed.)
ASP - Application Service Providing
The Ultimate Guide to Hiring rather than Buying Applications
2000. 320 pp. with 55 figs. and 11 tabs. Hardc. DM 98,00
ISBN 3-528-03148-4

What is ASP? - What's in it for you? - Secure ASPs - ASP tutorials -
Case studies - Research results

SCN Education B.V. (Ed.)
Webvertising
The Ultimate Internet Advertising Guide
2000. 270 pp. with 42 figs. and 13 tabs. Hardc. DM 98,00
ISBN 3-528-03150-6

Effectiveness of Banner advertising - Webvertising tutorials - Advantages and disadvantages of Webvertising - Defining the online audience - Interactive marketing relationships - How to integrate Webvertising into your media plan - Branding on the Net

SCN Education B.V. (Ed.)
Mobile Networking with WAP
The Ultimate Guide to the Efficient Use
of Wireless Application Protocol
2000. 392 pp. with 147 figs. and 23 tabs. Hardc. DM 98,00
ISBN 3-528-03149-2

Introduction to WAP - Mobile networking on the Internet - Resource utilization in wireless multimedia networks - WAP solutions - WAP tutorials

vieweg
Abraham-Lincoln-Straße 46
65189 Wiesbaden
Fax 0611.7878-400
www.vieweg.de